A Thematic Approach to Second and Thi

KINGDOM

Move forward and master

2

Aly Allsopp, Seanagh McCarthy and Ciara Morris

educate.ie

Acknowledgements

Together we wish to thank the team at educate.ie for their support and hard work in bringing the Kingdom series to life. In particular, a special thanks to Sinéad, Carolyn and Liz who shared our vision.

It brings us great joy to thank our valued students and colleagues. We dedicate this book to the teachers who inspired us and to inspiring teachers everywhere.

To my best friends, my amazing parents. Mary, for always being in my corner and for showing me what it means to be strong and fearless. And my wonderful Dad, for teaching me the true meaning of kindness. You mean more to me than you will ever know.

Aly Allsopp

I would like to thank my wonderful parents for my love of education, my brothers for their inspiration, my friends for their enthusiasm, and my husband for his invaluable support and encouragement.

Seanagh McCarthy

I would like to offer my heartfelt thanks to my incredible family and friends for their continued advice and encouragement. In particular, I would like to thank my husband and best friend, Geoff, for his unwavering belief, support and wisdom.

Ciara Morris

Introduction

Welcome to *Kingdom 2* – Junior Cycle English for Second and Third Year.

This book and its accompanying title for First Year English, *Kingdom 1*, complete the *Kingdom* series.

Kingdom 2 features nine fully developed thematic units to prepare students for their final written examination in English. Through thematic study, students will encounter and create texts in many different forms and develop a strong understanding of the common ideas and experiences that can create links between texts of different styles. The thematic units are:

1. Home is Where the Heart is
2. The World Around Me
3. Tracing My Travels
4. Courage Through Conflict
5. Breaking Barriers
6. Mapping Milestones
7. Let Freedom Ring
8. Facing Challenges
9. Looking Back

The themes of *Kingdom 2* are designed to allow you to easily draw comparisons with and complement the study of Junior Cycle novels, dramas and poetry. Featured extracts are regularly used as a springboard to pose a question on a studied text, reflecting the style of the written exam.

Kingdom 2 maintains the features and assessment structure of *Kingdom 1* with the 3 ups answering technique, 'Focus on …' feature, dedicated 'Language skills' and 'How to …' pages and assessment at the end of every unit covering written and oral assessment, CBA and exam preparation and grammar. Questions and tasks are consistently organised under five key headings:

◖ Discuss
◖ Understand
◖ Explore
◖ Investigate
◖ Create

Skills and knowledge built up through the study of *Kingdom 1* are regularly reinforced. The 'Flashback' feature reminds students of content covered in *Kingdom 1*, while the 'Remember how to …' pages give students a chance to revise key skills learned in First Year. A broad variety of material allows mixing and matching of old favourites with fresh, new and exciting texts to suit the skills and interests of the class and reflect their experience of the world. Each thematic unit within *Kingdom 2* contains texts from a number of genres, always featuring a mix of fiction, poetry, media, drama and non-fiction extracts for a rich, in-depth exploration of the theme.

The *Kingdom 2* Portfolio provides opportunities for students to draft and redraft their own creative texts with success criteria provided as a guide for improvement. The Portfolio also offers practice exam-style questions with answer space reflecting the style of the written exam.

Completing the package are a Teacher's Resource Book and Teacher's CDs offering invaluable support for planning, teaching and assessing the course.

Written by practicing teachers who have guided their students through the Junior Cycle course and exam, the *Kingdom* series responds to the requirements of the specification, ongoing assessment and final exam; you the teacher; and the variety of students that you teach. The relevant, lively texts and tasks have been developed to assist your students in reaching their full potential in their study of English, becoming masters of their own kingdom.

Aly Allsopp, Seanagh McCarthy and Ciara Morris
March 2018

Tasks

 Discuss questions are designed to promote discussion, encourage students to think about the texts and prepare them to answer further questions.

 Understand questions are comprehension-style questions that check the student's understanding.

 Explore questions are higher-order questions that require the student to think more deeply about the text.

 Investigate questions ask the student to conduct their own research.

 Create tasks require the student to produce their own oral and written work.

Icons

 The work together icon indicates that a task should be performed in pairs or in groups.

 The 3 ups icon reminds students to use the 3 ups answering technique to structure their answer.

 The portfolio icon is used to indicate where the task is to be completed in the Portfolio. This work can be helpful for revision and can provide a base for their collection of texts for their classroom-based assessment.

 The redraft icon is used whenever a task asks students to improve something they have created already.

 The oral language icon is used to show where a task has an oral component.

 The CD icon appears where recorded material is available on the Teacher's CD.

Contents

THEME 2
The World Around Me 44

THEME 3
Tracing My Travels 92

THEME 4
Courage Through Conflict

140

THEME 5
Breaking Barriers

186

THEME 6
Mapping Milestones 232

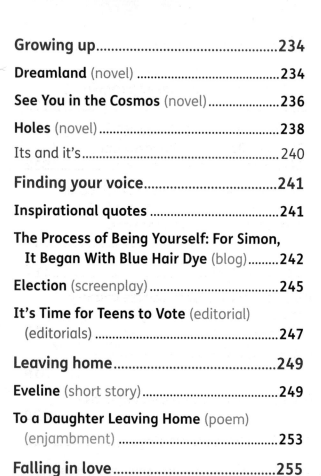

THEME 7
Let Freedom Ring 282

THEME 8
Facing Challenges 324

Language skills

How to...

Checklists

Answer questions

In *Kingdom 1* you learned the **3 ups**. These are three simple steps you can follow to ensure that you stick to the point and answer questions fully.

Example

The following extract is from comedian Sarah Millican's autobiography, *How to be Champion*.

> Growing up in South Shields, I went to Mortimer Primary and Comprehensive schools. Once, on my way there, I befriended a frog and was genuinely surprised after the bell went at the end of the day that he hadn't waited for me for the seven hours I'd been gone. Or, you know, gone about his day and then come back at 3.50 p.m. to meet me.

What kind of person was Sarah Millican as a child? Explain your answer.

 your answer by referring to the question and answer it in your own words.

In my opinion Sarah Millican was a friendly, innocent child who loved nature.

 your answer with evidence from the text.

She tells us that she 'befriended a frog' and was 'genuinely surprised' when it wasn't there to meet her after school.

 your answer by explaining how your evidence answers the question.

This shows that she was friendly, as she would make friends with anyone. This also suggests she was interested in nature, as some children might be scared of frogs. We also know that she was innocent, as she didn't understand that the frog wouldn't wait for her.

In my opinion Sarah Millican was a friendly, innocent child who loved nature. She tells us that she 'befriended a frog' and was 'genuinely surprised' when it wasn't there to meet her after school. This shows that she was friendly, as she would make friends with anyone. This also suggests she was interested in nature, as some children might be scared of frogs. We also know that she was innocent, as she didn't understand that the frog wouldn't wait for her.

 When you see this icon beside a question you should remember to use the **3 ups**.

Give a presentation

In *Kingdom 1* you learned how to give a presentation. Taking part in oral presentations as you use this book will help you to prepare for your first Classroom-Based Assessment on Oral Communication in Second Year. Your teacher will tell you more about this.

In your oral presentations, you should aim to communicate effectively and clearly in front of an audience. This is scary at first, but you will find it is a lot easier the more you prepare and practise.

Try not to rely too heavily on notes. Make eye contact with your audience to keep their attention. Practise at home before delivering your presentation to the class. A visual aid can help keep your presentation interesting and engaging for the audience, while acting as a guide for you to know what points you wanted to make.

Your teacher will examine your presentations and award you for the following:

- excellent communication skills
- well-chosen material
- good knowledge of your topic
- clear engagement with the audience.

Presentation checklist

- ✓ Research your topic well.
- ✓ Decide what you want your audience to know about the topic.
- ✓ Introduce your topic at the beginning of your presentation.
- ✓ Speak clearly and slowly – do not rush through your presentation.
- ✓ Engage with your audience – maintain eye contact, use humour and questions.
- ✓ Thank your audience for their attention at the end of your presentation.

Research

In *Kingdom 1* you learned how to carry out research. Here is a reminder of why you should carry our research and the steps you should follow when carrying out research.

Why research?

In order to fully inform yourself of a particular subject or topic, you must investigate the topic. This means finding out more about the topic you have chosen. Actively seeking out information is an important part of the learning process.

How do I begin?

Decide which form of research best suits your needs. For example, if you are researching a topic to present to your class, you may wish to find information from sources such as the library or the internet. If you are researching a topic that relates to your classmates, you might use an interview or survey to find out their opinions.

Primary research

Primary research is when you find information for yourself, instead of relying on other sources. Forms of primary research include:

- inviting someone to share their knowledge or experience by writing letters and sending emails
- carrying out an interview
- conducting a survey.

How do I carry out a survey?

1. **Make a list of relevant questions.**

    Work alone or with a group to decide which questions will help you to gather information.

2. **Ask the questions.**

    When you have chosen the questions, present them to the group. The group may fill out a paper or online questionnaire.

3. **Analyse the results.**

    Gather your results. You may wish to convert figures to percentages in order to present your findings later on.

4. **Present your findings.**

    Show your results using a table, graph or chart. You may also wish to quote responses to the questions as part of your presentation.

Secondary research

Secondary research is when you use sources to gather information. Forms of secondary research include:

- gathering official facts and statistics from organisations or groups
- watching documentaries
- reading information in books
- using the internet to find information.

How do I carry out an online search?

When carrying out an online search remember to use specific key words.

- You will have more success when you use **specific search terms**. *Causes of the First World War* is more effective than *Why did the First World War begin?*

- Place an **asterisk at the end of a word** to search for a variation of that key word. *France* First World War* will show variations of the word 'France', such as 'French'.

- Use **quotation marks to search for a phrase** rather than individual key words. *'Hitler's rise to power'* will show results including this entire phrase.

- Include the word **AND** in capital letters to show **two search results**. *Painters AND sculptors* will show results for both key words.

- Include the word **OR** in capital letters to show **two similar results**. *Hotels OR Hostels in Galway* will show both options for accommodation.

- Include the word **NOT** in capital letters to **filter particular results**. *Dublin Restaurants NOT Italian* will show results that do not include Italian restaurants.

Make sure the information you are gathering is from reliable sources. Use more than one source of information to cross-reference, ensuring the details you have found are accurate.

Keep a record of where your information came from, such as webpages or names of books and authors.

When researching, remember ...

1. Be clear about your topic.
Before thinking about the kind of research you will carry out, you must decide on your topic.

2. Make a list/use headings.
Consider the kind of information you would like to find beforehand. Use headings to help you.

RESEARCH

3. Record the most useful information.
Do not copy and paste lots of information. Make a note of the most interesting or useful facts.

4. Save the information as you go along.
You may wish to use images, video links or an exact statistic or quote. Save the details of your sources in a file and remember to save regularly.

5. Use information that is relevant.
Report back to your class when you have completed your research and gathered all of the relevant information. You should arrange your information in a clear and logical way.

Remember how to...

Draft and redraft

In *Kingdom 1* you learned how to draft and redraft your work. As part of your Junior Cycle English course, you are required to create a collection of written pieces throughout Second and Third Year. In Third Year you will select two of your best written pieces to be assessed. Your teacher will tell you more about this.

Writing your first draft

1. Firstly you must come up with an idea. Jot ideas down or use lists or bullet points if you prefer.
2. Consider the features and language style for the genre you are writing in.
3. Start writing! Try to think about your sentence structure before you start each sentence. At the end of the paragraph or section, read back over it. For example, if you were writing a piece of personal writing, you could use the following checklist for your paragraphs:
   ✓ Are you happy to stop where you did?
   ✓ Is there a topic sentence?
   ✓ Have you used the proper indentation?

Editing your work

1. Proofread your first draft to ensure that you have made no spelling, grammar or punctuation errors. Use a different-coloured pen to make any changes needed.
2. Make sure you have included the correct features of the genre you are writing in. For example, if you are writing an article make sure you include a headline, or if you are writing a diary entry make sure you include the date.
3. Reread your paragraph and make a note of any changes you would like to make. For example, could you add more description to draw your readers in?
4. Ask a peer to read over your work.
5. Listen to their feedback on your work and change any area that you feel you could improve.
6. Read over your piece one last time to ensure that there are no spelling or grammar mistakes and that you are happy with all the changes.

Writing your next draft(s)

1. Rewrite your work neatly, taking in all of the corrections and changes you marked on your first draft. Do not forget to give this piece the same title, but this time add 'Draft 2'. You can have as many drafts as you like!
2. When you are happy with your work, proofread your final draft one last time to guarantee that you have not missed any spelling or grammar mistakes.

Theme 1

Home is Where the Heart is

What is home?

We use the term 'home' to describe the place where we live. For many of us, home is much more than a building or place. Home is the feeling of belonging that everyone craves. The people we love will often represent home to us.

Why study this theme?

The famous writer Maya Angelou said, 'The ache for home lives in all of us. The safe place where we can go as we are and not be questioned.' One of our most basic needs is for a feeling of love and belonging. No matter what shape your home takes, the sense of belonging it gives is something to be prized. It is important to study this theme to gain an appreciation for the people and places we call home. In studying this theme we will also learn about the many different places people call home.

Learning intentions

- Learn about different types of homes.
- Appreciate the importance of a sense of belonging.

Writing With Purpose

- Read and write articles and personal essays.

Poetry and Song

- Study a song and a selection of poems with the theme of home.

Fiction

- Explore the prologue and opening of two novels and read and write your own short stories.

Stage and Screen

- Encounter a film script and a speech from a Shakespearean play.

Media and Advertising

- Examine a print advertisement and media images.

Language Skills

- Revise capital letters, full stops, apostrophes and commas.

Discuss

1. Which image do you feel best represents home?
2. Why did you choose this image?
3. What image would you add to the selection to represent home?

Create

 Write your own definition of 'home' in the space provided on page 104 of your Portfolio, by completing the sentence 'Home is ...'. You will return to this definition later on.

My idea of home

Everyone has a different idea and understanding of home. For some, home is simply a place that gives them shelter. For others, home is where their loved ones are.

This advertisement for Dutch Boy paint presents an image of the 'perfect home'.

As you examine the advertisement, ask yourself the following questions.

◖ Is there really such a thing as a perfect home?

◖ What is your idea of the perfect home?

Discuss

1. What do you notice about **(a)** the colours used in this advertisement **(b)** the style and size of the house and **(c)** the family members?
2. What do you imagine the inside of this house looks like?
3. Do you think this advertisement was made recently or in the past? Give reasons for your answer.

 Understand

1. Revise the features of advertising by writing a definition of each of the following features in your own words.
   (a) Slogan
   (b) Copy
   (c) Buzz words
   (d) Caption
   (e) Celebrity endorsement
2. Identify the target audience for Dutch Boy paint. Refer to the advertisement in your answer.

 Explore

1. According to the advertisement, the happiest moment of the day comes when you 'reach the place called home'. Do you agree with this sentiment?
2. Think of all the happy moments you have celebrated at home, such as Christmas and birthdays. Describe one of the happiest times in your home.
3. Would you like to live in a house like this? Give two reasons for your answer.
4. Explain why it is important to have a place to call home.

 Investigate

Use your research skills to find some other print advertisements for Dutch Boy paint. Bring them in to discuss with your class.

 Create

Design a print advertisement for your ideal home.

Examine advertising

Advertisers use certain devices to make their product, service or issue stand out. Some of these features of advertising are used in online, print, television and radio advertisements. Refer back to this list when writing about and discussing advertisements throughout Second and Third Year.

- **Brand:** the name of the company or product. The brand helps consumers to identify what is being advertised. For example: Adidas (sportswear), BMW (cars), Kellogg's (cereals).

- **Logo:** a design, symbol or image that is unique to a particular brand. For example: the Nike swoosh, the Twitter bird.

- **Copy:** any writing or text included in an advertisement. Copy will often include buzz words or emotive language. For example: free, best, new.

- **Caption:** a heading used to introduce the product, service or issue. For example: Cleans better than other leading brands.

- **Slogan:** a short, memorable phrase. Many brands repeat their slogan or catchphrase throughout several advertisements. It ensures that the brand is recognisable. For example: 'I'm Lovin' It', 'Every Little Helps', 'Because You're Worth It'.

- **Colours and images:** most advertisements use colour and images to visually appeal to consumers. For example: red for Coca-Cola, blue for Pepsi.

- **Target market:** the group targeted by the advertisement. This is based on age, gender, interests and lifestyle. For example: advertisements for baby products target families and mothers in particular.

- **Celebrity endorsement:** celebrities often appear in advertisements or promote products through social media for a fee. Celebrity endorsement can make a product more popular and desirable. For example: Rory McIlroy endorses Nike products.

 Understand

1. Identify three of the above features in the advertisement for Dutch Boy paint on page 2.

2. Suggest one more example of each of the features of advertising listed above. Refer to advertisements that you are familiar with in your answers.

The following poem attempts to define what home is and suggests that home is more than bricks and mortar. Instead home is defined by the warm welcome we receive from those who love us.

Home is where there's one to love us
By Charles Swain

Home's not merely four square walls,
Though with pictures hung and gilded;
Home is where Affection calls,
Filled with shrines the Heart hath builded!
Home! – go watch the faithful dove,
Sailing 'neath the heaven above us;
Home is where there's one to love!
Home is where there's one to love us!

Home's not merely roof and room –
It needs something to endear it;
Home is where the heart can bloom,
Where there's some kind lip to cheer it!
What is home with none to meet,
None to welcome, none to greet us?
Home is sweet – and only sweet –
Where there's one we love to meet us!

 **Flashback** Rhyme is similar sounding words in poetry or song.

 Discuss

   1. Choose two lines that rhyme in the poem and share your choice with a partner.
   2. How does the poet's use of rhyme contribute to the poem?

5

Understand

1. **(a)** Match each word with the correct definition.

Merely	To give cause for love
Gilded	Something special, usually worshipped
Shrine	Simply, just
Endear	Something covered in gold, usually a frame

 (b) Add these words to your vocabulary builder on pages 1–2 of your Portfolio.

(c) Put each of these words into a sentence.

2. What does the speaker mean when he says 'Home's not merely roof and room'?

 Explore

1. In your opinion, does the poet succeed in defining home in this poem?

2. The speaker asks a rhetorical question in the second stanza. Locate the question. What effect does this question have?

 3. In your view, what is the message of the poem? Do you agree with this message? (For information on how to use the 3 ups see page xv.)

 Create

1. Write about your own home and what it means to you.

2. Imagine you are living away from home. Write a letter to someone at home, telling them what you miss most about your home now that you are away from it. Use the checklist below to help you write your letter.

Personal letters
- ✓ Sender's address
- ✓ Date
- ✓ Greeting
- ✓ First person
- ✓ Casual/personal language
- ✓ Sign-off

Analyse poetry

Poets use certain techniques and devices when writing poems. Some of these techniques are also used in other forms of writing, such as fiction and drama. Refer back to this list when writing about and discussing the poems you study throughout Second and Third Year.

- **Alliteration:** when words that begin with the same sound are placed beside or close to one another.
- **Allusion:** an indirect or subtle reference to something.
- **Assonance:** repetition of broad vowel sounds.
- **Enjambment:** run-on lines.
- **Hyperbole:** exaggeration for emphasis.
- **Imagery:** descriptive language that appeals to the senses.
- **Mood:** the main feeling or atmosphere in the poem.
- **Metaphor:** when one thing is described as being something else.
- **Onomatopoeia:** when words sound like their meaning.
- **Personification:** when something non-human is given human qualities.
- **Repetition:** when a word or phrase appears more than once.
- **Rhyme:** similar-sounding words.
  - End rhyme occurs when words at the end of lines rhyme.
  - Internal rhyme occurs when words within the lines rhyme.
  - Rhyming couplets are pairs of lines that rhyme.
- **Rhythm:** the beat of a poem.
- **Sibilance:** the repetition of 's' sounds.
- **Simile:** a comparison that uses the words 'like', 'as' or 'than'.
- **Subject:** the focus of the poem, what it is about.
- **Symbols:** images that represent something else.
- **Theme:** the central issue or concern explored in a poem.
- **Title:** what the poem is called.
- **Tone:** the attitude in a poem.

 Understand

1. Work in groups to come up with examples of each of the above techniques and devices.
2. Return to the poem 'Home is where there is one to love us' on page 5.
   (a) Pick out three poetic techniques used by the poet.
   (b) What is the effect of each technique?

Readers are given an insight into Matilda's difficult home life in the following extract from Roald Dahl's novel *Matilda*.

Matilda

Matilda's parents owned quite a nice house with three bedrooms upstairs, while on the ground floor there was a dining-room and a living-room and a kitchen. Her father was a dealer in second-hand cars and it seemed he did pretty well at it.

'Sawdust,' he would say proudly, 'is one of the great secrets of my success. And it costs me nothing. I get it free from the sawmill.'

'What do you use it for?' Matilda asked him.

'Ha!' the father said. 'Wouldn't you like to know.'

'I don't see how sawdust can help you to sell second-hand cars, Daddy.'

'That's because you're an ignorant little twit,' the father said. His speech was never very delicate but Matilda was used to it. She also knew that he liked to boast and she would egg him on shamelessly.

'You must be very clever to find a use for something that costs nothing,' she said. 'I wish I could do it.'

'You couldn't,' the father said. 'You're too stupid. But I don't mind telling young Mike here about it seeing he'll be joining me in the business one day.' Ignoring Matilda, he turned to his son and said, 'I'm always glad to buy a car when some fool has been crashing the gears so badly they're all worn out and rattle like mad. I get it cheap. Then all I do is mix a lot of sawdust with the oil in the gear-box and it runs sweet as a nut.'

'How long will it run like that before it starts rattling again?' Matilda asked him.

'Long enough for the buyer to get a good distance away,' the father said, grinning. 'About a hundred miles.'

'But that's dishonest, Daddy,' Matilda said. 'It's cheating.'

'No one ever got rich being honest,' the father said. 'Customers are there to be diddled.'

Mr Wormwood was a small ratty-looking man whose front teeth stuck out underneath a thin ratty moustache. He liked to wear jackets with large brightly coloured checks and he sported ties that were usually yellow or pale green. 'Now take mileage for instance,' he went on. 'Anyone who's buying a second-hand car, the first thing he wants to know is how many miles it's done. Right?'

'Right,' the son said.

'So I buy an old dump that's got about a hundred and fifty thousand miles on the clock. I get it cheap. But no one's going to buy it with a mileage like that, are they? And these days you can't just take the speedometer out and fiddle the numbers back like you used to ten years ago. They've fixed it so it's impossible to tamper with it unless you're a ruddy watchmaker or something. So what do I do? I use my brains, laddie, that's what I do.'

'How?' young Michael asked, fascinated. He seemed to have inherited his father's love of crookery.

'I sit down and say to myself, how can I convert a mileage reading of one hundred and fifty thousand into only ten thousand without taking the speedometer to pieces? Well, if I were to run the car backwards for long enough then obviously that would do it. The numbers would click backwards, wouldn't they? But who's going to drive a flaming car in reverse for thousands and thousands of miles? You couldn't do it!'

'Of course you couldn't,' young Michael said.

'So I scratch my head,' the father said. 'I use my brains. When you've been given a fine brain like I have, you've got to use it. And all of a sudden, the answer hits me. I tell you, I felt exactly like that other brilliant fellow must have felt when he discovered penicillin. "Eureka!" I cried. "I've got it!"'

'What did you do, Dad?' the son asked him.

'The speedometer,' Mr Wormwood said, 'is run off a cable that is coupled up to one of the front wheels. So first I disconnect the cable where it joins the front wheel. Next, I get one of those high-speed electric drills and I couple that up to the end of the cable in such a way that when the drill turns, it turns the cable *backwards*. You got me so far? You following me?'

'Yes, Daddy,' young Michael said.

'These drills run at a tremendous speed,' the father said, 'so when I switch on the drill the mileage numbers on the speedo spin backwards at a fantastic rate. I can knock fifty thousand miles off the clock in a few minutes with my high-speed electric drill. And by the time I've finished, the car's only done ten thousand and it's ready for sale. 'She's almost new,' I say to the customer. 'She's hardly done ten thou. Belonged to an old lady who only used it once a week for shopping.'

'Can you really turn the mileage back with an electric drill?' young Michael asked.

'I'm telling you trade secrets,' the father said. 'So don't you go talking about this to anyone else. You don't want me put in jug, do you?'

'I won't tell a soul,' the boy said. 'Do you do this to many cars, Dad?'

'Every single car that comes through my hands gets the treatment,' the father said. 'They all have their mileage cut to under ten thou before they're offered for sale. And to think I invented that all by myself,' he added proudly. 'It's made me a mint.'

Matilda, who had been listening closely, said, 'But Daddy, that's even more dishonest than the sawdust. It's disgusting. You're cheating people who trust you.'

'If you don't like it then don't eat the food in this house,' the father said. 'It's bought with the profits.'

'It's dirty money,' Matilda said. 'I hate it.'

Two red spots appeared on the father's cheeks. 'Who the heck do you think you are,' he shouted, 'the Archbishop of Canterbury or something, preaching to me about honesty? You're just an ignorant little squirt who hasn't the foggiest idea what you're talking about!'

'Quite right, Harry,' the mother said. And to Matilda she said, 'You've got a nerve talking to your father like that. Now keep your nasty mouth shut so we can all watch this programme in peace.'

They were in the living-room eating their suppers on their knees in front of the telly. The suppers were TV dinners in floppy aluminium containers with separate compartments for the stewed meat, the boiled potatoes and the peas. Mrs Wormwood sat munching her meal with her eyes glued to the American soap-opera on the screen. She was a large woman whose hair was dyed platinum blonde except where you could see the mousy-brown bits growing out from the roots. She wore heavy make-up and she had one of those unfortunate bulging figures where the flesh appears to be strapped in all around the body to prevent it from falling out.

'Mummy,' Matilda said, 'would you mind if I ate my supper in the dining-room so I could read my book?'

The father glanced up sharply. '*I* would mind!' he snapped. 'Supper is a family gathering and no one leaves the table till it's over!'

'But we're not at the table,' Matilda said. 'We never are. We're always eating off our knees and watching the telly.'

'What's wrong with watching the telly, may I ask?' the father said. His voice had suddenly become soft and dangerous.

Matilda didn't trust herself to answer him, so she kept quiet. She could feel the anger boiling up inside her. She knew it was wrong to hate her parents like this, but she was finding it very hard not to do so. All the reading she had done had given her a view of life that they had never seen. If only they would read a little Dickens or Kipling they would soon discover there was more to life than cheating people and watching television.

Another thing. She resented being told constantly that she was ignorant and stupid when she knew she wasn't. The anger inside her went on boiling and boiling, and as she lay in bed that night she made a decision. She decided that every time her father or her mother was beastly to her, she would get her own back in some way or another. A small victory or two would help her to tolerate their idiocies and would stop her from going crazy. You must remember that she was still hardly five years old and it is not easy for somebody as small as that to score points against an all-powerful grown-up. Even so, she was determined to have a go. Her father, after what had happened in front of the telly that evening, was first on her list.

Understand

1. What does Mr Wormwood do with sawdust?
2. How does Mr Wormwood 'knock fifty thousand miles off the clock'?
3. Find evidence to support the view that Mr Wormwood is cruel to his daughter.
4. Where do the family eat their supper?
5. How old is Matilda?

Explore

1. Compare and contrast Matilda's home with your own.
2. Matilda tells her father that his actions are 'dishonest'. Do you agree with her view?
3. We are told that Matilda 'could feel the anger boiling up inside her'. Describe how you would feel if you were Matilda.
4. Suggest one way Matilda might 'score points' against her father. Use your imagination!

Investigate

 Film

 Musical

 Book

1. Identify the possible target audience for each of these images.

 2. Which of the images is most appealing, in your opinion?

3. Basing your answer on the images alone, would you prefer to watch the film, see the musical or read the book?

Create

 Choose one of the images accompanying the extract on pages 8–10. Fill in the character profile on page 3 of your Portfolio of the character depicted in the image you have chosen.

Capital letters and full stops

Capital letters should be used when:

◖ **starting a sentence:** *The team were ready to win!*

◖ **using the personal pronoun 'I':** *I will not give up.*

◖ **writing days of the week, months of the year and holidays:** *We do our Christmas shopping on the second Saturday in December.*

◖ **naming countries, languages, nationalities and religions:** *Sweden, Spanish, Irish, Hinduism.*

◖ **naming people and titles:** *President Higgins.*

◖ **naming companies and organisations:** *Dunnes Stores.*

◖ **naming places and monuments:** *I cannot wait to see the Colosseum when I go to Italy.*

◖ **writing titles of books, poems and songs:** *The Fault in Our Stars.*

◖ **abbreviating:** *My favourite show is on RTÉ tonight.*

Full stops show where a sentence ends.

It is important to include full stops in your writing; otherwise your sentences will be too long and confusing.

Donegal is one of the most beautiful places in Ireland. It boasts a wonderful coastal landscape. I would highly recommend that you visit while you are here.

Notice the full stops placed at the end of the sentences. Without them, this would be a very long statement.

 Understand

 1. Work in pairs to find an example of where Dahl uses capital letters for **(a)** a person's name, **(b)** the name of a place and **(c)** the start of a sentence in the extract from *Matilda* on pages 8–10.

2. Write out the following sentences, inserting the correct capital letters.

   (a) My dad and i walk our dog every evening.

   (b) we had the holiday from hell, i am never going camping again!

   (c) My dream job would be to work for nasa.

   (d) the best film i have ever seen is called *mrs doubtfire*.

   (e) coca-cola have the best advertisements.

   (f) My friend scarlett was born in london.

3. Write out the following passage, inserting capital letters and full stops where required.

   > the book said that vermeer died penniless when he was in his forties, and that almost nothing was known about his life no one understood why such a fabulous painter had made only thirty-five works of art no one knew who the people he painted were, or why he painted the things he did no one knew how he became an artist

This poem captures what appears to be an ordinary moment in the poet's young life. Heaney remembers spending time alone with his mother, peeling potatoes in a comfortable silence.

In a shift of tone, the poem moves forward in time to when his mother has passed away. He acknowledges that the time spent carrying out this chore was the closest they had been to each other.

Sonnet - Petrarchan Sonnet

When All the Others Were Away at Mass

By Seamus Heaney

When all the others were away at Mass
I was all hers as we peeled potatoes.
They broke the silence, let fall one by one
Like solder weeping off the soldering iron:
Cold comforts set between us, things to share
Gleaming in a bucket of clean water.
And again let fall. Little pleasant splashes
From each other's work would bring us to our senses.

Octave (octet)
first eight lines

the poet always change focus between the octave & the sestet.

So while the parish priest at her bedside
Went hammer and tongs at the prayers for the dying
And some were responding and some crying
I remembered her head bent towards my head,
Her breath in mine, our fluent dipping knives–
Never closer the whole rest of our lives.

Sestet
last six lines

 **Tone** is a poet's attitude towards the subject matter of a poem.

 Discuss

1. What chores do you usually carry out in your house?

2. Do you agree that ordinary moments with people we love can sometimes create the most valuable memories?

 Understand

1. What weekly chore do Heaney and his mother engage in while the others are at Mass?

2. What does Heaney do while the priest says 'prayers for the dying'?

3. Locate the point in the poem where the tone changes.

4. Find two examples of images that appeal to the senses in this poem.

 Explore

 1. Do you agree that the time Heaney spent with his mother was special? Support your answer with evidence from the poem.

2. Describe your response to the poem. Begin your answer with the following statement: While reading the poem I ...

 3. Choose a poem that you have studied as part of your Junior Cycle English course that focuses on a relationship.

   (a) Name the poem and the poet.

   (b) What did you learn about the relationship described in the poem?

 Create

In this poem, Heaney explores a memory from his childhood. Write a paragraph about an important memory from your own childhood.

Sadly, for many people throughout the world, home is not a safe, warm and comfortable place. The following images of less conventional homes have been shared in the media recently. These images show us that many people go through life without having a permanent place to call home.

Tent city, Australia

People are calling these tent cities home in parts of Australia.

Syrian refugee camp, Turkey

People are being forced to flee their homes to escape conflict in Syria.

Apollo House, Dublin

In 2016, a disused office building in Dublin was temporarily occupied and used to shelter people without a home.

Understand

1. Choose two adjectives to describe how you felt when looking at the images. Explain your choices.
2. Describe what home looks like for someone living in one of the places shown above.
3. What slogan is used in the image of Apollo House?

Explore

1. Do you think life is difficult for people living in the places shown in these images? Give reasons for your answer.

2. The second image of a Syrian refugee camp shows some young children. In what ways are their childhoods different to yours?

Investigate

Work in groups to find out more about one of the following topics:

◖ the homeless crisis in Ireland

◖ the Syrian refugee crisis.

Discuss your findings with the class. (For information on how to carry out research see page xvii.)

Create

Imagine you have moved into one of the places shown on page 15. Write your diary entry after your first night at your new home in the space provided on page 4 of your Portfolio. Include information about:

◖ where you lived before

◖ how you felt during your first night at your new home

◖ how it is different (better or worse) than your previous home

◖ your fears or hopes for the future.

Use the checklist below to help you.

Diary entries

✓ Date
✓ 'Dear Diary' format
✓ Reference to time and place
✓ Written in the first person
✓ Detailed account of events
✓ Description of thoughts, feelings and emotions
✓ Informal, conversational language
✓ Sign off

Memories of home

The place we call home may change throughout our lives. People will sometimes move to a new house or even a new country out of choice or necessity. Many people will have special memories of home, especially when thinking back to a place that they have left behind.

The title of the following poem uses the feminine form of the French word *emigré*, meaning emigrant. In the poem, a person who has been displaced remembers their home country. The speaker's memory of the place of their birth, although blurred with time, is dominated by 'an impression of sunlight'.

Try to locate the parts of the poem relating to the place the speaker once called home.

The Emigrée

By Carol Rumens

There once was a country … I left it as a child
but my memory of it is sunlight-clear
for it seems I never saw it in that November
which, I am told, comes to the mildest city.
The worst news I receive of it cannot break
my original view, the bright, filled paperweight.
It may be at war, it may be sick with tyrants,
but I am branded by an impression of sunlight.

The white streets of that city, the graceful slopes
glow even clearer as time rolls its tanks
and the frontiers rise between us, close like waves.
That child's vocabulary I carried here
like a hollow doll, opens and spills a grammar.
Soon I shall have every coloured molecule of it.
It may by now be a lie, banned by the state
but I can't get it off my tongue. It tastes of sunlight.

I have no passport, there's no way back at all
but my city comes to me in its own white plane.
It lies down in front of me, docile as paper;
I comb its hair and love its shining eyes.
My city takes me dancing through the city
of walls. They accuse me of absence, they circle me.
They accuse me of being dark in their free city.
My city hides behind me. They mutter death,
and my shadow falls as evidence of sunlight.

 **Imagery** is descriptive language that appeals to our senses (sight, sound, smell, taste and touch).

 Understand

1. How does the speaker describe their memory of their home?
2. Do you think the speaker in this poem is male or female? Give one reason for your answer.

 Explore

 1. Use evidence from the poem to suggest one possibility for the 'worst news' the speaker receives about their home.

 2. What is your understanding of the speaker's admission that 'It may by now be a lie'?

 3. Select one image from the poem that stands out to you. What makes this an effective image?

4. 'Some poems vividly bring a place to life for the reader.'
   Choose a poem that you have studied that describes a place.
   (a) Name the poem and the poet.
   (b) Discuss how the poet brings this place to life in the poem.

 Investigate

 Work in groups to read the poem aloud and choose one image that stands out. Use your research skills to find pictures to represent this image and explain your choice to the class.

The following speech is taken from *The Tempest* by William Shakespeare. Caliban lives on an island which he calls his own. It is the only home he has ever known. In this speech, Caliban says that his home was taken from him when Prospero and his daughter, Miranda, arrived on the island.

The Tempest

Caliban: I must eat my dinner.

This island's mine, by Sycorax my mother,

Which thou tak'st from me. When thou cam'st first,

Thou strok'st me, and made much of me, wouldst give me

Water with berries in't, and teach me how

To name the bigger light, and how the less,

That burn by day and night. And then I loved thee,

And showed thee all the qualities o'th'isle,

The fresh springs, brine-pits, barren place and fertile.

Cursed be I that did so! All the charms

Of Sycorax – toads, beetles, bats light on you!

For I am all the subjects that you have,

Which first was mine own king; and here you sty me

In this hard rock, whiles you do keep from me

The rest o'th'island.

Sycorax:
*Caliban's mother,
a witch*

sty:
*lock up or
contain like
an animal*

 Understand

1. What could Caliban mean when he says the following:
   - 'thou tak'st from me'
   - 'I loved thee, / And showed thee all the qualities o'th'isle'
   - 'I am all the subjects that you have'
   - 'here you sty me'?

2. How do you know that Caliban thinks of the island as his home?

3. What are the 'qualities o'th'isle' Caliban showed to his new master?

4. According to Caliban, how does Prospero treat him?

5. Besides his home, what has Caliban lost since Prospero and Miranda's arrival?

Explore

 1. Is there evidence to suggest that Caliban once saw Prospero as a parent or father figure? Explain the significance of this.

 2. Explain why someone might pity Caliban.

3. Caliban believes that he belongs on the island. Why does it matter that a person feels a sense of belonging, in your opinion?

4. Name the play that you have studied as part of your Junior Cycle English course. Think about a character who, at some point in the play, engaged your sympathy. What made you feel sorry for the character you have chosen?

 Investigate

1. (a) Interview members of your own family, asking what home means to them. With permission, you may like to record the interview. Use the checklist to help you.

 (b) Write up three of the most interesting questions and responses from the interview you carried out with a family member in the space provided on page 5 of your Portfolio.

 (c) Complete the reflection task on pages 6–7 of your Portfolio.

Interviews
- ✓ Transcript or dialogue format
- ✓ Clear purpose
- ✓ Probing questions
- ✓ Word-for-word answers
- ✓ Relevation of private thoughts and personal moments

 Create

 Prepare a three-minute presentation on the importance of home in your life. Your presentation could include details about:
- the place you call home
- your favourite part of your home
- why home is important to you
- family members and pets.

(For information on how to make presentations, see page xvi.)

A prologue is written at the beginning of some novels. Prologues introduce the story and give some background or context.

The following extract is the prologue to the novel *The Year the Gypsies Came* by Linzi Glass. The narrator hints at the difficulty and tension between her parents. Here, she tells us that the gypsies came to stay and changed her family's life forever.

The Year the Gypsies Came

My family was, in a way, not unlike the city in which we lived, Johannesburg; *eGoli* it is called in Zulu – the 'golden one'. A city surrounded for nearly a hundred miles by colossal piles of grey rock and fine yellow sand. Man-made mountains so dramatic in their shape that they resemble giant chopped-off pyramids towering over the city. Like some fabulous creation of a forgotten civilization rather than the work of sweaty gold miners burrowing like moles deep within the earth to get at the hidden treasure. Spectacular and magical, these mammoth monuments glisten over the city. But if you should feel compelled to look closer at them, to touch their shimmering forms, you will find, as you approach, that the particles blowing off them sting your cheeks. And when you reach to touch them, to hold a cluster of the gold in your hand, it will crumble and run through your fingers like sand. The illusion of a family held together as ours was is not unlike a mine dump. It is just dust.

We lived, my parents, my fifteen-year-old sister, Sarah, and I, not quite thirteen, at 99 Winslow Lane, a great old rambling house that sat on two acres of wild and abundant garden in an older neighbourhood of Johannesburg. Winslow Lane was a street of curves and bends. Dark curves, where the homes, set against lush foliage, spoke of stillness and soft air. A road with houses on one side and bluegum woods on the other. Beyond the woods was Zebra Lake, named because of its closeness to the city zoo, which stood on the far side of the murky water. It was not unusual for me to fall asleep with the faint roar of a lion or the laugh of a hyena coming across the lake in the quiet of the night, transporting me in dreams to a tent in the most uninhabited part of the bush. For our house, while firmly planted in suburbia, stood on the edge of the wild.

In those vibrant years of the sixties my parents used a powerful formula that kept our family together. As soon as the tension between them became unbearable, they would invite a house guest to come and stay with us. As if by magic, the presence of the new arrivals eased the strain between them, and for as long as there were outsiders living with us the dust of their discontent would briefly settle, and our house would seem to shimmer.

In the spring of 1966, there was no one living with us, and the tension between my parents was left to germinate and grow like untended weeds: in the bedrooms, the kitchen, in the dark spaces behind the curtains and in the hallway cupboards. It was then that the gypsies came.

germinate: *begin to grow*

But our gypsies were not black-eyed girls in scarlet shawls with silver loops through their ears. There was no shaggy dog, no swarthy men with handkerchiefs round their necks, dancing wildly in the moonlight. They were a family of four. Wanderers, without roots, without course or direction; nomads, lost in a suburban wilderness. Yet for me they were, and always will be, gypsies. For they came to us that spring in a caravan and cast a spell over us, and changed our lives forever.

swarthy: *dark-complexioned*

Understand

1. When did the gypsies come to stay?
2. Explain why the narrator often heard the 'faint roar of a lion' as she fell asleep.
3. The author makes effective use of simile in this prologue.
   (a) What is a simile?
   (b) Find an example of simile in the extract.
   (c) Explain why you find this example effective.

 ## Explore

 1. Do you find the narrator's home life appealing? Give reasons for your answer.

 2. Do you agree that the extract is rich in descriptive detail and imagery? Refer to the extract in your answer.

3. What theme does the author establish in the opening of her novel and how does she achieve this?

 ## Investigate

Use your research skills to find out more about Johannesburg in South Africa under the headings below.

◖ Location
◖ Population
◖ Landscape
◖ Attractions

 ## Create

Choose a novel that you enjoyed and write a prologue for it. Your prologue should provide context for the story that will follow.

A place to belong

For many people, home is not defined by a physical structure. Instead, it is a feeling of belonging. Feeling accepted and loved by others is one of the key factors in making someone feel like they belong.

The following personal essay is told from the perspective of a student who shares his experience of starting secondary school. At first, the writer feels out of place, but things change and school gradually becomes a place where the writer feels he belongs.

Where I belong

When I first came to this school, I did not fit in. For some people starting a new school feels like the first steps on a great adventure. This was not true in my case. I was afraid that it would be a new school and the same old me.

I was not very popular in my old school – and by not very I mean not at all. All of the other students played sports, but I did not. Try as I might, I just could not get the hang of them. To be honest, I never had an interest in sports. When they picked teams I hung back and often ended up on the bench. I knew I was a team player, but just not as part of a sports team. This meant that I was often alone at lunchtime, as the others ran after a ball.

My real passion is music. If you gave me a choice between a choir and a scrum, there would be no contest. Some people think that all boys play sports and all boys are good at them. In my opinion, the best part of any sporting event is the national anthem. The only part I would ever want to play on All-Ireland day would be as part of the band, proudly leading the teams on to the pitch.

I got a guitar for Christmas when I was nine and in many ways it has been my best friend. My guitar never made me feel like I was not good enough or I did not belong. My guitar makes me feel special. It has taught me to persevere and listen. Sometimes, when I hear a song on the radio, I just cannot wait to get home to the safety of my room to see if I can pick out the chords and bring it to life.

Until I came to this school it was just me in my bedroom with my guitar. It is all well and good to work on your solo material, but everyone knows you have got to be in a band first. I mean, John Lennon would not have achieved success if he had not been a Beatle.

When I started school here the last thing I expected was to become part of a band. In fact, other than being a member of my family, I had never been a member of anything before.

It was the wording on the poster that caught my eye: 'Tired of playing solo? Ready to rock as part of a team? Contact davelovesdrumming@ gmail.com.'

I carefully took down the email address in my school journal and I could barely wait to get home to make contact with Dave.

It turns out Dave was in my year too but, being so shy, I had not noticed him before. Of course I had to audition. It was scary, but almost as soon as I began playing, Dave joined in on the drums and before I knew it we were in sync.

Now we have a bass player called Sinéad and we are writing some of our own songs. I have even started to sing. I feel that at last I have found my voice. Last month we entered the school talent show and received a standing ovation. The principal asked us to play at an Open Day and even students in other years started saying 'hi' to me on the corridor. I went from zero to hero in a matter of months!

Do not get me wrong, I have not changed. I am still me, but now I feel like a better me. I have my own team, and for the first time I feel like I belong.

 Understand

1. How did the writer feel when he started school?
2. Describe the poster that caught the writer's eye.
3. How does the writer go from 'zero to hero'?

 Explore

1. Choose three adjectives to describe how a person might feel when they receive a standing ovation and explain your choice.
2. The writer says that, for some, starting school is 'a great adventure'. Do you agree with this viewpoint? Write about your own experience.
3. In your view, why is it important to be accepted and to belong?

 Create

Write a personal essay using the title 'Where I Belong'. Include the features of personal writing in the checklist.

Personal writing
✓ Write in the first person
✓ Write from your perspective
✓ Share and reflect on your own experiences
✓ Describe your feelings, thoughts and opinions

The following article tells readers about the Homeless World Cup, and how it can offer a sense of belonging to those without a place to call home.

Soccer helps the lost find a place to belong

Some people find their salvation in religion. But Scotsman Davie Duke found his on the soccer field.

In 2001, the death of his father sent him into a downward spiral. Duke struggled with alcohol and depression. By 22, he was homeless.

'I always remember just feeling so alone,' he said.

At a shelter, he saw a recruiting poster for the Homeless World Cup, a soccer tournament for homeless people. Duke made the team, and while the 2004 tournament was a thrill, he realised that the training for it had been the real catalyst for changing his life.

'The structure of training, the camaraderie with my teammates, having positive role models – it all got me back into a positive place,' said Duke, now 36.

In 2009, he started Street Soccer Scotland to share what he'd learned with others.

Every week, his organisation provides free soccer clinics to more than 1,000 people from disadvantaged backgrounds. Participants may be struggling with homelessness or addiction; some are refugees experiencing social isolation.

'When you're homeless or on the edge of society, often you don't feel part of anything,' Duke said. 'But football gives you a place where you belong ... and that's when change happens.'

Duke also partners with organisations that offer assistance with housing, addiction and mental health. But at its heart, Street Soccer is about giving people a chance to connect with others and move themselves beyond difficult times.

'We tell them "It's not about what's happened yesterday. It's about what you do tomorrow",' Duke said. 'That's the best inspiration for anyone.'

 Understand

1. **(a)** Use your dictionary to find a definition for each of the following words:

   ◄ camaraderie   ◄ catalyst   ◄ isolation.

    (b) Add these words to your vocabulary list on pages 1–2 of your Portfolio.

2. Where does Davie Duke come from?

3. What happened to Davie Duke in 2001?

4. According to Duke, what got him 'back into a positive place'?

Explore

1. In your view, is the message in this article hopeful? Explain your answer.

2. Davie Duke says 'When you're homeless or on the edge of society, often you don't feel part of anything'. Explain why this could be the case.

Create

1. **(a)** Duke says that the best inspiration for anyone is to realise that 'It's not about what's happened yesterday. It's about what you do tomorrow'.

   Write an inspirational speech entitled 'It's Never Too Late' in the space provided on pages 8–9 of your Portfolio. Include Duke's quote in your speech. Use the checklist below to help you write your speech.

Speeches

✓ Introduce yourself and your topic

✓ Involve your audience throughout your speech

✓ Use persuasive language to inspire your audience

✓ Ask rhetorical questions to make your audience think

✓ Strengthen your speech with some relevant facts and statistics

✓ Win your audience over by making them laugh

(b) Deliver your speech to your classmates, then fill out the checklist on page 9 of your Portfolio.

Commas

Commas affect the flow of your writing. Use commas to add pauses to your sentences. Can you find an example of where commas are used in the previous article?

Use a comma to separate parts of a sentence.

On the road below the cars were at a standstill.

Without a comma, it sounds like the road is below the cars.

On the road below, the cars were at a standstill.

Notice where the comma is placed. Does the sentence become clearer?

Use a comma to separate items in a list (until you come to the last item in a list, which is indicated by 'and').

The baker used flour butter eggs and sugar.

It is difficult to separate the ingredients without a comma.

The baker used flour, butter, eggs and sugar.

Notice where the comma is placed. Does the sentence become clearer?

Use a comma to separate adjectives.

The boy was thoughtful kind and loving.

Without a comma, the adjectives run into one another.

The boy was thoughtful, kind and loving.

Notice where the comma is placed. Does the sentence become clearer?

Use two commas to add information to the middle of a sentence.

The sales assistant despite his frown was very helpful.

There are two commas missing from this sentence. This makes it difficult to understand.

The sales assistant, despite his frown, was very helpful.

Notice how two commas have been placed before and after the interruption. Does the sentence become clear as a result?

 Understand

1. Write out each of these sentences, inserting commas in the correct places.

   (a) Maeve shoved the large heavy door shut.

   (b) Ms Johnstone come in.

   (c) It really isn't fair is it?

   (d) John Green has written many books including *Paper Towns The Fault in Our Stars* and *Looking for Alaska*.

   (e) Jack shoved his clothes shoes towels and sun cream into his suitcase while his taxi driver beeped impatiently.

   (f) Laura Lucy Leanne and Louise volunteered to tidy up.

   (g) The novel written by J. K. Rowling was a huge success.

   (h) Paul who was really annoyed roared at the passers-by.

 2. Return to the speech that you wrote for the Create task on page 26. Use the list above to check that you have used commas correctly throughout your writing. Redraft your speech, correcting any errors. (For information on how to draft and redraft see page xix.)

Leaving home

Many people leave the place where they grew up to find a home elsewhere. There are numerous reasons for this. Young adults may seek independence as they leave for college, employment or travel. Others have little choice, leaving home to escape conflict or in the hope of finding a better life elsewhere.

The following extract is taken from the novel *The Road Home* by Rose Tremain. Here, we are introduced to Lev who is leaving his home in Eastern Europe to find work in London. The opening of the novel traces the beginning of Lev's journey away from home.

The Road Home

On the coach, Lev chose a seat near the back and he sat huddled against the window, staring out at the land he was leaving: at the fields of sunflowers scorched by the dry wind, at the pig farms, at the quarries and rivers and at the wild garlic growing green at the edge of the road.

Lev wore a leather jacket and jeans and a leather cap pulled low over his eyes and his handsome face was grey-toned from his smoking and in his hands he clutched an old red cotton handkerchief and a dented pack of Russian cigarettes. He would soon be forty-three.

After some miles, as the sun came up, Lev took out a cigarette and stuck it between his lips, and the woman sitting next to him, a plump, contained person with moles like splashes of mud on her face, said quickly: 'I'm sorry, but there is no smoking allowed on the bus.'

Lev knew this, had known it in advance, had tried to prepare himself mentally for the long agony of it. But even an unlit cigarette was a companion – something to hold on to, something that had promise in it – and all he could be bothered to do now was to nod, just to show the woman that he'd heard what she'd said, reassure her that he wasn't going to cause trouble; because there they would have to sit for fifty hours or more, side by side with their separate aches and dreams, like a married couple. They would hear each other's snores and sighs, smell the food and drink each had brought with them, note the degree to which each was fearful or unafraid, make short forays into conversation. And then later, when they finally arrived in London, they would probably separate with barely a word or a look, walk out into a rainy morning, each alone and beginning a new life. And Lev thought how all of this was odd but necessary and already told him things about the world he was travelling to, a world in which he would break his back working – if only that work could be found. He would hold himself apart from other people, find corners and shadows in which to sit and smoke, demonstrate that he didn't need to belong, that his heart remained in his own country.

Focus on ... figurative language

Figurative language is language that uses words or expressions with a meaning that is different from the literal definition.

We use figures of speech to say something that does not need to be understood literally. For example, 'This jacket cost me an arm and a leg.' In this example the speaker is using figurative language because they did not literally use their arm and leg as payment for the jacket.

When a writer uses a metaphor they are speaking figuratively. They say one thing but mean something different. Rose Tremain uses figurative language when she tells us that Lev 'would break his back working'.

 Work in small groups to come up with as many examples of figurative language as you can. Share your examples with your classmates.

Understand

1. Locate the underlined words in the extract. Use your dictionary to find a definition of each word and add these to the vocabulary list on pages 1–2 of your Portfolio.
2. Why is Lev leaving his home country?
3. How old is Lev?
4. Describe the landscape observed in the opening paragraph.

Explore

1. How do you think Lev is feeling as he travels away from home?
2. Lev recognises that both he and his fellow passenger have 'separate aches and dreams'. What do you think these might be?

3. The extract is from the opening pages of the novel *The Road Home*. Do you think it is a good opening? Explain your answer.

Create

Lev has just arrived in London. Continue the story as he begins his new life in a strange and unfamiliar place.

Apostrophes

Find one instance where the author makes use of an apostrophe in the extract from *The Road Home* on page 28. Turn to a partner and explain why the author used an apostrophe. Check the information below to see if you are correct.

Apostrophes are used to show ownership.

When using an apostrophe to show that something belongs to someone, you should place the apostrophe before the 's'.
Richard's room is painted blue.

When using an apostrophe to show that something belongs to more than one person, you should place the apostrophe after the 's' at the end of the plural word.
The girls' changing room was cramped.

Some plural words, such as children, sheep and feet, do not end in 's'. In this case, you should add an apostrophe and an 's' after the word to indicate ownership:
The children's playground will close at 6 p.m.

Apostrophes are used to show where a letter is missing.

Sometimes two words are brought together and an apostrophe is used to replace the missing letter(s). This is known as a contraction.

I'm = I am

She'll = She will

They'd = They would

It's = It is

Joe's top

 Understand

1. Use contractions to replace the underlined words in the following sentences.
   (a) <u>You are</u> the best.
   (b) <u>They will</u> be pleased with the result.
   (c) People say <u>it is</u> taking part that matters.
   (d) <u>I would</u> hope for better.
   (e) <u>They are</u> going to be late.

2. Write out the following passage, adding apostrophes to the underlined words.

   > <u>Toms</u> sister was two hours late. Their <u>parents</u> car was not parked outside. The <u>boys</u> heart began to race as he thought the worst. Had something happened? The <u>dogs</u> bowls were still on the floor, untouched. <u>Toms</u> head turned towards the door as he heard a key and <u>strangers</u> voices outside. 'Move quickly, before <u>were</u> spotted,' he heard them say.

 3. Return to the story that you wrote for the Create task on page 29. Use the information above to check that you have used apostrophes correctly throughout your writing. Redraft your story, correcting any errors.

In this poem, Philip Larkin explores what happens when people who have lived in a home leave it behind. We are not given the exact reasons for the departure of those who once lived there, but the personified home has been abandoned and left to 'wither'.

Home is so Sad
By Philip Larkin

Home is so sad. It stays as it was left,
Shaped to the comfort of the last to go
As if to win them back. Instead, bereft
Of anyone to please, it withers so,
Having no heart to put aside the theft

And turn again to what it started as,
A joyous shot at how things ought to be,
Long fallen wide. You can see how it was:
Look at the pictures and the cutlery.
The music in the piano stool. That vase.

 **Personification** is when something non-human is given human qualities.

 Discuss

1. Do you agree with Larkin's sentiment in the title?
2. Are there times when 'Home is so sad'?

 Understand

1. **(a)** Use your dictionary to find a definition for each of the following words:
   - bereft
   - wither
   - joyous.

 (b) Add these words to your vocabulary builder on pages 1–2 of your Portfolio.

   (c) Put each of these words into a sentence.

2. How does the home try to win back those who once lived there?
3. Find evidence to show that the home is personified in this poem.

 Explore

 1. Why might the home have been left behind by those who once lived there?

 2. Do you agree that 'Home is so Sad', as stated in the title of this poem?

3. Look at the last two lines of the poem. Using evidence in these lines, describe what life might have been like when this home was lived in.

 Create

Using personification to bring the home to life, write a descriptive passage from the point of view of the abandoned home.

- What was your life like before everyone left?
- What has happened to you since?
- What effect has it had on you?

Returning home

Sometimes there is nothing better than coming home. Reuniting with friends, family and home comforts brings joy to many when they have been away. It is often true that people do not appreciate their home until they have left it.

Some of the best songs ever written are inspired by feelings of love. In this song, Joni Mitchell expresses her love and longing not for a person, but for the place she calls home.

Pay particular attention to the lyrics that are underlined.

California

Sitting in a park in Paris, France
Reading the news and it sure looks bad
They won't give peace a chance
That was just a dream some of us had
Still a lot of lands to see
But I wouldn't want to stay here
It's too old and cold and settled in its ways here

Oh, but California
California, I'm coming home
I'm going to see the folks I dig
I'll even kiss a sunset pig
California, I'm coming home

I met a redneck on a Grecian isle
Who did the goat dance very well
He gave me back my smile
But he kept my camera to sell
Oh the rogue, the red red rogue
He cooked good omelettes and stews
And I might have stayed on with him there

But my heart cried out for you, California
Oh California I'm coming home
Oh make me feel good rock'n roll band
I'm your biggest fan
California I'm coming home

Oh it gets so lonely
When you're walking
And the streets are full of strangers
All the news of home you read
Just gives you the blues
Just gives you the blues

So I bought me a ticket
I caught a plane to Spain
Went to a party down a red dirt road
There were lots of pretty people there
Reading *Rolling Stone*, reading *Vogue*
They said, 'How long can you hang around?'
I said a week, maybe two
Just until my skin turns brown

Then I'm going home to California
California I'm coming home
Oh will you take me as I am
Strung out on another man
California, I'm coming home

Oh it gets so lonely
When you're walking
And the streets are full of strangers
All the news of home you read
More about the war
And the bloody changes
Oh will you take me as I am?
Will you take me as I am?
Will you?
Will you take me as I am?
Hmmm mmmmm

Take me as I am

Discuss

1. Discuss the parts of the song where you feel Joni Mitchell is expressing a desire to return to California, the place she calls home.
2. Have you ever been homesick?
3. Have you ever missed a place or a person?
4. Have you looked forward to being welcomed home?

Understand

1. How does Joni Mitchell feel about California?
2. How do you know that Joni Mitchell is excited about the prospect of returning to California?
3. Find two examples of poetic techniques in this song.
4. Based on the song lyrics, which of the following images best matches your impression of California? Give one reason for your choice.

Explore

1. Write about the importance of the underlined parts of the song. What is the significance of these lines?
2. Do you agree that poems and songs share similarities? Suggest at least two similarities that they share.

Create

1. **(a)** Choose a song that you love and write down your favourite lyrics. Examine these lyrics carefully and highlight the parts that:
   - use poetic devices
   - include well-chosen words or phrases
   - express feelings
   - tell a story.

(b) Read the lyrics of your song to your class as though it were a poem. See if your classmates can guess which song you have chosen. After they have guessed, you may like to play a recording of the song or sing your own version.

The following scene is from the end of the film *The Wizard of Oz*. In the final scenes, Dorothy wants to make her way home to Kansas.

 Break into groups of six, assign parts and act out the scene. One person should read the stage directions. Make a note of the codes used in the stage directions.

The Wizard of Oz

MCS – Tin Man, Scarecrow and Lion grouped about Dorothy – she speaks – they ask her to stay with them – then the Scarecrow reacts, points up o.s. –

DOROTHY

Oh, now I'll never get home!

LION

Stay with us, then, Dorothy. We all love you.
We don't want you to go.

DOROTHY

Oh, that's very kind of you – but this could never be like Kansas. Auntie Em must have stopped wondering what happened to me by now. Oh, Scarecrow, what am I going to do?

SCARECROW

Look – here's someone who can help you!

MS – A group of Oz men react as they look up o.s. – they bow out of the scene – suddenly Glinda appears in the scene – Camera TRUCKS BACK to LEFT OVER HEADS of the bowing Oz people as she moves down the steps and up onto the platform to Dorothy, Tin Man, Lion and Scarecrow –

CS – Dorothy, Glinda and Scarecrow on the platform – Dorothy speaks with Glinda – Camera PULLS BACK to enter Tin Man and Lion – Tin Man speaks –

DOROTHY

Oh, will you help me? Can you help me?

GLINDA

You don't need to be helped any longer. You've always had the power to go back to Kansas.

DOROTHY

I have?

SCARECROW

Then why didn't you tell her before?

GLINDA

Because she wouldn't have believed me. She had to learn it for herself.

TIN MAN

What have you learned, Dorothy?

MCU – Dorothy – Lion behind her – she speaks –

DOROTHY

Well, I – I think that it – that it wasn't enough just to want to see Uncle Henry and Auntie Em – and it's that – if I ever go looking for my heart's desire again, I won't look any further than my own backyard. Because if it isn't there, I never really lost it to begin with! Is that right?

MCS – Tin Man, Dorothy, Glinda, Scarecrow and Lion on platform – they speak – Glinda points down to Dorothy's slippers –

GLINDA

That's all it is!

SCARECROW

But that's so easy! I should have thought of it for you.

TIN MAN

I should have felt it in my heart.

GLINDA

No. She had to find it out for herself. Now, those magic slippers will take you home in two seconds!

DOROTHY

Oh ...

CS – Dorothy and Glinda – Scarecrow in b.g. – Dorothy reacts, speaks – turns about – begins to cry as she realizes she will lose her three friends – Camera PANS her LEFT to Tin Man – she wipes his tears away – gives him his oil can and then kisses him – then Camera TRUCKS FORWARD slightly as she says goodbye to the Lion – PANS right slightly as she turns to the Scarecrow – hugs him – then steps back to Glinda as Camera PANS slightly –

DOROTHY

… Toto, too?

GLINDA

Toto, too.

DOROTHY

Oh, now?

GLINDA

Whenever you wish.

DOROTHY

Oh, dear – that's too wonderful to be true! Oh, it's – it's going to be so hard to say goodbye. I love you all, too. Goodbye, Tin Man. Oh, don't cry. You'll rust so dreadfully. Here – here's your oil can. Goodbye.

TIN MAN

Now I know I've got a heart – 'cause it's breaking.

DOROTHY

Oh – Goodbye, Lion. You know, I know it isn't right, but I'm going to miss the way you used to holler for help before you found your courage.

LION

Well – I would never've found it if it hadn't been for you.

DOROTHY

I think I'll miss you most of all.

GLINDA

Are you ready now?

DOROTHY

Yes. Say goodbye, Toto.

MS – Dorothy waves Toto's paw at the Tin Man, Lion and Scarecrow – then speaks to Glinda – Glinda instructs her –

DOROTHY

Yes, I'm ready now.

GLINDA

Then close your eyes, and tap your heels together three times.

MCU – Dorothy's heels as she CLICKS them together three times –

MCU – Dorothy and Glinda – Glinda instructs her – waves her wand – Dorothy closes her eyes – Camera TRUCKS in to a BIG CU of Dorothy – she speaks – the scene darkens behind her –

GLINDA

And think to yourself – 'There's no place like home; there's no place like home; there's no place like home.'

DOROTHY

There's no place like home. There's no place like home. There's no place like home. There's no place like home.

LAP DISSOLVE TO: ELS – The Munchkins waving goodbye from the gates of the Munchkin Village –

DOROTHY (O.S.)

There's no place like…

CS – The Witch laughing –

DOROTHY (O.S.)

… home. There's no place …

MCS – The Wizard at the control panel in the Throne Room – he turns, looks o.s. to f.g. – reacts – pulls the curtain –

DOROTHY (O.S.)

… like home. There's no place like home.

MS – Glinda leading the Munchkins in a dance – Munchkins in the b.g. –

DOROTHY (O.S.)

There's no place like home.

MCU – Lion GROWLING –

MS – The Tin Man BREAKING in the door of the Witch's Tower Room –

DOROTHY (O.S)

There's no place like home.

MS – Hickory's Wind Machine on the Gale farm –

DOROTHY (O.S)

There's no place like home.

 Understand

1. Name three characters that appear in the scene.
2. According to Glinda, what did Dorothy need to learn for herself?
3. What phrase does Dorothy repeat as she clicks her heels together?

 Explore

 1. How do you think Dorothy felt when she was saying goodbye to her friends?

 2. In your view, does Dorothy believe that 'there's no place like home'? Explain your answer.

3. Think about a film that you have studied as part of your Junior Cycle English course. Describe the setting of your studied film.

 Investigate

Use your research skills to find out the meaning of the following types of camera shots (note: some are written as codes):

◀ MCS   ◀ CS   ◀ panning

◀ MCU   ◀ OS   ◀ dissolve.

Create

1. **(a)** Write an outline of a plot inspired by one of the images below in the space provided on page 10 of your Portfolio.

(b) Write an important moment or scene from your plot outline in the form of a film script in the space provided on pages 11–12 of your Portfolio. Model your script on *The Wizard of Oz* extract. Include:

◖ stage direction

◖ characters' names

◖ dialogue

◖ camera shots.

(c) Write a second draft of your film script in the space provided on pages 104–105 of your Portfolio.

Examine film

Film scripts come to life on screen through the use of the features below.

Framing

Everything you see on screen has been framed through the camera lens.

Camera shots

There are various ways for a camera to frame a shot. These shots can determine our understanding of plot, setting and character.

- **Wide shots** are often used in the opening sequence of a film. A wide shot will show some of the landscape, which establishes setting.
- **Mid shots** show characters from a medium distance. These shots often capture relationships and interaction between characters.
- **Close-up shots** may be used to exaggerate detail and draw the viewer's attention towards something. This may include the significance of a certain object. It may also show a facial expression to highlight a character's thoughts and emotions.

Camera movements

You will notice the frame changes, which help to move the plot forward.

- **Panning** is when the camera moves horizontally from one side to the other.
- **Zooming** is when the camera lens focuses in on something to show it in more detail.
- **Tracking** is when the camera moves through or with the action.

Music and sound effects

Music and sound can be used to set the tone and establish the atmosphere or mood of a scene.

Lighting

Lighting is an important tool in setting the scene.

- Dark lighting can create an ominous atmosphere.
- Bright lighting can create a happy atmosphere.

Through clever lighting, viewers learn more about characters and what may be in store for them.

- Characters may appear frightening and sneaky when lit from below, as they are cast in shadow.
- Characters may appear innocent and trustworthy when lit from above, as they are fully revealed.

 Understand

1. Look back at the script on pages 35–39 and identify one piece of information in the instruction that relates to **(a)** camera shots and **(b)** camera movements.
2. Think of the opening scene in a film you have studied or watched recently.
   - **(a)** Identify one of the camera shots used.
   - **(b)** Describe one of the camera movements.
   - **(c)** What sort of music or sound effect is used?
   - **(d)** How is lighting used?

Reviewing home is where the heart is

Reflect and review

1. **(a)** Take a look at the images on page 1. Consider the association each image has with the theme of 'home'. Rank the images from most relevant (1) to least relevant (6).

   (b) Share the image that you feel ranks the highest. Explain your choice and listen as others share their choice with you.

   (c) What image would you choose to replace the image that you feel ranks the lowest? Describe the image you would replace it with and explain your choice.

2. Fill in the unit review on pages 13–14 of your Portfolio.

Language skills

1. Write out the following passage, making corrections as you go.

   > the girls looked awfully bored to me i saw them on the sun-roof yawning and painting their nails and trying to keep up their bermuda tans and they seemed bored as hell i talked with one of them and she was bored with yachts and bored with flying around in aeroplanes and bored with skiing in switzerland at christmas and bored with the men in brazil

2. **(a)** What do each of the following film terms mean:
   - framing
   - wide shot
   - zooming
   - lighting?

   (b) What is the effect of each of these techniques?

3. Write a paragraph about a film that you have studied or enjoyed. Refer to the techniques listed above in your answer.

Oral assessment

Prepare a two-minute speech entitled 'What Home Means to Me'.
- Carefully consider what home means to you.
- Plan what you would like to say.
- Write your speech.
- Practise the delivery of your speech. Make sure it is two minutes long.

When you are ready, deliver your speech to your classmates.

Written assessment

1. Write a poem entitled 'The Perfect Home' in the space provided on page 15 of your Portfolio.

   ◖ Think carefully about your idea of 'the perfect home'.

   ◖ Decide which poetic devices you would like to use.

   ◖ Use imagery that appeals to at least two of the senses.

2. **(a)** 'Home is much more than bricks and mortar.'

   Write a speech responding to this statement in the space provided on pages 16–17 of your Portfolio. Do you agree that home is much more than a building or a place?

   (b) Redraft your speech in the space provided on pages 106–107 of your Portfolio.

Exam skills

1. Think about what home is like for the central character in a novel or short story that you have studied.

   (a) Name the novel or short story, the author and the central character.

   (b) Where does your central character call home?

   (c) Would you like to be part of their world? Refer to the novel or short story in your explanation.

   (d) How is your chosen character's life affected by the world in which they live?

   Write your answer in the space provided on pages 130–131 of your Portfolio.

Theme 2

The World Around Me

What is the world around me?

The world around me focuses on how we interact with the world in our daily lives. It looks at how people find their own place in the world, considers changes that are occurring in the world, explores the different experiences people have and reflects on the beauty of our surroundings.

Why study this theme?

It is important to find your own place in this world. It is also important to be aware of the experiences of others. This will give you an insight into the impact humans can have on the world and highlight what you can do to preserve and improve the world for future generations. Finally, it is important to take the time to appreciate the beauty of the world around us.

Learning intentions

◖ Consider how people find their place in the world.

◖ Reflect on how the world is changing.

◖ Explore other people's worlds.

◖ Appreciate the beauty of the world.

Writing With Purpose

◖ Discover the features and language style of reports.

◖ Explore the conservation of Earth through a blog post.

◖ Read an inspiring speech.

Poetry and Song

◖ Experience the beauty of nature through personification.

Fiction

◖ Experience other worlds.

Stage and Screen

◖ Focus on creating a world on stage.

Media and Advertising

◖ Discover the importance of finding humour in the world around you.

◖ Examine the progress of technology through a feature article.

Language Skills

◖ Learn about possessive adjectives and pronouns.

Discuss

1. How do you think all of the images above are linked?
2. How are science and nature connected?
3. Through what medium do you think we connect and communicate with one another most often?

Create

 Write your own definition of 'the world around me' in the space provided on page 27 of your Portfolio by completing the sentence 'The world around me is ...'. You will return to this definition later on.

My place in the world

The world is a big place and at times it can be hard for us to figure out where we fit in. However, one of the greatest things about the world is that it provides us with so many different opportunities.

 The world we live in presents us with choices. In the following poem, Robert Frost explores how the decisions you make will lead you down a particular path in life.

The Road Not Taken

By Robert Frost

Two roads diverged in a yellow wood,
And sorry I could not travel both
And be one traveler, long I stood
And looked down one as far as I could
To where it bent in the undergrowth;

Then took the other, as just as fair,
And having perhaps the better claim,
Because it was grassy and wanted wear;
Though as for that, the passing there
Had worn them really about the same,

And both that morning equally lay
In leaves no step had trodden black.
Oh, I kept the first for another day!
Yet knowing how way leads on to way,
I doubted if I should ever come back.

I shall be telling this with a sigh
Somewhere ages and ages hence:
Two roads diverged in a wood, and I—
I took the one less traveled by,
And that has made all the difference.

diverged: branched off; moved in a different direction

undergrowth: small trees and plants that grow beneath larger trees

fair: promising; favourable

trodden: walked on

hence: from this time

Understand

1. Why does the speaker say that he is sorry?
2. What reason does the speaker give for choosing this particular path?
3. Why does the speaker doubt he will ever come back?

Explore

 1. In what season do you think this poem is set? Give reasons for your answer.

 2. Does the speaker think that both roads are similar? Explain your answer.

 3. Which image from the poem do you think is most memorable? Explain your choice.

 4. Do you think the speaker regrets his choice, or do you think he is happy about it?

 5. In your opinion, is a forked road an effective metaphor for choices in life?

Create

 1. **(a)** Write a blog entry aimed at teenagers in which you give advice about making choices in life in the space provided on pages 18–19 of your Portfolio. Offer advice on how to make a decision and how best to avoid regretting your choice. Remember to include the features of a blog entry in the checklist below.

> ### Blogs
> ✓ Title
> ✓ Date
> ✓ Your name
> ✓ Opinions
> ✓ First person
> ✓ Information
> ✓ Informal and conversational language

(b) There is a space at the end of your blog for comments. Pass your blog entry to the person sitting next to you and ask them to fill out the comment section on your blog.

Reports

A report is a written account of an investigation that has been carried out.

Reports can help us to make sense of the world around us. They give us information that is clear, factual and unbiased to make recommendations based on the facts that were uncovered.

Features

◖ Date
◖ Title
◖ Introduction
◖ Findings
◖ Information
◖ Facts
◖ Statistics
◖ Conclusion
◖ Sign off

Language

◖ Factual
◖ Formal
◖ Unbiased

◖ A report should have an **introduction** that clearly states the purpose of the report (why it has been conducted) and how the information was gathered (surveys, interviews, etc.).

◖ The report should then list the **findings**. The findings should be stated as facts. For example, '73% of students said they disliked the uniform'.

◖ After the information has been stated, the findings of the report should be summed up in the **conclusion**.

◖ Finally, a list **recommendations** of changes or improvements that could be made based on the information in the report should be given.

Read the following report on well-being in school compiled by a pair of students for their principal.

Report on well-being in our school

To: Mr O'Reilly, principal

Completed by: Alice Courtney and Polly Francis, members of the Student Council

Date: 29 January 2019

Introduction

The school principal requested an investigation into the well-being of students. He asked that we write a report on the area of wellness within the school environment. This report was conducted using a survey of sample students from each year group. 20 randomly selected students from each year group were surveyed – a total of 120 students across the school.

Findings

The results of the survey showed that 67% of the students surveyed find that keeping up with their school work, hobbies and friendships can overwhelm them and take a toll on their well-being.

The main reasons students feel this way are as follows:

- 32% said that they are not designating any time to themselves.
- 39% mentioned this was due to their poor time-management skills.
- 29% are not aware of any coping skills they can use to deal with pressure.

Of the 120 students surveyed, 94 said that they would welcome suggestions on how best to take care of their well-being.

Conclusion

The findings have highlighted the reasons behind students feeling overwhelmed as being a lack of time out for themselves, not wisely using their time and a lack of awareness regarding coping mechanisms.

Recommendations

In order to improve the well-being of students, we have come up with the following suggestions:

- Meditation Mondays: open meditation sessions at lunchtime on Mondays in the Oratory.
- One SPHE class per term should be dedicated to helping students to organise a timetable for their studies, after-school activities and hobbies, in an effort to better manage their time.
- Information booklets and posters should be designed to offer students support and advice on coping with stress.

Signed: *Alice Courtney*
Polly Francis

Title

Name of the person who commissioned the report
Names of the people who completed the report

Date

States the reason for the report

Explains how the research was carried out

Results from the investigation

Facts and statistics

Information presented as percentages

Highlights what the results from the investigation show

Lists recommendations for improvements based on the findings of the report

Understand

1. Who requested that this report be carried out?
2. What method did the students use to carry out their investigation?
3. What did the statistics from the investigation show?
4. On what date was this report submitted?
5. What recommendations does the report suggest would be useful in improving well-being among students?

 ## Explore

 Work in groups to come up with some other recommendations that could improve the well-being of students.

 ## Investigate

 Work in groups to create and distribute a survey to the class to find out information about your how your peers use social media. Consider the areas of investigation below.

◖ How many hours do students spend on social media?
◖ Does this affect completing homework assignments?
◖ Which social media platform is the most popular?
◖ Would students like to cut down on their use of social media?

Create

Using the information that you obtained from your survey, write a report for your school principal on students' social media usage in the space provided on pages 20–21 of your Portfolio.

Sometimes the way we perceive the world can change after a certain event or experience.

 In the following story by Roald Dahl, the narrator's view of people changes after she and her mother have an unusual encounter with an elderly man.

The Umbrella Man

I'm going to tell you about a funny thing that happened to my mother and me yesterday evening. I am twelve years old and I'm a girl. My mother is thirty-four but I am nearly as tall as her already.

Yesterday afternoon, my mother took me up to London to see the dentist. He found one hole. It was in a back tooth and he filled it without hurting me too much. After that, we went to a café. I had a banana split and my mother had a cup of coffee. By the time we got up to leave, it was about six o'clock.

When we came out of the café it had started to rain. 'We must get a taxi,' my mother said. We were wearing ordinary hats and coats, and it was raining quite hard.

'Why don't we go back into the café and wait for it to stop?' I said. I wanted another of those banana splits. They were gorgeous.

'It isn't going to stop,' my mother said. 'We must get home.'

We stood on the pavement in the rain, looking for a taxi. Lots of them came by but they all had passengers inside them. 'I wish we had a car with a chauffeur,' my mother said.

Just then a man came up to us. He was a small man and he was pretty old, probably seventy or more. He raised his hat politely and said to my mother, 'Excuse me, I do hope you will excuse me …' He had a fine white moustache and bushy white eyebrows and a wrinkly pink face. He was sheltering under an umbrella which he held high over his head.

'Yes?' my mother said, very cool and distant.

'I wonder if I could ask a small favour of you.' he said. 'It is only a very small favour.' I saw my mother looking at him suspiciously. She is a suspicious person, my mother. She is especially suspicious of two things – strange men and boiled eggs. When she cuts the top off a boiled egg, she pokes around inside it with her spoon as though expecting to find a mouse or something. With strange men she has a golden rule which says, 'The nicer the man seems to be, the more suspicious you must become.' This little old man was particularly nice. He was polite. He was well spoken. He was well dressed. He was a real gentleman. The reason I knew he was a gentleman was because of his shoes. 'You can always spot a gentleman by the shoes he wears,' was another of my mother's favourite sayings. This man had beautiful brown shoes.

'The truth of the matter is,' the little man was saying, 'I've got myself into a bit of a scrape. I need some help. Not much I assure you. It's almost nothing, in fact, but I do need it. You see, madam, old people like me often become terribly forgetful …'

My mother's chin was up and she was staring down at him along the full length of her nose. It is a fearsome thing, this frosty-nosed stare of my mother's. Most people go to pieces completely when she gives it to them. I once saw my own headmistress begin to stammer and simper like an idiot when my mother gave her a really foul frosty-noser. But the little man on the pavement with the umbrella over his head didn't bat an eyelid. He gave a gentle smile and said, 'I beg you to believe, madam, that I am not in the habit of stopping ladies in the street and telling them my troubles.'

'I should hope not, ' my mother said.

I felt quite embarrassed by my mother's sharpness. I wanted to say to her, 'Oh, Mummy, for heaven's sake, he's a very very old man, and he's sweet and polite, and he's in some sort of trouble, so don't be so beastly to him.' But I didn't say anything.

The little man shifted his umbrella from one hand to the other. 'I've never forgotten it before,' he said.

'You've never forgotten what?' my mother asked sternly.

'My wallet,' he said. 'I must have left it in my other jacket. Isn't that the silliest thing to do?'

'Are you asking me to give you money?' my mother said.

'Oh, goodness gracious me, no!' he cried. 'Heaven forbid I should ever do that!'

'Then what *are* you asking?' my mother said. 'Do hurry up. We're getting soaked to the skin standing here.'

'I know you are,' he said. ' And that is why I'm offering you this umbrella of mine to protect you, and to keep for ever, if … if only …'

'If only what?' my mother said.

'If only you would give me in return a pound for my taxi-fare just to get me home.'

My mother was still suspicious. 'If you had no money in the first place,' she said, 'then how did you get here?'

'I walked,' he answered. 'Every day I go for a lovely long walk and then I summon a taxi to take me home. I do it every day of the year.'

'Why don't you walk home now?' my mother asked.

'Oh, I wish I could,' he said. 'I do wish I could. But I don't think I could manage it on these silly old legs of mine. I've gone too far already.'

My mother stood there chewing her lower lip. She was beginning to melt a bit, I could see that. And the idea of getting an umbrella to shelter under must have tempted her a good deal.

'It's a lovely umbrella,' the little man said.

'So I've noticed,' my mother said.

'It's silk, ' he said.

'I can see that.'

'Then why don't you take it, madam,' he said. 'It cost me over twenty pounds, I promise you. But that's of no importance so long as I can get home and rest these old legs of mine.'

I saw my mother's hand feeling for the clasp on her purse. She saw me watching her. I was giving her one of my *own* frosty-nosed looks this time and she knew exactly what I was telling her. Now listen, Mummy, I was telling her, you simply *mustn't* take advantage of a tired old man in this way. It's a rotten thing to do. My mother paused and looked back at me. Then she said to the little man, 'I don't think it's quite right that I should take an umbrella from you worth twenty pounds. I think I'd just better *give* you the taxi-fare and be done with it.'

'No, no no!' he cried. 'It's out of the question! I wouldn't dream of it! Not in a million years! I would never accept money from you like that! Take the umbrella, dear lady, and keep the rain off your shoulders!'

My mother gave me a triumphant sideways look. There you are, she was telling me. You're wrong. He *wants* me to have it.

She fished into her purse and took out a pound note. She held it out to the little man. He took it and handed her the umbrella. He pocketed the pound, raised his hat, gave a quick bow from the waist, and said. 'Thank you, madam, thank you.' Then he was gone.

'Come under here and keep dry, darling,' my mother said. 'Aren't we lucky. I've never had a silk umbrella before. I couldn't afford it.'

'Why were you so horrid to him in the beginning?' I asked.

'I wanted to satisfy myself he wasn't a trickster,' she said. 'And I did. He was a gentleman. I'm very pleased I was able to help him.'

'Yes, Mummy,' I said.

'A *real* gentleman,' she went on. 'Wealthy, too, otherwise he wouldn't have had a silk umbrella. I shouldn't be surprised if he isn't a titled person. Sir Harry Goldsworthy or something like that.'

'Yes, Mummy.'

'This will be a good lesson to you,' she went on. 'Never rush things. Always take your time when you are summing someone up. Then you'll never make mistakes.'

'There he goes,' I said. 'Look.'

'Where?'

'Over there. He's crossing the street. Goodness, Mummy, what a hurry he's in.'

We watched the little man as he dodged nimbly in and out of the traffic. When he reached the other side of the street, he turned left, walking very fast.

'He doesn't look very tired to me, does he to you, Mummy?'

My mother didn't answer.

'He doesn't look as though he's trying to get a taxi, either,' I said.

My mother was standing very still and stiff, staring across the street at the little man.

We could see him clearly. He was in a terrific hurry. He was bustling along the pavement, sidestepping the other pedestrians and swinging his arms like a soldier on the march.

'He's up to something,' my mother said, stony-faced.

'But what?'

'I don't know,' my mother snapped. 'But I'm going to find out. Come with me.' She took my arm and we crossed the street together. Then we turned left.

'Can you see him?' my mother asked.

'Yes. There he is. He's turning right down the next street.' We came to the corner and turned right. The little man was about twenty yards ahead of us. He was scuttling along like a rabbit and we had to walk fast to keep up with him. The rain was pelting down harder than ever now and I could see it dripping from the brim of his hat onto his shoulders. But we were snug and dry under our lovely big silk umbrella.

'What is he up to?' my mother said.

'What if he turns round and sees us?' I asked.

'I don't care if he does,' my mother said. 'He lied to us. He said he was too tired to walk any further and he's practically running us off our feet! He's a barefaced liar! He's a crook!'

'You mean he's *not* a titled gentleman?' I asked.

'Be quiet,' she said.

At the next crossing, the little man turned right again.

Then he turned left.

Then right.

'I'm not giving up now,' my mother said.

'He's disappeared!' I cried. 'Where's he gone?'

'He went in that door!' my mother said. 'I saw him! Into that house! Great heavens, it's a pub!'

It was a pub. In big letters right across the front it said THE RED LION.

'You're not going in, are you, Mummy?'

'No,' she said. 'We'll watch from outside.'

There was a big plate-glass window along the front of the pub, and although it was a bit steamy on the inside, we could see through it very well if we went close.

We stood huddled together outside the pub window. I was clutching my mother's arm. The big raindrops were making a loud noise on our umbrella. 'There he is,' I said. 'Over there.'

The room we were looking into was full of people and cigarette smoke, and our little man was in the middle of it all. He was now without his hat and coat, and he was edging his way through the crowd towards the bar. When he reached it, he placed both hands on the bar itself and spoke to the barman. I saw his lips moving as he gave his order. The barman turned away from him for a few seconds and came back with a smallish tumbler filled to the brim with light brown liquid. The little man placed a pound note on the counter.

'That's my pound!' my mother hissed. 'By golly, he's got a nerve!'

'What's in the glass?' I asked.

'Whisky,' my mother said. 'Neat whisky.'

The barman didn't give him any change from the pound.

'That must be a treble whisky,' my Mummy said.

'What's a treble?' I asked.

'Three times the normal measure,' she answered.

The little man picked up the glass and put it to his lips. He tilted it gently. Then he tilted it higher … and higher … and higher … and very soon all the whisky had disappeared down his throat in one long pour.

'That's a jolly expensive drink,' I said.

'It's ridiculous!' my Mummy said. 'Fancy paying a pound for something to swallow in one go!'

'It cost him more than a pound,' I said. 'It cost him a twenty-pound silk umbrella.'

'So it did,' my mother said. 'He must be mad.'

The little man was standing by the bar with the empty glass in his hand. He was smiling now, and a sort of golden glow of pleasure was spreading over his round pink face. I saw his tongue come out to lick the white moustache, as though searching for one last drop of that precious whisky.

Slowly, he turned away from the bar and edged his way back through the crowd to where his hat and coat were hanging. He put on his hat. He put on his coat. Then, in a manner so superbly cool and casual that you hardly noticed anything at all, he lifted from the coat rack one of the many wet umbrellas hanging there, and off he went.

'Did you see that!' my mother shrieked. 'Did you see what he did!'

'Ssshh!' I whispered. 'He's coming out!'

We lowered our umbrella to hide our faces, and peered out from under it.

Out he came. But he never looked in our direction. He opened his new umbrella over his head and scurried off down the road the way he had come.

'So that's his little game!' my mother said.

'Neat,' I said. 'Super.'

We followed him back to the main street where we had first met him, and we watched him as he proceeded, with no trouble at all, to exchange his new umbrella for another pound note. This time it was with a tall thin fellow who didn't even have a coat or hat. And as soon as the transaction was completed, our little man trotted off down the street and was lost in the crowd. But this time he went in the opposite direction.

'You see how clever he is!' my mother said. 'He never goes to the same pub twice!'

'He could go on doing this all night,' I said.

'Yes,' my mother said. 'Of course. But I'll bet he prays like mad for rainy days.'

Plot is the sequence of events that make up the story in a piece of fiction. Most stories can be broken down into four main steps: situation, complication, problem or crisis point, resolution.

 Understand

1. In the case of each of the following, write the letter corresponding to the correct answer in your copy.

    (a) Why were the narrator and her mother in London?

        i. To go shopping   **ii.** To buy an umbrella   **iii.** To visit the dentist

    (b) What was the weather like when the narrator and her mother left the café?

        i. It was raining   **ii.** It was sunny   **iii.** It was windy

2. What reason does the girl give for thinking the man was a gentleman?

3. What does the narrator say that her mother is particularly suspicious about?

4. What does the old man want in return for the umbrella?

5. Where do the narrator and her mother follow the old man to?

6. There is a moment of discovery in this short story. When does this revelation happen and what is revealed?

Explore

 1. (a) What impression do you form of the old man when the girl and her mother first encounter him?

 (b) Did this impression change by the end of the story? Give a reason for your answer.

 2. How would you describe the relationship between the girl and her mother?

 3. Would you say there is humour in this short story? Explain your answer.

4. In your opinion, do you think what the old man is doing is clever or wrong? Give two reasons for your answer.

 5. Work with a partner to reduce this story into four main steps: situation, complication, problem or crisis point, resolution.

6. Think of an unexpected moment that surprised you in a novel or short story that you have studied.

(a) Name the novel or short story and the author.

(b) What impact did this moment have on a central character?

 Create

1. Write a short story inspired by the word 'discovery'. Use the checklist below to help you.

Short stories

✓ Plan the plot (situation, complication, problem or crisis point and resolution)
✓ Decide whether your story is going to be told in the first- or the third-person
✓ Choose a setting
✓ Use descriptive language that appeals to the senses
✓ Include dialogue
✓ Create interesting characters
✓ Show, do not tell

2. Imagine that the narrator and her mother decided to make a police report on the actions of the old man. Write the text of this report.

The world is a big place and thinking about this can sometimes make us feel very small.

In the following extract from *A Portrait of the Artist as a Young Man* by James Joyce, Stephen Dedalus is at study hall in his boarding school when he becomes preoccupied with deeper thoughts about the world around him.

A Portrait of the Artist as a Young Man

Sitting in the study hall he opened the lid of his desk and changed the number pasted up inside from seventy-seven to seventy-six. But the Christmas vacation was very far away: but one time it would come because the earth moved round always.

There was a picture of the earth on the first page of his geography: a big ball in the middle of clouds. Fleming had a box of crayons and one night during free study he had coloured the earth green and the clouds maroon ...

... He opened the geography to study the lesson; but he could not learn the names of places in America. Still they were all different places that had different names. They were all in different countries and the countries were in continents and the continents were in the world and the world was in the universe.

He turned to the flyleaf of the geography and read what he had written there: himself, his name and where he was.

> Stephen Dedalus
> Class of Elements
> Clongowes Wood College
> Sallins
> County Kildare
> Ireland
> Europe
> The World
> The Universe

That was in his writing: and Fleming one night for a cod had written on the opposite page.

> Stephen Dedalus is my name
> Ireland is my nation.
> Clongowes is my dwellingplace
> And heaven my expectation.

He read the verses backwards but then they were not poetry. Then he read the flyleaf from the bottom to the top till he came to his own name. That was he: and he read down the page again. What was after the universe? Nothing. But was there anything round the universe to show where it stopped before the nothing place began? It could not be a wall; but there could be a thin thin line there all round everything. It was very big to think about everything and everywhere. Only God could do that. He tried to think what a big thought that must be; but he could only think of God. God was God's name just as his name was Stephen. *Dieu* was the French for God and that was God's name too; and when anyone prayed to God and said *Dieu* then God knew at once that it was a French person that was praying. But, though there were different names for God in all the different languages in the world and God understood what all the people who prayed said in their different languages, still God remained always the same God and God's real name was God.

Discuss

1. Do you think this story would be more effective if it were written in the first person?
2. What do you imagine is 'after the universe'?

Understand

1. What picture was on the first page of Stephen's geography book?
2. In your opinion, why do you think Stephen could not learn the names of places in America?
3. What is the French word for God?

Explore

1. What age do you think Stephen is? Refer to the text to support your answer.
2. Summarise Stephen's thoughts about God in the last paragraph.

Create

Write the longest possible address for the location you are in right now.

For example:

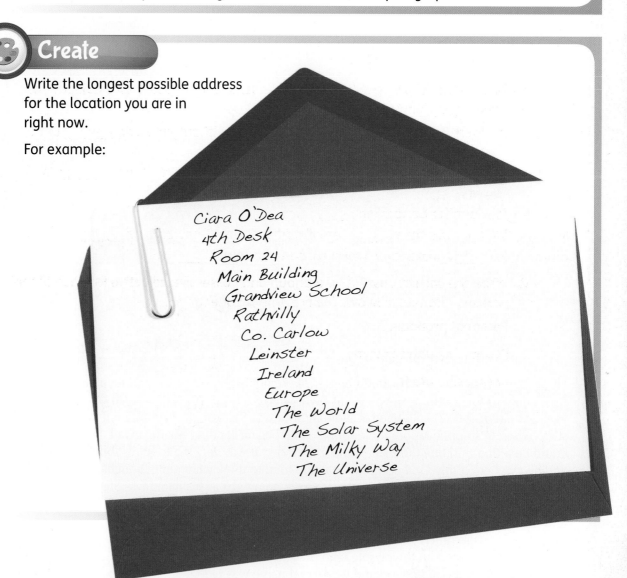

Ciara O'Dea
4th Desk
Room 24
Main Building
Grandview School
Rathvilly
Co. Carlow
Leinster
Ireland
Europe
The World
The Solar System
The Milky Way
The Universe

Possessive adjectives and pronouns

Possessive adjectives (e.g. my, your, her, its, his) **and possessive pronouns** (e.g. theirs, mine, yours, his, hers) **are both used to show possession or ownership of something.**

Possessive adjectives are always followed by a noun.

My shoes.

Your hair.

Possessive pronouns are not followed by a noun.

Yours are brighter.

Hers are cleaner.

 Understand

1. Rewrite the following sentences, putting in a correct possessive adjective or possessive pronoun where they are missing.

   (a) Mark has already eaten _____ slice of cake, but I'm saving _____ until later.

   (b) I do not understand why _____ wifi is not connecting when _____ is working.

   (c) Jennifer has broken _____ arm.

   (d) We gave them _____ email addresses and they gave us _____ .

   (e) _____ calculator is broken, can I borrow _____?

2. Write the correct possessive pronoun and possessive adjective for each of the personal pronouns below. The first one is done for you.

   Personal pronoun: I

   Possessive adjective: my

   Possessive pronoun: mine

   ◖ You   ◖ He   ◖ We

   ◖ It   ◖ She   ◖ They

Finding humour in the world around me

Humour is a necessary part of life. The world can sometimes be a difficult place to live. It is therefore important to see the funny side of life and to find humour in the world around us.

 **Focus on ... satire**

Satire is the use of humour and exaggeration to expose weaknesses, mostly regarding topical issues or ideas.

Usually, whatever is being criticised is exaggerated or ridiculed to such an extreme that it is wildly obvious to the audience. Satire can be used in all literary forms, and it is common in television, film and advertising. The main types of satire include:

◖ parody ◖ irony ◖ caricature.

Parody

Parodies are used mainly for entertainment purposes, but they are sometimes used to emphasise a point or persuade an audience.

In the following video, Irish sketch comedy group Foil Arms and Hog parody a well-known television advertisement.

🔗 https://youtu.be/MlIAbIuAn1c

 Explore

1. Why do you think the dentist keeps referencing the fact that he is a dentist?

 2. What makes this advertisement funny?

 3. What features of a real advertisement can you identify in this parody?

 Investigate

Use your research skills to find the original advertisement that Foil Arms and Hog are parodying here. How does the original compare with the parody?

 Create

 Think of a well-known advertisement that you could parody. In small groups, record a parody of your chosen advertisement to share with the class.

Irony

Irony is used to express a viewpoint which is usually the opposite of what is being said. For example, saying 'What a nice day' when it is raining. It is mostly used for humour and entertainment, but it can be used to emphasise a particular point. Irony also refers to oddly contradictory situations (situational irony).

Read the following headlines and see if you can identify the irony in each.

Pair Banned From All-You-Can-Eat Restaurant For Eating Too Much

Screening of Noah Cancelled After Cinema Theatre Floods

Anti-Piracy Group Accused of Stealing the Photo They Used in an Anti-Piracy Ad

Warehouse Worker Packing Stress Balls Punched His Boss in Face

 Discuss

1. Can you think of any other examples of irony?
2. Has anything ironic ever happened to you?

 Understand

Explain how each headline above is ironic.

 Explore

1. Which headline is your favourite? Give a reason for your answer.
2. Aside from entertainment value, what else would you use irony for?

 Create

 1. Work in groups to come up with some ironic newspaper headlines. Share these with the class.
2. Choose one of the headlines above, or one of the headlines that you came up with yourself, and write a humorous article to go with it.

Sarcasm

Sarcasm is the use of irony to mock. Sarcasm is used across all media platforms.

> Oh yes,
> I would love to go out in the rain to collect the cones from soccer practice.

Discuss

1. Can you recall the last time you heard someone using sarcasm? What did they say that was sarcastic?

2. When was the last time you used sarcasm? What did you say that was sarcastic?

Memes

Memes are a recent phenomenon. A meme is an image, video or piece of text that is copied and shared by internet users. Memes are often humorous and can be used to satirise the world around us.

YOU POST ALL YOUR PROBLEMS ON FACEBOOK?

THAT MUST SOLVE EVERYTHING!

Understand

1. Name the film the image is from.

2. What is the genuine message behind this meme?

3. What makes this meme sarcastic?

Create

  In pairs, come up with some text that could be added to the images below to create memes.

Caricature

A caricature is the exaggeration of a particular flaw or feature of someone for comic effect. A caricature can be visual or a written description.

In the poem 'Base Details', Siegfried Sassoon highlights the flaws of the major at the base: 'with his puffy petulant face'. This is an example of a caricature used in poetry.

 Discuss

1. What trait is the poet caricaturing in this quote?
2. How does the major come across in this quote?

 Explore

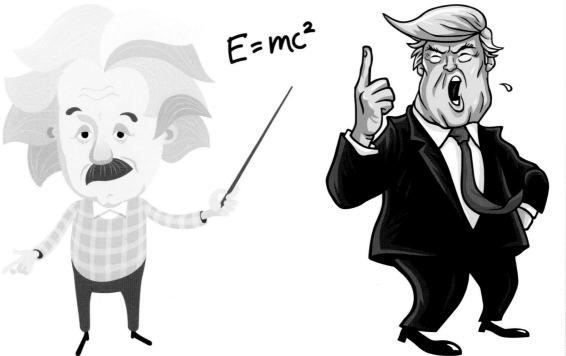

$$E=mc^2$$

1. Who do these caricatures represent?
2. What traits do you think these images are trying to capture?
3. Which caricature do you think is the better at representing the person being caricatured?
4. Is there anything in these caricatures that you would change to improve them?

 Create

 Design a front page for a newspaper or magazine in the space provided on page 22 of your Portfolio. Include one or more of the forms of satire you have just learned about. Remember, you will need:

- a catchy headline
- an image or a photo
- details about articles in the publication.

A changing world

The world around us is constantly changing. Some changes, such as evolution, are noticable only over long periods of time, whereas other changes, such as developments in technology, are more obvious.

Some of the biggest changes taking place in the world around us today are due to developments in technology. Technology is constantly advancing and altering the way we interact with the world and with one another.

The following feature article by Dennis Loctier explores advances in technology that could help people with disabilities and make the world more accessible.

A World without Limits

New technologies are blurring the boundaries between the real and the virtual world. The brain can control a machine, and even perceive it as its own body. Can that improve our lives?

At Barcelona University, scientists are working on a European Research Project to link a human brain to a robot using skin electrodes and video goggles so that the user feels they are actually in the android body wherever it is in the world.

The electrodes measure brain impulses enabling a person to control the robot's actions without moving their own limbs. The idea is to enable severely disabled people to enter the world via a real-life avatar.

Using a remote avatar, anyone can travel without leaving home. But to make the experience feel more realistic, several senses need to work together.

In a laboratory in Pisa, scientists are testing a chair that vibrates in time with 3D video playback, recreating some of the physical aspects of walking.

An even deeper immersion into the virtual world becomes possible with robotic exoskeletons that simulate physical interactions, and with advanced 3D projection systems.

Touching virtual objects, feeling their texture and weight will make the digital world more natural and easier to live in.

But what if virtual models could change the real world, making it more accessible? That's the goal of another European project involving hundreds of disabled people in several countries.

Scientists use cameras and sensors to study how physically impaired people move, getting a better idea of their average physical limitations.

The data is used to simulate how motor-impaired people cope with various tasks – such as opening the glove compartment in a car.

With these models, industrial designers will know in advance how safe and convenient their new products are, and can adapt them better for users with physical limitations.

Seeing the screen through the eyes of someone with advanced glaucoma, using the mouse as a person with tremors ... makes it easier to understand other people's physical challenges, helping us move towards a world without limits.

electrodes:
conductors through which electricity enters or leaves

android:
robot with a human-like appearance

avatar:
a figure representing a person

exoskeletons:
external supportive coverings

glaucoma:
condition that causes the gradual loss of sight

Focus on ... feature articles

A **feature article** is a piece of writing that focuses on a topic of interest.

Feature articles usually appear in magazines or newspapers. They focus on a smaller target audience than news articles. The language style can be emotive and subjective, allowing the writer to include more of their opinion. *based on ones personals opinions / feelings*

Feature articles can be humorous, informative, lighthearted or serious, depending on the style of the writer and the topic they are discussing.

Understand

1. What are scientists at Barcelona University working on?

2. What do the electrodes measure?

3. What will make the digital world more natural and easier to live in?

4. What do scientists use cameras and sensors to study?

5. According to the article, what makes it easier to understand other people's physical challenges?

6. What features of a feature article can you identify in this piece?

Investigate

Use your research skills to find out about a new breakthrough in technology (for example, self-driving cars, drone deliveries, brain implants to reverse paralysis, facial recognition systems to authorise payments). Try to find out the following information:

◖ who created the new technology

◖ what the new technology does

◖ when the new technology is likely to become widely available

◖ the impact the technology may have on society.

Create

1. Write a feature article about the new breakthrough in technology that you researched. Remember to include the features of a feature article in the checklist.

2. Imagine there was a worldwide electricity failure that lasted for a day. Write a diary entry for this day. Think of all the aspects of your daily life that would be affected by a lack of electricity.

Feature articles

✓ Headline

✓ Arresting opening

✓ Personal anecdotes

✓ Information and facts

✓ Opinions

✓ Humorous and engaging language

Our world has become smaller through advancements in technology. We can speak to friends and family across the globe through video calls and explore other countries through videos, photographs and applications like Google Maps, but is this really the same as seeing and feeling these adventures for ourselves?

In the following poem, Oscar Mann discusses all of the things he has experienced through screens.

My digital Utopia

Utopia:
an imagined place where
everything is perfect

By Oscar Mann

I know birds and bees
And magnificent trees
I have seen them on TV

I have climbed mountains
Despite my fear of heights
And have also mastered digital tides

There is nothing I don't know
And nowhere I can't go
There is nothing I need
Besides my 24/7 live feed

I have met some women
The greatest ones I've ever seen
Sitting inside my computer screen

And my conversations are special
Intelligent and profound
Now that I don't need to make a sound

There is nothing left to lose
And everything left to gain
There is nothing left untold
In my digital utopian world

Focus on ... **oxymorons**

An **oxymoron** is when two contradictory terms appear together.

For example: the walking dead, act natural.

Oxymorons can be used to place emphasis on an idea or to add to the emotion or mood of a piece of writing.

Work in pairs to identify an oxymoron in the 'Digital Utopia'. How does the oxymoron you found contribute to the poem?

Discuss

1. Is watching something on television or seeing it on your computer the same as experiencing it in real life, in your opinion? Why or why not?
2. Are there any types of interactions that you prefer to have via a computer?

Understand

1. What has the poet seen on television?
2. What does the poet say is the only thing he needs?
3. What does the poet not know?
4. What type of conversations is the poet having?
5. Where has the poet met 'the greatest women'?

Explore

 1. Identify the rhyming scheme used in this poem. What effect does this rhyming scheme have on the poem? Give two reasons for your answer.

 2. Would you agree that the title captures the message of the poem? Give two reasons for your answer.

Create

Write a short story about a character who is addicted to technology.

Environmental changes as a result of human activity are one of the biggest challenges the planet faces. The effects humans have on the world can be seen all around us. It is our duty to seek out more sustainable ways of living to protect our world for future generations.

In the following blog entry, Ramez Naam highlights some of the destruction that humans are causing to the world around us at this very minute.

https://blogs.scientificamerican.com/guest-blog/the-limits-of-the-earth-part-1-problems/

The Limits of the Earth

The world is facing incredibly serious natural resource and environmental challenges: Climate change, fresh water depletion, ocean over-fishing, deforestation, air and water pollution, the struggle to feed a planet of billions.

All of these challenges are exacerbated by ever rising demand – over the next 40 years estimates are that demand for fresh water will rise 50%, demand for food will rise 70%, and demand for energy will nearly double – all in the same period that we need to tackle climate change, depletion of rivers and aquifers, and deforestation …

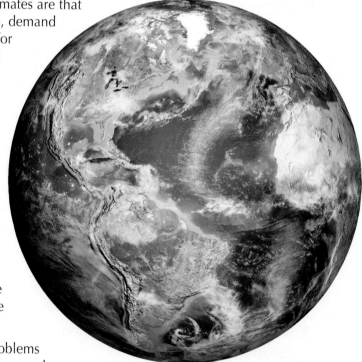

… The problem isn't economic growth, per se. Nor is the problem that our natural resources are too small. While finite, the natural resources the planet supplies are vast and far larger than humanity needs in order to continue to thrive and grow prosperity for centuries to come. The problem, rather, is the types of resources we access, and the manner and efficiency with which we use them.

And the ultimate solution to those problems is innovation – innovation in the science and technology that we use to tap into physical resources, and innovation in the economic system that steers our consumption.

Understand

1. **(a)** Use your dictionary to look up the underlined words in this blog entry.

   (b) Add the words and their definitions to the vocabulary builder on pages 1–2 of your Portfolio.

   (c) Put each of these words into a sentence.

2. According to the blog entry, what problems is the world currently facing?

3. What does the blog estimate will happen to demand for water and food over the next 40 years?

4. What does Ramez Naam suggest is the reason behind the challenges that the Earth faces?

5. According to Ramez Naam, what is the ultimate solution to the problems that the environment is facing?

Explore

1. Do you agree with the author that 'the ultimate solution to those problems is innovation'? Explain your answer. _Both bc it contains info on the topic but it also contains info that can persuaid the reader_

2. Do you think this blog entry is an example of informative or persuasive writing? Give reasons for your answer with reference to the content and style of the blog.

Investigate

Work in groups to research one of the challenges to the environment listed below.

- Global warming
- Ozone layer depletion
- Overpopulation
- Acid rain
- Deforestation
- Ocean acidification
- Urban sprawl

When you have found out as much as you can about your topic, work as a group to come up with a list of changes humans could make to help stop or prevent the issue.

Create

1. Use the information you researched and the solutions you came up with to create a conservation awareness poster to be displayed in your classroom.

2. Write a six-step guide for students about changes they could make in their daily lives to help conserve the environment.

We all have the capacity to change the world around us – either positively or negatively. Voicing our opinions can be a substantial tool in making a difference.

In the following speech, given at a New York University graduation ceremony, musician Pharrell Williams praises students for their activism and encourages them to use their education to serve humanity.

Pharrell Williams at NYU Graduation

Thank you. Hi everybody.

I want to thank all of you for this humbling experience today. This is major. It's super heavy and I'm very really grateful. My mom is a lifelong educator—so this is gonna be a really good look for me.

To be a part of a group like this is unimaginable. To speak on behalf of our group is an honor that I am not sure I am qualified for. Their accomplishments … The body of work represented on this stage is staggering. We have history-makers. Miracle-workers in their own way. If their names aren't on buildings yet, they're totally gonna be.

I'd like to say that I am forever a student, and its people like this that I'm forever grateful to learn from. They are fearless, boundless, multi-disciplined and multi-talented. They break down barriers and embody the focus and dedication that this planet needs—even if, for Mark Kelly, it means leaving from time to time.

Some may call them public servants, but their work is actually in the service of humanity and standing with them here today … and it's totally mind-blowing.

In this day and age, it's easy to lose sight of the fact that it's the people who serve humanity, that make the world really go around. Most social media and media itself would lead you to believe otherwise.

This group's work doesn't fuel gossip. Sadly, it doesn't generate a lot of clicks amongst a sea of headlines designed to bait. Their work is often too important to be boiled down to just a quick headline. Their work has never been more important, yet as a society, we seem to celebrate less important achievements far more frequently. I am glad to be a part of a moment that recognizes these people, the real movers and shakers.

Think about it … these great scientists, public servants, and activists cannot be bothered with building their Instagram followers. Or how many views they get on YouTube … But they are the real influencers. Their work makes us healthier, safer, more enriched, and more intelligent. Their work is designed to improve the quality of life for all people, not just themselves.

They are not motivated by attention. But rather, they are motivated by the idea of creating change. For the better.

I personally find that incredibly inspiring. I hope you do as well.

NYU—the school you all chose to attend—is going out of its way to honor this distinguished group. What will they honor you for someday? What will they honor you for?

Speaking to you guys today has me charged up. As you find your ways to serve humanity, it gives me great comfort knowing this generation is the first that understands that we need to lift up our women. Imagine the possibilities when we remove imbalance from the ether. Imagine the possibilities when women are not held back. Your generation is unravelling deeply entrenched laws, principles and misguided values that have held women back for far too long and therefore, have held us all back, the human race. The world you will live in will be a lot better for it.

Mark Kelly: an astronaut present at the ceremony

This is the first generation that navigates the world with the security and the confidence to treat women as equal. You are the first ever. Our country has never seen this before. It makes some people uncomfortable. But just imagine the possibilities.

Today is in many ways a celebration of higher education.

I am forever a student ... I believe it is a trait that we all share. Yet we live in a time when a great education is harder and harder to come by.

But like anything in life, if there is enough demand, somebody will supply it.

To the graduates, you might think your time in education is done, but after you leave here today, I am asking you to let your actions out there in the world ... fuel the demand for better and accessible education. Engage and inspire—either on an individual level or loudly within your communities. Talk about your accomplishments. Be humble, but not too humble. Don't be invisible.

Sidebar ... The days of being an anonymous activist or participant are over. How can we inspire if we are only behind the scenes? How will an anonymous donation ever inspire another? That was the way of the previous generations. No disrespect, but don't be like them.

Let your actions serve as an endorsement for education and watch the demand rise.

Shining a light on a group of individuals like these on stage also helps fuel the demand. It's why all of us standing here do what we do.

That same gene—those same feelings and adrenaline that fuel us—is inside all of you as well. Just like you, these recipients are brothers, sisters, sons, and daughters. We all put our pants on one leg at a time. We all have a daily commute, but we do so with an eye towards something much bigger. Serving humanity.

There is no humanity without education. There is no education without demand.

You are all walking endorsements for education. So please embrace that.

Thank you again to the students and the faculty at NYU. Thank you to all these remarkable individuals that I am up here standing with. For your service, leadership and inspiration. We are all forever grateful.

Thank you.

Understand

1. What reasons does Pharrell give for why this is a humbling experience for him?
2. What features of a typical speech can you identify in this piece?
3. What does Pharrell encourage the students to do once they graduate?

Explore

1. Pharrell addresses the students by telling them that they are 'the first ever'. What does he mean by this?

 2. In your opinion, would you consider this to be an inspirational speech? Give reasons for your answer.

Create

 1. **(a)** *This house believes that science destroys the mysteries of the world.*
In teams of two, decide whether you both want to oppose or propose the motion above. Work with your teammate to each write a two-minute debate speech. Each of you should use different points to support your argument. Include the features of debates in the checklist.

 (b) Read your debate speech aloud to the class.

 2. **(a)** Write a speech with the heading 'My hopes for the future of our world' in the space provided on pages 23–24 of your Portfolio.

 (b) Deliver your speech to your classmates, then fill out the checklist on page 24 of your Portfolio.

Debates

- ✓ Welcome the audience
- ✓ Introduce yourself
- ✓ Introduce the motion and say whether you are proposing or opposing
- ✓ Structured approach
- ✓ Statistics, facts and figures
- ✓ Engaging language
- ✓ Rhetorical questions
- ✓ Formal language
- ✓ Sum up main points in closing argument

Different worlds

We all experience the world around us in different ways. The lives and experiences of no two people are the same and we are all shaped by the society, culture and world we live in.

The following extract from *All the Light We Cannot See* by Anthony Doerr recounts the story of two teenagers during the Second World War: Marie-Laure, a blind girl in Nazi-occupied France, and Werner, a German orphan pressed into service by the Nazi army.

All the Light We Cannot See

Zero
7 August 1944

Leaflets

At dusk they pour from the sky. They blow across the ramparts, turn cartwheels over rooftops, flutter into the ravines between houses. Entire streets swirl with them, flashing white against the cobbles. *Urgent message to the inhabitants of this town*, they say. *Depart immediately to open country.*

The tide climbs. The moon hangs small and yellow and gibbous. On the rooftops of beachfront hotels to the east, and in the gardens behind them, a half-dozen American artillery units drop incendiary rounds into the mouths of mortars.

Bombers

They cross the Channel at midnight. There are twelve and they are named for songs: *Stardust* and *Stormy Weather* and *In the Mood* and *Pistol-Packin' Mama*. The sea glides along far below, spattered with the countless chevrons of whitecaps. Soon enough, the navigators can discern the low moonlit lumps of islands ranged along the horizon.

France.

Intercoms crackle. Deliberately, almost lazily, the bombers shed altitude. Threads of red light ascend from anti-air emplacements up and down the coast. Dark, ruined ships appear, scuttled or destroyed, one with its bow shorn away, a second flickering as it burns. On an outermost island, panicked sheep run zigzagging between rocks.

Inside each airplane, a bombardier peers through an aiming window and counts to twenty. Four five six seven. To the bombardiers, the walled city on its granite headland, drawing ever closer, looks like an unholy tooth, something black and dangerous, a final abscess to be lanced away.

The Girl

In a corner of the city, inside a tall, narrow house at Number 4 rue Vauborel, on the sixth and highest floor, a sightless sixteen-year-old named Marie-Laure LeBlanc kneels over a low table covered entirely with a model. The model is a miniature of the city she kneels within, and contains scale replicas of the hundreds of houses and shops and hotels within its walls. There's the cathedral with its perforated spire, and the bulky old Château de Saint-Malo, and row after row of seaside mansions studded with chimneys. A slender wooden jetty arcs out from a beach called the Plage du Môle; a delicate, reticulated atrium

ramparts:
defensive walls

gibbous:
when the illuminated part of the moon is greater than a semicircle and less than a circle

incendiary:
device designed to cause fires

mortars:
devices used to fire bombs at high angles

chevrons:
v-shaped lines or stripes on the sleeve of a uniform, indicating rank

emplacements:
platforms where guns are placed

abscess:
a collection of pus that builds up

lanced:
pricked or cut open

reticulated:
arranged in a network

vaults over the seafood market; minute benches, the smallest no larger than apple seeds, dot the tiny public squares.

Marie-Laure runs her fingertips along the centimeter-wide parapet crowning the ramparts, drawing an uneven star shape around the entire model. She finds the opening atop the walls where four ceremonial cannons point to sea. 'Bastion de la Hollande,' she whispers, and her fingers walk down a little staircase. 'Rue des Cordiers. Rue Jacques Cartier.'

In a corner of the room stand two galvanized buckets filled to the rim with water. Fill them up, her great-uncle has taught her, whenever you can. The bathtub on the third floor too. Who knows when the water will go out again.

galvanized:
coated with iron
or steel

Her fingers travel back to the cathedral spire. South to the Gate of Dinan. All evening she has been marching her fingers around the model, waiting for her great-uncle Etienne, who owns this house, who went out the previous night while she slept, and who has not returned. And now it is night again, another revolution of the clock, and the whole block is quiet, and she cannot sleep.

She can hear the bombers when they are three miles away. A mounting static. The hum inside a seashell.

When she opens the bedroom window, the noise of the airplanes becomes louder. Otherwise, the night is dreadfully silent: no engines, no voices, no clatter. No sirens. No footfalls on the cobbles. Not even gulls. Just a high tide, one block away and six stories below, lapping at the base of the city walls.

And something else.

Something rattling softly, very close. She eases open the left-hand shutter and runs her fingers up the slats of the right. A sheet of paper has lodged there.

She holds it to her nose. It smells of fresh ink. Gasoline, maybe. The paper is crisp; it has not been outside long.

Marie-Laure hesitates at the window in her stocking feet, her bedroom behind her, seashells arranged along the top of the armoire, pebbles along the baseboards. Her cane stands in the corner; her big Braille novel waits facedown on the bed. The drone of the airplanes grows.

armoire:
ornate wardrobe

Braille:
a form of writing
using raised
dots, which blind
people can read
by touch

 **Flashback**   In **third-person narratives** the story is told by an unknown narrator who is not involved in the story.

 Understand

1. What do the leaflets floating through the sky have printed on them?

2. What were the bombers named after?

3. Where is Marie-Laure kneeling when she is introduced to us?

4. 'The night is dreadfully silent'. What does the narrator tell us that Marie-Laure is used to hearing?

 5. **(a)** Work in pairs to put four of the following words into sentences:

- ramparts
- mortars
- lanced
- gibbous
- chevrons
- reticulated
- incendiary
- abscess
- galvanise

 (b) Add the words above to the vocabulary builder on pages 1–2 of your Portfolio.

 Explore

 1. What would you say the atmosphere in France was like at this time, based on what you have read in this extract?

2. What impression do you get of Marie-Laure from the extract?

3. Based on what you have read, would you like to read more of this novel? Give two reasons for your answer.

4. What are the advantages of the author using a third-person narrative voice in this novel? Refer to the extract from *All The Light We Cannot See* in your answer.

 Investigate

 Work in groups to look up information about the occupation of France during the Second World War. Each group must present one piece of information to the class that is different to the group that has gone before them.

 Create

 Imagine Marie-Laure asked you to transcribe a diary entry for her on 7 August 1944, the date of the events in this extract. Write the diary entry that you think she would have wanted you to transcribe in the space provided on page 25 of your Portfolio.

The world around us is full of different destinations and places that we never knew existed. These places hold a mystery and a fascination.

In Kiran Milwood Hargrave's novel *The Island at the End of Everything*, Amihan lives with her mother on an island that is to be turned into a colony for people with leprosy. In the extract below Amihan describes the island.

The Island at the End of Everything

Culion Islands, The Philippines 1906.

There are some places you would not want to go.

Even if I told you that we have oceans clear and blue as summer skies, filled with sea turtles and dolphins, or forest-covered hills lush with birds that call through air thick with warmth. Even if you knew how beautiful the quiet is here, clean and fresh as a glass bell ringing. But nobody comes here because they want to.

My *nanay* told me this is how they brought her, but says it is always the same, no matter who you are or where you come from.

From your house you travel on horse or by foot, then on a boat. The men who row it cover their noses and mouths with cloths stuffed with herbs so they don't have to share your breath. They will not help you on to the boat although your head aches and two weeks ago your legs began to hurt, then to numb. Maybe you stumble towards them, and they duck. They'd rather you rolled over their backs and into the sea than touch you. You sit and clutch your bundle of things from home, what you saved before it was burned. Clothes, a doll, some books, letters from your mother.

Somehow, it is always dusk when you approach.

The island changes from a dark dot to a green heaven on the horizon. High on a cross-topped cliff that slopes towards the sea is a field of white flowers, looping strangely. It is not until you are closer that you see it forms the shape of an eagle, and it is not until you are very close

that you see it is made of stones. This is when your heart hardens in your chest, like petals turning to pebbles. Nanay says the white eagle's meaning is known across all the surrounding islands, even all the places outside our sea. It means: *stay away. Do not come here unless you have no choice.*

The day is dropping to dark as you come into the harbour. When you step from the boat, the stars are setting out their little lights. Someone will be there to welcome you. They understand.

The men who brought you leave straight away, though they are tired. They have not spoken to you in the days or hours you spent with them. The splash of oars fades to the sound of waves lapping the beach. They will burn the boat when they get back, as they did your house.

You look at the person who greeted you. You are changed now. Like flowers into stones, day into night. You will always be heavier, darkened, marked. Touched.

Nanay says that in the places outside, they have many names for our home. The island of the living dead. The island of no return. The island at the end of everything.

You are on Culion, where the oceans are blue and clear as summer skies. Culion, where sea turtles dig the beaches and the trees brim with fruit.

Setting is the time, place and type of world in which a story takes place.

 Understand

1. How does Amihan present the setting in the opening paragraph of the extract?
2. Why do the men cover their noses and mouths?
3. What examples does Amihan give of the bundle of things that you would bring with you from home?
4. According to Nanay, what does the white eagle shape of the island signify?
5. What does Nanay say are alternative names for this island?

 Explore

 1. Having read this extract, would it encourage you to read the rest of this novel? Give reasons for your answer.
 2. Would you like to visit the island of Culion? Explain your answer.

 Create

Write a persuasive paragraph encouraging people to visit Culion Island, based on the descriptive information above.

In the following extract, teenage dancer and actress Maddie Ziegler talks about how people make assumptions about her life and gives us a true insight into her world.

The Maddie Diaries

People think they know everything about me from *Dance Moms* or my Sia videos ...

... I get how people can make assumptions based on what they see or hear or read—it's easy to do that. Which is why I thought it was a really good idea to write a book. I may be only fourteen, but there are so many things I love and care about, and so many other sides of who I am. I want people to know the *real* me—the silly stuff, the serious stuff, and everything in between. I'm pretty sure you'll be surprised at some of what you learn. For example ...

- I'm an artist: I love to draw faces—especially eyes—and paint. I just did a watercolor self-portrait. To be honest, it didn't really look like me, but I had fun trying. I did a painting for my room—it's black and white and kind of abstract, with a flower dripping down the middle. I also did one for Kenzie's room of lips and a nose, and I painted Olaf for my baby cousin. In fact, I drew all these doodles throughout the book!

- I cannot leave my house without spraying on my favorite perfume. I love the sweet vanilla scent, and I spray on *a lot*. I spray it inside my arms, then on the back of my neck, and finally, I spray it in the air and walk through this cloud of perfume. My mom is always saying, 'Maddie, you don't need that much!' but I insist. Maybe it's because the dance studios are always so stinky that I feel the need to smell good!

- I don't wear my hair in a perfect bun all the time. In reality, a messy topknot is my go-to style when I'm not onstage. It's the easiest thing to do. I just scoop it and clip it up, without even looking in the mirror!

- When I was three or four years old, I broke my arm just when I was supposed to start horseback riding, so I couldn't. Looking back, I'm really glad that happened—even though at the time I remember being really upset. I might have been a horseback rider instead of a dancer! Things definitely happen for a reason, and I believe in fate.

- I have a wish list in my head of things I want to do, see, and be. And I believe in making wishes. Whenever my friends and I see the time 11:11 on a clock, we touch something blue and make a wish. I don't really know why, but it seemed like a good idea and it kinda stuck ... it's like a superstition now.

- Dancing didn't come naturally to me—I wasn't very good at it in the beginning, and I had to work really hard. It taught me an important lesson: Even if you're not good at something at first, don't give up. Someday you will look back and never believe how far you've come.

- I believe in taking time-outs every now and then. People think I am in the dance studio 24/7, every second of the day. I do dance every day, but I also have a home and friends that I hang with (more on that later). My family recently went to Aruba on vacation and I loved every minute of it (except for the sunburn—I looked like a lobster!). Sia taught me this: If you don't want to be doing what you're doing, if you're feeling overwhelmed or stressed and the passion isn't there, then it's okay to walk away for a little while. You're allowed to take a second to breathe; you don't have to keep going and going.

- I'm okay with being a loser. In the beginning of my competitive dancing, I always wanted to win and I'd get mad or upset if I didn't. But now I know that losing is good. It makes you work harder the next time and learn and grow from your mistakes. It makes you a better performer and a better person.

- Our dog Maliboo is a diva. Every night she has to go out at 4 a.m. to pee and my stepdad has to get up, go downstairs, and open the door for her. Technically, she's Mackenzie's dog, but there's no way my little sister is losing any beauty sleep ...

- I have a bedtime routine: I put a barrier of pillows around me so I feel comfy and protected, and I can only fall asleep if I watch TV before I go to bed. Right now, I'm binge-watching *Grey's Anatomy*.

- I have an amazing memory. Seriously, I don't forget anything—I remember things from when I was a toddler. I never kept a journal when I was little, because I didn't feel the need to write stuff down. But I can tell you every detail of what happened when I was younger and how I felt at that time—it's like hitting rewind, and it really comes in handy when you're writing a book!

And those are just a few things off the top of my head. My mom has also kept every picture of me over the years (even the embarrassing ones) in boxes, and a ton of those are in here, too. But I have a whole other reason for writing this book—one that doesn't involve me at all. It's about *you*. I want to encourage you to believe in yourself and follow your passion. Everyone has a talent and a gift; everyone can make an impact. I know I'm just a teenager, but if you haven't noticed, teens are changing the world. More than ever, we have a voice through social media and a way to connect, educate, and make a difference. We are the future, and girls especially are awesome. There is nothing that we can't do if we put our minds to it. See the possibilities and don't let stuff or people hold you back.

I always thought I would be 'just a competitive dancer.' But now, I realize that was only the beginning. I'm just figuring out what makes me happy and excited and pushing myself to try new things and stretch my wings. I guess my philosophy is 'Why not?' Why not do something that you've never done before? Why not dream big? Why not stand up for things you believe in? Sometimes you have to take a big, scary leap, and that's okay. Even if you fall on your butt, you've still soared.

Discuss

1. Do you think it is important for celebrities to write openly and honestly about their personalities and lifestyle?
2. How do you think this extract fits in to the theme of 'the world around me'?

Understand

1. List the possessive pronouns you can find in this extract.
2. What can Maddie not leave the house without doing?
3. What does Maddie tell us about the family dog Maliboo?
4. Does Maddie get upset when she loses a competition now?
5. What is Maddie's philosophy?

Explore

1. Which piece of information that Maddie gives about herself did you find most interesting? Explain your choice.
2. Does Maddie give any advice that you find inspiring?
3. Maddie tells us that she wrote this book because she wanted 'people to know the *real* me—the silly stuff, the serious stuff, and everything in between'. Do you think this is a good reason to write a memoir? Explain your answer.

Create

 Write three paragraphs that reveal aspects of your life and world in the space provided on page 26 of your Portfolio.

The weather plays a significant role in our world for crop production, survival of wildlife and tourism. Replicating weather on set can be a challenging task for the producer of a play.

In William Shakespeare's play *King Lear*, Lear has stepped down from his throne and divided his kingdom between his two eldest daughters, Goneril and Regan. Now, not wanting to care for their elderly father, his eldest daughters have thrown him out of the castle into the wilderness on a particularly stormy night with only his two loyal followers.

While reading this extract, try to come up with ways that you would bring this piece to life on stage.

King Lear

Enter Lear, Kent and the Fool

KENT	Here is the place, my lord; good my lord, enter.
	The tyranny of the open night's too rough
	For nature to endure.

tyranny: cruelty

(Storm still)

LEAR	Let me alone.
KENT	Good my Lord, enter here.
LEAR	Wilt break my heart?
KENT	I had rather break mine own. Good my lord, enter.
LEAR	Thou think'st 'tis much that this contentious storm
	Invades us to the skin; so 'tis to thee.
	But where the greater malady is fixed
	The lesser is scarce felt. Thou'dst shun a bear;
	But if thy flight lay toward the roaring sea
	Thou'dst meet the bear i'the mouth. When the mind's free
	The body's delicate; this tempest in my mind
	Doth from my senses take all feeling else

malady: sickness

Save what beats there. Filial ingratitude!
Is it not as this mouth should tear this hand
For lifting food to't? But I will punish home.
No, I will weep no more! In such a night
To shut me out! Pour on; I will endure.
In such a night as this! O Regan, Goneril!
Your old kind father, whose frank heart gave all!
O, that way madness lies; let me shun that;
No more of that!

Filial ingratitude:
ungrateful children

KENT   Good my lord, enter here.

LEAR   Prithee go in thyself; seek thine own ease.
This tempest will not give me leave to ponder
On things that would hurt me more; But I'll go in.
(To the Fool) In, boy, go first – You houseless poverty –
Nay, get thee in. I'll pray and then I'll sleep.

(Exit the Fool)

Poor naked wretches, whereso'er you are,
That bide the pelting of this pitiless storm,
How shall your houseless heads and unfed sides,
Your looped and windowed raggedness, defend you
From seasons such as these?

wretches:
*unfortunate or
unhappy people*

Understand

1. In the case of each of the following write the letter corresponding to the correct answer in your copy.

   (a) Who does Kent say cannot endure the storm?
      i. Lear's daughters
      ii. Nature itself
      iii. The Fool

   (b) What does Lear say is affecting him more than the storm?
      i. His hunger
      ii. The noise of Kent
      iii. His mind

   (c) What does Lear try to ignore?
      i. The storm
      ii. The thoughts of what his daughters have done to him
      iii. The advice that the Fool is giving him

2. What does Lear say he will do before he sleeps?

3. What does Lear acknowledge that the 'poor naked wretches' must endure?

Explore

1. Imagine you are directing a performance of this play. What tone would you instruct the actor playing Lear to use for the line 'Poor naked wretches, whereso'er you are, / That bide the pelting of this pitiless storm': pity, sorrow or anger? Explain your answer.

2. What do you think Lear might mean when he says 'But where the greater malady is fixed / The lesser is scarce felt'?

3. In your opinion, does the fact that this scene takes place in a storm add to its impact? Give two reasons for your answer.

 4. What is your impression of the relationship between King Lear and Kent? Explain your answer.

5. Select a scene from a play you have studied. Imagine that you have been asked to recreate a performance of this scene on stage. How would you bring the scene to life? Use the following prompts to guide you.

   ◖ Costume
   ◖ Lighting
   ◖ Sound effects
   ◖ Music
   ◖ Backdrop
   ◖ Stage direction
   ◖ Props

Create

Imagine you are Kent. Write an email to King Lear's two eldest daughters, Goneril and Regan. Tell them about his condition and let them know what you think of their actions towards their father. Remember to include the features in the checklist below.

Emails
✓ To/From
✓ Subject
✓ Greeting
✓ Sign-off

Appreciating the world around me

Nowadays our lives are busy and we can become too wrapped up in technology and our smartphones to notice the beauty of the world around us. It is important that we take moments to appreciate our surroundings and to enjoy all of the beauty that this world has to offer.

Wonders happen every day in the world around us, yet we are often too preoccupied and busy to notice them. The following social experiment, conducted by the *Washington Post Magazine*, explores people's perceptions, taste and priorities.

https://youtu.be/hn0Pu0_YWhw

A social experiment on perception and appreciation

Joshua Bell, one of the most talented musicians in the world, played six pieces of music by famous composer Bach for 45 minutes in the metro station. During those 45 minutes, it is estimated that 1,100 people walked through the station. People scurried past on their way to work. The person who paid most attention to the violinist was a three-year-old boy.

During the 45-minute set, only 6 people stopped and stayed for a while. Roughly 20 people gave him money, but continued to walk past the acclaimed violinist. He collected $32 in total. When he finished playing he packed up his violin and left to no applause or recognition.

Joshua Bell had just played one of the most intricate pieces of music on a violin worth $3.5 million.

Two days before Joshua Bell played in the subway, he had sold out a concert in Boston, where tickets averaged $100.

The Washington Post organised his incognito performance in the subway as part of a social experiment about perception, taste and the priorities of people.

 ## Discuss

 The experiment was aimed at addressing the questions below. Work in groups to read these questions and discuss your answers. Voice your group's opinion or experiences to the class.

1. Can we appreciate beauty in unusual settings?

2. Do we recognise talent in an unexpected context?

3. If we do not stop to listen and appreciate one of the greatest musicians of our time playing one of the most beautiful pieces of music, what else are we potentially missing out on?

4. Why do you think that the person who stopped the longest to appreciate the music was a three-year-old child? What does this tell us about habits in society?

5. Do you think that this was an interesting study to carry out?

 ## Investigate

 Work in groups to come up with an idea for a social experiment that you can carry out. Perhaps you could try to promote positivity, change the behaviour of people or simply observe if people will notice something out of the ordinary. Carry out your experiment and report your findings to the class.

 ## Create

Write a feature article for your school website encouraging students to appreciate the world around them.

In Willy Russell's play *Educating Rita*, Rita is a working-class housewife and hairdresser who wants to better herself by attending university. Her study of literature opens her eyes to new worlds, while her enthusiasm for the subject reignites her professor Frank's passion for teaching.

Educating Rita

It is lunchtime as Frank *enters.*

He puts down his things, switches on the radio (Radio Four) from which we hear the weather forecast directly preceding The World At One. Frank *takes out his lunch and sits at his desk eating and reading a book; the cover of which we recognise as being* Rubyfruit Jungle.

Rita suddenly bursts into the room, out of breath from running.

Frank switches off the radio.

Frank:	What are you doing here? It's Thursday, you ...
Rita:	I know I shouldn't be here, it's me dinner hour, but listen, I've got to tell someone, have y' got a few minutes, can y' spare – ?
Frank:	My God, what is it?
Rita:	I had to come an' tell y', Frank, last night, I went to the theatre! A proper one, a professional theatre.
Frank:	For God's sake, you had me worried, I thought it was something serious.

Rita:	It was, it was Shakespeare, I thought it was gonna be dead borin' but it wasn't – it was brilliant. I'm gonna do an essay on it.
Frank:	Come on, which one was it?
Rita:	' ... Out, out, brief candle!

> Life's but a walking shadow, a poor player
>
> That struts and frets his hour upon the stage
>
> And then is heard no more. It is a tale
>
> Told by an idiot, full of sound and fury
>
> Signifying nothing.'

Frank:	Ah, *Romeo and Juliet*.
Rita:	Tch. Frank! Be serious. I learnt that today from the book. Look, I went out an' bought the book. Isn't it great? What I couldn't get over is how excitin' it was. Wasn't his wife a cow, eh? An' that fantastic bit where he meets Macduff an' he thinks he's all invincible. I was on the edge of me seat at that bit. I wanted to shout out an' tell Macbeth, warn him.
Frank:	You didn't, did you?
Rita:	Nah. Y' can't do that in a theatre, can y'? It was brilliant though. It was like a thriller.
Frank:	Well, you'll have to go and see more Shakespeare.
Rita:	I'm goin' to. *Macbeth*'s a tragedy, isn't it?
Frank:	Yes, it is.

Rita:	Right.
	Beat
	Well I just – I just had to tell someone who'd understand.
Frank:	I'm honoured that you chose me.
Rita:	I better get back. I've left a customer in the shop. If I don't get a move on there'll be another tragedy.

 Focus on ... **acting**

Acting is the art of representing a fictional character.

Scripts are designed to be performed, rather than just read. Therefore, when studying drama, it can be important to act out the scenes you are reading.

 Work in pairs to perform the scene from *Educating Rita* together.

Read through the scene twice to get your tone of voice and expression just right.

Understand

1. What important information does Rita have to tell Frank?
2. Why, according to Rita, did she go to the theatre in the first place?
3. What did Rita want to do during the play?
4. Why does Frank say that he is honoured at the end of the extract?
5. Why does Rita say she has to hurry back?

Explore

 1. What impression do you get of Rita from the extract?

 2. Do you think that Frank is a good tutor, based on the extract?

 3. Do you think Rita is surprised by how she felt after watching *Macbeth*?

4. If you had the choice to audition for the part of Frank or Rita, which character would you want to play and why? Give three reasons for your answer.

5. How would you play the part of your chosen character to convince the director that you were suitable for this part? Give two reasons for your answer. You might refer to tone of voice, movement, costume, facial expression.

Create

 Work in small groups to write the next scene of this play. When you have finished, perform your piece for the rest of the class.

Focus on ... spoken word

Spoken word is a combination of a poem and a rap that is performed for an audience. It is poetry that is intended to be performed.

Spoken word is an oral skill that plays on words to create a message that is catchy and memorable. It relies on a heavy use of rhythm, improvisation, word play and slang.

In his spoken word short film *Look Up*, Gary Turk encourages people to look up from their smartphones and to engage with the world in a meaningful way.

🔗 https://youtu.be/Z7dLU6fk9QY

💬 Discuss

1. Do you think that using spoken word is effective in this short film?
2. In your opinion, what is the most important point that Gary makes in this film?
3. After watching this film do you feel differently about how you interact with your phone?
4. Can you think of any possible opportunities you may have missed as a result of being on your phone?
5. Do you know of any other spoken word videos you could share with the class?

🎞 Create

 Work in groups to create a spoken word poem about social media and how it can disconnect us from the world around us. When you have finished, perform your piece as a group for the rest of the class.

It is important to take time to appreciate the beauty of the natural world all around us. The following poem portrays the changing seasons and the effect they have on nature.

There Came a Day

By Ted Hughes

There came a day that caught the summer
Wrung its neck
Plucked it
And ate it.

Now what shall I do with the trees?
The day said, the day said.
Strip them bare, strip them bare.
Let's see what is really there.

And what shall I do with the sun?
The day said, the day said.
Roll him away till he's cold and small.
He'll come back rested if he comes back at all.

And what shall I do with the birds?
The day said, the day said.
The birds I've frightened, let them flit,
I'll hang out pork for the brave tomtit.

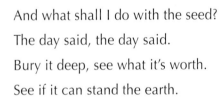

tomtit:
a small songbird

And what shall I do with the seed?
The day said, the day said.
Bury it deep, see what it's worth.
See if it can stand the earth.

What shall I do with the people?
The day said, the day said.
Stuff them with apple and blackberry pie –
They'll love me then till the day they die.

There came this day and he was autumn.
His mouth was wide
And red as a sunset.
His tail was an icicle.

 Poets use **repetition** to emphasise their point or to draw attention to an important theme.

 Discuss

1. Which season does your birthday fall in?
2. Which season do you prefer? Why?
3. How do you feel when the seasons change?

 Understand

1. What will the day do to summer?
2. What will happen to the birds in the fourth stanza?
3. What will the day do to the people in the sixth stanza?
4. The poet personifies the day in this poem. Find two examples where the poet uses personification to bring the day to life.

 Explore

1. How many times does the poet repeat 'the day said'? What effect does this have on the poem, in your opinion?
 2. What image from the poem stands out to you the most? Give two reasons for your answer.
3. Poetry can powerfully explore the theme of nature. Choose a poem that you have studied that explores the theme of nature.
   (a) Name the poem and the poet.
   (b) How does the poem explore the theme of nature?

 Create

1. Draw a picture to represent the day that the poet refers to in the final stanza.
2. Write a final stanza for 'There Came a Day' in which you detail what winter will do to nature.

Reviewing the world around me

Reflect and review

1. Take a look at the images on the first page of this unit. Consider the association each image has with the theme of 'the world around me'. Which image do you think best represents this unit? Explain your answer.

2. Can you think of any other pieces of literature that would fit well within this theme? Share your thoughts with the class.

3. Fill in the unit review on pages 27–28 of your Portfolio.

Language skills

Write a blog post about technology, nature, education or social media. Try to include at least two possessive pronouns, two possessive adjectives and three of the new words that you learned in this unit.

Oral assessment

Chose one of the topics below to write a spoken word poem about. Deliver this spoken word poem to your class.

- The future of technology will change our daily lives.
- Nature goes unappreciated in a society full of photographs.
- Spend an hour a day reading a book instead of scrolling through social media.

Written assessment

1. (a) Write a personal essay entitled 'The Wonders of My World' in the space provided on pages 29–30 of your Portfolio.

   (b) Redraft your personal essay in the space provided on pages 108–109 of your Portfolio.

Exam skills

1. 'The world that a novel is set in can greatly affect the choices or actions of a character.' Choose a novel you have studied in which a character's choices or actions are affected by the world in which they live.

   (a) Name the novel, the author and the character.

   (b) Describe the world the character lives in.

   (c) How has the world of your studied novel affected the choices or actions of this character?

   Write your answer in the space provided on pages 134–135 of your Portfolio

Theme 3

Tracing My Travels

What is travel?

Travel is the movement and journey through geographical locations. People travel for many reasons – to explore and experience different surroundings and cultures, to learn more about the world, to see beautiful sights, to have adventures and to discover new places.

Why study this theme?

As Saint Augustine once said, 'The world is a book, and those who do not travel, read only one page.' Travel allows us to gain a greater understanding of the world in which we live. Studying this theme will broaden your horizons and open your mind to new experiences and ideas.

Learning intentions

- ◖ Consider the advantages and disadvantages of travel.
- ◖ Look at how to prepare for travel.

Writing With Purpose
- ◖ Look at travel blogs.
- ◖ Learn how to write brochures.

Poetry and Song
- ◖ Explore the possible downsides of travelling.
- ◖ Study the advancement of travel beyond our world.
- ◖ Experience the richness and vibrancy of travel.

Fiction
- ◖ Analyse the implications of travel.
- ◖ Encounter foreshadowing.

Stage and Screen
- ◖ Revise how camera angles can capture a sense of place.
- ◖ Engage with stage direction and dialogue.
- ◖ Explore the benefits of having others visit us.

Media and Advertising
- ◖ Enhance your comparison skills.
- ◖ Analyse imagery.

Language Skills
- ◖ Learn how to avoid using double negatives.

Discuss

1. Do any of the images above remind you of an experience or memory you have of travelling?
2. Which image do you think best represents the theme of travel?
3. Come up with another image that you think could represent the theme of travel.

Create

Write your own definition of 'travel' in the space provided on page 35 of your Portfolio, by completing the sentence 'Travel is …'. You will return to this definition later on.

The desire to travel

Many people long to travel to new places, to have adventures, experience other cultures and view beautiful sights.

Our desire to travel and explore can be inspired by others. In the following extract from Ransom Riggs's novel *Miss Peregrine's Home for Peculiar Children*, the narrator tells us how his desire to explore new places was inspired by his grandfather.

Miss Peregrine's Home for Peculiar Children

I had just come to accept that my life would be ordinary when extraordinary things began to happen. The first of these came as a terrible shock and, like anything that changes you forever, split my life into halves: Before and After. Like many of the extraordinary things to come, it involved my grandfather, Abraham Portman.

Growing up, Grandpa Portman was the most fascinating person I knew. He had lived in an orphanage, fought in wars, crossed oceans by steamship and deserts on horseback, performed in circuses, knew everything about guns and self-defence and surviving in the wilderness, and spoke at least three languages that weren't English. It all seemed unfathomably exotic to a kid who'd never left Florida, and I begged him to regale me with stories whenever I saw him. He always obliged, telling them like secrets that could be entrusted only to me.

regale:
amuse with
talk

When I was six I decided that my only chance of having a life half as exciting as Grandpa Portman's was to become an explorer.

He encouraged me by spending afternoons at my side hunched over maps of the world, plotting imaginary expeditions with trails of red pushpins and telling me about the fantastic places I would discover one day. At home I made my ambitions known by parading around with a cardboard tube held to my eye, shouting, 'Land ho!' and 'Prepare a landing party!' until my parents shooed me outside. I think they worried that my grandfather would infect me with some incurable dreaminess from which I'd never recover – that these fantasies were somehow inoculating me against more practical ambitions – so one day my mother sat me down and explained that I couldn't become an explorer because everything in the world had already been discovered. I'd been born in the wrong century and I felt cheated.

inoculating:
vaccinating

Flashback In **first-person narratives** the story is written in the first person (I) and told from the point of view of a character who is involved in the story.

Discuss

1. When you were younger, what did you want to be when you grew up?
2. Has this changed now that you are older?
3. Was there anything that you believed when you were younger that you no longer believe?

Understand

1. What is the name of the narrator's grandfather?
2. What does the narrator tell us about his grandfather's life?
3. How did the narrator's grandfather encourage his passion for discovery?
4. What did the narrator decide to become when he was six?
5. What were the narrator's parents worried about?
6. What does the narrator's mother sit him down to tell him?

Explore

1. What kind of person was Grandpa Portman, in your opinion?
2. Were the speaker's parents right to be worried that his grandfather would infect him 'with some incurable dreaminess' that he would never recover from? Explain your answer.
3. Do you agree that you cannot be an explorer in this day and age? Why or why not?
4. **(a)** Rewrite the first two paragraphs of this extract as a third-person narrative.

   (b) What are the advantages and disadvantages of first-person narratives?

Create

1. 'Everything in the world has already been discovered.' Imagine that you have discovered a new country. Draw a picture of what you envisage this new country to look like.

2. Work in pairs to write the dialogue that took place between the boy and his mother when she told him that he could not become an explorer. When you have finished, act your dialogue out for the rest of the class.

The lyrics in the following song, written by Leslie Bricusse, explore the fabulous places in the world that the songwriter would love to visit and experience for herself.

Fabulous Places

There are so many fabulous faraway places to see

Such as Mexico, Sweden, Hawaii, Japan and Capri

There are so many exciting and wonderful places

Mountains and jungles, deserts and oases

Pleasant as home is, it isn't what Rome is, so why stay there?

When there are so many fabulous faraway places to see

Why should Spain and Tahiti and Rio, just be only names to you and me?

I feel certain there's people we'd be glad to know there

So tell me why don't we get up and go there

Go to those fabulous places where we long to be

Like Bangkok, Hong Kong, Paris and Venice

Tokyo and Cairo and Lisbon and London

Wonderful fabulous places we're longing to see

There are so many simply incredible places to see

When I think of the warm Caribbean, I see a new world for you and me

I'd give anything just to have one single day there

And once we get there, I know that we'll stay there

Stay in those fabulous places where we long to be

Like Bangkok, Hong Kong, Paris and Venice

Tokyo and Cairo and Lisbon and London

Siam, Sienna, Vienna, Verona, Java, Jamaica, Bombay, Barcelona

Show me those fabulous places, we're longing to see

Discuss

1. Is there a place that you long to visit? Why do you want to go there?
2. Are there any places mentioned in the song that you would not want to visit? Why?

Understand

1. Identify the rhyming scheme in this song.
2. List each place mentioned in the song in alphabetical order.

Investigate

Research one of the places mentioned in the song. Find out the size, population, history and main attractions of this destination.

Create

1. Use the information you have researched in the Investigate task above to create a poster advertising the place as a holiday destination.
 2. Work in pairs to write another verse for this song that deals with places that have cold climates and captures why you would long to be there.

When we cannot visit the destinations that we desire to go to, we can travel to places in our imagination without ever leaving home. Edna St Vincent Millay's poem 'Travel' explores this idea.

Travel

By Edna St Vincent Millay

The railroad track is miles away,
And the day is loud with voices speaking,
Yet there isn't a train goes by all day
But I hear its whistle shrieking.

All night there isn't a train goes by,
Though the night is still for sleep and dreaming,
But I see its cinders red on the sky,
And hear its engine steaming.

My heart is warm with the friends I make,
And better friends I'll not be knowing;
Yet there isn't a train I wouldn't take,
No matter where it's going.

Discuss

1. Does the speaker seem reluctant to travel?
2. Do you think the speaker has done much travelling?

 Understand

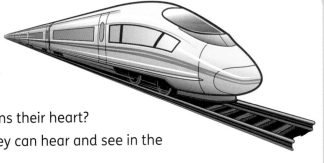

1. How far away is the railroad track?
2. What noises does the speaker hear in the first verse?
3. What does the speaker tell us warms their heart?
4. What does the speaker imagine they can hear and see in the second verse?
5. What does the speaker tell us they would take in the final verse?

 Explore

1. Name and explain two poetic features that you can identify in this poem.
 2. Which line do you think best suggests that the poem deals with the theme of travel? Give reasons for your choice.
3. In your opinion, what does the speaker mean by 'And better friends I'll not be knowing'?

 Create

Create your own poem entitled 'Travel'. Try to use the same rhyming scheme that Edna St Vincent Millay uses in this poem.

Double negatives

A double negative is when two negatives come together and cancel each other out.

'I did nothing' and 'I didn't do anything' both mean the same thing.

If we change this sentence to 'I didn't do nothing', it becomes a double negative. Technically, if you 'didn't do nothing', then you must have done something!

Generally, you should avoid using double negatives as they can be confusing. However, they are sometimes used in song lyrics or poetry to make a particular point.

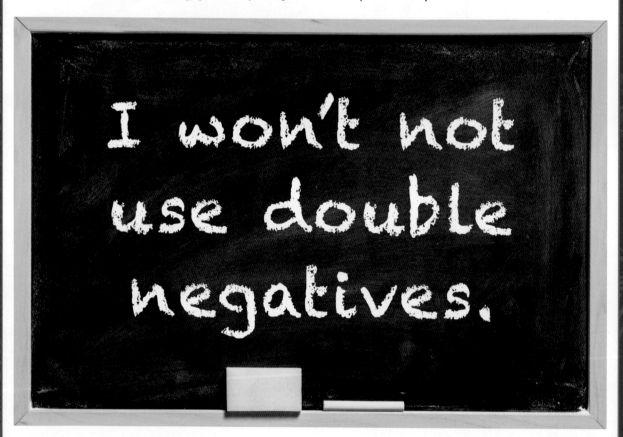

I won't not use double negatives.

 Discuss

1. Identify a double negative in the poem 'Travel' on page 98.
2. Think of the famous song 'We Don't Need No Education' by Pink Floyd. How is this a double negative? What does the sentence actually mean?

 Understand

Rewrite the following sentences, correcting the double negatives.

1. I cannot find my keys nowhere.
2. You cannot see no one in this crowd.
3. We have not never seen a house that big.
4. That attitude will not get you nowhere.
5. There are not no presents left to unwrap.

Methods of travel

Travel has evolved throughout the years. We all love going on holidays and the excitement surrounding getting there. Imagine how travelling would have been years ago when there were no airplanes, boats or cars. Imagine how long it would take to get from the city to the countryside by horse or by foot.

Focus on ... infographics

An **infographic** is a graphic visual representation of information or data.

Infographics are used to present a large amount of information in an easy, fast and accessible way. Infographics should be visually appealing, creative, sharable and contain information that is easy to digest.

The following infographic explores the evolution of transportation methods over time.

The Evolution of Travel

559 CE
First manned
kite glide

1783 CE
First manned
hot air balloon
flight

1852 CE
First engine-
powered
airship flight

1903 CE
First engine-
powered
airplane flight

2004 CE
First privately funded
human spaceflight
in the SpaceShipOne

2000 BCE
Chariots
were used for
transportation

1400s CE
Use of horse-
drawn coaches
in Europe

1769 CE
First steam engine
car capable of
human transport

1908 CE
Ford model T
went into
production

1980s CE
US and Europe
demonstrated
driverless cars

1500 BCE —⌁— 1500 CE 1550 CE 1600 CE 1650 CE 1700 CE 1750 CE 1800 CE 1850 CE 1900 CE 1950 CE 2000 CE 2050 CE

750 BCE
Earliest
identified use
of mast ships

1400s CE
Europeans
explored the
world via ships

1770s CE
Steam engines
were used to
power boats

1891 CE
First cruise liner
created for
pleasure voyages

2002 CE
First cruise ship
to serve as a
residental community

Understand

1. According to the infographic, what was the earliest mode of transport?
2. In what year was the earliest identified use of mast ships?
3. What model of car went into production in 1908?
4. In what year did steam engines begin to power boats?

Investigate

1. **(a)** Work in groups to research one of the following modes of transport:
   - road
   - water
   - rail
   - air.

   Try to find the answers to the following questions.
   - What was the original form of this transport?
   - Who invented it?
   - How has it improved in recent years?
   - How often is it used?
   - What is it mainly used for nowadays?

   (b) In your groups, create a presentation on the history of this form of transport and present it to your class.

Create

Work in small groups to create an infographic on one of the following topics:
- human rights
- education
- world languages
- tourism.

Due to advancements in technology, methods of travel are evolving extremely quickly. The following article traces the personal experience of one man's relationship with cars and travel over a span of 80 years.

Clonmel driver finally makes switch to electric cars – at age 100

Walsh learned to drive in a Ford Model T in 1930s but Nissan Leaf is his first brand new car

He learned to drive in a Ford Model T more than 80 years ago, and now he's made the switch to an electric car at the age of 100.

Clonmel man John Walsh must be one of the few drivers anywhere able to compare the two.

He started driving in the 1930s behind the wheel of his father's Ford Model T and has just bought a Nissan Leaf.

It's the first brand new car he has ever bought – a spending decision partly influenced by the low interest rates he's getting on his savings, but also reflecting concern for the environment.

Mr Walsh, who celebrates his 101st birthday on September 10th, was told by Nissan the zero emissions Leaf would have brought him fuel savings worth €120,000 if the car had existed for his whole motoring life.

'I would never have dreamt of buying a car at this stage', he said. 'My motivation was to do something to improve the environment and to conserve the supply of fossil fuels. The banks are paying no interest, so I decided to spend my money on an EV to do my own little bit to protect the environment.'

He intends to use the car for trips into town and to visit friends.

'There are a few places that I'd like to visit soon like Dungarvan, Holy Cross or Mount Melleray Abbey, which is quite a special place and somewhere I used to visit quite a bit in earlier years.'

Mr Walsh, who retired as chief accountant with Bulmers in 1981, said another goal is to make a trip to Foynes to visit the place where he grew up and first sat behind the wheel of a car as a teenage driver.

He said he was 'about 15 or 16 years old' when he first drove his father's Model T around the garage at the BP installation in Foynes where his father was manager.

'He had a few of them in his day and we used them to go back to Cork. It was a hell of a journey, 70 miles each way, driving 20mph at best. We had two accidents and I wasn't in either, which was quite the achievement.'

He said he can vividly recall how fuel shortages led to the collapse of private and public transport during World War II, forcing him to take up cycling. He was working in Dublin at the time and used to cycle to Limerick where he met and first dated his late wife Brigid (Ciss).

Mr Walsh said his first car was an early second hand VW. 'It had cable brakes and you had to anticipate stopping. That was around 1953. I drove a company car from 1960 until I retired.

'I am convinced that we have to do something about global warming and pollution. I am a late convert to environmental protection and a bit of a late starter driving an electric car but this is my way of playing my part. My son also enjoys driving the car on longer distances, but I have priority on it.'

 ## Discuss

1. 'It was a hell of a journey 70 miles each way ...' Would this be considered 'a hell of a journey' today? Give reasons for your answer.
2. What do you think cars will look like in 70 years?

 ## Understand

1. What is the headline of this article?
2. What was the first car that John Walsh learned to drive?
3. What reason does John give for buying an electric car?
4. Where does John plan on driving his new car to?
5. What does John tell us about his experience of driving to Cork?

 ## Investigate

 Conduct a survey to find out what mode of transport members of your class take to school. Create a bar chart to represent the various modes of transport that students use to get to school.

 ## Create

1. Write a report on the findings from your survey on modes of transport used to get to school. Make some recommendations of alternative transportation modes students could use.
2. Create a print advertisement to promote a car of the future.

Preparing to travel

Researching and educating yourself on a destination you are intending to visit can be really beneficial in organising a trip. Advice on travel can come from a tour operator, a friend or relative, a travel blog, brochure or guidebook.

There are numerous travel blogs dedicated to informing the public about specific destinations and recommending attractions to see.

The following blog post from journalistontherun.com gives information about the Maldives as a holiday destination.

Journalist on the run
Travel. Educate. Inspire.

Top Maldives points of interest you must visit

While the tiny islands in the Maldives are most popular thanks to their beautiful, white sandy beaches and tropical waters, there are also plenty of top Maldives points of interest to check out if you're feeling curious.

From spectacular water sports to visiting the Male fish market and Tsunami memorial, the Maldives is an ideal destination for all types of travellers. Below are some of the must-visit attractions in the Maldives that are well worth taking an afternoon away from your island paradise for.

Male

Male, the Maldives capital city, is often visited during the week or on the last day of a holiday. Despite being a relatively small city, Male is home to many interesting museums and mosques. Male's museums house many precious artifacts procured by the famous explorer Thor Heyerdahl when he first visited the Maldives. He also founded the Singapore Bazaar in Male, which is popular for traditional handicrafts showcasing the talents and skills of the locals. Just off Male's shoreline is a submarine that offers the opportunity to explore the hidden reefs of the island – a unique attraction in the Maldives!

Esjehi Art Gallery

This art gallery is situated in Male, just on the right side of the also popular Sultan Park. The Esjehi Art Gallery is simply an ideal treat for those who greatly appreciate art. It is located in one of the oldest and most prominent buildings in Male. It's relatively small compared to other art galleries in other countries, but it has a decent and fascinating collection of art, making it a must-see place during your Maldives holiday.

Maldives Fish Market

The Maldives Fish Market is a must-see attraction and this is proven by the crowd that never fails to visit. It is one of the most crowded attractions in the Maldives. Globetrotters visit to sample the delicious fresh fruits, vegetables, tuna, dried fish and other varieties of fish that the place offers. The market is unbelievably clean, despite the wet and perishable goods on offer. The Maldives Fish Market is one of the top things to do in the Maldives.

Understand

1. What reason does the blogger give for the Maldives being so popular?
2. What is Male home to?
3. What was founded by Thor Heyerdahl?
4. What does the submarine off the shore of Male offer you the opportunity to do?
5. Where is the Esjehi Art Gallery located?
6. According to the blogger, what is one of the most crowded attractions in the Maldives?
7. List three items that the blogger tells us are available to purchase from the fish market.

 Investigate

Research a place in the world that you would like to visit. Look up travel blogs to help you gain inspiration. There are a few travel blogs listed below to help you get started.

🔗 www.keepcalmandtravel.com

🔗 tipsforfamilytrips.com

🔗 www.thisistheplaceiwastellingyouabout.com

🔗 youngadventuress.com

🔗 www.travelforteens.com

 Create

 1. **(a)** Write a blog post about the place that you researched for the Investigate task above in the space provided on page 31 of your Portfolio. Tell your readers your reasons for choosing this particular place.

 (b) Redraft your blog entry in the space provided on pages 110–112 of your Portfolio. Make sure to include features of a blog and to check for spelling and grammar mistakes.

Brochures

A brochure is an advertising document that contains both information and images about a particular product, place, event or service. It is usually produced as a booklet to provide details on what is being advertised.

Features	Language
◖ Imagery	◖ Persuasive
◖ Detailed information	◖ Descriptive
◖ Contact details	◖ Engaging
	◖ Lively

Read the following brochure.

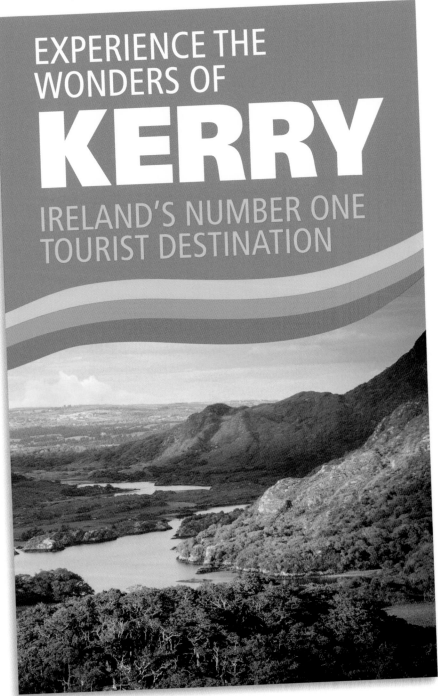

Catchy heading

Subheading with further details

Attractive image

Kerry boasts spectacular views throughout. There are numerous walks and cycles for enthusiastic adventure seekers, or, if you fancy a leisurely holiday, the views are equally impressive on the wonderful coastal drives.

With lots to see and do, from historic attractions to wildlife interactions, Kerry will provide you with a holiday of a lifetime. Our watersports include:

- sailing
- canoeing
- windsurfing
- surfing
- jetskiing
- paddle boarding
- kayaking
- kitesurfing.

When the day's activities are complete and you are ready to wind down, the towns and villages can offer you plenty of restaurants and cafés to enjoy dinner or a tasty snack.

Afterwards, you can enjoy the traditional nightlife and music of County Kerry first hand.

Carefully chosen information to persuade the reader

Conversational language

Directly addresses the reader

Bullet points

Engaging language

What are you waiting for?
Start your Kerry adventure today!

Book an exciting and memorable trip that caters for all the family.

Don't delay – book today!
Discounts available for family packages.

Persuasive language

Contact us for further information:
Tel: 066 123 4560
Email: info@kerrytravels.ie
Website: www.kerrytravels.com
Or tweet us: @kerrytravels

Booking information and contact details

Understand

1. What is the heading of this brochure?
2. What is the subheading of this brochure?
3. Outline three pieces of information that the brochure provides about Kerry.
4. What does the brochure suggest you can do when the day's activities are over?
5. How can you contact Kerry Travels for further information?
6. Give two examples of persuasive writing used in this brochure.

 Explore

 In your opinion, does the brochure successfully advertise Kerry? Give two reasons for your answer.

 Create

1. Write an email to Kerry Travels enquiring about a weekend holiday for you and your family. Tell the tour agent the types of activities that you would be interested in and ask for two restaurant recommendations. Remember to use the correct layout for an email.
2. Design a brochure to advertise your school to potential students.
 3. Below are some images that could appear on the covers of brochures. In pairs, select one image and create a brochure to advertise this destination.

Sometimes, we can have intentions to travel and explore the world from a young age, and can spend many years preparing for these adventures.

In the following extract from *Gulliver's Travels* by Irish author Jonathon Swift, Gulliver tells us how he had been preparing to travel for many years and that he took time to acquire numerous skills that would be useful.

Gulliver's Travels

My father had a small estate in Nottinghamshire; I was the third of five sons. He sent me to Emanuel College in Cambridge at fourteen years old, where I resided three years, and applied myself close to my studies: but the charge of maintaining me (although I had a very scanty allowance) being too great for a narrow fortune, I was bound apprentice to Mr. James Bates, an eminent surgeon in London, with whom I continued four years; and my father now and then sending me small sums of money, I laid them out in learning navigation, and other parts of the mathematics, useful to those who intend to travel, as I always believed it would be some time or other my fortune to do. When I left Mr. Bates, I went down to my father; where, by the assistance of him and my uncle John, and some other relations, I got forty pounds, and a promise of thirty pounds a year to maintain me at Leyden: there I studied physic two years and seven months, knowing it would be useful in long voyages.

Soon after my return from Leyden, I was recommended by my good master, Mr. Bates, to be surgeon to the *Swallow*, Captain Abraham Pannell, commander; with whom I continued three years and a half, making a voyage or two into the Levant, and some other parts. When I came back, I resolved to settle in London, to which Mr. Bates, my master, encouraged me, and by him I was recommended to several patients. I took part of a small house in the Old Jury; and being advised to alter my condition, I married Mrs. Mary Burton, second daughter to Mr. Edmond Burton, hosier in Newgate-street, with whom I received four hundred pounds for a portion.

But, my good master Bates dying in two years after, and I having few friends, my business began to fail; for my conscience would not suffer me to imitate the bad practice of too many among my brethren. Having therefore consulted with my wife, and some of my acquaintance, I determined to go again to sea. I was surgeon successively in two ships, and made several voyages, for six years, to the East and West–Indies, by which I got some addition to my fortune. My hours of leisure I spent in reading the best authors, ancient and modern, being always provided with a good number of books; and when I was ashore, in observing the manners and dispositions of the people, as well as learning their language, wherein I had a great facility by the strength of my memory.

scanty:
small

eminent:
high-ranking

physic:
medicine

resolved:
decided

hosier:
manufacturer or seller of stockings and tights

portion:
money given to a husband by his wife's family on marriage

Discuss

1. How do you prepare when you are travelling to a new destination?
2. What is the most exciting part of travelling to a new destination?
3. Have you ever heard about *Guilliver's Travels*? You may have read the book or seen the film. Share what you know about the story.

 Understand

1. Where did Gulliver attend school?
2. Who recommended that Gulliver become a surgeon?
3. How many voyages did Gulliver make while he was a surgeon?
4. What did he spend his leisure hours at sea doing?
 5. Put the following words into sentences, then add them you your vocabulary builder on pages 1–2 of your Portfolio.
   ◖ Scanty
   ◖ Eminent
   ◖ Resolved

 Explore

 1. What impression do you form of Gulliver having read this extract? Give two reasons for your answer.

 2. Would this extract encourage you to read the novel *Gulliver's Travels*? Give two reasons for your answer.

3. Gulliver tells us that he reads 'the best authors, ancient and modern'. If this novel was set today, name two books you imagine Gulliver reading. Explain your choices.

 Create

Write a list of guidelines that you think would be helpful to assist someone who is preparing to travel to a new place.

Before travelling to a new place, it can be important to prepare by researching the culture and learning some useful phrases in the country's native language.

The following Irish short film, *Yu Ming is ainm dom*, is about a young Chinese man, Yu Ming, who travels to Ireland and tries to overcome the language barrier by learning the language.

https://youtu.be/ JqYtG9BNhfM

 ## Understand

1. When Yu Ming spins the globe, where does his finger land?
2. What book does Yu Ming rent from the library in preparation for his journey?
3. What saying does Yu Ming repeat to himself in the mirror?
4. What mode of transport does Yu Ming take from the airport to the city centre?
5. What is the confusion when Yu Ming tries to check in to Isaac's hostel?
6. What does Yu Ming ask for when he enters the pub?
7. What does Paddy explain to Yu Ming about the language barrier he is facing in Ireland?
8. How long did Yu Ming spend learning Irish?
9. Where does Yu Ming end up working at the end of the short film?

 ## Explore

1. In small groups, discuss what you think the message behind this short film is. Write a list of other preparations Yu Ming could have made before deciding to move to Ireland.
2. In your opinion, do you think Yu Ming is lonely during his trip to Ireland? Give two reasons for your answer.
3. In your opinion, would you say this film has a happy ending? Give two reasons for your answer.

 ## Create

 Imagine you are Yu Ming. Write an email home after your first day in Ireland.

Travelling to new worlds

For some, travel is more than just a leisure activity. Instead, it can be a chance to discover and explore new worlds. In the past, explorers sought to chart new territories on Earth. Nowadays, there are few parts of the world that remain unexplored, and explorers look beyond Earth to other planets and the mysteries of outer space.

Christopher Columbus was an Italian explorer, navigator and coloniser. For many years, he was credited with discovering America, although America was actually discovered by its indigenous population and the vikings were the first Europeans to reach its shores.

Watch the following video biography of Christopher Columbus's life.

www.biography.com/video/christopher-columbus-mini-biography-6831683604

 ## Understand

1. In what year was Columbus born?
2. What inspired Columbus to sail west in an effort to reach India?
3. Who gave Columbus the money for his voyage?
4. Name the three ships that Columbus set sail with.
5. After two months of sailing, where did Columbus reach?
6. What did Columbus force the indigenous people to do?
7. Why was Columbus arrested?
8. What did Christopher Columbus die believing?

 ## Investigate

 Work in small groups to research a famous explorer of your choice. Below are some suggestions.

- Roald Amundsen
- Neil Armstrong
- Juan Garrido
- Isabelle Eberhardt
- Captain James Cook
- Hernan Cortes
- Gertrude Bell
- Sir Francis Drake
- Marco Polo

Use the following headings to guide your research:

- Year of birth
- Early life
- Voyages/quests
- Discoveries
- Legacy
- Year of death

 ## Create

 Work in your groups to create a short video biography about the explorer you have researched. Come up with 10 questions for the class to answer after they have watched your video biography.

The following song from Disney's *Aladdin* explores the excitement and sense of adventure that can come from exploring somewhere new.

A Whole New World

I can show you the world

Shining, shimmering, splendid

Tell me, princess, now when did

You last let your heart decide?

I can open your eyes

Take you wonder by wonder

Over, sideways and under

On a magic carpet ride.

A whole new world

A new fantastic point of view

No one to tell us no

Or where to go

Or say we're only dreaming

A whole new world

A dazzling place I never knew

But when I'm way up here

It's crystal clear

That now I'm in a whole new world with you

(Now I'm in a whole new world with you)

Unbelievable sights

Indescribable feeling

Soaring, tumbling, freewheeling

Through an endless diamond sky

A whole new world

(Don't you dare close your eyes)

A hundred thousand things to see

(Hold your breath; it gets better)

I'm like a shooting star

I've come so far

I can't go back to where I used to be

A whole new world

(Every turn, a surprise)

With new horizons to pursue

(Every moment, red-letter)

I'll chase them anywhere

There's time to spare

Let me share this whole new world with you

A whole new world

(A whole new world)

That's where we'll be

(That's where we'll be)

A thrilling chase

(A wondrous place)

For you and me.

Flashback   **Alliteration** is a sound effect created when words that begin with the same sound are placed beside or close to one another in a sentence.

 Understand

1. Identify and list three adjectives in the lyrics of 'A Whole New World'.
2. List three prepositions in the song.
3. Find three examples of alliteration in the lyrics.

 Explore

 Work with a partner to identify any similarities and differences between this song and 'Fabulous Places' on page 96 using the worksheet on pages 32–33 of your Portfolio.

 Create

Think of a whole new world that you could create. In groups design a poster to advertise this new world. Use the following prompts to help you envisage your world.

◖ In what era is your world located? Past, present, future?
◖ Where is your world located? A new planet, a different galaxy?
◖ Who inhabits your world? Demons, fairies, unicorns or something else?
◖ What is the government system of your world? Monarchy, republic, dictatorship?
◖ What is the weather like in your world?
◖ What technology is available in your world?
◖ What landscape does your world have?

Travel can extend beyond our Earth and into space. Outside of Earth there is an unlimited amount of exploring and discovering to be undertaken.

Song in Space

By Adrian Mitchell

When man first flew beyond the sky

He looked back into the world's blue eye.

Man said: What makes your eye so blue?

Earth said: The tears in the ocean do.

Why are the seas so full of tears?

Because I've wept so many thousand years.

Why do you weep as you dance through space?

Because I am the mother of the Human Race.

A note from the poet: Educational Health Warning. None of these poems or any other work by Adrian Mitchell is to be used in connection with any examination or test whatsoever. But I'm glad if people who like them read them aloud, sing them, dance them or act them in schools. And even happier if they choose to learn any of them by heart.

 **Rhythm** is the way beats are arranged in a poem or song.

Discuss

1. What do you think would be the biggest challenge in travelling into space?
2. What would be most exciting thing about space travel?
 3. (a) What is the rhythm of this poem? Work with a partner to read through the poem and tap the beat.
   (b) How does this rhythm contribute to the poem?

 Understand

1. What did the man who first flew beyond the sky see when he looked back?
2. What questions does the man ask planet Earth?
3. (a) What human characteristic does the poet give to planet Earth?
   (b) What is the name of this poetic device?

 Explore

 1. In your opinion, who says the final line of the poem: 'Because I am the mother of the human race'? Give a reason for your answer
2. Do you think dialogue within a poem is effective? Give one reason for your answer.

 Investigate

 1. (a) Work in groups to research one of the space missions listed below.

   ◀ Pioneer 10 & 11   ◀ Rosetta   ◀ Spirit and Opportunity
   ◀ Chandra   ◀ Hubble   ◀ Voyager
   ◀ Viking   ◀ Spitzer   ◀ Apollo
   ◀ Juno   ◀ New Horizons   ◀ Dawn

   Try to find out the following information about your chosen mission:
   ◀ when the mission took place
   ◀ the reason(s) for this mission
   ◀ who was selected to go on this mission
   ◀ how long the mission lasted
   ◀ the outcome of this mission.

 (b) Work with your group to create a short presentation to be delivered to your class on the mission that you have researched.

 Create

 Work in pairs to continue the conversation between Earth and man. Give them each three more lines that you think could be added to this poem. Do not forget to adhere to the rhyming pattern Adrian Mitchell uses in the poem.

Our understanding of space and our interaction with space missions has advanced remarkably in the past number of years.

Listen to the following broadcast from Tallaght Community School, where a group of students make contact with an astronaut on the International Space Station.

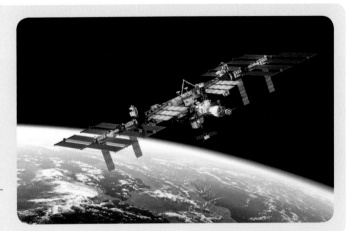

www.newstalk.com/podcasts/
Moncrieff/Highlights_from_
Moncrieff/206185/Tallaght_Kids_Talk_
To_The_International_Space_Station

 Discuss

1. How do the students feel after speaking with the International Space Station?
2. If you had the opportunity to ask Paolo Nespoli a question, what would you ask?

 Understand

1. Who did Tallaght Community School successfully communicate with?
2. What speed was the astronaut on the International Space Station travelling at when the students made contact?
3. What did the students build for the event?
4. What questions did the students want to ask the International Space Station?
5. How many years have the students been preparing for this event?
6. What adjectives did the teachers use to describe the atmosphere in the school?
7. What time did they make the connection?
8. How would you describe the tone of voices of the students in the school during this broadcast?
9. Does the International Space Station have a black box like an aircraft?
10. What does Paolo Nespoli say he will miss the most about life on the International Space Station when the mission is complete?
11. How many voices can you hear during the broadcast?
12. Are there any sound effects or music used during this broadcast? Does this contribute to your listening experience?

 Create

Write a short story centred around a mission to space with the title 'The Sky Is the Limit'.

The universe is home to trillions of celestial bodies that, thanks to science and technology, we now know much more about.

A solar system consists of a star and the planets that travel around it. The following inforgraphic gives information about our solar system.

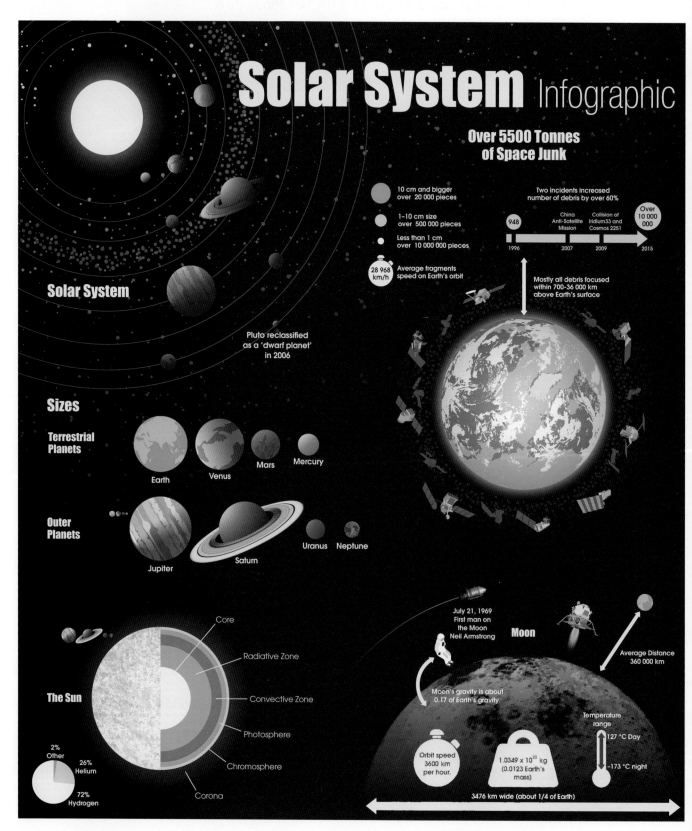

Understand

1. According to the infographic, what was Pluto reclassified as in 2006?
2. According to the infographic, what is the Sun made up of?
3. Which planet is closest to the Sun?
4. What is the Moon's orbit speed?
5. Where is the debris above the Earth's surface mostly focused?
6. List the planets mentioned in this infographic in alphabetical order.
7. What is the average distance between Earth and the Moon?
8. Which two incidents increased the amount of debris in the solar system?

Explore

1. In your opinion, is there any information missing from this infographic that you would like to know?
2. Is there any information in this infographic that you think could be explained more clearly?

 3. Which of the following words would you use to describe this infographic?
   - Informative
   - Educational
   - Clear
   - Limited

   Explain your choice.

Investigate

Can you find any other information that you think would be suitable to add to this infographic? Share the relevant information you found with the class.

Create

 Work in groups to create a new infographic with all the extra material you have researched.

Chris Hadfield is a retired Canadian astronaut who has flown in two space missions and served as commander of the International Space Station. He shares his experiences in his autobiography, *An Astronaut's Guide to Life on Earth.*

An Astronaut's Guide to Life on Earth

The windows of a spaceship casually frame miracles. Every 92 minutes, another sunrise: a layer cake that starts with orange, then a thick wedge of blue, then the richest, darkest icing decorated with stars. The secret patterns of our planet are revealed: mountains bump up rudely from orderly plains, forests are green gashes edged with snow, rivers glint in the sunlight, twisting and turning like silvery worms. Continents splay themselves out whole, surrounded by islands sprinkled across the sea like delicate shards of shattered eggshells.

Floating in the airlock before my first spacewalk, I knew I was on the verge of even rarer beauty. To drift outside, fully immersed in the spectacle of the universe while holding onto a spaceship orbiting Earth at 17,500 miles per hour—it was a moment I'd been dreaming of and working toward most of my life. But poised on the edge of the sublime, I faced a somewhat ridiculous dilemma: How best to get out there? The hatch was small and circular, but with all my tools strapped to my chest and a huge pack of oxygen tanks and electronics strapped onto my back, I was square. Square astronaut, round hole.

The cinematic moment I'd envisioned when I first became an astronaut, the one where the soundtrack swelled while I elegantly pushed off into the jet-black ink of infinite space, would not be happening. Instead, I'd have to wiggle out awkwardly and patiently, focused less on the magical than the mundane: trying to avoid snagging my spacesuit or getting snarled in my tether and presenting myself to the universe trussed up like a roped calf.

Gingerly, I pushed myself out headfirst to see the world in a way only a few dozen humans have, wearing a sturdy jetpack with its own thrusting system and joystick so that if all else failed, I could fire my thrusters, powered by a pressurized tank of nitrogen, and steer back to safety. A pinnacle of experience, an unexpected path.

Square astronaut, round hole. It's the story of my life, really: trying to figure out how to get where I want to go when just getting out the door seems impossible. On paper, my career trajectory looks preordained: engineer, fighter pilot, test pilot, astronaut. Typical path for someone in this line of work, straight as a ruler. But that's not how it really was. There were hairpin curves and dead ends all the way along. I wasn't destined to be an astronaut. I had to turn myself into one.

sublime:
of great excellence or beauty

mundane:
ordinary

trussed:
tied

thrusters:
small rocket engines used to make alterations in flight paths

pinnacle:
most successful point

trajectory:
path of an object moving under force

preordained:
decided beforehand

Discuss

1. Do you know of any other autobiographies written by explorers?
2. Are you familiar with any biographies written about explorers?

 Understand

1. According to Chris Hadfield, what happens every 92 minutes?
2. What does Chris compare islands to from his view of the Earth?
3. How fast does Chris tell us that the spaceship is orbiting Earth?
4. What dilemma does Chris face as he is about to complete his first spacewalk?
5. If all else failed, how would Chris return to safety?
6. What features of a typical autobiography do you recognise in this extract?

 Explore

 1. 'The first paragraph of this extract is rich in descriptive imagery.' Do you agree with this statement? Give reasons for your answer.

 2. What impression do you form of Chris, having read this extract?

 Create

 Imagine that you are an astronaut or an explorer. Write an extract from your autobiography in the space provided on page 34 of your Portfolio. Be sure to include the features of an autobiography listed.

Autobiographies
- ✓ Personal details
- ✓ Facts and information
- ✓ Written in the first person
- ✓ Narrative style
- ✓ Revelation of secrets and private events
- ✓ Honest tone
- ✓ Descriptive writing
- ✓ Informal language

Welcoming travellers

Travelling to a new place can sometimes be disorientating. People can feel overwhelmed by their new surroundings. This is why it is always important to make visitors feel welcome, and to help them have a positive experience on their travels.

The following extract from Ted Hughes's play *The Coming of the Kings* explores the fact that, as exciting as it is to travel, it can be equally as enjoyable to host visitors who travel to you.

The Coming of the Kings

FORTUNE-TELLER: I read here

That the greatest good luck in a million year

Is coming your way.

INNKEEPER: What? Where? *When?*

FORTUNE-TELLER: (*still studying the WIFE's palm*):

Today.

WIFE: Today?

FORTUNE-TELLER: The King Of Men

Is going to visit your inn – today.

INNKEEPER: What? What's that? What do you say?

FORTUNE-TELLER: Be prepared.

INNKEEPER: A king?

FORTUNE-TELLER: *Three* kings.

INNKEEPER: Beyond my wildest imaginings!

To stay with us here?

FORTUNE-TELLER: To visit this inn.

A new age is going to begin

From what occurs at this inn today.

And you will be famous for ever.

WIFE: For ever!

INNKEEPER: Now who's stupid? Now who's clever?

I bought this inn ten years ago

For this moment. What else do you know?

FORTUNE-TELLER: Prepare.

WIFE: Three kings!

INNKEEPER: When we've had them,

Every night after, we'll be crammed full.

We'll be on the map, the fashionable

Most famous inn in Bethlehem.

We'll make a fortune!

WIFE: (*in great excitement*):

        Get the place clean.

        Some of those rooms aren't fit to be seen.

        Scrub them, sweep them, quick, quick, quick, and

        Get the flea-powder.

INNKEEPER: Get the chickens

        Out of the bath.

WIFE: Get all the dogs

        And their pups out of the beds and the hogs

        And the hoglets out of the cupboards and scatter

        Disinfectant. What's the matter?

INNKEEPER: (*he is standing almost in a trance*):

        This is the greatest day of my life!

WIFE: And as usual you've to thank your wife.

        Get a move on.

They dash into the inn. Through what follows, the WIFE is throwing bundles of rags, broken chairs, picture frames, etc. out of the windows. Soon the INNKEEPER re-emerges dressed and begins to carry the junk into the shed. But first:

FORTUNE-TELLER: I told them no more than the true.

 **Flashback** **Stage directions** are instructions written in a script that describe how the stage should look and how the actors should speak and behave.

 ## Discuss

What well-known story is this play based on?

 ## Understand

1. Who does the fortune teller say will be visiting the inn today?
2. How long ago did the innkeeper buy the inn?
3. What does the innkeeper say will happen to his inn after his visitors have stayed?
4. What does the innkeeper say that the inn will now be known as?
5. What does the innkeeper suggest needs to be done with the chickens?
6. What does the wife start throwing out the windows?

 ## Explore

1. Choose two words that you think best describe the fortune teller and explain why you have selected these words.
 2. What is your impression of the innkeeper's wife, having read the extract?
3. What do we learn about the characters from reading the stage directions? Explain your answer.
4. Think of a scene from a play that you have studied that was charged with emotion.
   (a) Name the play and the playwright.
   (b) What emotion was present in this scene?
   (c) How did the playwright convey this emotion?

 ## Create

 1. **(a)** Work in small groups to imagine what you think happens next in this play. Write the script for the next scene. Remember to include stage directions in your script.
 (b) When you have finished writing your script, act it out for the rest of your class.

Imagine how lonely travelling would have been in the past. A traveller on horseback would have been alone and cold, without any lights on the road, any satellite navigation or any form of communication.

The Listeners

By Walter de la Mare

'Is there anybody there?' said the Traveller,
    Knocking on the moonlit door;
And his horse in the silence champed the grasses
    Of the forest's ferny floor:
And a bird flew up out of the turret,
    Above the Traveller's head:
And he smote upon the door again a second time;
    'Is there anybody there?' he said.
But no one descended to the Traveller;
    No head from the leaf-fringed sill
Leaned over and looked into his grey eyes,
    Where he stood perplexed and still.
But only a host of phantom listeners
    That dwelt in the lone house then
Stood listening in the quiet of the moonlight
    To that voice from the world of men:
Stood thronging the faint moonbeams on the dark stair,
    That goes down to the empty hall,
Hearkening in an air stirred and shaken
    By the lonely Traveller's call.
And he felt in his heart their strangeness,
    Their stillness answering his cry,
While his horse moved, cropping the dark turf,
    'Neath the starred and leafy sky;
For he suddenly smote on the door, even
    Louder, and lifted his head:—
'Tell them I came, and no one answered,
    That I kept my word,' he said.
Never the least stir made the listeners,
    Though every word he spake
Fell echoing through the shadowiness of the still house
    From the one man left awake:
Ay, they heard his foot upon the stirrup,
    And the sound of iron on stone,
And how the silence surged softly backward,
    When the plunging hoofs were gone.

champed:
a noise made while biting or chewing

smote:
struck with force

phantom:
appearance or illusion

thronging:
filling a place in great numbers

127

Understand

1. What did the traveller say as he knocked on the door?
2. What is the horse doing as the traveller knocks on the door?
3. What colour are the traveller's eyes?
4. What did the traveller feel in his heart?

Explore

1. Name two poetic devices that you recognise in the poem and provide quotes from the poem to illustrate each example. How effectively do these poetic devices contribute to the poem?
2. What time of the day do you imagine this poem is set? Give two reasons for your answer.
3. Which of the following words best describes the atmosphere of the poem? Give a reason for your choice.
   - Lonely
   - Eerie
   - Quiet
4. What do you understand by the quote 'A host of phantom listeners'?
5. In your opinion, who do you think the listeners in this poem are?

6. Work in pairs to come up with an alternative title for this poem.

Create

Imagine there are two ghosts living in this house. Write the dialogue that takes place between the two ghosts after the traveller has left.

The dangers of travel

Although travel is usually a positive thing, it is sometimes dangerous to travel to unknown places without carrying out research beforehand. When travelling, you should always keep someone informed of your whereabouts for your safety and protection.

 Travelling to new destinations can be perilous, as Billy Weaver discovers in Roald Dahl's short story below.

The Landlady

Billy Weaver had travelled down from London on the slow afternoon train, with a change at Swindon on the way, and by the time he got to Bath it was about nine o'clock in the evening and the moon was coming up out of a clear starry sky over the houses opposite the station entrance. But the air was deadly cold and the wind was like a flat blade of ice on his cheeks.

'Excuse me,' he said, 'but is there a fairly cheap hotel not too far away from here?'

'Try The Bell and Dragon,' the porter answered, pointing down the road. 'They might take you in. It's about a quarter of a mile along on the other side.'

Billy thanked him and picked up his suitcase and set out to walk the quarter-mile to The Bell and Dragon. He had never been to Bath before. He didn't know anyone who lived there. But Mr Greenslade at the Head Office in London had told him it was a splendid city. 'Find your own lodgings,' he had said, 'and then go along and report to the Branch Manager as soon as you've got yourself settled.'

Billy was seventeen years old. He was wearing a new navy-blue overcoat, a new brown trilby hat, and a new brown suit, and he was feeling fine. He walked briskly down the street. He was trying to do everything briskly these days. Briskness, he had decided, was *the* one common characteristic of all successful businessmen. The big shots up at Head Office were absolutely fantastically brisk all the time. They were amazing.

There were no shops on this wide street that he was walking along, only a line of tall houses on each side, all of them identical. They had porches and pillars and four or five steps going up to their front doors, and it was obvious that once upon a time they had been very swanky residences. But now, even in the darkness, he could see that the paint was peeling from the woodwork on their doors and windows, and that the handsome white façades were cracked and blotchy from neglect.

Suddenly, in a downstairs window that was brilliantly illuminated by a street-lamp not six yards away, Billy caught sight of a printed notice propped up against the glass in one of the upper panes. It said BED AND BREAKFAST. There was a vase of pussy-willows, tall and beautiful, standing just underneath the notice.

He stopped walking. He moved a bit closer. Green curtains (some sort of velvety material) were hanging down on either side of the window. The pussy-willows looked wonderful beside them. He went right up and peered through the glass into the room, and the first thing he saw was a bright fire burning in the hearth. On the carpet in front of the fire, a pretty little dachshund was curled up asleep with its nose tucked into its belly.

The room itself, so far as he could see in the half-darkness, was filled with pleasant furniture. There was a baby-grand piano and a big sofa and several plump armchairs; and in one corner he spotted a large parrot in a cage. Animals were usually a good sign in a place like this, Billy told himself; and all in all, it looked to him as though it would be a pretty decent house to stay in. Certainly it would be more comfortable than The Bell and Dragon.

On the other hand, a pub would be more congenial than a boarding-house. There would be beer and darts in the evenings, and lots of people to talk to, and it would probably be a good bit cheaper, too. He had stayed a couple of nights in a pub once before and he had liked it. He had never stayed in any boarding-houses, and, to be perfectly honest, he was a tiny bit frightened of them. The name itself conjured up images of watery cabbage, rapacious landladies, and a powerful smell of kippers in the living-room.

rapacious: greedy

After dithering about like this in the cold for two or three minutes, Billy decided that he would walk on and take a look at The Bell and Dragon before making up his mind. He turned to go.

And now a queer thing happened to him. He was in the act of stepping back and turning away from the window when all at once his eye was caught and held in the most peculiar manner by the small notice that was there. BED AND BREAKFAST, it said. BED AND BREAKFAST, BED AND BREAKFAST, BED AND BREAKFAST. Each word was like a large black eye staring at him through the glass, holding him, compelling him, forcing him to stay where he was and not to walk away from that house, and the next thing he knew, he was actually moving across from the window to the front door of the house, climbing the steps that led up to it, and reaching for the bell.

He pressed the bell. Far away in a back room he heard it ringing, and then *at once* – it must have been at once because he hadn't even had time to take his finger from the bell-button – the door swung open and a woman was standing there.

Normally you ring the bell and you have at least a half-minute's wait before the door opens. But this dame was a like a jack-in-the-box. He pressed the bell – and out she popped! It made him jump.

She was about forty-five or fifty years old, and the moment she saw him, she gave him a warm welcoming smile.

'*Please* come in,' she said pleasantly. She stepped aside, holding the door wide open, and Billy found himself automatically starting forward into the house. The compulsion or, more accurately, the desire to follow after her into that house was extraordinarily strong.

'I saw the notice in the window,' he said, holding himself back.

'Yes, I know.'

'I was wondering about a room.'

'It's *all* ready for you, my dear,' she said. She had a round pink face and very gentle blue eyes.

'I was on my way to The Bell and Dragon,' Billy told her. 'But the notice in your window just happened to catch my eye.'

'My dear boy,' she said, 'why don't you come in out of the cold?'

'How much do you charge?'

'Five and sixpence a night, including breakfast.'

It was fantastically cheap. It was less than half of what he had been willing to pay.

'If that is too much,' she added, 'then perhaps I can reduce it just a tiny bit. Do you desire an egg for breakfast? Eggs are expensive at the moment. It would be sixpence less without the egg.'

'Five and sixpence is fine,' he answered. 'I should like very much to stay here.'

'I knew you would. Do come in.'

She seemed terribly nice. She looked exactly like the mother of one's best school-friend welcoming one into the house to stay for the Christmas holidays. Billy took off his hat, and stepped over the threshold.

'Just hang it there,' she said, 'and let me help you with your coat. There were no other hats or coats in the hall. There were no umbrellas, no walking-sticks – nothing.

'We have it *all* to ourselves,' she said, smiling at him over her shoulder as she led the way upstairs. 'You see, it isn't very often I have the pleasure of taking a visitor into my little nest.'

The old girl is slightly dotty, Billy told himself. But at five and sixpence a night, who gives a damn about that? 'I should've thought you'd be simply swamped with applicants,' he said politely.

'Oh, I am, my dear, I am, of course I am. But the trouble is that I'm inclined to be just a teeny weeny bit choosy and particular – if you see what I mean.'

'Ah, yes.'

'But I'm always ready. Everything is always ready day and night in this house just on the off-chance that an acceptable young gentleman will come along. And it is such a pleasure, my dear, such a very great pleasure when now and again I open the door and I see someone standing there who is just *exactly* right.' She was half-way up the stairs, and she paused with one hand on the stair-rail, turning her head and smiling down at him with pale lips. 'Like you,' she added, and her blue eyes travelled slowly all the way down the length of Billy's body, to his feet, and then up again.

On the first-floor landing she said to him, 'This floor is mine.'

They climbed up a second flight. 'And this one is *all* yours,' she said. 'Here's your room. I do hope you'll like it.' She took him into a small but charming front bedroom, switching on the light as she went in.

'The morning sun comes right in the window, Mr Perkins. It *is* Mr Perkins, isn't it?'

'No,' he said. 'It's Weaver.'

'Mr Weaver. How nice. I've put a water-bottle between the sheets to air them out, Mr Weaver. It's such a comfort to have a hot-water bottle in a strange bed with clean sheets, don't you agree? And you may light the gas fire at any time if you feel chilly.'

'Thank you,' Billy said. 'Thank you ever so much.' He noticed that the bedspread had been taken off the bed, and that the bedclothes had been neatly turned back on one side, all ready for someone to get in.

'I'm so glad you appeared,' she said, looking earnestly into his face. 'I was beginning to get worried.'

'That's all right,' Billy answered brightly. 'You mustn't worry about me.' He put his suitcase on the chair and started to open it.

'And what about supper, my dear? Did you manage to get anything to eat before you came here?'

'I'm not a bit hungry, thank you,' he said. 'I think I'll just go to bed as soon as possible because tomorrow I've got to get up rather early and report to the office.'

'Very well, then. I'll leave you now so that you can unpack. But before you go to bed, would you be kind enough to pop into the sitting-room on the ground floor and sign the book? Everyone has to do that because it's the law of the land, and we don't want to go breaking any laws at *this* stage in the proceedings, do we?' She gave him a little wave of the hand and went quickly out of the room and closed the door.

Now, the fact that his landlady appeared to be slightly off her rocker didn't worry Billy in the least. After all, she was not only harmless – there was no question about that – but she was also quite obviously a kind and generous soul. He guessed that she had probably lost a son in the war, or something like that, and had never got over it.

So a few minutes later, after unpacking his suitcase and washing his hands, he trotted downstairs to the ground floor and entered the living-room. His landlady wasn't there, but the fire was glowing in the hearth, and the little dachshund was still sleeping in front of it. The room was wonderfully warm and cosy. I'm a lucky fellow, he thought, rubbing his hands. This is a bit of all right.

He found the guest-book lying open on the piano, so he took out his pen and wrote down his name and address. There were only two other entries above his on the page, and, as one always does with guest-books, he started to read them. One was a Christopher Mulholland from Cardiff. The other was Gregory W. Temple from Bristol.

That's funny, he thought suddenly. Christopher Mulholland. It rings a bell.

Now where on earth had he heard that rather unusual name before?

Was he a boy at school? No. Was it one of his sister's numerous young men, perhaps, or a friend of his father's? No, no, it wasn't any of those. He glanced down again at the book.

Christopher Mulholland   231 Cathedral Road, Cardiff.

Gregory W. Temple   27 Sycamore Drive, Bristol.

As a matter of fact, now he came to think of it, he wasn't at all sure that the second name didn't have almost as much of a familiar ring about it as the first.

'Gregory Temple?' he said aloud, searching his memory. 'Christopher Mulholland? ...'

'Such charming boys,' a voice behind him answered, and he turned and saw his landlady sailing into the room with a large silver tea-tray in her hands. She was holding it well out in front of her, and rather high up, as though the tray were a pair of reins on a frisky horse.

'They sound somehow familiar,' he said.

'They do? How interesting.'

'I'm almost positive I've heard those names before somewhere. Isn't that queer? Maybe it was in the newspapers. They weren't famous in any way, were they? I mean famous cricketers or footballers or something like that?'

'Famous,' she said, setting the tea-tray down on the low table in front of the sofa. 'Oh no, I don't think they were famous. But they were extraordinarily handsome, both of them, I can promise you that. They were tall and young and handsome, my dear, just exactly like you.'

Once more, Billy glanced down at the book. 'Look here,' he said, noticing the dates. 'This last entry is over two years old.'

'It is?'

'Yes, indeed. And Christopher Mulholland's is nearly a year before that – more than *three years* ago.'

'Dear me,' she said, shaking her head and heaving a dainty little sigh. 'I would never have thought it. How time does fly away from us all, doesn't it, Mr Wilkins?'

'It's Weaver,' Billy said. 'W-e-a-v-e-r.'

'Oh, of course it is!' she cried, sitting down on the sofa. 'How silly of me. I do apologise. In one ear and out the other, that's me, Mr Weaver.'

'You know something?' Billy said. 'Something that's really quite extraordinary about all this?'

'No, dear, I don't.'

'Well, you see – both of these names, Mulholland and Temple, I not only seem to remember each one of them separately, so to speak, but somehow or other, in some peculiar way, they both appear to be sort of connected together as well. As though they were both famous for the same sort of thing, if you see what I mean – like ... like Dempsey and Tunney, for example, or Churchill and Roosevelt.'

'How amusing,' she said. 'But come over here now, dear, and sit down beside me on the sofa and I'll give you a nice cup of tea and a ginger biscuit before you go to bed.'

'You really shouldn't bother,' Billy said. 'I didn't mean you to do anything like that.' He stood by the piano, watching her as she fussed about with the cups and saucers. He noticed that she had small, white, quickly moving hands, and red finger-nails.

'I'm almost positive it was in the newspapers I saw them,' Billy said. 'I'll think of it in a second. I'm sure I will.'

There is nothing more tantalising than a thing like this which lingers just outside the borders of one's memory. He hated to give up.

'Now wait a minute,' he said. 'Wait just a minute. Mulholland ... Christopher Mulholland ... wasn't *that* the name of the Eton schoolboy who was on a walking-tour through the West Country, and then all of a sudden ...'

'Milk?' she said. 'And sugar?'

'Yes, please. And then all of a sudden ...'

'Eton schoolboy?' she said. 'Oh no, my dear, that can't possibly be right because *my* Mr Mulholland was certainly not an Eton schoolboy when he came to me. He was a Cambridge undergraduate. Come over here now and sit next to me and warm yourself in front of this lovely fire. Come on. Your tea's all ready for you.' She patted the empty place beside her on the sofa, and she sat there smiling at Billy and waiting for him to come over.

He crossed the room slowly, and sat down on the edge of the sofa. She placed his teacup on the table in front of him.

'*There* we are,' she said. 'How nice and cosy this is, isn't it?'

Billy started sipping his tea. She did the same. For half a minute or so, neither of them spoke. But Billy knew that she was looking at him. Her body was half-turned towards him, and he could feel her eyes resting on his face, watching him over the rim of her teacup. Now and again, he caught a whiff of a peculiar smell that seemed to emanate directly from her person. It was not in the least unpleasant, and it reminded him – well, he wasn't quite sure what it reminded him of. Pickled walnuts? New leather? Or was it the corridors of a hospital?

'Mr Mulholland was a great one for his tea,' she said at length. 'Never in my life have I seen anyone drink as much tea as dear, sweet Mr Mulholland.'

'I suppose he left fairly recently,' Billy said. He was still puzzling his head about the two names. He was positive now that he had seen them in the newspapers – in the headlines.

'Left?' she said, arching her brows. 'But my dear boy, he never left. He's still here. Mr Temple is also here. They're on the third floor, both of them together.'

Billy set down his cup slowly on the table, and stared at his landlady. She smiled back at him, and then she put out one of her white hands and patted him comfortingly on the knee. 'How old are you, my dear?' she asked.

'Seventeen.'

'Seventeen!' she cried. 'Oh, it's the perfect age! Mr Mulholland was also seventeen. But I think he was a trifle shorter than you are, in fact I'm sure he was, and his teeth weren't *quite* so white. You have the most beautiful teeth, Mr Weaver, did you know that?'

'They're not as good as they look,' Billy said. 'They've got simply masses of fillings in them at the back.'

'Mr Temple, of course, was a little older,' she said, ignoring his remark. 'He was actually twenty eight. And yet I never would have guessed it if he hadn't told me, never in my whole life. There wasn't a *blemish* on his body.'

'A what?' Billy said.

'His skin was *just* like a baby's.'

There was a pause. Billy picked up his teacup and took another sip of his tea, then he set it down again gently in its saucer. He waited for her to say something else, but she seemed to have lapsed into another of her silences. He sat there staring straight ahead of him into the far corner of the room, biting his lower lip.

'That parrot,' he said at last. 'You know something? It had me completely fooled when I first saw it through the window from the street. I could have sworn it was alive.'

'Alas, no longer.'

'It's most terribly clever the way it's been done,' he said. 'It doesn't look in the least bit dead. Who did it?'

'I did.'

'*You* did?'

'Of course,' she said. 'And have you met my little Basil as well?' She nodded towards the dachshund curled up so comfortably in front of the fire. Billy looked at it. And suddenly, he realized that this animal had all the time been just as silent and motionless as the parrot. He put out a hand and touched it gently on the top of its back. The back was hard and cold, and when he pushed the hair to one side with his fingers, he could see the skin underneath greyish- black and dry and perfectly preserved.

'Good gracious me,' he said. 'How absolutely fascinating.' He turned away from the dog and stared with deep admiration at the little woman beside him on the sofa. 'It must be most awfully difficult to do a thing like that.'

'Not in the least,' she said. 'I stuff *all* my little pets myself when they pass away. Will you have another cup of tea?'

'No, thank you,' Billy said. The tea tasted faintly of bitter almonds, and he didn't much care for it.

'You did sign the book, didn't you?'

'Oh, yes.'

'That's good. Because later on, if I happen to forget what you were called, then I can always come down here and look it up. I still do that almost every day with Mr. Mulholland and Mr ... Mr ...'

'Temple,' Billy said, 'Gregory Temple. Excuse my asking, but haven't there been *any* other guests here except them in the last two or three years?'

Holding her teacup high in one hand, inclining her head slightly to the left, she looked up at him out of the corners of her eyes and gave him another gentle little smile.

'No, my dear,' she said. 'Only you.'

Focus on ... foreshadowing

Foreshadowing is a warning or an indication about a future event.

This literary device is used in films or stories to give the reader an expectation of what is to come.

The student got dressed in a hurry and ran from his house. 'I feel like I am forgetting something,' he said to himself.

In the example above, the reader is made aware of the possibility that there is something unsettling the student. He has alluded to the idea that he may have forgotten something. This could feature again later in the story when he realises what he has forgotten.

Discuss

Can you identify any examples of foreshadowing in this story?

Understand

1. Where is Billy Weaver travelling from?
2. What is Billy wearing when he arrives in London?
3. (a) What is the name of the pub that is recommended to Billy?
   (b) What stopped Billy from going to look at it?
4. Describe what Billy can see when he looks into the bed and breakfast.
5. How much does the landlady charge Billy for a night at the bed and breakfast?
6. What unusual thing does Billy notice when he steps into the bed and breakfast?
7. What two names were already in the guestbook?
8. How does Billy react to the names written in the guestbook?
9. What does the landlady tell Billy about Mr Mulholland?
10. What is the reason for the dog being so still?
11. How many guests has the landlady had in the past three years?

Explore

 1. What impression do you form of Billy from the opening of the story (page 129)?

2. In your opinion, when does the complication in this short story present itself?

 3. The writer uses moments of foreshadowing in the story to create suspense and mystery. How do the moments of foreshadowing reveal clues about the story?

4. According to Billy, the landlady's smell reminded him of 'pickled walnuts? New leather? Or was it the corridors of a hospital?' What does this suggest about the landlady?

5. What do you think happened to the previous guests who stayed in this bed and breakfast?

6. In your opinion, what could Billy have done to keep himself safe from harm on this journey?

7. Think of an unexpected moment that shocked you in a novel or short story that you have studied.

   (a) Name the novel or short story and the author.

   (b) What were the events that led up to this moment?

   (c) What happened that shocked you?

   (d) Why did this moment shock you?

 Investigate

1. Billy says that his tea 'tasted faintly of bitter almonds'. Use your research skills to find out why something might have a bitter almond taste.

   (a) Does the information you discovered give you any clues about what may have happened to the guests who stayed at the bed and breakfast?

   (b) What does this information tell us about what might happen to Billy?

 Create

1. At the beginning of the short story, Billy Weaver has taken a train from London to Bath. Write a paragraph describing the setting and the atmosphere on his train journey.

2. This story ends quite suddenly. Write a paragraph predicting what you think happens next.

The following films both deal with potential dangers that can be encountered while exploring.

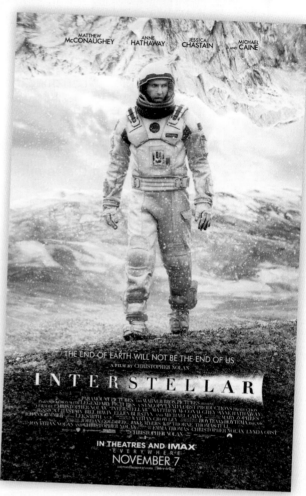

Discuss

1. Are there any similarities between these two posters?
2. In what ways do you think these films might differ?

Explore

1. Which poster catches your attention more effectively? Explain your answer.
2. What one suggestion could you give to improve the poster that you think is less effective?
3. Which film has a more interesting title?
   Give one reason for your answer.

Create

Write a review for a film you have seen that deals with the theme of travel or exploration. Use the checklist to help you.

Reviews

✓ Introduction
✓ Description
✓ Judgement
✓ Recommendation

Reviewing tracing my travels

Reflect and review

1. Take a look back to the images at the start of this unit (page 93).
   (a) Which was your favourite?
   (b) Which one best represented what we learned?
   (c) Are there any images that you would add?
2. Fill in the unit review on pages 35–36 of your Portfolio.

Language skills

Correct the double negatives in the sentences below.

1. The pilot hasn't got nowhere to land.
2. She doesn't have nothing.
3. He never goes with nobody.
4. I don't want to travel nowhere.
5. That won't do you no good.
6. You can't see no one in this room.
7. She doesn't have nothing.
8. I don't have nobody.
9. I couldn't walk no more.
10. I never wanted nothing.

Oral assessment

Imagine you are stranded on a desert island. What three items would you want to have with you? Show them to the class, either in physical form or in pictures, and explain your reason for having chosen each item.

Written assessment

1. **(a)** Write a short story based on the theme of 'travel' in the space provided on pages 37–38 of your Portfolio. Include foreshadowing in your story.
   (b) Redraft your story in the space provided on pages 112–113 of your Portfolio.

Exam skills

1. Think of a poem that you have studied that explores the theme of travel.
   (a) Name the poet and the poem.
   (b) Discuss how the poet explores the theme of travel in this poem.
   (c) What image do you find most effective in this poem?
   Write your answer in the space provided on pages 136–137 of your Portfolio.

Theme 4

Courage Through Conflict

What is conflict?

Conflict occurs when there is a struggle of some kind. There are many causes of conflict. Sometimes, people disagree with each other. At times, people experience confusion or uncertainty, which can be defined as internal conflict. In studied texts, like novels, plays and films, conflict refers to an obstacle preventing the protagonist from achieving success. Conflict may not always refer to an argument, but to a problem that should be resolved in some way. War is when conflict occurs between nations or groups and escalates into violence. Many of the texts that you will encounter throughout this unit depict life during war.

Why study conflict?

Sadly, conflict is part of the human experience. We will all experience conflict in some form during our lives. It is important to be able to resolve conflict effectively and to examine our attitudes towards war and violence. Some of the best-known poems in the English language were borne out of war and the struggles that people were forced to endure as a result. A lot can be gained from studying literature that deals with this theme.

Learning intentions

- Learn about different types of conflict.
- Assess the impact of war on people's lives.

Writing With Purpose
- Read an interview and a review.

Poetry and Song
- Study a selection of poems that deal with the theme of conflict.

Fiction
- Read about different experiences of conflict.

Stage and Screen
- Explore scenes from a modern play, a Shakespearean play and a film.

Media and Advertising
- Learn about war propaganda.
- Discover how to read visual texts.

Language Skills
- Revise the past and present tenses.
- Learn how to avoid common spelling mistakes.

 Discuss

1. Choose one of the images above that you feel best represents conflict. Why did you choose this image?

2. What sort of image would you like to add to the selection above to represent the theme of conflict?

3. Can you remember the poem 'Base Details' by Siegfried Sassoon from First Year? What was it about?

4. Have you seen any films set during a war?

 5. Can you think of examples of conflict? With a partner, try to come up with a scenario involving a conflict. How could this conflict be resolved?

 Create

 Write your own definition of 'conflict' in the space provided on page 42 of your Portfolio, by completing the sentence 'Conflict is …'. You will return to this definition later on.

What sort of conflict is shown in each of
the following images?

 Create

1. **(a)** Write a short story inspired by one of the images shown above.
   - ◖ Plan your story – make sure it involves conflict.
   - ◖ Introduce and describe your setting in detail.
   - ◖ Consider how you will resolve the conflict – remember that not all stories have happy endings!

    (b) Ask a peer to read over your work. Listen to their feedback and edit (add, take away or change) anything that you feel you could improve. Read over your piece one last time to ensure there are no spelling or grammar mistakes and that you are happy with all of the changes, then write your second draft.

Interpersonal conflicts

Interpersonal conflicts are conflicts that occur between two or more people. We will all experience interpersonal conflicts in our lives, whether it is with our peers, our family or even with strangers.

Many people experience conflict with their peers. It can be a good idea to reach out to a teacher for help in dealing with these conflicts.

In *The Bully* by Gene Kemp, Jim remembers being bullied in school when he spots his tormentor years later.

The Bully

Nearly empty classroom on second floor at lunch-time. Jim's busy copying out schoolwork. Houseman and gang march in. Houseman comes over to Jim. He looks really mad.

Houseman: You've had it. You grassed on me, you little sneak. Got me chucked out.

He starts hitting Jim, who gets to his feet, hands covering his head and tries to run, but Houseman's mates grab him, lifting Jim off his feet.

Gang Member: What shall we do to 'im, then? Give 'im a good kicking?

Houseman: No! Let's chuck him out the window.

Jim struggles furiously. As they open the window and try to lift him out he hears the door open.

Jim: Help! Save me! Help!

The door shuts again. They swing him out of the window, holding his legs. He sees the ground spinning around a long way down below and closes his eyes.

Gang Member: You'd better not drop 'im. It'll mean Borstal for us.

Houseman: I don't care. I want to kill 'im.

Borstal: detention centre for young offenders

The door opens again. Mr. Tomkins appears with Dave and some classmates. Houseman drops Jim back in the classroom and rushes away. Mr. Tomkins helps Jim up.

Mr. Tomkins: Are you all right?

Jim splutters, unable to reply.

Mr. Tomkins: You sure you're all right?

Jim: *(stammering)* I thought ... he was going ... I ... thought... he ... was ... going ... to ... kill ... me ...

. . . .

Bus stop in first scene.

Jim the Narrator: That was the last time I'd seen him until today. The last years at school were better after he'd gone.

As I stared at Houseman in the bus queue he turned and looked at me. I tensed, wondering if he'd do anything, but he didn't seem to recognise me. His eyes were glazed over and he looked rather depressed and lifeless. Perhaps he was on drugs or something. He looked scruffy, a bit like a down-and-out.

He'd forgotten me, but I would never forget him. Never.

 ## Understand

1. Where does the action take place in the first scene?

2. Houseman says 'You grassed on me' and 'got me chucked out'. Explain the terms 'grassed on' and 'chucked out'.

3. How does Jim try to defend himself?

4. What happens when Mr Tomkins arrives?

 ## Explore

 1. Jim sees Houseman years later. What is your view of Houseman, based on Jim's description?

2. Jim says that he 'would never forget' Houseman. Why do you think Jim feels this way?

3. Imagine the first scene coming to life on stage. What tips would you offer the actor playing Houseman?

 ## Create

 1. **(a)** Imagine the moment when Houseman began picking on Jim. In pairs, discuss what you think happened when they met for this first time. Try to imagine:
   ◖ the moment when Jim first saw Houseman
   ◖ Houseman's actions
   ◖ how Jim felt.

(b) When you have shared your ideas, work with your partner to write the script of the scene in which Jim and Houseman first meet. Model your script on the scenes above. Do not forget to include stage directions.

 (c) When you have finished writing your script, perform your scene for the class.

Examine stagecraft

Each play you see at the theatre is designed and crafted using some or all of the elements of stagecraft from the list below. When staging a play, a director will consider the following technical elements in order to make the scene or setting appear authentic.

- **Set:** the scenery or furniture used on stage.
- **Backdrop:** a cloth that hangs at the back of the stage, often with scenery painted on it.
- **Props:** moveable objects used on stage. Props can be moved or used by the actors as part of the plot.
- **Sound effects:** sounds, such as music, gunfire or rain, are used to bring a scene to life. These sounds will often indicate what is happening off-stage.
- **Lighting:** lights are used to create atmosphere and mood. A spotlight is often used to light actors delivering an important speech, such as a soliloquy or monologue. Darkness is an effective tool in creating tension.
- **Costumes:** costumes contribute to the production and inform the audience of the time-period of the play. The costumes may reflect a character's status (crowns and furs for kings) or situation (chains and rags for a prisoner).
- **Hair and make-up:** hair and make-up can also be used to highlight a character's status or situation. For example, a character could be given pale make-up and tangled hair to show that they are unwell.

 Explore

1. Look back at the bus stop scene from *The Bully* on page 144.
   (a) What costume, hair and make-up would you give the actor playing Houseman? Give reasons for your choices.
   (b) What lighting and sound effects would you use in this scene? Explain your choice.
   (c) Suggest one prop that you think would be useful in this scene. Give a reason for your answer.

 Create

 Design the stage set for the classroom scene from *The Bully* on page 143. Use the template on page 39 of your Portfolio to sketch your ideas. Consider the backdrop and props.

As we move through life, we are bound to encounter conflict in one form or another. No matter what the circumstances, it is important that we keep our cool and avoid using violence in any form. The following poem by Rita Ann Higgins examines conflict within a family. In it, the speaker alludes to a conflict between father and son.

As you read the poem, try to find the source of conflict.

It Wasn't the Father's Fault

By Rita Ann Higgins

His father
him hit
with a baseball bat
and he was
never right since.

Some say
he was never right
anyway.

Standing
behind the kitchen table
one Sunday before Mass
his mother said,

'If Birdie Geary
hadn't brought
that cursed baseball bat
over from America,

none of this would have happened.'

Discuss

 Work in pairs to discuss the following statements:
- ◖ You should always feel safe with your family.
- ◖ Spending time with family has its difficulties.
- ◖ Parents do not always get it right.

Understand

1. Identify the cause of conflict in this poem.
2. Who does the mother hold responsible for the incident described?

Explore

1. Find two poetic techniques used in the poem. Do you think these techniques are effective?
2. The mother is 'standing behind the kitchen table' when she speaks. Why is this detail significant?

3. How do you know that the son was badly affected by his father's actions?
4. Suggest an alternative title for this poem. Explain your choice.
5. Choose a poem that you have studied that deals with conflict in some way. Perhaps the speaker had a difficult decision to make or maybe the poem recalls a disagreement of some kind.
   (a) Name the poem and the poet.
   (b) What kind of conflict is there in the poem?
   (c) How was the conflict dealt with in the poem?
   (d) Choose one image that stood out to you in this poem and explain your choice.

                                    OR

Choose a poem that you have studied that deals with a serious incident within a family unit.
   (a) Name the poem and the poet.
   (b) How does the poet portray the incident, the family or both?
   (c) Choose one image from the poem that you found effective and explain your choice.
   (d) What did you learn from this poem?

Create

1. Write a poem that deals with the theme of conflict.
2. You have been given the opportunity to interview one member of the family portrayed in this poem.
   (a) Which family member would you choose? Explain your choice.
   (b) Write the text of the interview in transcript format.

Sometimes, people get off to a bad start because of a misunderstanding of some kind. Often, people find that they get along better once they take the time to understand more about each other's circumstances.

The following extract is from the beginning of the short story 'Thank You, Ma'am' by Langston Hughes. It introduces conflict between a young boy and an older woman.

Listen to the extract being read. As you listen, try to locate the moment of conflict.

Thank You, Ma'am

She was a large woman with a large purse that had everything in it but a hammer and nails. It had a long strap, and she carried it slung across her shoulder. It was about eleven o'clock at night, dark, and she was walking alone, when a boy ran up behind her and tried to snatch her purse. The strap broke with the single tug the boy gave it from behind. But the boy's weight and the weight of the purse combined caused him to lose his balance. Instead of taking off full blast as he had hoped, the boy fell on his back on the sidewalk and his legs flew up. The large woman simply turned around and kicked him right square in his blue-jeaned sitter. Then she reached down, picked the boy up by his shirtfront, and shook him until his teeth rattled.

After that the woman said, 'Pick up my pocketbook, boy, and give it here.'

She still held him tightly. But she bent down enough to permit him to stoop and pick up her purse. Then she said, 'Now ain't you ashamed of yourself?'

Firmly gripped by his shirtfront, the boy said, 'Yes'm.'

The woman said, 'What did you want to do it for?'

The boy said, 'I didn't aim to.'

She said, 'You a lie!'

By that time two or three people passed, stopped, turned to look, and some stood watching.

'If I turn you loose, will you run?' asked the woman.

'Yes'm,' said the boy.

'Then I won't turn you loose,' said the woman. She did not release him.

'Lady, I'm sorry,' whispered the boy.

'Um-hum! And your face is dirty. I got a great mind to wash your face for you. Ain't you got nobody home to tell you to wash your face?'

'No'm,' said the boy.

'Then it will get washed this evening,' said the large woman, starting up the street, dragging the frightened boy behind her.

He looked as if he were fourteen or fifteen, frail and willow-wild, in tennis shoes and blue jeans.

The woman said ...

Understand

1. Describe the woman introduced in the opening paragraph.
2. What is the first sign of conflict in this story?
3. How does the woman react to what the boy does?
4. According to the narrator, approximately how old is the boy?
5. Choose three adjectives to describe the boy and explain your choice.

Explore

 1. The boy says that he is sorry for what he has done. Do you think the woman should believe him?

 2. The boy is frightened. Why do you think he feels this way?

3. The boy tried to steal the woman's purse. What could have motivated the boy to do this?

Create

1. **(a)** The story above is incomplete. Try to imagine what happens next.
   - What does the woman say?
   - What does she do?
   - What happens to the boy?
   - Does the conflict continue?
   - How does the story end?

   Write an ending to the story in the space provided on page 40 of your Portfolio.

  (b) When you have written your ending, compare it to the original by Langston Hughes, which your teacher will play for you.

   How does it compare to the ending you have imagined? Write your answer in the space provided on page 41 of your Portfolio.

Internal conflict

As well as conflict with others, many people experience internal conflict when they struggle with feelings of confusion, uncertainty or self-doubt.

 In this scene from *The Winter's Tale* by William Shakespeare, the King of Sicily, Leontes, is experiencing internal conflict as he wrongly believes that his wife, Hermione, has been unfaithful with his best friend Polixenes, King of Bohemia.

In this scene, Leontes instructs his servant, Camillo, to kill Polixenes. The pair argue before Camillo reluctantly agrees.

The Winter's Tale

LEONTES
Ha' you not seen, Camillo –
But that's past doubt; you have, or your eyeglass
Is thicker than a cuckold's horn – or heard –
For to a vision so apparent Rumour
Cannot be mute – or thought – for cogitation
Resides not in that man that does not think –
My wife is slippery? If thou wilt confess,
Or else be impudently negative,
To have nor eyes, nor ears, nor thought, then say
My wife's a hobby-horse, deserves a name
As rank as any flax-wench that puts to
Before her troth-plight – say't, and justify't.

Leontes insults his wife, Hermione, and implies she is a cheater who cannot be trusted

CAMILLO
I would not be a stander-by to hear
My sovereign mistress clouded so without
My present vengeance taken. 'Shrew my heart,
You never spoke what did become you less
Than this, which to reiterate were sin
As deep as that, though true.

Camillo defends the Queen, referring to her with respect

LEONTES
Is whispering nothing?
Is leaning cheek to cheek? Is meeting noses?
Kissing with inside lip? Stopping the career
Of laughter with a sigh? – a note infallible
Of breaking honesty! Horsing foot on foot?
Skulking in corners? Wishing clocks more swift?
Hours minutes? Noon midnight? And all eyes
Blind with the pin and web but theirs, theirs only,
That would unseen be wicked? Is this nothing?
Why then the world and all that's in't is nothing,
The covering sky is nothing, Bohemia nothing,

Leontes shares his 'proof' with Camillo

	My wife is nothing, nor nothing have these nothings
	If this be nothing.
CAMILLO	Good my lord, be cured
	Of this diseased opinion, and betimes,
	For 'tis most dangerous.
LEONTES	Say it be, 'tis true.
CAMILLO	No, no, my lord!
LEONTES	It is – you lie, you lie!

I say thou liest, Camillo, and I hate thee,
Pronounce thee a gross lout, a mindless slave,
Or else a hovering temporizer that
Canst with thine eyes at once see good and evil,
Inclining to them both. Were my wife's liver
Infected as her life she would not live
The running of one glass.

Leontes, tormented with jealousy, becomes angry with Camillo

CAMILLO   Who does infect her?

LEONTES Why, he that wears her like a medal, hanging
About his neck, Bohemia, who, if I
Had servants true about me that bare eyes
To see alike mine honour as their profits,
Their own particular thrifts, they would do that
Which should undo more doing. Ay, and thou,
His cupbearer, whom I from meaner form
Have benched and reared to worship, who mayst see
Plainly as heaven sees earth and earth sees heaven
How I am galled, mightst bespice a cup
To give mine enemy a lasting wink,
Which draught to me were cordial.

Leontes refers to Polixenes as Bohemia

He asks Camillo to poison Polixenes's drink

CAMILLO
Sir, my lord,
I could do this, and that with no rash potion,
But with a ling'ring dram that should not work
Maliciously, like poison; but I cannot
Believe this crack to be in my dread mistress,
So sovereignly being honourable.
I have loved thee –

Camillo does not want to carry out Leontes's request because he believes Hermione is honourable

LEONTES
Make that thy question, and go rot!
Dost think I am so muddy, so unsettled,
To appoint myself in this vexation! Sully
The purity and whiteness of my sheets –
Which to preserve is sleep, which being spotted
Is goads, thorns, nettles, tails of wasps –
Give scandal to the blood o'th' prince, my son,
Who I do think is mine and love as mine,
Without ripe moving to't? Would I do this?
Could man so blench?

Leontes lashes out, refusing to accept that he is wrong and his wife is innocent

CAMILLO
I must believe you, sir;
I do, and will fetch off Bohemia for't –
Provided that when he's removed your highness
Will take again your Queen as yours at first,
Even for your son's sake, and thereby for sealing
The injury of tongues in courts and kingdoms
Known and allied to yours.

Camillo says he will do as Leontes asks, provided he does not punish Hermione

LEONTES
Thou dost advise me
Even so as I mine own course have set down.
I'll give no blemish to her honour, none.

CAMILLO
My lord, go then, and with a countenance as clear
As friendship wears at feasts keep with Bohemia
And with your Queen. I am his cupbearer;
If from me he have wholesome beverage,
Account me not your servant.

Camillo advises Leontes to remain friendly towards Polixenes and Hermione, and promises to poison Polixenes

LEONTES
This is all.
Do't, and thou hast the one half of my heart;
Do't not, thou splitt'st thine own.

Leontes threatens to kill Camillo if he does not kill Polixenes

CAMILLO
I'll do't, my lord.

LEONTES
I will seem friendly, as thou hast advised me. *Exit*

Understand

1. Find quotes to support the following:
   - Leontes believes that his wife has been unfaithful.
   - Camillo believes the Queen is innocent.
   - Leontes and Camillo are in conflict.
   - Leontes is certain that Polixenes is to blame.
   - The King instructs Camillo to poison Polixenes.
   - Leontes threatens Camillo.

2. Choose a moment in the scene where the tension is highest. Describe what is happening in this moment.

 Explore

 1. Does Camillo really want to poison Polixenes?

 2. Why does Camillo experience internal conflict at the end of this scene?

 3. Do you think that Camillo will carry out the King's wishes?

4. Write about a moment of conflict in the play that you have studied as part of your Junior Cycle English course.
   (a) Name the play and playwright.
   (b) Describe the moment of conflict.
   (c) How is the conflict made clear to the audience?
   (d) How is the conflict resolved?

 Create

 1. **(a)** In pairs, rewrite this scene.
   - Update the scene by setting it in a new location and time.
   - The dialogue should reflect the new setting.
   - Use stage directions to explain how the characters should move and speak during the moments of conflict.

 (b) Perform your scene for your classmates.

Present tense and past tense

Language skills

The present tense describes:

◖ **things that are happening right now**

◖ **things that happen on a regular basis.**

The past tense describes things that have already happened.

It is important to identify the tense in which you are writing. A common mistake is to jump between different tenses.

✗ *My heart beats fast as I ran.*

✓ **Present tense:** *My heart beats fast as I run.*

✓ **Past tense:** *My heart beat fast as I ran.*

When you are telling a story, decide whether your narrator is describing events as they are happening (present tense) or looking back on events that have already taken place (past tense).

Verb	Present tense	Past tense
Do	I do	I did I have done
See	I see	I saw I have seen
Write	I write	I wrote I have written
Teach	I teach	I taught I have taught
Bring	I bring	I brought I have brought

 Understand

1. Write sentences using the past tense of the following words:
   ◖ do   ◖ write   ◖ bring   ◖ find   ◖ take
   ◖ see   ◖ teach   ◖ go   ◖ eat   ◖ sneak.

2. The following passage is written from the point of view of Leontes.

> I see my wife flirting with Polixenes right under my nose! She writes him secret love-letters. He brings her gifts and thinks I do not see but I do! I see everything. I will bring them to justice and prove their guilt. I will show that Hermione is lying when she says 'I do nothing wrong'.

   (a) Identify all of the verbs in this extract.
   (b) Rewrite the extract, changing all verbs into the past tense.

Victims of war

There are many victims of war – both those who are actively involved, such as soldiers, and others who are not involved, such as citizens of war-torn countries. Such people have had their lives uprooted by terrible, and often violent, conflicts.

Read the following interview with Luma Mohed, a Syrian woman who raises orphaned children in war-torn Syria.

Raising Kids During War: A Syrian Mom's Story

Since 1999, Luma Mohed has helped raise 17 orphaned, abandoned and other vulnerable children at the SOS Village in Aleppo. But since the war in Syria broke out in 2011, life as a mother has taken on a host of new challenges—especially when she, her children, and the entire SOS Village were forced to evacuate their homes due to security threats.

As the war in Syria enters its 6th year, we sat down with Luma, an SOS Mother, to ask her what it's like to be a mother today in Syria.

Describe how life at the SOS Village in Aleppo became more and more challenging from when the war began in March 2011 until you and your family were evacuated in August 2012. What changes did you notice to your life and the lives of your children?

At that time, the security situation became more and more dangerous at the SOS Village in Aleppo. First, we started to hear bombs and bullets from far away. But after the clashes between the regular army and armed groups moved closer to us, we started to see the mortars pass over the village. The situation was extremely dangerous so we had no choice but to evacuate the children to the SOS Village in Damascus.

Why was it necessary to evacuate the children in August 2012? At that time, what were some of the biggest risks to the children's safety?

The kids started to feel unsafe, especially when the sound of the explosions became very loud. We left the village a month before armed groups entered it. Many people were killed after we left the town.

What has been the most difficult thing for you to deal with, as a mother, during the war?

It has been challenging to deal with children who have come to the Village after the war began. These children experience trauma because of the war. For example, one of my children was trapped under a newly destroyed building before he was rescued. I don't know how long he was trapped until they got him out. When he joined us at the SOS Village, he was unable to talk or to laugh. He was so sad and crying all the time. It took him a long time to speak with us.

What do your children need most that you are unable to provide for them because of the war?

Because the security situation is so bad, I can't raise them in a safe environment as I did with my older kids. I used to take my kids on picnics, and we attended many parties and activities. But we can't do this regularly anymore. We can only go to specific areas.

 Discuss

1. Share your understanding of the word 'war'.
2. What do you know about wars that have taken place?
3. What do you know about the conflict in Syria?

 Understand

In the case of each of the following, write the letter corresponding to the correct answer in your copy.

1. When did Luma start raising orphaned children?
    (a) 2011
    (b) 1999
    (c) 2012

2. When were the children evacuated?
    (a) April 2012
    (b) August 2012
    (c) October 2012

3. Where did the children go when they were evacuated?
    (a) Aleppo
    (b) Damascus
    (c) Daraa

Explore

1. What evidence is there to suggest that the children have been traumatised by their experience of war?

2. What happened to make the children feel unsafe?

3. Choose three words to describe how the children might have felt and explain your choices.

4. Based on your reading of this interview, do you think that war is fair or unfair? Explain your answer in detail.

Investigate

Use your research skills to find out more about the war in Syria. Try to find the following:

- the location of Syria on a map
- images of Syria before and during the war
- when the war began
- why the war began
- news reports
- video clips.

Gather your findings to share with your classmates.

Create

Organise a class debate on the issue of war. Work together to build an argument for or against one of the following motions:

- *This house believes that every country should have an army.*

OR

- *This house believes that war is necessary.*

The following review was written by The Lightning Readers – *The Guardian* newspaper's children's book reading group.

Hitler's Canary by Sandi Toksvig – review

This book is based on events that took place during the Second World War and the experiences of the author's father during the war.

Bamse, the main character, lives in Denmark with his family. The story follows Bamse and his family throughout their terrible fight for freedom when the Germans invade Denmark. This emotional yet humorous story tells of a daring escape and the differences – even the smallest ones – that people can make.

Our group's favourite character was Marie, the mother, due to her optimism and ability to get her family out of many sticky situations with her excellent improvisation and acting skills. We all agreed that the characters felt very real to us, even though the story was set a long time ago and in a different country.

We had lots of favourite moments, including humorous, tense and sad ones. Marquell thought that the cow dung taxi was really funny and Daniel liked a particularly intense and sad moment in which Tomas sacrificed himself to the Germans, so the rest of the group would not be captured.

Most of The Lightening Readers really enjoyed this book. We felt lots of different emotions whilst reading it and some of the group felt gripped by the story all the way through. Those that weren't too keen on the book commented that the foreign words, for example place names, made it difficult to follow. They also felt that it may have been a little long for them.

The Lightening Readers would recommend this book to ages 10+ and award it 3 stars.

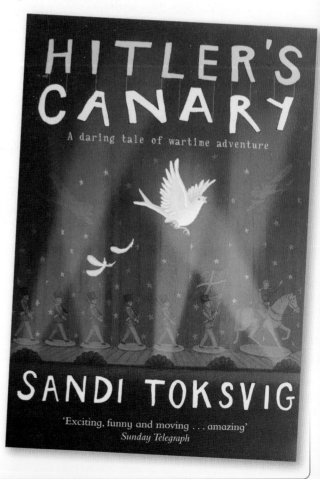

Understand

1. Name the title and the author of the book reviewed in this article.
2. What do you learn about the setting of the novel from the review?
3. **(a)** Who have the reviewers chosen as their favourite character?

   (b) Why have they chosen this character?
4. What group of readers may be interested in this book, according to the reviewers?

Explore

1. The novel is described as 'emotional' and 'humorous'. Which of these qualities would you enjoy most in a novel?
2. Suggest two reasons why someone might like to read a novel set during a war.

3. Look carefully at the images of the book cover that accompany the review. Which book cover do you find more appealing? Explain your answer.

Investigate

Visit your local library to borrow a copy of *Hitler's Canary* by Sandi Toksvig.

1. Are there any recommendations included on the cover or inside of the book?
2. What is written in the blurb?
3. Does the book include any information about the author?
4. Read the book for yourself – do you agree with the reviewers' thoughts on the novel?

Create

Write a review of a novel you have read as part of your Junior Cycle English course.

◖ Introduce the novel and author.
◖ Give readers a sense of the characters, setting and story without revealing too much.
◖ Identify the theme of the novel.
◖ Give your recommendation to others – who might enjoy this novel?
◖ Give a star rating.

The following song was written in response to the Vietnam War. Listen to Edwin Starr performing the song and discuss the view of war explored throughout. Is the song pro-war or anti-war? https://youtu.be/dQHUAJTZqF0

War

(War, what is it good for?) Absolutely nothing
(War, what is it good for?) Absolutely nothing
(War, what is it good for?) Absolutely nothing

War is something that I despise
Because it means destruction of innocent lives
War means tears in thousands of mothers' eyes
When their sons go out to fight and lose their lives
I said

(War) good God y'all
(What is it good for?) Absolutely nothing, say it again
(War, what is it good for?) Absolutely nothing

(War), It ain't nothing but a heartbreaker
(War), Friend only to the undertaker
War is the enemy of all mankind
The thought of war blows my mind
War has caused unrest, within the younger generation
Induction then destruction. Who wants to die?

(War) good God y'all
(What is it good for?) Absolutely nothing, say it, say it, say it
(War, what is it good for?) Absolutely nothing

(War), It ain't nothing but a heartbreaker
(War), Its only friend is the undertaker
War has shattered many young men's dreams
Made them disabled, bitter and mean
Life is much too short and precious to be fighting wars these days
War can't give life it can only take it away

(War) good God y'all
(What is it good for?) Absolutely nothing, say it
(War, what is it good for?) Absolutely nothing

Listen to me
(War), It ain't nothing but a heartbreaker
(War), Friend only to the undertaker
Peace, love and understanding
Tell me, is there no place for them today?
They say we must fight to keep our freedom
But Lord knows there's gotta be a better way

(War) good God y'all
(What is it good for?) You tell me, say it, say it, say it, say it
(War) good God y'all
(What is it good for?) Stand up and shout it (Nothing)

Understand

Identify the poetic technique used in each of the following lines:

◖ (War), It ain't nothing but a heartbreaker / (War), Friend only to the undertaker'

◖ 'Who wants to die?'

◖ War is the enemy to all mankind'

◖ 'The thought of war blows my mind'

Explore

1. Does the songwriter approve or disapprove of war? How do you know?

2. Do you agree that war is good for 'absolutely nothing'? Give reasons for your answer.

3. **(a)** According to Edwin Starr, what happens to young men's dreams?

   (b) Why might this be the case?

Investigate

1. **(a)** Use your research skills to learn more about the Vietnam War. Try to find out the following information:

   ◖ when it began and when it ended

   ◖ which countries were involved

   ◖ the cause of the conflict

   ◖ images of the war

   ◖ images of Vietnam then and now

   ◖ links to videos or articles about the war.

   (b) Share your findings in groups. Work together to discover more about the effects of war. How many people died in the Vietnam War?

Create

Write a speech in which you emphasise the importance of peace, love and understanding in the world today.

Read visual texts

It has been said that a picture paints a thousand words. Photographs capture a moment in time and can contain both obvious and hidden details in one image. Visual texts can be provocative, informative and stimulating.

In the exam you may be asked to respond to a visual text, or during your classroom-based assessments you may choose to use a picture or photograph as inspiration for your presentation and/or one of your written pieces. Refer back to this list when writing about and discussing visual texts.

- **Subject:** what does the image capture?
  - **An object:** identify the central object. Describe the appearance and placement of the object. Who does it belong to? Why is it there?
  - **A person:** look closely at the person's facial expression and body language. Try to read their mind – what are they feeling or thinking?
  - **People:** if there is more than one person, try to guess the relationship or connection between them. Look closely at the facial expressions and body language. Do they know each other? If so, how?
- **Focus:** what is the main draw or where is your attention directed? Is your attention directed towards one particular part of the image?

- **Placement and order:** in the same way that a poet emphasises an idea using techniques like imagery and repetition, an artist or photographer will emphasise an idea by presenting their image in a particular way. Ask yourself, what elements make up the image? How are these placed? Do they relate?
- **Size of objects within the image:** does one object or person dominate the image? Are other objects or people hidden? Sometimes the most interesting part of a visual text is the background detail.
- **Examine the use of colour.**
  - **Colour:** what colours stand out to you? Why has the artist or photographer chosen the colours? What do you associate with the colours?
  - **Lack of colour:** is the image lacking in colour? Why has the artist or photographer chosen to present the image without colour? While an image may be lacking in colour, there may be significance to shade or shadow.

Use the list on page 162 to 'read' the image below, then answer the questions that follow.

 ## Understand

1. What is the subject of this image?
2. What object or person is in focus? What does this tell you about this particular object or person?
3. Explain what you see in the foreground of the picture.
4. Are the colours of the main subject in contrast with other colours in the photograph?

 ## Explore

1. **(a)** What is the occupation of the main subject of the photograph?
   (b) How do you know?
   (c) Would you like to do this job? Why/Why not?

 ## Investigate

 Work in pairs to learn more about a recent news story or event. Find an image that relates to the news story or event to share with your class. Explain the relevance of the image.

 ## Create

Write a diary entry from the perspective of the subject of this photograph.

'The Boy' is set in Afghanistan, a place that has been greatly affected and damaged by war. The speaker is taken through the city by a boy who lives there.

Take turns reading the poem aloud in pairs.

The Boy

By PJ Harvey

Boy speaks,   *Follow me.*
Through the old   city streets
   you follow him   past the tents
through the fog   and excrement.

   Smile at him.   He smiles back
   leads you past   wooden shacks
and open gutters.   Don't fall in.
   Put your feet   in his footprints.

Bullet holes   in the walls
   form a map   of the world.
Giant door   with a key.
Boy turns;   *Follow me.*

Young boy   in your face
   every loss   I can trace.
   Follow you   enter in.
Put my feet   in your footprints.

Understand

1. What experience does the speaker share with the boy?
2. How do you know that the boy's life has been affected by war?
3. Find two poetic techniques used in this poem.

Explore

1. In what way is the boy's home different to your own? Make a detailed comparison.
2. 'Young boy in your face, / every loss I can trace'. What is the speaker referring to in these lines?
3. Choose an image from the poem that you find striking. Why does it stand out to you?
4. Comment on the structure of 'The Boy'. Is it unusual?

Create

Write a poem inspired by one of images of war below. Refer to the list of poetic techniques on page 7, as you may like to include some of these in your own poem.

Soldiers of war

People choose to go to war for a great many reasons – some are motivated by a love for their country, some want to fight for a cause they are passionate about, some join the army as a way to support loved ones at home and some are drafted into military service.

drafted: compulsory recruitment

In the following extract from Shakespeare's *Henry V*, King Henry delivers a powerful speech to rally his soldiers in the midst of a siege.

Henry V

HENRY   Once more unto the breach, dear friends, once more;

Or close the wall up with our English dead!

In peace, there's nothing so becomes a man

As modest stillness and humility;

But when the blast of war blows in our ears,

Then imitate the action of the tiger:

Stiffen the sinews, summon up the blood,

sinews: tendons or ligaments

Disguise fair nature with hard-favour'd rage;

Then lend the eye a terrible aspect:

Let pry through the portage of the head,

portage: carrying

Like the brass cannon; let the brow o'erwhelm it,

As fearfully as doth a gallèd rock

O'erhang and jutty his confounded base,

confounded: damned

Swill'd with the wild and wasteful ocean.

Now set the teeth, and stretch the nostril wide,

Hold hard the breath, and bend up every spirit

To his full height. On, on, you noblest English,

Whose blood is fet from fathers of war-proof:

fet: drawn

Fathers that, like so many Alexanders,

Have in these parts from morn till even fought,

And sheathed their swords for lack of argument:

Dishonour not your mothers: now attest

That those whom you called fathers did beget you.

Be copy now to men of grosser blood,

And teach them how to war. And you, good yeoman,

yeoman: servant

Whose limbs were made in England, show us here

The mettle of your pasture; let us swear

mettle: spirit and resilience

That you are worth your breeding – which I doubt not:

For there is none of you so mean and base,

base: immoral

That hath not noble lustre in your eyes.

I see you stand like greyhounds in the slips,

Straining upon the start. The game's afoot:

Follow your spirit; and upon this charge,

Cry 'God for Harry, England, and Saint George!'

lustre:
shine

Focus on ... monologues

A **monologue** is a long speech by one character in a play or film.

Monologues usually reveal the character's true feelings and desires. A monologue may be addressed to other characters or the audience.

 ## Understand

1. Choose two quotes to suggest that Henry V's speech encourages soldiers to fight with honour.
2. What true feelings are expressed by Henry V in this monologue?
3. How would you describe this monologue? Select one of the following and explain your choice.

   ◖ Patriotic   ◖ Passionate   ◖ Inspiring

 ## Explore

1. Former British Prime Minister, Winston Churchill, quoted from Henry V's monologue when delivering a speech to the people of Britain during the Second World War. Choose an appropriate quote from the monologue which people could relate to at that time. Explain your choice.
2. Why is it important for leaders to boost morale and keep people's spirits up in times of war?
3. Imagine you are directing the actor playing the part of Henry V. How would you instruct him to deliver these lines? Consider:

   ◖ tone of voice   ◖ movement and gestures
   ◖ facial expression   ◖ body language.

 ## Investigate

Find a monologue in a play or film you have studied.

◖ Which character is speaking?

◖ What is revealed?

◖ Select the line from the monologue that you find most revealing.

'The Target' was published in 1919 after the First World War. The poem is told from the point of view of a young soldier who has just shot and killed an enemy soldier.

This poem is a dramatic monologue from the soldier's point of view, as he is the only speaker and the poem reveals his thoughts and feelings.

 Take turns reading 'The Target' aloud in pairs.

The Target

By Ivor Gurney

I shot him, and it had to be
One of us! 'Twas him or me.
'Couldn't be helped' and none can blame
Me, for you would do the same

My mother, she can't sleep for fear
Of what might be a-happening here
To me. Perhaps it might be best
To die, and set her fears at rest

For worst is worst, and worry's done.
Perhaps he was the only son ...
Yet God keeps still, and does not say
A word of guidance any way.

Well, if they get me, first I'll find
That boy, and tell him all my mind,
And see who felt the bullet worst,
And ask his pardon, if I durst.

All's a tangle. Here's my job.
A man might rave, or shout, or sob;
And God He takes no sort of heed.
This is a bloody mess indeed.

Discuss

 Which of these statements do you agree with most? Discuss your views in pairs.

- Those who are left behind suffer greatly during war.
- People should show empathy and love in times of war.
- War is a bloody mess.

Understand

1. What is revealed in the opening line of the poem?
2. In the fourth stanza, what does the soldier tell us that he intends to do if he is killed in battle?
3. What does the soldier describe as 'a bloody mess'?
4. Find two examples of enjambment in this poem.

Explore

 1. The soldier says 'none can blame / Me'. Do you think he blames himself or feels some guilt at what he has done?

 2. What could be the soldier's reason for thinking 'it might be best / To die'?

 3. Do you think the soldier feels let down or abandoned by God?

 4. How do you think the soldier's mother feels?

 5. Who do you feel more sympathy for, the soldier speaking in poem or the one who died?

Create

Imagine you are one of the soldiers depicted in this poem. Write a letter home to your mother on the morning before the shooting took place.

Take turns reading 'An Irish Airman Foresees his Death' aloud in pairs. The Irish airman who speaks in this poem risks his life for Britain during the First World War. Do you think he struggles with his identity as a result?

An Irish Airman Foresees his Death

By W. B. Yeats

I know that I shall meet my fate
Somewhere among the clouds above;
Those that I fight I do not hate,
Those that I guard I do not love;
My country is Kiltartan Cross,
My countrymen Kiltartan's poor,
No likely end could bring them loss
Or leave them happier than before.
Nor law, nor duty bade me fight,
Nor public men, nor cheering crowds,
A lonely impulse of delight
Drove to this tumult in the clouds;
I balanced all, brought all to mind,
The years to come seemed waste of breath,
A waste of breath the years behind
In balance with this life, this death.

 Understand

1. Identify the rhyming scheme in this poem.
2. The airman knows that he will die in action. Find the line that supports this statement.
3. Say how the airman feels about:
   (a) those he fights against   **(b)** those he fights for.
4. Was the airman forced to join the war?

 Explore

 1. What is the 'impulse of delight' that drove the speaker to join the war as an airman, in your opinion?

2. How do you know that the airman accepts his death?

3. This poem is a dramatic monologue. What qualities does it share with the poem 'The Target' (page 168)?

In pairs, read the poem 'Comrades' by Eva Gore-Booth aloud. Look carefully at the title of the poem, what do you think the word 'comrades' means?

Comrades

By Eva Gore-Booth

The peaceful night that round me flows,
Breaks through your iron prison doors,
Free through the world your spirit goes,
Forbidden hands are clasping yours.
The wind is our confederate,
The night has left her doors ajar,
We meet beyond earth's barrèd gate,
Where all the world's wild Rebels are.

confederate: ally

 Understand

1. How is the night described in the first line?
2. Find an example of personification in this poem.

 Explore

 1. Do you think the speaker considers herself one of 'the world's wild Rebels'?

 2. Do you think the speaker longs to be with the person addressed in the poem? Give reasons for your answer.

 Investigate

This poem is written to the poet's sister Constance Markievicz, who was imprisoned for her part in the 1916 Easter Rising. Use your research skills to find out more about Constance Markievicz. Try to find out the following information:

◄ date and place of birth and death
◄ her involvement in the Easter Rising
◄ images of and articles about Constance Markievicz
◄ video links or media files with information about Markievicz
◄ information about her sister, the poet Eva Gore-Booth.

When you have gathered the information, share your findings with your class.

Key spellings

Many of the following words are misspelled because they are synonyms or sound similar.

Were	Where	Wear	We're
Past tense of 'to be' *We were the winners.*	**In what place?** *Where will we meet?*	**To have something (clothes, etc.) on** *I have nothing to wear!*	**Contraction: we are** *We're so proud of you!*

To	Too	Two
Motion in the direction of *We are going to school.*	**Excessively or also** *Don't go too far!* *Can I come along too?*	**The number 2** *I have two brothers.*

There	Their	They're
Statement or placement *There are 30 students in my class.* *Put your schoolbag over there.*	**Possessive adjective** *The children took their bikes to the park.*	**Contraction: they are** *I love puppies, they're so cute!*

Your	You're
Possessive adjective *Is this your house?*	**Contraction: you are** *You're a star!*

Our	Are
Possessive pronoun *We are staying with our grandparents.*	**Plural and second person singular of 'to be'** *We are going to Italy this summer.*

👍 Understand

Write out the following sentences in your copy, adding the correct words to fill the blanks.

1. *were   where   wear   we're*

   We _____ really excited when our parents told us _____ we will be going on holidays this year! _____ going to Florida for three weeks. I will get to _____ all of my favourite summer clothes. I cannot wait!

2. *to   too   two*

   I am going _____ a match on Friday. My grandad got me _____ tickets so I can take a friend with me _____.

3. *there   their   they're*

   _____ are just two days to go until Christmas. Children have written _____ letters and now _____ getting ready to leave carrots out for the reindeer!

4. *your   you're*

   I can't believe you have slept in! Didn't you hear _____ alarm? _____ going to be late for school at this rate.

5. *our   are*

   _____ you free on Saturday? We would love you to come to _____ house for a party.

The following extract is taken from a novel called *The Silver Donkey* by Sonya Hartnett. In the extract, two sisters find a stranger in the woods. They are very excited at their discovery, especially when they learn that the man is a soldier.

The Silver Donkey

'Who's there?' cried the man, and then repeated it in a language that the sisters understood. '*Qui est là?* Who's there?'

He looked towards Marcelle and Coco and must have seen two skinny, flash-eyed little girls, wild as kittens born under stables, the taller dressed in her brother's hand-me-downs, the smaller rumpled as a street urchin – but then he looked to the mouldery soil and up into the trees, and behind himself towards the distant sea. He searched about frantically, as if the sisters were fleet butterflies and could alight anywhere. He scrambled backwards in the dirt, covering his knees in mud. 'Who is there?' he asked again.

Marcelle and Coco stared. They had never met someone so frightened of them. They felt regretful, and sorry for him. 'It's just us,' said Marcelle. 'No one else.'

The man stopped scrabbling and became very still. He gazed towards a woodpigeon which perched above Marcelle's head. 'I can't see you,' he said nervously. 'I'm blind. Who are you?'

That the man was blind was some compensation for his not being dead: Pascal had never found or even met a blind man. The girls, emboldened, peered more closely at their discovery, stepping from the shadows like fawns. They saw that the man had untidy brown hair and that his face was rather dirty. Coco, who had a sparrow's quick eyes, saw that he held something silver and enticing in his palm, something that twinkled and glimmered. Marcelle saw that, although he wore tatty old-man's clothes, the man himself was not very old – in fact he was young, as young as some of the fishermen's sons who raced small skiffs in the bay. His blue eyes shone and his cheeks were smudged with downy whiskers that the girls' father called baby-fluff. 'I'm Marcelle,' she told him. 'I'm ten. This is my sister Coco. She's eight. Her real name is Thérèse, but everybody calls her Coco.'

'Because I have hair like a black poodle's,' explained Coco.

Marcelle felt compelled to expand on this. 'When I was little and Coco was a baby and she had curly hair like a poodle's, Madame Courbet at the end of the road had a tiny black poodle named Coco, so that was the name I gave Thérèse – Coco.'

'I see,' said the man, huddling against a tree.

'And Coco – the poodle – got stolen,' added Coco.

'Yes, she did, she got stolen. Everyone said Mademoiselle Bloom took her – Coco the poodle, I mean – because Coco disappeared exactly on the day Mademoiselle Bloom went to live in Paris, and she was always fond of Coco – the poodle, I mean – so everyone said that Mademoiselle Bloom was to blame. But that was a long time ago.'

'When I was a baby,' said Coco. 'Coco would be old old old now – the dog.'

'And now Madame Courbet doesn't have a dog at all,' said Marcelle. 'Not a poodle or a bulldog or a dachshund or anything. She says her heart is broken for Coco.'

'But everyone still calls me Coco,' Coco pointed out.

'Except when you're naughty or when something is very serious,' her sister reminded her. 'Then we call you Thérèse.'

'Yes,' admitted the little girl. 'When I am in trouble, I'm Thérèse.'

The young man turned his head from one sister to the other, following the voices as if they were birds. He wondered what to say. 'That's a sad story, about the dog.'

'Yes, it is,' agreed Marcelle.

'Do you still have hair like a poodle's, Coco?'

'Oh, yes!'

The man nodded thoughtfully. 'Then I know what it looks like, even though I can't see it.'

Coco smiled deeply, and tugged at a ringlet. She was insufferably proud of her hair.

'What are you doing here, anyway?' asked Marcelle, wishing to change the subject.

A frown crossed the man's face. 'I'm trying to go home. My brother is very ill. He is only eleven years old. His name is John. The doctors don't think he has long to live. My mother wrote saying that he wakes at night with a fever, calling out for me. She wrote that I should hurry home.'

Marcelle and Coco were soft-hearted, and the man's words caused their hearts to pang. 'Where is your home?' asked Marcelle.

The man twisted on his knees, and pointed in the direction of the sea. 'Across the Channel. Up the beach. Climb a narrow path between the rocks and walk three miles down a chalky road. When you reach a five-railed gate bordered on each side by oaks as big as churches, that's my home. You can see the chimneys from the road. John's window is on the ground floor, third from the right.'

Marcelle considered. She knew that the Channel was very wide, and could be choppy and dangerous. She knew that three miles was a long distance to walk. 'How will you get across the sea, up the path and along the chalky road?' she asked. 'You're all alone. You're blind.'

The man looked stricken. 'Yes, I am.'

'Are you a soldier?' asked Coco unexpectedly.

The man hunkered against the tree. 'Why do you ask that?'

'Well, you are a bit like a soldier. You have a soldier's blanket and soldier's boots. And once there were soldiers who slept a night in our village and they spoke in a funny way, the same way that you do.'

'It's called an accent,' said Marcelle with superiority.

The man was fidgeting, casting his blind gaze about. The fascinating silver thing remained closed in his hand, gleamy as a fishhook, hidden as a jewel. He said, 'I am a soldier – well, I used to be. I'm not one any more.'

'Why not? Because You're blind?'

The soldier nodded wonkily. 'That must be the reason.'

'We could help you go home, Monsieur.' Marcelle stepped a little nearer. 'You must come with us to our house – we will each hold one of your hands, and guide you – and Papa will know how you can get home, I'm sure.'

'No! No!' The soldier waved his arms. 'You can't tell anyone about me – you mustn't!'

The sisters were startled, their eyes opened wide, but they were not afraid. Coco asked, 'Why mustn't we?'

'Because … Why, because …' The soldier looked helpless, his hands dropped in his lap. 'Because other people might not understand about John, and his being ill, and his calling for me feverishly at night. People might say I should go back to soldiering and forget about my brother, since he's only a boy, and sickly, and since there's a war being fought.'

The soldier seemed badly worried, and was chewing his lip; Marcelle, who had noticed many injustices in the world, thought he was probably right about what other people would say. No one seemed to care about anything except the dreary war; nothing else appeared important any more. At any rate, it suited her to keep the soldier a secret: it felt nice to know something that Pascal did not. 'Did you hear, Thérèse?' She addressed her sister imperiously. 'Don't say a word to anybody. Not even to Mama or Papa.'

'I shan't,' swore Coco regally, lifting her chin.

'Maybe you should run home,' sighed the soldier, his fingers shifting over the beguiling object in his hand: Coco craned on tiptoes but couldn't see it properly. 'Maybe it would be best if you forgot about me.'

Marcelle shook her head – there was no point having a secret if one promptly forgot about it. Then, recalling that the soldier couldn't see, she said, 'We won't tell anyone – we promise, Monsieur! We can bring you food, and something to drink. We have to go to school today, but we could bring you something afterwards. Bread and jam, and some cognac or wine. Would you like that?'

In the past few days the soldier had eaten just a handful of biscuits and had drunk only dew; he was, as a result, parched and famished. The promise of a decent meal made him feel boneless and weak. 'I am hungry,' he admitted. 'I would like something to eat.'

'Then we'll bring it,' said Marcelle. 'Later – after school. You lie in the shade and rest, and wait for us to return.'

The soldier wiped his grimy face and smiled. Already his stomach was rumbling. He leaned against the tree trunk, bundled up against the cold. 'Remember, you must not tell anybody that I'm here. Not yet. Not yet.'

'We'll remember,' said Marcelle.

'What's your name?' asked Coco: her eyes were still fastened on the soldier's closed hand, on the slivers of silver that were glowing between his folded fingers.

'My name is Lieutenant,' the soldier answered. 'Lieutenant Shepard.'

Coco thought 'Lieutenant' was a strange name for a person to have, even a person with an accent hiding in the woods: but her mother often said there was no accounting for some people, so Coco dismissed the thing as unaccountable. There was something more important buzzing in her mind. She asked, 'What have you got in your hand?'

The soldier turned his face in the direction of her voice. He did not reply immediately, as if judging whether some things weren't best kept to himself. The girls waited, tense as cats. Then the soldier unfurled his fingers and held up the thing that had hidden in his palm. The object caught the morning light and threw it sparkling into the trees. The girls drew a breath, their hearts leaping; they trampled quickly closer, scuffing up the leaves. There, on the soldier's palm, stood a shining silver donkey. It was small as a mouse, and just as perfect. Its legs were slender as twigs; it gazed through a fringe of carved lashes. It had four sturdy hooves, two fine, pointed ears, knobbly knees, a scruffy mane, and a smooth, rounded muzzle. Its waggly tail was tipped with a kink of silvery hair. It seemed ready to canter across the soldier's shoulder and away into the forest. It was the most beautiful thing that Marcelle and Coco had ever seen. 'Oh!' gasped Coco. 'How darling! Can I have it?'

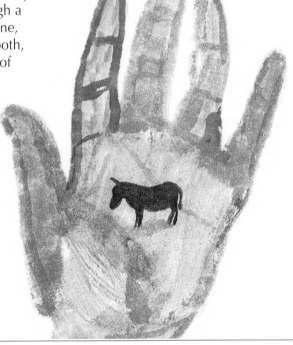

Her sister smacked her; the soldier only smiled. 'I'm sorry, Coco,' he said. 'I need it, you see. It's my good-luck charm.'

'Oh!' Coco's eyes felt melded to the exquisite thing. 'And – is it? Is it lucky, Monsieur?'

The soldier's hand trembled as he stroked the donkey's back, but he was still smiling. 'I think so, Coco,' he replied. 'I believe it is.'

Understand

1. What language do the children understand at the start of the extract?
2. How are **(a)** the girls and **(b)** the man described?
3. What do you learn about the setting of the story in this extract?
4. How did Coco get her name?
5. **(a)** Who is the man?

   (b) Why is he trying to go home?
6. Describe the man's good-luck charm.

 Explore

 1. What makes the girls think that the man is a soldier?

2. How do you imagine a soldier might look?

3. Why do you think the soldier does not want the girls to tell anyone that he is there?

 4. What obstacles does the soldier face in his effort to return home?

 Investigate

It is very likely that the soldier in this story is absent without leave (AWOL). This means that he did not have permission to leave the army.

1. Find out what happened to soldiers who went AWOL during the First World War.
2. Discuss the consequences for soldiers who went AWOL. Do you think the punishment was fair?

 Create

1. Write a short story in which someone acts without permission. For example, your character might go somewhere their parents do not allow them to go. What happens when they are found out?
2. Have you ever done something that you were not allowed to do? Write a personal essay based on this experience.
   - Did you feel guilty?
   - Were you caught?
   - What consequences did you face?

The following advertisement for Sainsbury's supermarket is more like a short film. The advertisement shows how the soldiers stopped fighting on Christmas Day 1914, during the First World War. Along the front line, many soldiers from both sides sang, shook hands and exchanged items with one another.

 https://youtu.be/NWF2JBb1bvM

Understand

1. Name the two soldiers who shake hands.
2. The soldiers sing a song at the beginning of the advertisement. What is the song called?
3. What gifts do the soldiers exchange?
4. What game do the soldiers play?
5. What features of advertising are used in this television advertisement?

Explore

1. What is the main message in this advertisement, in your opinion?
2. How did you feel while watching this advertisement?
3. How is this advertisement different to other television ads?

Investigate

 Watch the story behind the advertisement, then work with a partner to discuss the following: https://youtu.be/2s1YvnfcFVs

1. 'Even at the toughest of times, in the heat of war and at the most dreadful occasions there can be great humanity'. Do you agree that there can be great humanity in the darkest of times? Share some examples.
2. Discuss the benefits of:
   (a) charity   **(b)** support   **(c)** human contact.
3. Share your ideas on what else people need in times of darkness, destruction or war.

Create

 1. **(a)** Work in small groups to write the news segment reporting on the Christmas truce that took place between soldiers in 1914. The news should be current, so write as though you are informing the public about this event for the first time.

 (b) When you have written your news segment, one person should assume the role of newsreader. This person should read the news report that you have written. You could use a visual recording tool such as iMovie to record your news report for television or an audio recording tool such as AudioBoom to record your news report for radio.

The speaker in this poem addresses their loved one who left to fight in the Vietnam War.
Look out for the use of poetic techniques as you read the poem.

But You Didn't

By Merrill Glass

Remember the time you lent me your car and I dented it?
I thought you'd kill me ...
But you didn't.

Remember the time I forgot to tell you the dance was
formal, and you came in jeans?
I thought you'd hate me ...
But you didn't.

Remember the times I'd flirt with
other boys just to make you jealous, and
you were?

I thought you'd drop me ...
But you didn't.
There were plenty of things you did to put up with me,

to keep me happy, to love me, and there are
so many things I wanted to tell
you when you returned from
Vietnam ...
But you didn't.

Discuss

1. In pairs, discuss the emotional impact of this poem.
    (a) What feelings does the poem evoke?
    (b) Choose three words to describe the mood created in this poem. Share your chosen words with the rest of the class.

Understand

1. What did the speaker do to the car?
2. Who do you think the speaker addresses in this poem?
    (a) Her husband
    (b) Her brother
3. **(a)** How often is the title repeated as a line throughout the poem?
    (b) Where is this line most effective?

Explore

1. Do you think the speaker feels regretful?
2. The person addressed in the poem did not return from Vietnam.
    (a) What do you think happened to him?
    (b) How do you think the speaker felt when she found out?
3. What do you think the speaker might have wanted to say to this person upon his return from war?
4. What do you know about the Vietnam War?

Create

Write the diary entry the speaker or the speaker's husband would have written on the day he left for Vietnam.

War propaganda

Propaganda is information of a biased or misleading nature used to promote a political cause or point of view. Propaganda is often used during conflicts to create hatred against an enemy and to encourage people to sign up to fight or contribute to the war effort.

'Dulce et Decorum Est' by Wilfred Owen was first published in 1920 following the First World War.

In pairs, try to work out the language in which the title of the poem is written. Does it look familiar?

Dulce et Decorum Est
By Wilfred Owen

Bent double, like old beggars under sacks,
Knock-kneed, coughing like hags, we cursed through sludge,
Till on the haunting flares we turned our backs
And towards our distant rest began to trudge.
Men marched asleep. Many had lost their boots
But limped on, blood-shod. All went lame; all blind;
Drunk with fatigue; deaf even to the hoots
Of tired, outstripped Five-Nines that dropped behind.

Five-Nines:
a type of German artillery shell

Gas! GAS! Quick, boys!—An ecstasy of fumbling,
Fitting the clumsy helmets just in time;
But someone still was yelling out and stumbling,
And floundʼring like a man in fire or lime …
Dim, through the misty panes and thick green light,
As under a green sea, I saw him drowning.

In all my dreams, before my helpless sight,
He plunges at me, guttering, choking, drowning.

If in some smothering dreams you too could pace
Behind the wagon that we flung him in,
And watch the white eyes writhing in his face,
His hanging face, like a devilʼs sick of sin;
If you could hear, at every jolt, the blood
Come gargling from the froth-corrupted lungs,
Obscene as cancer, bitter as the cud
Of vile, incurable sores on innocent tongues,—
My friend, you would not tell with such high zest
To children ardent for some desperate glory,
The old Lie: Dulce et decorum est
Pro patria mori.

The 'old Lie' that Wilfred Owen refers to in this poem is written in Latin. 'Dulce et decorum est / Pro patria mori' means 'it is sweet and honourable to die for your country'.

This statement is ironic because the poem proves that it is not sweet or honourable to die for your country. Wilfred Owen describes the horror of war, recalling the awful things he has witnessed during the First World War.

Similes compare one thing to another, using the words 'like' or 'as' or 'than'.

Understand

1. **(a)** How are the soldiers described in the first stanza?

   (b) Do you pity them? Explain your answer.

2. Identify the poetic technique used in each of the following:

   (a) 'Gas! GAS!'

   (b) 'And watch the white eyes writhing in his face'

   (c) 'An ecstasy of fumbling ... yelling out and stumbling'.

Explore

1. What is the poet's attitude towards war? How do you know?

2. Wilfred Owen experienced war first-hand as a soldier. Do you agree that his description of war is realistic and honest?

3. Pick out two similes that you find striking in the poem. Why do these images appeal to you?

4. Wilfred Owen makes use of vocabulary with negative associations. Pick out words that show:
   ◖ disease and sickness   ◖ difficulty breathing   ◖ exhaustion.

Create

Turn this poem into a short story. Add extra details about the terror of war. Consider:
◖ narrative voice – first or third person
◖ plot and action – including conflict
◖ setting – where the action takes place
◖ characters – introduce and develop three main characters
◖ ending – the resolution to your story.

During the Second World War, posters were produced to encourage people, particularly women, to play their part in the war efforts. Some of the images have become iconic.

This poster was produced in the United States in 1943 during the Second World War.

This poster was produced in Britain in 1941 during the Second World War.

Discuss

1. Which of the posters do you like better?
2. In what way are the posters persuasive?
3. Why might posters like these have been necessary?

 Understand

1. Describe the images used in both posters.
2. What are the posters asking women to do?

 Explore

1. Identify the target audience in both cases.
2. Choose two features of advertising used in one of the posters and explain how these features are effective.
 3. Which of the posters do you like best? Explain your choice.
4. You have been asked to choose one of the images for a new campaign or advertisement this year.
   (a) Which of the images would you choose?
   (b) Why would you choose this image?
   (c) What sort of campaign or advertisement would the image suit?

 Investigate

Posters like these are examples of war propaganda. Use your research skills to find one more example of war propaganda to share with the class. You may like to dedicate a Padlet page to the theme of war, where you can share media files as well as images.

 Create

 1. **(a)** In groups, create a similar poster for use during a war in the past. Your poster may promote the war effort or be in opposition to the war.
   - List the advertising techniques that you will use.
   - Choose the image that you will use.
   - Create a catchy, memorable slogan.
   - Work as a team to create your poster.
 (b) When you have finished making your poster, present it to the class. Explain why this poster may have been used as war propaganda.

Reviewing courage through conflict

Reflect and review

1. **(a)** Take a look at the four images at the start of this unit (page 141). Consider the association each image has with the theme. Rank the images in order from most relevant (1) to least relevant (4).

   (b) Share the image that you feel ranks the highest. Explain your choice and listen as others share their choice with you.

   (c) What image would you choose to replace the image that you feel ranks the lowest? Describe the image you would replace it with and explain your choice.

2. Fill in the unit review on pages 42–43 of your Portfolio.

Language skills

1. In this chapter, you revised the past tense. The following passage is written in the present tense. Rewrite it in the past tense.

   > It's hard being left behind. I wait for Henry, not knowing where he is, wondering if he's okay. It's hard to be the one who stays.
   >
   > I keep myself busy. Time goes faster that way.
   >
   > I go to sleep alone, and wake up alone. I take walks. I work until I'm tired. I watch the wind play with the trash that's been under the snow all winter.

2. Write a sentence using any three of the words shown below. When you have written your sentence, read it out loud. Can your classmates identify the correct spellings of the words used?

   ◖ Were/Wear
   ◖ Your/You're
   ◖ Their/There
   ◖ Too/To
   ◖ Our/Are

Oral assessment

1. Recite a poem relating to the theme of conflict. You may recite a poem that you have written, studied or sourced yourself.

2. Carry out a class debate on the following motion: *This house believes that war destroys lives.*

Written assessment

1. **(a)** Write a newspaper report on the outbreak of a war (past, present or imaginary) in the space provided on pages 44–45 of your Portfolio.

   (b) Redraft your news report in the space provided on pages 114–115 of your Portfolio.

Exam skills

1. 'War poetry is moving because it is real.'

   Choose a poem that you have studied that deals with the theme of war.

   (a) Name the poem and the poet.

   (b) How is the theme of war dealt with in this poem?

   (c) Choose two poetic techniques used in the poem. Describe the effects of both techniques.

   (d) You have been asked to read a poem at an event commemorating those who fought in wars. Explain why you would or would not choose to read the poem named in the previous pages at this event.

   Write your answer in the space provided on pages 136–138 of your Portfolio.

Theme 5

Breaking Barriers

What are barriers?

We are surrounded by barriers in our everyday lives. Sometimes these barriers are there to protect us. Other times they stop us from getting where we want to be. These barriers can be physical, in the form of walls and borders, or non-physical, such as prejudice or emotional barriers that separate us from our goals. In this unit we will explore different types of barriers and how they can be broken down.

Why study this theme?

It is important to study this theme to gain an understanding of the barriers people can face. In doing so, we can understand how these barriers can be broken down or overcome.

Learning intentions

- Reflect on and understand the different types of barriers people can face.
- Explore how barriers can be overcome.

Writing With Purpose

- Explore first-hand accounts of prejudice and barriers.
- Read an interview with someone who overcame a barrier to achieve success.
- Learn the features and language style of memoirs.

Poetry and Song

- Compare different viewpoints.

Fiction

- Read fiction with the theme of barriers.

Stage and Screen

- Explore how barriers can be used as symbols.
- Examine how flashbacks can strengthen our understanding of a character.

Media and Advertising

- Read an article about people's reactions to a barrier.
- Analyse images and an advertisement.

Language Skills

- Recognise and use synonyms and antonyms.
- Use a thesaurus.

 Discuss

1. Which of the images above best represents your understanding of a barrier? Explain your choice.

2. Give three words to describe each of the images above.

3. What kinds of barriers have you experienced in your own life?

4. How did you overcome these barriers?

 Create

 Write your own definition of 'barriers' in the space provided on page 56 of your Portfolio, by completing the sentence 'Barriers are …'. You will return to this definition later on.

Borders

Physical barriers, such as borders and walls, are used to mark territory. These types of barriers can be used to protect people, but also to hold people captive or to prevent others from gaining access. Many countries share land mass but are separated by borders. Authorisation is often required to enter a country.

People sometimes try to cross borders illegally to enter a country that offers more opportunities, or to seek shelter from conflict and persecution. The following short story by Pam Muñoz Ryan is about a father and son who are trying to illegally cross the border from Mexico into the United States.

First Crossing

Early Sunday morning, Coyote Lady came down the stairs into the basement room. She wore a dress like the ones Marco's mother wore for church, a floral print with a white collar, although it was much bigger than any dress his mother owned. Her face was scrubbed clean of makeup, and she looked like someone's aunt or a neighborhood woman who might go to mass every day.

'Today is a big football game, professional, in San Diego. La Migra will be eager to get people into the U.S. in time for the game. We start moving you in one hour, one at a time. The wait will not be bad at the border this morning. But later today, closer to game time, it will be *horrible*.'

La Migra: (Spanish) immigration

Marco looked at Papá. He did not want to be separated from him.

Papá said, 'How?'

'In a car,' said Coyote Lady. 'We hide you. If I take only one across at a time, the car doesn't ride low in the back and does not look suspicious. I drive in a different lane each time. As you can see, we are having trouble with the usual ways, so we try this. It has worked before, especially on a busy day.'

Marco didn't like the idea of being away from Papá. What would happen if Papá got across and he didn't? Or what if he couldn't find Papá on the other side? Then what would he do? He didn't like this part of the journey. Suddenly, he wished he'd stayed at home another year in Jocotepec.

As if reading his mind, Papá said, 'I will go before you, Marco. And I will wait for you. I will not leave until you arrive. And if you don't arrive, I will come back to Tijuana.'

Marco nodded.

Coyote Lady gave orders and told a woman to get ready to go. Every hour she stuck her head inside the room and called out another person.

Papá and Marco were the last of the group to go. They walked outside.

In the alley, the trash cans had been pushed aside to make room for an old car, a sedan. Flashlight Man waited beside the car, but he wasn't wearing his usual black uniform. Instead he had on jeans, a blue-and-white football jersey, and a Chargers cap. He lifted the hood.

Inside, a small rectangular coffee table had been placed next to the motor, forming a narrow ledge. Two of the wooden legs disappeared into the bowels of the car and two of the legs had been cut short and now provided the braces against the radiator and motor.

'Okay,' he said. 'You lie down in here. It only takes a half hour. There is a van waiting for you in Chula Vista that will take you to your destinations.'

Papá climbed up. Flashlight Man positioned his feet and legs so they would not touch the motor. Papá put his head and upper body on the tiny tabletop, curling his body to make it smaller. For an instant before the hood was closed, Papá's eyes caught Marco's.

Marco turned away so he wouldn't have to see his father humbled in this manner.

'*Vámanos*,' said Coyote Lady, and she wedged into the driver's seat. Flashlight Man sat on the passenger side. A Chargers football banner and blue pompoms sat on the dashboard as further proof of their deception. The car backed out of the alley and left. Marco closed the gate behind them.

He paced up and down the alley. They had said it would take an hour roundtrip. The minutes crawled by. Why did Papá agree to do this? Why did he resign himself to these people? 'It is the way it is,' Papá had said. Marco went back into the basement room and walked in circles.

After one hour, he put in a tape, *Aladdin*, and tried to pay attention as the characters sang about a whole new world. It was so easy in the video to get on a flying carpet to reach a magical place. *Where is this new world? Where is Papá? Did he get through?* Marco had never once heard a story of someone crossing over under the hood of a car. He tried to imagine being inside, next to the engine. His stomach churned. *Where is my magic carpet?*

The door opened suddenly. Flashlight Man was back. 'Let's go,' he said.

The car was already positioned in the alley with the hood up. Coyote Lady took Marco's backpack and threw it in the trunk. Marco climbed up on the bumper and swung his legs over the motor, then sat on the makeshift ledge. Flashlight Man arranged Marco's legs as if he were in a running position, one leg up, knee bent. One leg straighter, but slightly bent. Marco slowly lowered himself onto his side and put his head on the tabletop. Then he crossed his arms around his chest and watched the sunlight disappear to a tiny crack as the hood was closed.

'Don't move in there,' said Flashlight Man.

Don't worry, thought Marco. *My fear will not permit me to move.*

The motor started. The noise hurt his ears, and within minutes it was hot. The smell of motor oil and gasoline accosted his nostrils. He breathed through his mouth, straining his lips towards the slit where the light crept through for fresh air. The car moved along for about ten minutes until they reached the lanes of traffic that led to the border crossing. Then it was stop and go. Stop and go. Marco's legs began to cramp, but he knew not to move one inch. He tried not to imagine what would happen if he rolled onto the inner workings of the car.

The car lurched and stopped, over and over. Marco wanted to close his eyes, but he was afraid that he would get dizzy or disoriented. He watched the small crack between the car and hood as if it were his lifeline. A flash of color obliterated his line of sunlight as a flower vendor stopped in front of the car, trying to make one last sale to those in the car next to them. 'Flores, flores! You buy cheap!'

Flores:
(Spanish) *flowers*

The line of cars started to move again, but the flower vendor continued to walk in front of their car. Coyote Lady pressed on the horn. Marco's body trembled as the sound reverberated through his body. He inched his hands up to cover his ears. The vendor stepped out of the way, and the car began to move faster.

Marco never knew when they actually crossed the line. He only knew when the car began to speed up on the freeway. His body pulsed with the vibrations of the car. Afraid to close his eyes, he watched beads of moisture move across the radiator, as if they had the ability to dance. Marco could not feel his right foot. It had fallen asleep. Panic crept into his chest and seized his muscles. He slowly pressed his hand back and forth across his chest to relieve the tightness. 'No worries,' he whispered. 'No worries.'

The car stopped and shook with a door being slammed. Marco heard someone fiddling with the hood latch. Light streamed into his eyes, and he squinted. Flashlight Man pulled him from the car and handed over his backpack. Marco stumbled from his dead foot, and his body still rocked with the feeling of the moving car. He looked around. He was in a parking lot behind an auto shop. Papá was waiting.

'We made it,' said Papá, clapping Marco on the back. 'We're in Chula Vista.'

Marco said nothing. He couldn't hear what Papá had said because of the noise in his ears, as if they were filled with cotton and bees. He felt as if he'd been molested, his body misappropriated. He pulled away from Papá's arm and climbed into the waiting van, this one with seats and windows. The door slid shut. Marco turned his face to the window and saw Coyote Lady and Flashlight Man driving away.

The others in the van smiled and talked as if they'd all just come from a party. The relief of a successful crossing seemed to have unleashed their tongues. Marco listened as they talked of their jobs in towns he'd never heard of before: Escondido, Solana Beach, Poway, Oceanside. Papá told them that he and his son were going to Encinitas to work in the flower fields and that it was his son's first time crossing over. Faces turned toward Marco.

Marco cringed, his discomfort showing. *Why did he have to mention me?*

One of the men laughed out loud. 'At least you were not rolled inside a mattress like I was on my first time!'

'Or like me,' said a young woman, grinning. 'They dressed me as an *abuelita*, a grandmother, with a wig and old clothes and had me walk across with another woman's identification. I was shaking the entire time.'

Marco could only force a smile, but everyone else laughed.

Stories spilled from their lips about their first times or their friend's or family member's: hiding inside hollowed-out bales of hay, cramped inside a hide-a-bed sofa from which the bed frame had been removed, buried in the middle of a truckload of crates filled with cackling chickens. Marco found himself chuckling and nodding in co-misery. An almost giddy air seemed to prevail as they all reveled in one another's bizarre stories and sometimes life-threatening circumstances.

He found himself eager to hear of each exploit and began feeling oddly proud and somehow connected to this unrelated group. A strange camaraderie seemed to

molested: assaulted or abused

misappropriated: dishonestly taken or stolen

camaraderie: friendship; sharing something in common

permeate the air, and when one man told how he was hidden in a door panel of a truck, smashed in a fetal position for one hour, and thought he might suffocate, Marco laughed the hardest.

permeate:
spread throughout

As the people were dropped off in towns along the way north, they shook hands with Marco and Papá and left them with the words *'Buena suerte,'* good luck. When Papá and Marco were the only ones left in the van and the driver finally headed up Freeway 5 toward Encinitas, Papá grinned at him. 'Okay now?'

Marco nodded. 'Okay.' He looked out the window at the people in the cars on the freeway. They were all headed somewhere in the United States of America. Marco wondered how many were headed to a whole new world.

Understand

1. What is the barrier that Marco and his father face?

2. Where are Marco and his father trying to get to?

3. Why was Marco separated from his father?

4. What names are given to the people who help Marco and his father travel across the border?

5. Why does Marco struggle to hear his father once they arrive in the parking lot?

6. Describe another way that the characters in the extract have been smuggled across the border in the past.

7. **(a)** Put each of the words below into a sentence.
   - Misappropriated
   - Camaraderie
   - Permeate

   (b) Add these words to your vocabulary builder on pages 1–2 of your Portfolio.

Explore

1. What kind of relationship do you think Marco and his father have?

2. Marco watches a Disney film while waiting in the basement room. What do you think is the general theme or message that he takes from this film?

Investigate

People often travel to other countries for seasonal work, but do not stay permanently. Look up the most common types of seasonal work in Ireland and suggest reasons why these sectors may need extra workers at certain times of year.

Create

1. Write the diary entry Marco would have written after the events in this story took place.

2. Work in groups to design a welcome pack for a person arriving in Ireland. Think about what they might need. For example, a language guide, clothes and basic knowledge about currency, sign posts and road signs.

In the following personal essay, Krystal A. Sital details the challenges she faced as an illegal immigrant in the United States.

When Immigration Agents Came Knocking

On that particular evening back in 2003, my parents were in the car together returning home from work — my mother was a babysitter, my father an electrician — when they noticed three men in suits reading the labels on the mailboxes in front of our building. This was on the urban streets of New Jersey, against a backdrop of dilapidated buildings, and they immediately assumed who it was.

dilapidated: *run-down*

'Go in your bedroom and hide,' my mother hissed over the phone. 'Immigration is here. Do not open the door.' My younger sister, Kim, was only 12, and I was 16, a junior in high school. When I relayed the message to her, we both grinned. Our family had a dark sense of humor, and even though we were residing in the United States illegally, this sounded like just the kind of prank she would play on us.

'Krys,' she said, 'this is not a joke! I am sitting outside with your father. They are going upstairs right now. Hide!' Her voice was too serious, too worried. Not a tremor of a laugh vibrated in her words. So I shut my sister in our bedroom, turned off all the lights and locked the windows. We lived in a third floor walk-up in Bayonne. It would take them a couple of minutes to get up there, so I stood behind the door of our apartment and peered through the peephole. I could hear footsteps on the wooden stairs — not the weary ascension of the old Egyptian lady and her husband who lived across the hallway or the skip of the little Puerto Rican boy below us or the cheerful whistle of the African-American woman on the first floor.

It was when the tops of their heads floated above the railing that I really believed my mother's words. Having gone through the motions of locking the apartment down, I was still hoping it was all an elaborate gag. I felt the unlawfulness of our status in this country acutely. As far as I knew, they could, and had every right to, remove us from our apartment and send us back to our country, Trinidad and Tobago.

The three came one behind the other down the narrow corridor. I trapped a breath in my chest and stepped away from the door just as the one in front raised a fist to rap his knuckles where my face had been.

I had heard stories of immigration officers not even bothering to knock but kicking down the door and sweeping every family member into an unmarked white van. I was terrified that would happen now. My back was against the wall of the kitchen, and I wanted so desperately to close the short distance between me and the locked door of my bedroom, but I knew a creaking board could signal our presence. I yearned to be next to my sister, our shoulders touching and heads inclining toward each other in our dark closet. Instead I stood next to the door, letting air out of my chest one miniature puff at a time.

Although the apartment's imperfections were many, from the lack of space to the falling plaster, we called it home. My mother sewed curtains, glued wallpaper and repaired the ceiling; my father rebuilt cupboards, ran new lights and retiled the bathroom. Under normal circumstances, these updates would fall on the landlord's shoulders, but we flew under the radar, so it was done on our own.

Each knock on the door sent a cold stab through my body. I clutched my belly, feeling the sharpness of my nails, something to ground me. Having finally succeeded somewhat in assimilating into American culture, we weren't sure what would happen if we were sent back. My parents brought us to the United States knowing this could happen once our visas expired. We had abandoned the tangerine skies of the islands for New Jersey at a violent time in our country. My father, a police officer there, believed it was worth the risk to live in the safety of the States.

assimilating:
adapting

At one point, I heard the men step away, and I braced myself for the crashing of the door. But all I heard was the familiar creaking of stairs as they descended. I listened till the door of the building slammed closed behind them before I checked the peephole and released a trembled breath. An empty corridor.

I dug my sister out of our room, held onto her and cried until our parents came and gathered us up. We left the apartment, but there was really nowhere else for us to go, so we returned that evening. For a long time we waited in fear for them to come back. We were always cognizant of our surroundings, always vigilant in a way that was just below the surface.

cognizant:
aware

Eventually we would gain legal status, and over time the fear was layered over by everyday life — worrying about grades, fencing practice, the attention of boys — until a knock at the door was finally transformed into a joke. 'Be careful,' my mother said, 'it might be Immigration.' The fear was still there, but we had to move on.

Understand

1. What is the age difference between Krys and Kim?
2. How does Krys describe the tone of her mother's voice?
3. Where is Krys's family originally from?
4. What stories has Krys heard about immigration?
5. Why can't Krys's family ask the landlord to carry out renovations on the apartment?
6. Why did Krys's father believe moving to New Jersey was the right thing to do?
7. What did Krys and Kim do when the immigration officers left?
8. What features of a typical personal essay can you identify in this piece?

Explore

1. Which word from the choices below would you say best describes the atmosphere in Krys's apartment during the visit from the immigration officers? Give two reasons for your answer.
   - Tense
   - Frightening
   - Nerve-wracking

2. What barriers do you think Krys and Kim face in their day-to-day lives as immigrants living in the United States?

Investigate

1. Look at recent news articles. Find out as much as you can about real accounts of immigrants trying to flee their own country in search of a better life. Share your findings with the class.

2. In recent years the world has seen large groups of people fleeing their countries in search of shelter. Use your research skills to find out what Ireland has done to tackle the refugee crisis. Do you think it is enough?

Create

Write a letter to Krys responding to this event and telling her how reading about it made you feel in the space provided on page 46 of your Portfolio.

In war, borders often change as territories are conquered or lost.

 The following song by Mike Harding tells a story from the Western Front. The Western Front was the line along which most of the battles during the First World War took place between Britain and Germany. It was an area of meandering trenches and battlefields, stretching from the North Sea to the Swiss border with France. (Think back to the Sainsbury's advertisement on page 177, which deals with the same events.)

Christmas 1914

Christmas Eve in 1914

Stars were burning, burning bright

And all along the Western Front

Guns were lying still and quiet.

Men lay dozing in the trenches,

In the cold and in the dark,

And far away behind the lines

A village dog began to bark.

Some lay thinking of their families,

Some sang songs while others were quiet

Rolling fags and playing brag

To while away that Christmas night.

But as they watched the German trenches

Something moved in No Man's Land

And through the dark came a soldier

Carrying a white flag in his hand.

Then from both sides men came running,

Crossing into No Man's Land,

Through the barbed-wire, mud and shell holes,

Shyly stood there shaking hands.

Fritz brought out cigars and brandy,

Tommy brought corned beef and fags,

Stood there talking, singing, laughing,

As the moon shone on No Man's Land.

Christmas Day we all played football

In the mud of No Man's Land;

Tommy brought some Christmas pudding,

Fritz brought out a German band.

When they beat us at football

We shared out all the grub and drink
And Fritz showed me a faded photo
Of a dark-haired girl back in Berlin.

For four days after no one fired,
Not one shot disturbed the night,
For old Fritz and Tommy Atkins
Both had lost the will to fight.
So they withdrew us from the trenches,
Sent us far behind the lines,
Sent fresh troops to take our places
And told the guns 'Prepare to fire'.

And next night in 1914
Flares were burning, burning bright;
The message came along the trenches
Over the top we're going tonight.
And the men stood waiting in the trenches,
Looking out across our football park,
And all along the Western Front
The Christian guns began to bark.

Understand

1. What are the soldiers doing to occupy themselves in the first stanza?
2. What was the soldier from no man's land carrying?
3. Where did the men stand shaking hands?
4. **(a)** Who are 'Fritz' and 'Tommy'?

   (b) What did Fritz and Tommy bring out?
5. What did the soldiers do on Christmas day?

 Explore

 1. Which image from this song do you find most memorable? Give a reason for your answer.
2. 'For four days after no one fired.' Why do you think this was the case?
3. Do you think that the soldiers in this song broke down barriers? Give a reason for your answer.
 4. '"Christmas 1914" is a song with a powerful message.' Do you agree with this statement? Give two reasons for your answer.

 Investigate

1. Look at a map to see where most of the fighting in the First World War took place. Can you suggest why it may have taken place where it did?
2. Find some images or photos of no man's land and any other relevant information online or from your history books to share with the class.

 Create

1. You have been asked to select three images to accompany a performance of this song. What three images would you choose? Explain why you chose each image.
2. Imagine you are a soldier in the trenches. Write a diary entry, detailing your experience of Christmas day 1914.

Walls

A wall is a structure that encloses or divides something. Walls can be real, physical structures, but they can also be figurative. This means that you cannot see them but they still exist. Sometimes walls exist in society, dividing people based on race, religion, gender or wealth.

The Berlin Wall was constructed in 1961 to divide East and West Germany during the Cold War. It was heavily guarded and acted as a barrier between the two sides. Families were divided until it came down in 1989.

The following article from *The Guardian* is a collection of different first-person experiences of the Berlin Wall.

Berlin Wall – readers' memories: 'It's hard to remember how scary the Wall was'

Barb Dignan was living in Germany when the Wall was being built

'I was a 14-year-old army dependant living in a German neighbourhood of Bad Kreuznach, Germany. My father was a major; my mother was German. No one had televisions on our street; news came by human contact, newspapers, and telephones. The night the Wall went up (the beginning of the process, anyway), my family was in our home. We began to hear people outside yelling, crying, louder and louder. We went into the street to witness tragic panic and fear. Neighbours were telling each other (and us) that they had relatives in East Berlin – they had tried to contact them, but couldn't – that no one knew what was happening. Rumours spread. Some thought their relatives had been killed, or would soon be killed. I had never witnessed anything like this. Everyone cried. As time went on, neighbours told us they thought their loved ones behind the wall were lost to them for good … I'm sure some of those 'lost' relations died over that period. That night is etched in my permanent memory.'

Tina Bain was visiting her pen friend in Berlin in the summer of 1961

'I came to Berlin as a 15-year-old girl visiting my German pen friend Elke. I stayed in Borsigwalde, in the then French sector. Many people were leaving the eastern part of Berlin and the authorities decided to stop this by closing the borders and then building the Wall. The whole atmosphere was one of fear and panic, people stocking up on food and worrying about loved ones on the other side. My parents back in the UK worried that I wouldn't be able to get out. I had never seen tanks in the streets before and I was very frightened.

I did get home and lost touch with Elke. In 1989 she advertised for me in a Manchester newspaper, saying we were together at the building of the Wall and she wanted to be reunited with me at the ending of it. I flew to Berlin in early 1990, had a great reunion with Elke and did my share of breaking down the Wall, crossed into the east at Checkpoint Charlie and met a young East German girl who then came to stay with me in England for a few months. I have been back in Berlin several times since and am here now for Elke's 70th birthday. It's a wonderful city and I am so glad to have had this 53-year relationship with it.'

Sebastian Merrick visited his aunts in Berlin

'I grew up in England with aunts in Berlin who had lived through the Wall being erected, the airlift, the import of US jazz by the "Amis" (Americans), and the different buzz in the British and French sectors; the Wall to me was a terrifying reality that had always been there. And there was not only one Wall, there were two: there was nothing more imaginatively fearsome than "der Todestreifen" – the Death Strip between inner and outer walls – where my teenage mind pictured desperate hopefuls running from spotlights and dodging machine-gun fire only to be hunted down and torn apart by vicious German Shepherds. Swimming the river border always seemed the better option and we heard of a few who were successful.

We knew one other who had somehow got out, with deals being done behind the scenes, but he

seemed mentally scarred and only half able to live. Looking back now it is hard to remember how scary the Wall was. West Berlin tried to be as normal as possible. There were cultural festivals thrown by the Amis and the Brits. KaDeWe – the enormous department store – showed off its success; West Berliners had a certain mindset of resilience. But as a teenage visitor in the late '70s it was hard to appreciate that this was one of the most improbable things in European history. The Wall was simply there; it was their problem, but in one sense a normality. One section of the Wall was however not 'normal'. Somewhere in the south-west was a small enclave of West Berlin. We visited a local summer beer festival there – but the road leading to this little village has the Wall on both sides! My teenage mind boggled. How did that work? Who had agreed to that? Were guns being trained on us from both sides? I managed to get one visit to East Berlin in my early 20s. The mystery and fearfulness went with me as I went through passport control, allowed in for just one day. My vague memories are of empty streets, the derelict cathedral, basic food in a canteen-type restaurant on the Spree [the local river], and out of curiosity I visited the street which had my name, Sebastianstraße, which was brutally chopped in two by the Wall.'

Manny Reyes contrasts West and East Berlin

'I'm from the Philippines and I first visited Berlin in 1986, aged 28. I was invited to attend a film conference in Mannheim, West Germany, and afterwards, I made a side trip to see Berlin. To get from Frankfurt to West Berlin, we had to enter East Germany. It was my first time to encounter those stern, no-nonsense East German border officials. They boarded the train as soon as we entered East Germany, scrutinized the passports of all the passengers to make sure no East German civilians or Allied military personnel were on board and disembarked before the train entered West Berlin. My first impression of West Berlin was that it wanted to be everything that East Berlin was not. It was decadent and unapologetically capitalist. East Berlin, on the other hand, still had buildings that had bullet holes from the Second World War. I visited again in 1988 – I'd often take the bus to the Reichstag area because the Berlin Wall ran directly behind it. The Brandenburg Gate was also nearby, but was on the East Berlin side. One time I remember going over a sign that said, "verboten" [forbidden], to take a close-up of a graffiti that had been painted on the Berlin Wall. I thought the sign was silly because the section of the Wall behind it was heavily vandalised. No sooner had I stepped over the sign when, suddenly, the window of the East German watchtower behind the Wall slid open. The border guard yelled, "Halt!" [stop] and he really meant it. So I quickly stepped back, having learned my lesson that those "verboten" signs had to be taken seriously.'

Understand

1. In what year was the Berlin Wall built?

2. In what year did the Berlin Wall come down?

3. Why was it nearly impossible to stay in contact with people on the other side of the wall?

4. Why did Elke get in touch with Tina in 1989?

5. What does 'verboten' mean?

6. Explain what the Death Strip was in your own words.

 Explore

1. On which side of the Berlin Wall would you rather have lived, East or West? Explain your answer.

2. How do you think the people of Berlin felt when the Wall finally came down?

 Create

1. 'No one had televisions on our street; news came by human contact, newspapers, and telephones.'

   Write three paragraphs discussing the advantages and disadvantages of 24-hour news coverage and access to live news updates via online platforms in modern society.

2. Write a short story inspired by one of the accounts in this article.

One of the most common forms of communication between people on different sides of the Berlin Wall was letter writing. Read the short translation from a letter that an East German boy wrote to his penpal in 1989.

'Someday the Wall will fall' – Letter from an East German Penpal

A week ago we had a very nice yet sad farewell party. Two couples whom I know well have finally received their permit to emigrate to West Germany, after three years of waiting. Such a farewell was definitely sad, but we're all agreed that someday the walls will fall and we'll all see each other again. I'm so looking forward to that.

 Understand

1. Why was the farewell party described as 'sad'?
2. How would you describe the writer's tone in this letter?
3. What evidence from the letter suggests that it was not easy to cross between East and West Germany?

 Create

1. Imagine your family and friends have been divided by a wall or barrier and you are forbidden from crossing over to see them. Write a letter to a loved one describing your feelings.

 2. Write a speech to be delivered to your class based on your own experience of barriers or walls.

In the following play by James Saunders, the characters live on an island that is divided by a wall.

Over The Wall

N: There was once an island, if you believe it, on which lived a people no better and no worse than most. They had enough to eat, without stuffing themselves, everyone had a day's work (which in those times was considered a great blessing), the old were looked after, as long as they didn't outstay their welcome, and the young were respected as individuals — within reason. All this had been so for as long as anyone could remember, and so they hoped it would continue. For, while they were not exactly happy, they were not exactly unhappy either. And as they said to each other when they bothered to talk about it:

1: If it was good enough for my father it's good enough for me. That's what my father used to say, and it's what I say too.

2: Absolutely. Leave well alone, that's my motto.

3: We should count our blessings. It's better than it was in the bad old days.

4: Mind you, it's not so good as it was in the good old days.

5: But things could always be worse. That's what we should think of.

6: They could always be better, of course.

5: But they could always be worse.

7: At least we're allowed to work all day.

8: And we're allowed not to work on Saturday and Sunday.

9: And we've got the vote. We didn't have that in the bad old days.

6: *(female)* We didn't have it in the good old days.

N: So they counted their blessings and rested content. Now what made this island different from any other you might have in mind was a wall, which ran across the island a bit more than halfway down and which had been there as long as anyone could remember, and as long as anyone they could remember could remember. Forever, in fact, as far as they knew or cared. They called it 'The Wall', and if they ever talked about it they said things like:

1: There's always been a Wall and there always will be, that's the way things are. It's a fact of nature. There's nothing you can do about it.

2: There must be a purpose in it, that's what I say. Everything has its purpose: wars, walls, it's all meant.

3: There are things beyond us. A higher Wall, I mean Will. Someone's in charge up there. The great Wall-Builder in the sky. He knows what's best for us. Leave it to Him, that's what I say.

6: Or Her.

4: After all, when you think of us — human beings — crawling on the earth ... I mean humility's called for. It's not for us to seek to understand the sublime purpose.

5: *Of* which the Wall is part.

sublime: divine

4: *Of* which the Wall is part.

1: It was good enough for my father, and it's good enough for me. That's what my father used to say. Leave it at that. Nuff said.

N: So they went on with their business, working as they were allowed to through the week, and on Saturdays and Sundays working, as they were allowed to, at what they called their leisure activities. This wall, now, was not quite straight but curved outwards, so that you could never see the two ends of it together. Not that it had ends for, as the fishermen knew, it continued, when it reached the sea, back along both shores to meet itself again at the far end of the island, so encircling the half of it – a bit more than half.

7: Lor, Jarge, yon Wall goos roit raing the oisland.

8: Oi knoos thaat, Taam. Tis a well-knoon faact.

N: So they spoke when they fished. High it was, and smooth, and impregnable, and how it got there no one knew. There were theories, of course.

9: There is no doubt that it was constructed in the Neo-plasticene Age by primitive tree-worshippers, to enclose the sacred grove of the earth-goddess …

1: It was built of course, by invading Venusians, as a navigational aid and to protect the space-ships from marauding dinosaurs.

2: Obviously a natural outcrop of rock, pushed up by volcanic activity and then worn smooth by the wind and rain, an interesting phenomenomenom.

3: It's a figment of the imagination. The Wall only exists in our minds. If we stopped thinking it was there it wouldn't be.

N: No one could prove this theory wrong.

4: I walked into it last night in the dark. Look at the bump on my forehead.

3: Psychosomatic. You *imagined* it was there, so when you got to where you imagined it was you walked into it and imagined you hurt yourself. It stands to reason.

impregnable:
could not be crossed over or broken down

Neo-plasticene:
invented word suggesting a geological era in the distant past

marauding:
attacking

figment:
invention

4: It still hurts.

3: You think it does.

N: But since it seemed to make not much difference, if you thought you walked into it, whether you were really hurt or only thought you were, people tried not to. Except for one poor fellow who so convinced himself that the wall was imaginary that he took a flying leap at where it was, or wasn't, and dashed his brains out. Or so it seemed.

5: Excuse me, I'm conducting a survey. May I ask what *you* think is on the other side of the Wall?

6: I don't want to talk about it. I think it's disgusting. There's enough nasty *this* side of the Wall, never mind the *other* side of the Wall.

7: It's like a beautiful garden, with fruit hanging down and bambis and pretty flowers. And you don't have to wear any clothes.

8: It's like a sort of a ooze, a sort of — like a — ooze, sort of.

9: Nothing.

5: Nothing?

9: Nothing. Everything finishes at the Wall. Then there's nothing.

1: The fifth dimension.

2: Ethereal vibrations.

3: That is to say, beyond the Wall the laws of space-time as we know them no longer operate. Call it ethereal vibrations, call it the fifth dimension, call it a rolypoly pudding …

1: In other words, as far as we're concerned it doesn't exist in there — if one can say 'in there' for a 'there' which doesn't exist, and therefore cannot be said to be either *in* or *there*. As for *what* doesn't exist …

3: It's like a mathematical point really …

9: Like I said, nothing.

2: Don't know.

3: Don't know.

4. Don't know.

6. Don't care.

N: So there it was. Or wasn't, or was in a different way, or seemed to be.

1: Mum!

2: What?

1: What's over the Wall?

2: You wash your mouth out with soapy water! I'll give you over the Wall! Wait till I tell your father!

3: Dad!

4: What?

3: What's over the Wall?

Ethereal vibrations: heavenly sounds

4: Ask your teacher. What d'you think I pay rates and taxes for? To teach you myself?

3: I asked my teacher.

4: Well?

3: Said to get on with my algebra.

4: Well, then, do what your teacher says.

3: But what *is* over the Wall?

4: The toe of my boot. Get on with your homework.

3: I've done my homework. What *is* over the —?

4: Then do something else. Can't you see I'm trying to watch telly?!

N: Or whatever it was they watched in those days; it wasn't telly.

4: Can't you see I'm trying to watch the goldfish?

5: Can't you see I'm trying to get this ferret out of my trousers? Can't you see I'm trying to invent the wheel?

7: — cook the joint?

8: — bath the baby?

9: — darn my socks?

4: —frame a photo of my mother?

5: — write a sonnet?

6: — make a fortune?

7: — get my head out from between these railings?

8: — bury the cat?

9: — dig a well starting at the bottom?

N: Or whatever. And so, in short, on the whole, more or less, without splitting hairs, broadly speaking, in a nutshell, they ignored it.

1: Pretended it wasn't there.

N: Well no, they couldn't do that. Because it was. No, they just ... ignored it; as you might ignore a gatecrasher at a party whom nobody knows and nobody wants to, who turns up in the wrong gear with a nasty look on his face and what looks like a flick knife sticking out of one pocket.

3: It's ridiculous.

2: What is?

3: It's stupid. I can't believe it. It's ludicrous. Here we are with a great Wall across the island and we don't even know why and no one seems to care.

2: It's not for us mere mortals to ask why.

ludicrous:
laughable or
ridiculous

3: Why not?

2: Because we're mere mortals, that's why not.

3: I'm not a mere mortal, I'm a rational human being.

5: We're not meant to understand everything, you know.

3: Why not, who says so?

6: There's enough needs putting right *this* side of the Wall, never mind the *other* side of the Wall.

7: Get on with your work and think yourself lucky. Thinking about the Wall won't do you any good.

8: Do some leisure activities, take your mind off it. Do some healthy outdoor pursuits.

4: All you do is talk about the Wall. Wall, Wall, Wall, that's all I get from you.

2: Leave wall alone, I mean leave well alone, that's my advice.

1: Ignorance was good enough for your father and it ought to be good enough for you.

4: Who do you think you are anyway? God or somebody?

3: I want to know what's on the other side!!

5: Next please. Well, now, what seems to be the matter with you?

3: I'm having a bit of trouble, doctor.

5: What sort of trouble? Stick out your tongue.

3: It'th athout the Thall ...

5: Put your tongue in.

3: It's about the Wall. All I want to know ...

5: Bowel movements all right?

3: Yes, thanks. All I want to know is what's on the other side, that seems reasonable enough to me, only —

5: Sleeping all right, are you? Getting the old beauty sleep?

3: I dream about walls. Only no one else seems to be bothered, only me, so I —

5: Eating all right, are you? Getting the old nosh down?

3: Yes, I'm eating. Or if in fact it's that there's something wrong with everybody else. And it's turning into a bit of —

5: How's the pains in the leg? Pains in the leg all right?

3: They're fine. Into a bit of an obsession. Because, I mean, you don't just ignore something like that. I mean I'm not a mere mortal I'm a rational human being and it could be important, I mean, *look* at the flaming thing, I mean *look* at it, there it is, look, there!

5: Any neuralgia, headache, backache, loss of breath, vomiting, congenital idiocy, piles, trouble with the waterworks, spots before the eyes, dizzy spells?

3: D — I —Z — Z —

5: Falling hair, loss of weight, gain of weight, tenseness, got a drink problem have you, smoking too much, hallucinations, palpitations, eructations, on drugs are you, can you read the top line, overdoing it at work perhaps, worrying about the work, about the spouse, about where to go for your holiday, about the mortgage, about the value of the pound, about the political situation, about your old mother, about the kids, kids playing you up are they, not doing well at school, got a drink problem have they, smoking, on drugs are they, suffering from loss of weight, falling hair, got any worries have you?

3: Yes!

5: Have you seen a priest?

3: Yes. She didn't know either.

5: Didn't know what? They're not supposed to know, they're supposed to give comfort. Seen a psychiatrist, have you, consulted a shrink?

3: He said it was my mother.

5: Well there you are. Here's a prescription. Take some four times a day, and if there's any left over rub it on your chest. Or your mother's chest. I don't care.

3: What's wrong with me, doctor?

5: You're a nut. Get out, you're wasting my time.

N: So out he got, this nut, taking his obsession with him, and the doctor turned thankfully to the next patient, a nice simple case who'd put his thumb out trying to plant beans in hard ground.

5: Put your thumb out, have you? How's your bowel movements? Sleeping all right?

3: I'm going to start an Association for Investigating The Wall In Order To See What's On The Other Side. The AFITWIOTSWOTOS. Catchy title. They'll flock to join. Then we'll get somewhere.

N: But they didn't. And after a while he disbanded the association, with the full agreement of the members — himself. But he didn't give up.

3: All right. I'm on my own. So be it. But I'm going to find out what's on the other side of That Wall. If it kills me.

N: And for the next thirty of forty years he did nothing but think about the Wall. He read books, consulted sages, took measurements, drew diagrams, worked out theories, studied history, biology, theology, psychology, astrology, cogitated, meditated and did a bit of yoga on the side. He lost his friends of course.

6: Oh, don't invite *him*. He'll only talk about the Wall.

N: His marriage went for a Burton.

4: Wall, Wall, Wall, nothing but Wall! I'm sick of Wall! And I'm sick of you too! I'm going home to father!

N: Slam. His kids turned delinquent.

7: What are you doing tonight?

neuralgia:
nerve pain, often originating in the head

congenital idiocy:
extreme stupidity originating at birth

eructations:
belches

delinquent:
young person who has committed a crime

8: Thought I'd cripple a few fuzz.

7: We did that last night.

N: Until finally, old, alone and penniless, he decided on the direct approach, and built his great invention: a sort of a catapult, quite novel in those times, which could hurl an object, or a person, up to an enormous height. He tried it on a rock, which disappeared into the blue, and then, one day, surrounded by curious bystanders, sat his own skinny, threadbare, old body where the rock had been.

3: Wind it up, then.

N: They did.

3: When I say three, pull the lever. One … two … thr … ooww!

N: They did, only too glad to get rid of this nut, this disruptive influence, so they could get back to watching their goldfish and planting their beans.

9: There he goes!

1: Look at his rags flapping!

2: Bald head glinting in the sun!

4: Better than fireworks!

5: Coo!

N: Up he went, up, up, up, until looking down… we surmise … he saw the whole gold of that sunny day, the whole spread of the earth and seas, saw the tiny moving figures of people and the infinite distances of space. And it looked good.

3: I'm up! I'm over! I can see! I can see over! Its… It's… It's… Aaah!

N: A heart attack — we surmise. But in any case he was too far away for those on the ground to hear him. And as he dwindled into what seemed like a mathematical point, and disappeared, those on the ground shook their heads, or giggled, and went back to their beans, and their goldfish.

Focus on ... allegories

An **allegory** is a story with a hidden meaning – usually to teach a moral lesson.

For example, the story of 'The Tortoise and the Hare' is an allegory because it is designed to teach a lesson about how perseverance and hard work will win in the end.

 Work with a partner to come up with some other examples of allegories.

Discuss

1. Why do you think the Wall was built?
2. What do you think is on the other side of the Wall?
 3. With a partner, discuss what you think the message of this story might be.

Understand

1. **(a)** Match each of the following terms with their definition. Use the dictionary to help you.

Optimist	Someone who believes in equal rights between the sexes
Pessimist	Someone who offers theories and views on profound questions about life
Philosopher	Someone who is negative and assumes the worst
Feminist	Someone who is hopeful and positive

   (b) Put each of these words into a sentence of your own.

   (c) Add these words to the vocabulary builder on pages 1–2 of your Portfolio.

   (d) Which characters in the play are best represented by each of these terms?

2. What is character 2's motto? Do you agree with it?

3. Name one theory about what is on the other side of the Wall.

4. Where does the Wall end?

5. **(a)** What is the AFITWIOTSWOTOS?

   (b) Come up with a better name for the AFITWIOTSWOTOS.

6. What do the people suspect happened to the man who catapulted over the Wall?

Explore

1. 'The old were well looked after, as long as they didn't outstay their welcome.' What does this mean, in your opinion?

2. Do you think that the Wall may be a symbol for something else? Explain your answer.

3. People have become so used to the Wall that they have started ignoring it. Only one person seems to be curious as to what is on the other side. What reasons might someone have for not wanting to know what is on the other side of a wall or barrier?

4. What is the message in this play, in your opinion? Explain your answer.

5. Imagine you are the director of *Over the Wall*. Describe how you would stage this play.

   (a) How would you represent the Wall on stage?

   (b) What kind of clothing and props would you give the actors?

   (c) How would you portray the time and place of the play?

Investigate

Look at places throughout the world and across history where walls have been built and people divided. Choose one wall or barrier and write a news article describing what its purpose was, where it was constructed and if it was eventually broken down.

Create

1. Think of a time where you have come up against a wall or barrier and not known what was on the other side. Write the opening to a short story inspired by the title 'Over the Wall'.

2. Barriers or walls aren't always used to divide us, sometimes they are there to protect us. Organise a class debate on the following motion: *This house believes that good fences make good neighbours.*

3. (a) Think about a time when you put up a barrier or a wall between yourself and someone else. Ask yourself:

   ◀ Why was this barrier necessary?

   ◀ What kind of things might you miss out on if you did not break down the barrier?

   ◀ Why was it hard to break down this barrier?

   Write a personal essay outlining your views in the space provided on pages 47–48 of your Portfolio.

   (b) Redraft your personal essay in the space provided on pages 116–117 of your Portfolio.

Prejudice

Prejudice is another type of barrier people can face. Prejudice is an unfavourable opinion that is not based on reason or experience. People can face prejudice for many reasons, including race, religion and gender. It is important that we work as a society to break down prejudices.

Anti-Semitism is hostility towards or hatred against Jewish people. The Holocaust was the persecution and murder of European Jews by Nazi Germany and its collaborators.

Anne Frank, a German-born Jewish victim of the Holocaust, was forced into hiding with her family in 1942 when she was 12 years old. The hiding place was a concealed room behind a bookcase in her father's workplace. Anne kept a diary of the events up until her arrest in 1944. Anne died in the Bergen-Belsen concentration camp in 1945.

Her diary was translated from its original Dutch and published with the help of her father, Otto, the only surviving member of the Frank family.

The Diary of a Young Girl

Wednesday, 8 July 1942

Dearest Kitty,

I'll begin by telling you what happened Sunday afternoon.

At three o'clock … the doorbell rang. I didn't hear it, since I was out on the balcony, lazily reading in the sun. A little while later Margot appeared in the kitchen doorway looking very agitated. 'Father has received a call-up notice from the SS,' she whispered. 'Mother has gone to see Mr van Daan.' (Mr van Daan is Father's business partner and a good friend.)

I was stunned. A call-up: everyone knows what that means. Visions of concentration camps and lonely cells raced through my head. How could we let Father go to such a fate? 'Of course he's not going,' declared Margot as we waited for Mother in the living room. 'Mother's gone to Mr van Daan to ask whether we can move to our hiding place tomorrow. The van Daans are going with us. There will be seven of us altogether.' Silence. We couldn't speak. The thought of Father off visiting someone in the Jewish Hospital and completely unaware of what was happening, the long wait for Mother, the heat, the suspense – all this reduced us to silence.

Thursday, 9 July 1942

Dearest Kitty,

… Here's a description of the building … A wooden staircase leads from the downstairs passage to the second floor. At the top of the stairs is a landing, with doors on either side. The door on the left takes you up to the spice storage area, attic and loft in the front part of the house. A typically Dutch, very steep, ankle-twisting flight of stairs also runs from the front part of the house to another door opening onto the street.

The door to the right of the landing leads to the 'Secret Annexe' at the back of the house. No one would ever suspect there were so many rooms behind that plain grey door. There's just one small step in front of the door, and then you're inside. Straight ahead of you is a steep flight of stairs. To the left is a narrow hallway opening onto a room that serves as the Frank family's living-room and bedroom. Next door is a smaller room, the bedroom and study of the two young ladies of the family. To the right of the stairs is a 'bathroom', a windowless room with just a sink. The door in the corner leads to the lavatory and another one to Margot's and my room … Now I've introduced you to the whole of our lovely Annexe!

Friday, 9 October 1942

Dearest Kitty,

Today I have nothing but dismal and depressing news to report. Our many Jewish friends and acquaintances are being taken away in droves. The Gestapo is treating them very roughly and transporting them in cattle-trucks to Westerbork, the big camp in Drenthe to which they're sending all the Jews. Miep told us about someone who'd managed to escape from there. It must be terrible in Westerbork. The people get almost nothing to eat, much less to drink, as water is available only one hour a day, and there's only one lavatory and sink for several thousand people. Men and women sleep in the same room, and women and children often have their heads shaved. Escape is almost impossible; many people look Jewish, and they're branded by their shorn heads.

If it's that bad in Holland, what must it be like in those faraway and uncivilized places where the Germans are sending them? We assume that most of them are being murdered. The English radio says they're being gassed. Perhaps that's the quickest way to die.

I feel terrible. Miep's accounts of these horrors are so heartrending …

Fine specimens of humanity, those Germans, and to think I'm actually one of them! No, that's not true, Hitler took away our nationality long ago. And besides, there are no greater enemies on earth than the Germans and the Jews.

Understand

1. What was Anne doing when the doorbell rang?
2. Who does Anne share a room with?
3. Why does Anne only have 'dismal and depressing news to report'?
4. How does Anne describe the conditions in Westerbork?
5. According to the radio, what was happening to the Jewish people?
6. List three features of typical diary entries that you recognise in these diary entries, and provide examples for each.

Explore

1. 'We couldn't speak.' What caused Anne and Margot to feel this way?
2. Earlier in her diary, Anne wrote that she intended to express her deepest feelings in her diary. Having read the three extracts above, do you think that she achieves this?

Investigate

Anne Frank was a victim of prejudice. Use your research skills to find out more information about Anne Frank and the barriers she faced. Share your information with the class.

Create

In the second diary entry, Anne uses descriptive language to convey what her hiding place looked like. Using her descriptions, sketch an image of what you imagine her hiding place to look like in the space provided on page 49 of your Portfolio.

Synonyms

In pairs, think of as many words as you can that have the same meaning as each of the words listed below:

◖ small

◖ received

◖ whispered

◖ dismal

◖ acquaintance.

You have just learned how to use a synonym.

A synonym is a word or phrase that means the same thing as another word or phrase.

For example, 'large' is a synonym for 'big'.

Using synonyms helps to vary your vocabulary and prevent it from being repetitive and boring.

If you are looking for a synonym for a word, use a **thesaurus**. You search for the word in the same way as in a dictionary, but this time a list of alternatives is offered rather than a definition.

 Understand

1. Which word is a synonym for 'fast'?
   - (a) Slow
   - (b) Run
   - (c) Quick
   - (d) Sit

2. Which word is a synonym for 'boring'?
   - (a) Short
   - (b) Long
   - (c) Near
   - (d) Dull

3. Which word is a synonym for 'angry'?
   - (a) Furious
   - (b) Happy
   - (c) Cold
   - (d) Wide

4. Write a synonym for each of the words below.
   - (a) Smile
   - (b) Amazing
   - (c) Interesting
   - (d) True
   - (e) Bad
   - (f) Hate
   - (g) Look
   - (h) Take
   - (i) Silent
   - (j) Delicious
   - (k) Move
   - (l) Strange
   - (m) Nice
   - (n) Fear
   - (o) Shout
   - (p) Sad
   - (q) Big
   - (r) Good
   - (s) Tell
   - (t) Old
   - (u) Young

5. Find synonyms for the following words found in the extracts from *The Diary of a Young Girl* on pages 211–212:
   - ◖ dismal
   - ◖ agitated
   - ◖ speak
   - ◖ lovely
   - ◖ transporting
   - ◖ terrible.

A refugee is a person who has been forced to leave their country in order to escape war, persecution or a natural disaster. Unfortunately, refugees often experience prejudice when they go to a new country.

 The following poem explores people's attitudes to refugees.

Refugees

By Brian Bilston

They have no need of our help

So do not tell me

These haggard faces could belong to you or me

Should life have dealt a different hand

We need to see them for who they really are

Chancers and scroungers

Layabouts and loungers

With bombs up their sleeves

Cut-throats and thieves

They are not

Welcome here

We should make them

Go back to where they came from

They cannot

Share our food

Share our homes

Share our countries

Instead let us

Build a wall to keep them out

It is not okay to say

These are people just like us

A place should only belong to those who are born there

Do not be so stupid to think that

The world can be looked at another way

Understand

1. Who are 'they' in the first line?
2. In your own words, how does this poem describe refugees?
3. Which of the words below best describes the speaker's attitude? Choose one and explain your choice.

   ◖ Angry   ◖ Welcoming
   ◖ Dismissive   ◖ Helpful

4. Can you find any words or phrases repeated in this poem? What effect does this have on you as a reader?

Explore

1. With a partner, take turns reading this poem aloud. One person should read the poem from the top to the bottom (speaker 1) and the other person should read it from the bottom to the top (speaker 2).

   (a) Do you see a different viewpoint?
   (b) Answer the Understand questions again, based on the second viewpoint.

2. Complete the table on page 50 of your Portfolio.

Create

1. Rewrite the poem in the form of two diary entries, one for each speaker. Add in punctuation. Use the following example to get you started:

> Dear Diary,
> They have no need of our help, so do not tell me these haggard faces could belong to you or me. Should life have dealt a different hand …

2. Write a letter to the Taoiseach outlining how you think we could help refugees from other countries. Use the checklist to help you.

Formal letters
✓ Sender's address
✓ Recipient's address
✓ Date
✓ Greeting
✓ First person
✓ Professional and formal language
✓ Introductory paragraph
✓ Details/information
✓ Closing statement
✓ Sign-off

People who belong to a particular country are referred to as 'citizens'. In the following poem, Dave Calder explores what it means to be a citizen and the barriers people who have moved from one country to another may face.

Citizen of the World
By Dave Calder

when you are very small
maybe not quite born
your parents move
for some reason you may never understand they move
from their own town
from their own land
and you grow up in a place
that is never quite your home

and all your childhood people
with a smile or a fist say
you're not from here are you
and part of you says fiercely yes I am
and part of you feels no I'm not
I belong where my parents belonged

but when you go to their town, their country
people there also say
you're not from here are you
and part of you says no I'm not
and part of you feels fiercely yes I am

and so you grow up both and neither
and belong everywhere and nowhere much the same
both stronger and weaker for the lack of ground
able to fly but not to rest
and all over the world, though you feel alone
are millions like you, like a great flock of swallows
soaring or falling exhausted, wings beating the rhythm
of the wind that laughs at fences or frontiers,
whose home is itself, and the whole world it moves over.

frontiers:
borders

Discuss

1. What does being a citizen mean to you?
2. How do you define where you belong or what country you are a citizen of?

Understand

1. According to the poem, what does it mean to be a 'citizen of the world'?
2. What do you think the line 'with a smile or a fist' means?
3. What barriers do people face in this world, according to the speaker?
4. There are many oxymorons in the fourth stanza. Make a list of these oxymorons.

Explore

1. With a partner, find an example of personification in the poem and discuss whether you think this example is effective.
2. 'and all over the world, though you feel alone / are millions like you, like a great flock of swallows'

   Rewrite this sentence, replacing the simile with another comparison. For example, 'like a swarm of bees'.
3. Which of the images below do you think would best accompany a reading of this poem? Explain your choice.

4. **(a)** Read back over this poem and 'Refugees' on page 214. There is a lack of punctuation in both poems. Why do you think this is?

   (b) Find some other poetic devices that both poems have in common and suggest why both poets may have used these devices.

Create

Write an article for your school magazine describing what you feel it means to be a citizen of the world.

Antonyms

An antonym is a word that is opposite in meaning to another.

Bad and good   full and empty   right and wrong   noisy and quiet

 Understand

1. Match the words in with their antonyms.

Day
Cheap
Dark
Tight
Fearful
Break
Capture
Soft

Fix
Fearless
Release
Expensive
Hard
Light
Loose
Night

2. Find an antonym for each of the following words and put them into sentences.
   Use a thesaurus or dictionary to help you.

   (a) Energetic   **(e)** Tall   **(i)** Smooth
   (b) Wide   **(f)** Shout   **(j)** Frightened
   (c) Far   **(g)** Winning   **(k)** Depart
   (d) Hatred   **(h)** Helpless   **(l)** Excitedly

 3. There are antonyms in the poem 'Citizen of the World' on page 216. Work with a
   partner to find the antonyms in this poem.

It is important to try to overcome prejudices and to make everyone feel included and accepted. The following images both promote inclusivity in society.

Explore

1. Choose one image and describe it orally to your partner.
2. Which image do you think is more effective in encouraging inclusivity? Explain your answer.
3. Discuss each image under the headings below.

   ◀ Copy   ◀ Colour   ◀ Visuals/images

Investigate

Discuss the idea of inclusivity with your classmates and find some suggestions on how to encourage it in school. Write a report outlining your findings.

Create

Create a digital presentation to accompany one of images above in a campaign to encourage inclusivity.

People can experience prejudice in society for many different reasons. Some people experience prejudice due to their sexual orientation.

The following advertisement for Smart Communications aired in the Philippines. It explores how difficult it can be for people in same-sex relationships to come out to their family.

https://www.youtube.com/watch?v=CHp-9aSQrk0

 Explore

1. Why do you think the son is reluctant to become friends with his father on Facebook?
2. Do you think this is an effective advertisement for a mobile network? Give a reason for your answer.
3. Do you think the logo at the end of this advertisement is effective in promoting the brand?
4. In your opinion, have the father and son broken down barriers that may have been between them? Explain your answer.

 Create

Think about the message of this advertisement. Design a storyboard for an advertisement of your own, containing a similar message.

Overcoming barriers

As we have seen, there are many types of barriers in society. These barriers can be difficult to overcome. The following texts all deal with overcoming barriers.

In the following interview, Paralympic gold medallist Michael McKillop explains how he overcame barriers to achieve success.

Breaking Down Barriers to Become a Champion

Michael McKillop decided to make ability out of his disability, breaking down barriers to become double Paralympic gold medallist.

What makes a champion?

A champion is just like a cocktail made up of lots of little things to create a masterpiece. My training is a key element to that and also having a very strong belief in my own ability. But it's the team that I have surrounding me that makes up the rest of a champion. From my girlfriend, to my family and to my coaches and Paralympics Ireland, we all come together to be Team McKillop.

What does being involved in sport mean to you?

It gives me a chance to show my talent to the world and showcase the ability I have to perform at the highest level – regardless of having a disability.

Have you ever faced criticism, dealt with barriers to your success? (e.g. bullying in the playground when younger). How did you overcome these?

Growing up with a physical disability was tough as it was visible to the public. I stood out. I was different to all the other kids.

Yes, I was picked on at times, but I didn't allow those words to affect the way I lived. I realised after a while that everybody is different and I should be proud to be who I am and own my disability.

Can you tell us how you first got interested in athletics?

With my disability I was introduced to sport at a very young age as a form of physio.

I got involved with running through my mum and dad, they were both former athletes in their time. My father was an athletics coach at a local grammar school which I went on to attend.

Did you ever dream when you first started out that you would be on the international stage and winning gold medals for Ireland?

When I started athletics, I was competing against able-bodied athletes and saw myself as able-bodied. I wasn't aware of Paralympic sport at the time so it was difficult for me to envisage being on the international stage.

At what moment did you realise, hang on – I can make a career out of this?

When I attended my first major championships at the age of 15 – where I won two silver medals – it hit me that I could improve on this, and my aim since then has been to win gold at every other championship.

Has there ever been a moment(s) that you have doubted yourself, lost belief in what you can do?

Life has never been normal for me growing up as a Paralympic medalist. From the young age of 16 I have been expected to live my life as a world class athlete, I missed out on opportunities and experiences that every teenager usually experiences. With this I have found myself in dark places at times, trying to live up to people's expectations. But with the support of friends, family, my coaches and most importantly Nicole my girlfriend, I have got through this.

Your relationship with your mother was one of the moments that everyone remembers from London 2012. Can you tell us why her presenting you with your medal was such a special moment for you?

I never expected anything like that to happen during one of my medal ceremonies, when she walked out it put a massive smile on my face and made my heart beat a little faster. When she put the medal around my neck, I gave her a big hug it was a moment of reflection and relief. Through all of my mum's hard work while I was growing up and my hours spent training, it was in that moment that we proved to the world that with belief and determination, you can achieve anything. I may also have shed a little tear!

If you could revisit one moment in your career and go back and relive it – what would it be?

I am still yet to find a moment I would like to relive. One I want to experience is to run at a major championships in front of my girlfriend Nicole for the first ever time.

On the other hand, if you could revisit one moment in your career and go back and change it, what would it be?

I would like to change how I reacted after coming second in the IPC World Championships in 2006. I was a 16-year-old teenager and didn't know how to react to and deal with disappointment. Thankfully I've learned with age.

RIO 2016

How is your preparation for Rio 2016 going?

Things are currently going very well, me and my team have all the niggles under control and we are being consistent with my training. Crossing the line in Doha at last year's IPC World Championships, I showed to the world

and the people in my category that even though it had been one of the toughest years training and injury wise for me, I could still perform under pressure and still be the best athlete I can be.

What are your hopes for Rio from a performance point of view?

Now that I am an established athlete, there is that sense of expectation to win every race, but for me, I just need to go to Rio this summer and perform to my best ability and do my country proud.

Some other facts

Life after racing – what are your hopes for the future?

I want to become a well-known after-dinner and motivational speaker.

Who would you class as your inspiration and why?

My parents – they were the people who were faced with the challenges of raising a disabled child. I fully appreciate how daunting and tough this must have been. I owe everything to them.

Favourite quote: Believe and you will achieve.

Best advice you have been given: Be happy and do your best.

Understand

1. According to Michael, what makes a champion?
2. How did Michael become interested in athletics?
3. When did Michael realise that he could have a career in sport?
4. What barriers did Michael come up against?
5. How did Michael feel when his mother presented him with his medal?
6. What moment does Michael say he would like to change?
7. Who does Michael consider to be his inspiration?
8. What are Michael's hopes for his future career?
9. What features of a typical interview can you identify in this piece?

Explore

1. Which question, in your opinion, leads to the most revealing information about Michael? Give a reason for your answer.
2. If you could ask Michael one more question in this interview, what would it be and why?

3. 'Michael is a humble hero.' Do you agree with this statement? Give two reasons for your answer.

Create

Think of someone in your life who overcame a barrier. If possible, carry out an interview with this person, asking them about the barriers they overcame. If this is not possible, imagine how this interview might go, detailing both questions and answers. Write the transcript of the interview you have carried out (real or imaginary). Give details on how they overcame this barrier and what advice they would offer to others in the space provided on pages 51–52 of your Portfolio.

Memoirs

A memoir is a record of events or moments in a writer's life that had an impact on them. A memoir is similar to an autobiography in terms of style and features. The main difference is that an autobiography recounts an entire life, whereas a memoir only reflects on certain memories.

Features	Language
◖ Written in the first person ◖ Reveals thoughts and feelings ◖ Deals with the author's experiences	◖ Honest ◖ Descriptive ◖ Can be informal and conversational or formal, depending on the author's preference and the events being discussed

In her wartime memoir *One Pair of Feet*, Monica Dickens recounts her experiences as a nurse during the Second World War. In the following extract, she explains how the war broke down many barriers for women, as it allowed them enter the workplace.

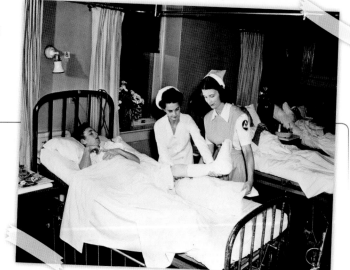

One Pair of Feet

One had got to be something; that was obvious. But what? It seemed that women, having been surplus for twenty years, were suddenly wanted in a hundred different places at once. The Suffragettes could have saved themselves a lot of trouble if they had seen this coming. Men's jobs were open to women and trousers were selling like hot cakes in Kensington High Street ... I could not make up my mind what to be. A lot of fanatics rushed into the most uncongenial jobs they could find, stimulated by a glow of self-sacrifice that lasted until the novelty wore off or the cold weather set in, but it seemed to me that, provided that it was just as useful, it was no less patriotic to do something enjoyable ... The Services? I didn't think my hips would stand the cut of the skirt and I wasn't too sure about my legs in wool stockings ... The Land Army? One saw oneself picking apples in a shady hat, or silhouetted against the skyline with a couple of plough horses, but a second look showed one tugging mangel-wurzels out of the frozen ground at five o'clock on a bitter February morning. Ministries and Bureaux? Apart from the question of my hips again (sitting is so spreading), they didn't seem to want me. Perhaps it was because I can only type with three fingers ... Nursing? The idea had always attracted me, even in peace-time, but I suppose every girl goes through that. It's one of those adolescent phases, like wanting to be a nun. It was reading *Farewell to Arms*, I think, that finally decided me, though what sort of hospital allowed such goings on, I can't imagine. However, that was the last war.

uncongenial:
unpleasant

mangel-wurzels:
a type of root vegetable

Farewell to Arms:
a novel by Ernest Hemingway set in the First World War

Understand

1. What was the dilemma Monica faced?
2. Name one type of profession Monica considered joining.
3. Why did Monica consider herself unsuitable for an administrative role?

 Explore

1. Do you agree with Monica's view that wanting to be a nurse is a phase that every girl goes through? Explain your answer.
2. What kind of person do you think Monica is? Give reasons for your answer.
3. What barrier do you think Monica faced in the past? Explain your answer.

 Investigate

1. 'The Suffragettes could have saved themselves a lot of trouble if they had seen this coming.'
   (a) Research the suffrage movement and find five interesting facts to share with the class.
   (b) Explain what you understand by this line.

 Create

1. Think of a time where you faced a difficult decision. Write your own memoir in the space provided on page 53 of your Portfolio. In it, you should outline how you felt at the time and explain how you came up with a solution.
2. Think of a famous figure from history or from contemporary society who faced a barrier in life. Write a memoir from their perspective, detailing an interesting aspect of your life.

The following short film, *New Boy*, is based on a short story by Roddy Doyle. In it, we see how Joseph, a young refugee, deals with the barrier of prejudice that he faces when he arrives in Ireland.

https://www.irishfilmboard.ie/directory/view/7604/new-boy

Focus on ... flashbacks

Flashbacks are used to explain a past event or provide relevant background information.

In films, the audience is aware of a flashback when some of the following things occur:

- the music or sound changes
- the setting or scene changes
- a caption appears with a date or year

In *New Boy*, flashback is used to tell us more about the central character, where he has come from and what barriers he has overcome.

 **Discuss**

1. What information does the audience gain from the flashback in *New Boy*?
2. Can you think of any other films that use flashbacks?

Understand

1. Which subject are the students studying at the beginning of the film?
2. What do the students say when the lesson in Joseph's home country finishes?
3. Why do you think the teacher selects Seth Quinn to do the sum on the board?
4. How many goals does Joseph tell his father he scored in the last game?
5. Why do you think Christian Kelly does not punch Joseph?
6. How do the boys bond in the end?
7. If you were to show this film to a group of First Years, what is the overall message you would hope that they would come away with?

Explore

1. Why do you think Christian Kelly makes an insulting remark to Joseph?
2. From whose perspective do we understand the story?
3. What technique does the director use to indicate that a flashback is taking place?
4. What differences do you notice between the education system in Ireland and the education system in Joseph's home country?
5. Would you agree that there are moments of humour in this film? Give reasons for your answer.
6. What is your impression of the Irish teacher in this film? Do you think she could have handled the situation better? If so, what could she have done?
7. Choose two adjectives to describe Hazel, and explain your choices.
8. Which adjective listed below do you think best describes this film? Give two reasons for your answer.
   ◀ Touching
   ◀ Thought-provoking
   ◀ Memorable
9. How is the theme of breaking barriers relevant to this film?
10. What feelings were you left with at the end of this film?

Create

1. Write a review of *New Boy*.
2. You have been asked to select a film to show for an anti-bullying campaign. Give three reasons why you believe *New Boy* would be a good choice for this event.

3. Write a six-step survival guide for a first day in a new school in the space provided on page 54 of your Portfolio.

The following poem describes a different planet that seems to have overcome many of the barriers that we face in today's world. However, the speaker faces a barrier that is preventing her from going to live there.

Another Planet

By Dunya Mikhail

I have a special ticket
to another planet
beyond this Earth.
A comfortable world, and beautiful:
a world without much smoke,
not too hot
and not too cold.
The creatures
are gentler there,
and the governments
have no secrets.
The police are nonexistent:
there are no problems
and no fights.
And the schools
don't exhaust their students
with too much work
for history has yet to start
and there's no geography
and no other languages.

And even better:
the war
has left its 'r' behind
and turned into love,
so the weapons sleep
beneath the dust,
and the planes pass by
without shelling the cities,
and the boats
look like smiles
on the water.
All things
are peaceful
and kind
on the other planet
beyond this Earth.
But still I hesitate
to go alone.

Understand

1. Name three things that are different about this new planet, compared to our own.
2. Why are the police not needed on this planet?

 Explore

 1. Offer an alternative title for this poem. Explain your answer with reference to the poem.

2. What does the fact that 'there's no geography and no other languages' suggest about the people on this new planet?

3. What do the lines 'the war / has left its "r" behind / and turned into love' mean, in your opinion?

4. Why do you think the speaker hesitates 'to go alone'? Give reasons for your answer.

 5. Would you like to travel to the planet described in this poem? Explain your answer.

 Create

 1. Create your own poem with the same message as 'Another Planet' in the space provided on page 55 of your Portfolio. Use a similar format to this poem.

2. 'If we could break down all barriers, then we could open ourselves up to other worlds and opportunities.'

Using 'Another Planet' as a model, and in whatever format you wish, create your own world where barriers, borders and walls have been broken down.

Reviewing breaking barriers

Reflect and review

1. Look back at the images at the start of the unit. Consider the association each image has with the theme. Rank the images in order from most relevant (1) to least relevant (4).

2. Share the image that you feel ranks the highest. Explain your choice and listen as others share their choice with you.

3. What image would you choose to replace the one that you feel ranks the lowest? Describe the image you would replace it with and explain your choice.

4. 'Before I built a wall, I'd ask myself what I was walling in or walling out.' (Robert Frost)

   Do you agree with this statement? Discuss the texts that you have studied throughout this unit in your answer.

5. Fill in the unit review on pages 56–57 of your Portfolio.

Language skills

1. Identify the relationships between the following pairs of words. Are they antonyms or synonyms?

   ◀ Happy   Content
   ◀ Light   Dark
   ◀ Smooth   Rough
   ◀ Short   Brief
   ◀ Sick   Unwell

2. Give an antonym and a synonym for each of the following words:

   ◀ intelligent
   ◀ certain
   ◀ break
   ◀ wall
   ◀ inequality
   ◀ build
   ◀ challenge.

Oral assessment

Prepare a two-minute presentation entitled 'The Barriers in My Life'. You may use visual aids or make a digital presentation if you wish. If you are using visual aids, carefully consider what each image means to you.

- Plan what you would like to say.
- Write your speech.
- Practise the delivery of your speech. Make sure it is two minutes long.

When you are ready, deliver your speech to your classmates.

Written assessment

1. **(a)** Write a short story entitled 'Breaking Barriers' in the space provided on pages 58–59 of your Portfolio.

   (b) Redraft your short story in the space provided on pages 118–119 of your Portfolio.

Exam skills

1. Think about a poem you have studied that deals with the theme of barriers.
   (a) Name the poem and the poet.
   (b) Describe the barrier.
   (c) Do you think the poet's use of language is effective in describing this barrier? Give reasons for your answer.

   Write your answer in the space provided on pages 139–140 of your Portfolio.

Theme 6

Mapping Milestones

What are milestones?

Our lives unfold in many different ways, but the phases we go through, such as childhood, puberty, adulthood and old age, are common to all of us. Each time we encounter a new milestone, it signals a time of change in our lives.

Why study milestones?

It is important to recognise your growth as a person and to be proud of your progress. There are many joys and challenges involved in reaching each new milestone. Our experiences shape who we are and how we think and feel. Studying what other people have to say about these milestones can help us to understand our own experiences and prepare for moments yet to come.

Learning intentions

- Explore different milestones that occur in our lives.

Writing With Purpose
- Learn about documentaries.
- Read a blog post about finding your true self.

Poetry and Song
- Explore the effects of love and loss.

Fiction
- Look at a variety of milestones through the journey of life.

Stage and Screen
- Read monologues and soliloquies about life experiences.

Media and Advertising
- Discover how to express our voice through editorials.

Language Skills
- Understand the difference between 'its' and 'it's'.

 Discuss

1. Choose one of the images above that you feel best represents milestones. Why did you choose this image?

2. Can you think of any other images that would convey the theme of milestones?

3. Do you think each experience of love and/or loss shapes who we are as people?

 Create

 Write your own definition of 'milestones' in the space provided on page 73 of your Portfolio, by completing the sentence 'Milestones are ...'. You will return to this definition later on.

Growing up

Childhood is an important milestone in everyone's life. During this time, we create our first memories and learn important life lessons. When we become teenagers, we begin to seek independence as we experience more of the world.

Sibling rivalry is part of growing up. In the following extract from *Dreamland* by Sarah Dessen, the protagonist Caitlin discusses her relationship with her sister Cass.

Dreamland

When I was four and Cass was six, she whacked me across the face with a plastic shovel at our neighborhood park. We were in the sandbox, and it was winter: In the pictures, we're in matching coats and hats and mittens. My mother loved to dress us alike, like twins, since we were only two years apart. We *did* look alike, with the same round face and dark eyes and the same brown hair. But we weren't the same, even then.

The story goes like this: Cass had the shovel and I wanted it. My mother was sitting watching us on a bench with Boo, who had her camera and was snapping pictures. This was at Commons Park, the small grassy area in the center of our neighborhood, Lakeview. Besides the sandboxes it also had a swing set, one of those circular things you push real fast and then jump on—a kind of manual merry-go-round – and enough grass to play baseball or kickball. Cass and I spent most of the afternoons of our childhood at Commons Park, but the shovel incident is what we both always remembered.

Not that we ourselves recalled it that well. We had just heard the story recounted so many times over the years that it was easy to take the details and fold them into our own sparse memories, embellishing here or there to fill in the blanks.

It is said that I reached for the shovel and Cass wouldn't give it to me, so I grabbed her hand and tried to yank it away. A struggle ensued, which must have looked harmless until Cass somehow scraped one hard plastic edge across my temple and it began to bleed.

This moment, *the* moment, we have documented in one of Boo's photos. There is one picture of Cass and me playing happily, another of the struggle over the shovel (I'm wailing, my mouth a perfect O, while Cass looks stubborn and determined, always a fighter), and finally, a shot of her arm extended, the shovel against my face, and a blur in the left corner, which I know is my mother, jumping to her feet and running to the sandbox to pull us apart.

Apparently, there was a lot of blood. My mother ran through the winding sidewalks of Lakeview with me in her arms, shrieking, then took me to the hospital where I received five tiny stitches. Cass got to stay at Boo and Stewart's, eat ice cream, and watch TV until we got home.

The shovel was destroyed. My mother, already a nervous case, wouldn't let us leave the house or play with anything not plush or stuffed for about six months. And I grew up with a scar over my eye, small enough that hardly anyone ever noticed it, except for me. And Cass.

As we grew older, I'd sometimes look up to find her peering very closely at my face, finding the scar with her eyes before reaching up with one hand to trace it with her finger. She always said it made her feel horrible to look at it, even though we both knew it wasn't really her fault. It was just one more thing we had in common, like our faces, our gestures, and our initials.

Discuss

1. Can you think of a time when you had a row with a sibling, a cousin or a friend?

2. Do you think we are quicker to forgive the ones we love than the ones we don't?

Understand

1. In what season is this extract set?

2. What do the two sisters have in common?

3. What was their mother doing when this incident took place?

4. How does Cass feel now when she looks at the scar on her sister's face?

5. How did their mother react to the incident **(a)** when it happened and **(b)** afterwards?

Explore

1. Do you agree that sibling fights are a part of growing up? Give a reason for your answer.

2. In your opinion, do you think their mother's reaction to the fight was fair?

3. Do you think Cass regrets her actions? Give a reason for your answer.

Create

1. Write a short story with the title 'Dreamland'.

2. Imagine you are Caitlin. Write an email to Cass in which you tell her that you forgive her for the incident in the sandbox all those years ago in the space provided on page 60 of your Portfolio.

As we grow up, we often long to reach certain milestones and have more independence than our parents or guardians agree with. In the following extract from Jack Cheng's novel *See You in the Cosmos*, two siblings discuss their changing relationship with their mother. Their conversation is written in transcript form.

See You in the Cosmos

ALEX: I know what you mean. It's like when someone thinks I'm still nine or ten years old. I hate that because I'm eleven, not nine. I'm in middle school, not fourth grade. And I'm probably at least thirteen in responsibility years!

TERRA: It's a big difference, isn't it? They just don't get it.

ALEX: They just don't get it.

TERRA: I don't know what happened though, it wasn't always like this.

ALEX: Like what?

TERRA: With my mom. Our relationship was a lot different. I used to tell her everything. If there was … something I'd done that I knew she wouldn't approve of – like, some hard decision that'd I made on my own, I'd tell her about it afterwards. And I felt that at least she understood why I made the choices I did, even if she wasn't always happy about them.

ALEX: Was one of the choices to move to your own apartment? She wasn't happy probably because she knew she was going to really miss you.

TERRA: Mmm … yeah, I guess. But it's just that sometimes parents don't want to accept that their kids are growing up. It's like they think, I don't know, they think if we grow up, then we stop being their kids or something. But that's their whole job! It's to raise us to be independent! They just have such a hard time facing it, you know? Facing the truth.

Discuss

1. Do you think teenagers are responsible enough to be treated like adults?
2. Do you think teenagers should have more say in decisions that affect their lives?
3. If you had the power to make changes for young people, what would you change?

Understand

1. What age is Alex?
2. How has Terra's relationship with his mom changed?
3. What reason does Alex put forward for why Terra's mother wasn't happy with his decision to move into his own apartment?
4. What does Terra believe is the a job of a parent?
5. According to Terra, what do parents not want to accept?

Explore

1. In your opinion, what does Alex mean when he says 'I'm probably at least thirteen in responsibility years'?
2. Do you agree with Terra that a parent's 'whole job' is 'to raise us to be independent'? Explain your answer.

Create

 Write a debate speech proposing or opposing the following motion in the space provided on pages 61–62 of your Portfolio: *This house believes that the sole job of a parent is to raise their children to be independent.*

Life can take us on very interesting paths. Who we are, where we are from and the experiences we go through all influence us as people. Part of growing up can be realising that life isn't always fair, and learning life lessons from any negative experiences that we may have.

In the following extract from *Holes* by Louis Sachar, Stanley Yelnats is being taken to a juvenile detention camp for a crime that he did not commit.

Holes

Stanley Yelnats was the only passenger on the bus, not counting the driver or the guard. The guard sat next to the driver with his seat turned around facing Stanley. A rifle lay across his lap

Stanley was sitting about ten rows back, handcuffed to his armrest. His backpack lay on the seat next to him. It contained his toothbrush, toothpaste, and a box of stationery his mother had given him. He'd promised to write to her at least once a week.

He looked out the window, although there wasn't much to see – mostly fields of hay and cotton. He was on a long bus ride to nowhere. The bus wasn't air-conditioned, and the hot, heavy air was almost as stifling as the handcuffs.

Stanley and his parents had tried to pretend that he was just going away to camp for a while, just like rich kids do. When Stanley was younger he used to play with stuffed animals, and pretend the animals were at camp. Camp Fun and Games he called it. Sometimes he'd have them play soccer with a marble. Other times they'd run an obstacle course, or go bungee jumping off a table, tied to broken rubber bands. Now Stanley tried to pretend he was going to Camp Fun and Games. Maybe he'd make some friends, he thought. At least he'd get to swim in the lake.

He didn't have any friends at home. He was overweight and the kids at his middle school often teased him about his size. Even his teachers sometimes made cruel comments without realizing it. On his last day of school, his math teacher, Mrs Bell, taught ratios. As an example, she chose the heaviest kid in the class and the lightest kid in the class, and had them weigh themselves. Stanley weighed three times as much as the other boy. Mrs. Bell wrote the ratio on the board, 3:1, unaware of how much embarrassment she had caused both of them.

Stanley was arrested later that day.

He looked at the guard who sat slumped in his seat and wondered if he had fallen asleep. The guard was wearing sunglasses, so Stanley couldn't see his eyes.

Stanley was not a bad kid. He was innocent of the crime for which he was convicted. He'd just been in the wrong place at the wrong time.

It was all because of his no-good-dirty-rotten-pig-stealing-great-great-grandfather!

He smiled. It was a family joke. Whenever anything went wrong, they always blamed Stanley's no-good-dirty-rotten-pig-stealing-great-great-grandfather.

Supposedly, he had a great-great-grandfather who had stolen a pig from a one-legged Gypsy, and she put a curse on him and all his descendants. Stanley and his parents didn't believe in curses, of course, but whenever anything went wrong, it felt good to be able to blame someone.

Things went wrong a lot. They always seemed to be in the wrong place at the wrong time.

 Discuss

1. Have you ever been wrongfully accused of something?
2. Suggest a reason why you think Stanley was arrested.
3. Do you think that challenging experiences in life can help to make you stronger?

 Understand

1. What items does Stanley's backpack contain?
2. What can Stanley see when he looks out the window?
3. What game did Stanley play when he was younger?
4. What did Stanley promise his mother he would do?
5. What was Stanley's family joke?

 Explore

 1. What was the atmosphere on the bus like?
2. Do you think that Mrs Bell was wrong to teach ratios in the way that she did? Explain your answer.
 3. From reading the above passage, what age do you imagine Stanley to be? Give a reason for your answer.
 4. Would this extract make you to want to read the rest of the novel *Holes*? Give reasons for your answer.

 Create

Write the diary entry that you imagine Stanley could have written the night before his journey to the juvenile detention camp.

Its and it's

There is often confusion between the use of 'its' and 'it's'.

'It's' is short for 'it is' or 'it has'.

It's the correct answer.

'Its' is a possessive adjective, indicating ownership.

The dog has a bone in its mouth.

Understand

Write out the following sentences in your copy, inserting either 'it's' or 'its'.

1. This dog must be lost. Where is _____ collar?
2. _____ obvious that we are going to get homework tonight.
3. Eithne decided to get a Saint Bernard puppy as _____ floppy ears are adorable.
4. George hates driving in the dark as _____ difficult to see the road signs.
5. _____ been a week since I last saw my watch. _____ definitely lost.
6. I don't think _____ going to rain today.
7. If _____ fine with you, I would rather go tomorrow.
8. The oven has _____ own timer.
9. The dog hurt _____ leg.
10. The tree loses _____ leaves every autumn.

Finding your voice

Our day-to-day life consists of ups and downs, times of hardships and times of happiness. Ultimately, life is very much about your experiences and how you relate to others. Being true to yourself and living your life the way you want can give you a great sense of freedom and happiness. It is important to find your voice and to have a say in how you live your life.

The following inspirational quotes are all about why it is important to live life your own way.

The biggest adventure you can ever take is to live the life of your dreams.
– Oprah Winfrey

Be yourself. Everyone else is already taken.
– Oscar Wilde

Why fit in when you were born to stand out?
– Dr Seuss

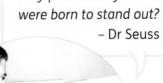

Always be a first-rate version of yourself, instead of a second-rate version of somebody else.
– Judy Garland

Life isn't about finding yourself, life is about creating yourself.
– George Bernard Shaw

Discuss

1. Which of the quotes is your favourite? Why?
2. Do you know any other inspirational quotes? What is it about these quotes that you find inspiring?

Create

 1. In pairs choose one of the inspirational quotes above or another inspirational quote that you like. Design a poster to accompany your chosen quote.

 2. **(a)** Work in groups to come up with your own inspirational quotes. Write your quotes on page 63 of your Portfolio and pass your Portfolios around for other groups to write in theirs until your page is full.

 (b) Share your inspirational quotes with the rest of the class.

In the following piece from lgbt.ie, Venezuelan journalist Simon talks about finding a look that made him feel like his true self.

○ ○ ○

← → ↻   🔒 http://lgbt.ie/blog/91/the-process-of-being-yourself-for-simon,-it-began-with-blue-hair-dye

LGBT Ireland

The Process of Being Yourself: For Simon, It Began With Blue Hair Dye

Being yourself is not always easy and can take a great deal of courage. Simon, a Venezuelan journalist living in Dublin, details his experience of overcoming fears and social obstacles in order to be more true to himself. Read about his journey below.

Hi, my name is Simon and I'm a Venezuelan journalist living in Dublin. I'm also a gay man with a lifelong fascination with Britney Spears. And two years ago I discovered that my 'natural' hair colour is blue.

It wasn't always like that of course. Like most people in the world, I was born with natural dark hair, a little greasy sometimes, and wavy when long. And it wasn't until my 'tween' years (10 or 11), when I saw the TV show *Buffy the Vampire Slayer*, when I decided I wanted my hair to be all white like Spike's. Once main villain/later soul mate of Buffy's, Spike was a bloody sexy English vampire with white blonde hair, Billy Idol style. I was OBSESSED.

But little me wasn't allowed to bleach and dye his hair. Mom said no very early on and that was that. I made it to college, in a different city and without adult supervision, but by then I wasn't brave enough. Life and a mostly Catholic/Latino society had made me very wary of expressing myself, I wasn't even out of the closet.

I came out in 2010, and moved to Dublin in 2013 and my hair was still pitch black. After so many years of being 'normal,' I kind of forgot about the whole white hair until one day in 2014, when talking about Buffy (as I often do) with a friend, she offered me to bleach my hair, she had done it dozens of times before and there was beer and pizza involved in the plan.

I was amazed by the opportunity. And slightly scared (very scared actually, I even told my boyfriend in a failed attempt of getting him to talk me out of it). I went up to her house and after 150 minutes of excruciating pain, my hair was a bright golden ball of hay. We used the highest developer (Level 40) but my Venezuelan hair was too dark to go white in only one session. Pains, logistics and a bruised ego made me refuse to do a second session and I decided instead to walk out on the street as a 'blonde'.

Despite my boyfriend's assurance, I wasn't comfortable with my new golden head, it wasn't pretty, trust me. So a few days later I went into a pharmacy and came out with a bottle of washable hair dye. The colour was called 'Washed-Up Mermaid' and the girl on the picture had a long mane of 'turquoise' hair. Pink and Peach were attractive options too but they had me at mermaid (did I say I'm very gay already?). 20 minutes after getting home my head was blue and has been so ever since. It took me maybe a couple of weeks but soon after, I realised that blue haired is who I wanted to be.

After changing my hair I became braver and more outgoing. I started to talk to people on the street more easily. I developed a stronger self-esteem not only based on my looks, but on the sense of finally achieving a childhood dream, and vanquishing my fears. The old little fears at least.

Being yourself is scary. I was afraid of my hair being damaged beyond repair. I was unsure what my mom and dad would say. I was told that employers might not take me seriously with blue hair. But I've never been happier. Sometimes people called me a Smurf trying to slag me, but not a day goes by without catching strangers noticing my hair with amusement, old ladies tell me how much they love my hair and little kids point their fingers with smiles and sharing their discovery with their parents.

Being yourself can also be exhausting. I have to redye my hair every two weeks if I want to keep the blue colour that I like. And every 10 weeks I have to bleach my head all over to avoid the black hair to come back. I'm careful of getting into swimming pools, I prepare my own conditioner with dye in it and I daily put on coconut milk to keep my hair healthy. But I realise now that I know a lot more about my hair and how to take care of it than before, and knowledge is power. I'm always ready to give advice to others who would like to do it and it's a cool conversation topic.

Being yourself is a never ending process. Not only because I need to keep dying my hair, but because I don't know when I will change my mind about it. I'm a firm believer in change, in adapting and constantly evolving. And there should be no shame in trying new things in hopes to find what will stick: joining a gym, dying your hair, volunteering for a cause you care about, trying out a new layout of your room.

Being yourself is a ride that we should all get on.

Discuss

1. Why do you think it can be hard for people to be themselves?
2. Do you think society puts obstacles in the way of us being able to live our lives the way we want to?
3. Do you think there is a stigma attached to the clothes we wear and the style and/or colour of our hair?
4. Blogs allow us to comment freely on the experiences of others anonymously. What problems do you think can arise from this?
5. Reflect back on a time in your life when you changed your appearance. Maybe it was a haircut or a particular style of clothing you wore. Share your experience with the class.

Understand

1. According to Simon, what is his 'natural' hair colour?
2. **(a)** In what year did Simon move to Dublin?

   (b) How many years ago was that?
3. What sparked Simon's decision to dye his hair?
4. What happened after Simon's first attempt to dye his hair?
5. How did Simon feel after dying his hair blue?
6. What is Simon a firm believer in?

 Explore

1. Which of the words below do you think best describes Simon?
   - Inspirational
   - Honest
   - Original

   Explain your choice.
2. In your opinion, do you agree that 'being yourself is a never ending process'?
3. Do you have a particular item of clothing that you believe best represents you? Describe this item. How does wearing this garment make you feel?

 Create

1. Write a comment in response to this blog post.
2. 'Being yourself is a ride we should all get on.' Using this quote as a title, write an article for your school website encouraging students to be themselves.

In the film *Election*, student Tammy Metzler delivers the following monologue when running for student body president.

Election

Who cares about this stupid election? We all know it doesn't matter who gets elected president of Carver. Do you really think it's gonna change anything around here? Make one single person smarter? Or happier? Or nicer? The only person it does matter to is the one that gets elected. The same pathetic charade happens every year and everyone makes the same pathetic promises, just so they can put it on their transcripts to get into college. So vote for me! Because I don't even want to go to college. And I don't care. And as president, I won't do anything. The only promise I will make is that, if elected, I will immediately dismantle the student government, so that none of us will ever have to sit through one of these stupid assemblies again! Or don't vote for me! Who cares? Don't vote at all!

Discuss

1. Have you ever been involved in a school election?
2. What would you like to have an opportunity to vote on?
3. Do you agree with Tammy that voting does not make a difference?

Understand

1. What does Tammy say candidates do every year?
2. According to Tammy, why do students run for election?
3. What does Tammy say she will do if she is elected?

Explore

 1. Do you think Tammy's election speech is refreshing and clever or poorly researched? Give a reason for your answer.

 2. What tone can you identify in this monologue? Explain your answer.

 3. Choose two words to describe Tammy and give reasons for your choices.

4. If you were in the audience and you had the opportunity to ask Tammy one question, what would it be?

Create

 1. **(a)** Write a speech that you could deliver to an audience if you were to run for class captain in your school, in the space provided on pages 64–65 of your Portfolio.

 (b) Deliver your speech to your classmates, then fill out the checklist on page 65 of your Portfolio.

The following editorial by 14-year-old Miriam Gold explores the idea that teenagers should be allowed to have a say in general elections.

It's Time for Teens to Vote

At sixteen years old, Jack Andraka discovered an inexpensive method to test for pancreatic cancer. At just fifteen, Louis Braille invented the Braille writing system, allowing the blind to read and write. Additionally, Malala Yousafzai was seventeen when she won the Nobel Peace Prize for promoting women's education in Pakistan. These teens show themselves to be innovators and inspirers, their work rivaling the achievements of our most celebrated adults. However, even with the potential that every teen holds, they are denied a voice in who governs their own country. As a politically aware high school student, I should be allowed to vote at sixteen in the November 2016 election because my opinion is no less valid than the adults who vote.

Throughout history, restricted voting has been a way for the government to stifle the voices of those they did not want to hear. In 1870, blacks were finally given the right to vote; and in 1920, Congress gave voting rights to women. Finally, Americans understood that no matter what group someone belonged to, their right to vote should be protected — except one group, teens. Through unfair voting law, teens are told that the fundamental rights of all Americans do not apply to them.

Many who deny teens' rights to vote believe teens will make uninformed decisions that will hurt the country. Although many teens may seem not to care about voting now, this could easily be changed. An extremely effective way to increase voting interest is 'to inoculate [teens] with a significant dose of meaningful responsibility and authority' (Epstein, Robert, *Saving Our Children and Families From the Torment of Adolescence*, 2010). If students are given the responsibility of a vote that will affect their life, most will become more invested in electing the best candidate.

inoculate: vaccinate

Although teens are not extended the rights of adults, they are still burdened with the responsibilities. In many states, 'A child, defined as a person under age 18, can be tried as an adult if the child was age 14 or older at the time of the offense' (Ohio State Bar Association, 'How Are Juveniles Tried as Adults?', 2016). If our society believes teens can handle the burden of adult responsibility, why are they believed undeserving of adult rights?

Not only do teens deserve the right to vote, their votes would prove constructive to society. Research shows political involvement by teens to 'trickle up' to their parents, increasing voter turnout, and, 'Empirical evidence suggests that the earlier in life a voter casts their first ballot, the more likely they are to develop voting as a habit' (FairVote, 'Lower The Voting Age', 2016). Low voter turnout is only worsening, but teen voting could help turn this issue around because countless teenagers like myself would be proud to fill out the ballots deciding our country's future.

Focus on ... editorials

An **editorial** is a newspaper article expressing the editor's, newspaper's or magazine's opinion on a topical issue.

Editorials differ from news articles as news articles should neutrally present facts or report other people's opinions, whereas an editorial expresses the opinions of the author.

Discuss

1. Have there been there any Irish elections or referendums that you would have liked to have been able to vote in?
2. If you were given the right to vote now, would you vote?
3. What do you think the legal minimum age of voting should be?
4. Would having the right to vote change your life?

Understand

1. According to Miriam, how have teens shown themselves to be 'innovators and inspirers'?
2. In what year did Congress give voting rights to women in America?
3. According to Miriam, why are teens not given the right to vote?
4. What does Miriam suggest would be an effective way to increase voting interest among teens?

Explore

1. How do you know that this is an editorial and not a news article? Give reasons to support your answer.

2. Would you agree that this extract is a persuasive piece of writing? Use reference from the text to support your answer.

3. This editorial won a contest for young writers. Do you think this was worthy of winning? Give reasons for your answer.

Investigate

Use your research skills to find other interesting editorials to share with your class.

Create

1. Write an editorial on an issue that matters to you in the space provided on pages 66–67 of your Portfolio.

2. Organise a class debate on the following motion: *This house believes that the legal voting age should be reduced to 16.*

Leaving home

Growing up and becoming independent is an important part of life. Leaving home can be a difficult decision for one to make. We leave everything that we are familiar with, the people we love and the places we know. On the other hand, leaving home can be a significant milestone, as it demonstrates our independence.

In the following short story by James Joyce, Eveline decides to leave her home, but struggles with going when the time comes.

Eveline

She sat at the window watching the evening invade the avenue. Her head was leant against the window curtains and in her nostrils was the odour of dusty cretonne. She was tired.

Few people passed. The man out of the last house passed on his way home; she heard his footsteps clacking along the concrete pavement and afterwards crunching on the cinder path before the new red houses. One time there used to be a field there in which they used to play every evening with other people's children. Then a man from Belfast bought the field and built houses in it – not like their little brown houses but bright brick houses with shining roofs. The children of the avenue used to play together in that field – the Devines, the Waters, the Dunns, little Keogh the cripple, she and her brothers and sisters. Ernest, however, never played: he was too grown up. Her father used often to hunt them in out of the field with his blackthorn stick, but usually little Keogh used to keep *nix* and call out when he saw her father coming. Still they seemed to have been rather happy then. Her father was not so bad then; and besides, her mother was alive. That was a long time ago; she and her brothers and sisters were all grown up; her mother was dead. Tizzie Dunn was dead, too, and the Waters had gone back to England. Everything changes. Now she was going to go away like the others, to leave her home.

Home! She looked round the room, reviewing all its familiar objects which she had dusted once a week for so many years, wondering where on earth all the dust came from. Perhaps she would never see again those familiar objects from which she had never dreamt of being divided. And yet during all those years she had never found out the name of the priest whose yellowing photograph hung on the wall above the broken harmonium beside the coloured print of the promises made to Blessed Margaret Mary Alacoque. He had been a school friend of her father. Whenever he showed the photograph to a visitor, her father used to pass it with a casual word:

'He is in Melbourne now.'

cretonne:
heavy cotton material

cripple:
a term formerly used to describe people with a physical disability. This term is no longer acceptable

nix:
a signal or warning given when someone is approaching

harmonium:
type of organ

She had consented to go away, to leave her home. Was that wise? She tried to weigh each side of the question. In her home anyway she had shelter and food; she had those whom she had known all her life about her. Of course she had to work hard, both in the house and at business. What would they say of her in the Stores when they found out that she had run away with a fellow? Say she was a fool, perhaps, and her place would be filled up by advertisement. Miss Gavan would be glad. She had always had an edge on her, especially whenever there were people listening.

'Miss Hill, don't you see these ladies are waiting?'

'Look lively, Miss Hill, please.'

She would not cry many tears at leaving the Stores.

But in her new home, in a distant unknown country, it would not be like that. Then she would be married – she, Eveline. People would treat her with respect then. She would not be treated as her mother had been. Even now, though she was over nineteen, she sometimes felt herself in danger of her father's violence. She knew it was that that had given her the palpitations. When they were growing up he had never gone for her, like he used to go for Harry and Ernest, because she was a girl, but latterly he had begun to threaten her and say what he would do to her only for her dead mother's sake. And now she had nobody to protect her. Ernest was dead and Harry, who was in the church-decorating business, was nearly always down somewhere in the country. Besides, the invariable squabble for money on Saturday nights had begun to weary her unspeakably. She always gave her entire wages – seven shillings – and Harry always sent up what he could, but the trouble was to get any money from her father. He said she used to squander the money, that she had no head, that he wasn't going to give her his hard-earned money to throw about the streets, and much more, for he was usually fairly bad of a Saturday night. In the end he would give her the money and ask her had she any intention of buying Sunday's dinner. Then she had to rush out as quickly as she could and do her marketing, holding her black leather purse tightly in her hand as she elbowed her way through the crowds and returning home late under her load of provisions. She had hard work to keep the house together and to see that the two young children who had been left to her charge went to school regularly and got their meals regularly. It was hard work – a hard life – but now that she was about to leave it she did not find it a wholly undesirable life.

She was about to explore another life with Frank. Frank was very kind, manly, open-hearted. She was to go away with him by the night-boat to be his wife and to live with him in Buenos Aires where he had a home waiting for her. How well she remembered the first time she had seen him; he was lodging in a house on the main road where she used to visit. It seemed a few weeks ago. He was standing at the gate, his peaked cap pushed back on his head and his hair tumbled forward over a face of bronze. Then they had come to know each other. He used to meet her outside the Stores every evening and see her home. He took her to see *The Bohemian Girl* and she felt elated as she sat in an unaccustomed part of the theatre with him. He was awfully fond of music and sang a little. People knew that they were courting and, when he sang about the lass that loves a sailor, she always felt pleasantly confused. He used to call her Poppens out of fun. First of all it had been an excitement for her to have a fellow and then she had begun to like him. He had tales of distant countries. He had started as a deck boy at a pound a month on a ship of the Allan Line going out to Canada. He told her the names of the ships he had been on and the names of the different services. He had sailed through the Straits of Magellan and he told her stories of the terrible Patagonians. He had fallen on his feet in Buenos Aires, he said, and had come over to the old country just for a holiday. Of course, her father had found out the affair and had forbidden her to have anything to say to him.

'I know these sailor chaps,' he said.

One day he had quarrelled with Frank and after that she had to meet her lover secretly.

palpitations: increased beating of the heart

The evening deepened in the avenue. The white of two letters in her lap grew indistinct. One was to Harry; the other was to her father. Ernest had been her favourite, but she liked Harry too. Her father was becoming old lately, she noticed; he would miss her. Sometimes he could be very nice. Not long before, when she had been laid up for a day, he had read her out a ghost story and made toast for her at the fire. Another day, when their mother was alive, they had all gone for a picnic to the Hill of Howth. She remembered her father putting on her mother's bonnet to make the children laugh.

Her time was running out but she continued to sit by the window, leaning her head against the window curtain, inhaling the odour of dusty cretonne. Down far in the avenue she could hear a street organ playing. She knew the air. Strange that it should come that very night to remind her of the promise to her mother, her promise to keep the home together as long as she could. She remembered the last night of her mother's illness; she was again in the close dark room at the other side of the hall and outside she heard a melancholy air of Italy. The organ-player had been ordered to go away and given sixpence. She remembered her father strutting back into the sickroom saying:

'Damned Italians! coming over here!'

As she mused the pitiful vision of her mother's life laid its spell on the very quick of her being – that life of commonplace sacrifices closing in final craziness. She trembled as she heard again her mother's voice saying constantly with foolish insistence:

'Derevaun Seraun! Derevaun Seraun!'

Derevaun Seraun: the end of pleasure is pain

She stood up in a sudden impulse of terror. Escape! She must escape! Frank would save her. He would give her life, perhaps love, too. But she wanted to live. Why should she be unhappy? She had a right to happiness. Frank would take her in his arms, fold her in his arms. He would save her.

She stood among the swaying crowd in the station at the North Wall. He held her hand and she knew that he was speaking to her, saying something about the passage over and over again. The station was full of soldiers with brown baggages. Through the wide doors of the sheds she caught a glimpse of the black mass of the boat, lying in beside the quay wall, with illumined portholes. She answered nothing. She felt her cheek pale and cold and, out of a maze of distress, she prayed to God to direct her, to show her what was her duty. The boat blew a long mournful whistle into the mist. If she went, tomorrow she would be on the sea with Frank, steaming towards Buenos Aires. Their passage had been booked. Could she still draw back after all he had done for her? Her distress awoke a nausea in her body and she kept moving her lips in silent fervent prayer.

fervent: passionate, intense

A bell clanged upon her heart. She felt him seize her hand:

'Come!'

All the seas of the world tumbled about her heart. He was drawing her into them: he would drown her. She gripped with both hands at the iron railing.

'Come!'

No! No! No! It was impossible. Her hands clutched the iron in frenzy. Amid the seas she sent a cry of anguish.

'Eveline! Evvy!'

He rushed beyond the barrier and called to her to follow. He was shouted at to go on but he still called to her. She set her white face to him, passive, like a helpless animal. Her eyes gave him no sign of love or farewell or recognition.

Discuss

1. Have you ever intended to go somewhere and at the last minute backed out of going?
2. Can you think of a time that you were away and felt homesick?

Understand

1. Who did Eveline used to play with in the field?
2. Where is Eveline going?
3. What nickname did Frank call Eveline?
4. Why did Eveline have to meet Frank secretly?
5. What promise did Eveline make to her mother?

Explore

 1. How does Joyce succeed in creating a sense of place in the opening paragraph?

 2. What kind of relationship do you think Eveline had with her father?

 3. In your opinion, which of the following words best describes Eveline?
   - Devoted
   - Caring
   - Romantic
   - Innocent

   Explain your choice.

4. In your opinion, why do you think Eveline decided not to go with Frank?
5. If you were transforming this short story into a short film, what could you do to make your audience aware of the inner conflict that Eveline is experiencing?

Create

1. Write the letter that Eveline wrote to Frank following on from this night, explaining what happened and why she didn't go with him.

 2. In this short story Eveline struggles with a difficult decision. Write a short story where the central character faces a difficult decision in the space provided on pages 68–69 of your Portfolio.

Relationships change as we grow up and become more independent. For parents, this can be a hard development to accept. The following poem focuses on the independence of a daughter from the point of view of her mother.

To a Daughter Leaving Home

By Linda Pastan

When I taught you
at eight to ride
a bicycle, loping along
beside you
as you wobbled away
on two round wheels,
my own mouth rounding
in surprise when you pulled
ahead down the curved
path of the park,
I kept waiting
for the thud
of your crash as I
sprinted to catch up,
while you grew
smaller, more breakable
with distance,
pumping, pumping
for your life, screaming
with laughter,
the hair flapping
behind you like a
handkerchief waving
Goodbye.

 **Flashback**   **Enjambment** is when a sentence or phrase runs from one line of poetry into the next.

 ## Discuss

1. Can you remember when you learned to ride a bike? Describe this experience.
2. At what stage in life do you think children start to become independent?
3. How do you think parents feel when their children become independent?

 ## Understand

1. How old was the daughter when her mother taught her to ride a bike?
2. What is the mother waiting for as her daughter cycles off?

 ## Explore

 1. Identify two poetic devices that are used in this poem and explain their effect.

2. In your opinion, why does the mother's mouth round in surprise when her daughter pulled ahead on the curved path?

3. Focus on the form of the poem on the page. Why do you think the poet shaped the poem in this way? What do you think this form represents?

 4. How effective do you think the ending of the poem is in capturing the message of this poem?

 5. 'The poem "To a Daughter Leaving Home" is about two milestones at once.'

Do you agree with this statement? Refer to the poem to support your answer.

 ## Create

1. Write the tweet that you imagine the mother would have written after her daughter has moved out of the family home.

 2. **(a)** In pairs, write the dialogue that you imagine took place between the daughter and her mother when she came back from having learned to ride her bike for the first time.

(b) Act out your dialogue for the class.

Falling in love

Falling in love can be a life-changing milestone. It can teach us a lot about caring for someone other than ourselves and gives us the opportunity to experience and explore new emotions.

Our love for someone can immortalise them long after they are gone. In the following poem, Shakespeare writes of his feelings for his beloved in an effort to keep the memory of his beloved's beauty alive forever.

Shall I Compare Thee

By William Shakespeare

Shall I compare thee to a summer's day?
Thou art more lovely and more temperate:
Rough winds do shake the darling buds of May,
And summer's lease hath all too short a date;
Sometime too hot the eye of heaven shines,
And often is his gold complexion dimm'd;
And every fair from fair sometime declines,
By chance or nature's changing course untrimm'd;
But thy eternal summer shall not fade,
Nor lose possession of that fair thou ow'st;
Nor shall death brag thou wander'st in his shade,
When in eternal lines to time thou grow'st:
     So long as men can breathe, or eyes can see,
     So long lives this, and this gives life to thee.

Focus on ... sonnets

A **sonnet** is a fourteen-line poem that has a specific rhythm and follows a formal rhyming scheme.

Shakespearean sonnets are written in iambic pentameter, which means that each line consists of ten syllables. A syllable is a unit of pronunciation with one vowel sound. This forms the entire word or part of the word. For example: 'aunt' has one syllable, 'grand-fath-er' has three syllables. In iambic pentameter every first syllable is stressed and every second syllable is unstressed. This creates a rhythm that sounds similar to a heartbeat:

da	dum	da	dum	da	dum	da	dum	da	dum
1	2	3	4	5	6	7	8	9	10
Shall	I	**comp**	are	**thee**	to	**a**	sum	**mer's**	day?

Read 'Shall I Compare Thee' aloud, and gently tap the rhythm as you read.

Shakespearean sonnets are divided into three quatrains (four lines of verse), and have a rhyming couplet at the end. The couplet is usually used to sum up the main ideas in the sonnet.

Understand

1. According to the speaker, why is summer not an adequate comparison for his beloved?
2. In your opinion, what is the 'eye of heaven'?
   (a) God   **(b)** The Sun   **(c)** The clouds
3. According to the speaker, what happens to eradicate the beauty of nature?
4. Why will the eternal beauty of the speaker's love never fade?
5. Number the 10 syllables in each line of the sonnet

 Explore

1. Shakespearean sonnets follow a specific rhyming scheme. Identify the rhyming scheme of a Shakespearean sonnet by writing out the rhyming scheme used in 'Shall I Compare Thee'. Does this rhyming scheme contribute to the mood of the sonnet?

 2. Which image do you think is most memorable in this sonnet? Explain your choice.

 3. Do you think this sonnet effectively captures the theme of love? Give a reason for your answer.

4. You have been asked to visually represent this sonnet. Describe the three images would you choose and explain your reasons for each choice.

 Create

 Swap your Portfolio with your partner and write a title for each other's sonnets in the space provided on page 70. When you have written titles for each other, swap your Portfolios back and write a sonnet based on the title that your partner has given you. You must conform to the rhyming scheme of the Shakespearean sonnet.

It can be difficult to capture the essence of a relationship or express the power of love. For this reason, poets sometimes rely on metaphors to portray love. In the following poem, Seamus Heaney conveys a loving relationship that has developed and strengthened.

Watch the following recording of Seamus Heaney introducing and reading 'Scaffolding':
https://youtu.be/fNYBwF7lKLA

Scaffolding
By Seamus Heaney

Masons, when they start upon a building,
Are careful to test out the scaffolding;

Make sure that planks won't slip at busy points,
Secure all ladders, tighten bolted joints.

And yet all this comes down when the job's done
Showing off walls of sure and solid stone.

So if, my dear, there sometimes seem to be
Old bridges breaking between you and me,

Never fear. We may let the scaffolds fall,
Confident that we have built our wall.

Flashback   **Metaphors** describe something as though it is something else.

 Understand

1. According to the poem, what comes down when the job is done?
2. Summarise what this poem is about in your own words.

 Explore

1. Who do you think this poem was written for?
2. What has scaffolding got to do with love?
3. Why does the speaker reassure his beloved that 'we may let the scaffolds fall'?
4. In the recording, what do you think Heaney meant when he described his poem as 'confident and innocent'?

 Create

Think of a suitable metaphor to convey love. Write a 10-line poem that includes this metaphor. Follow the rhyming scheme Heaney uses in 'Scaffolding'.

Documentaries

A documentary is a film, television or radio programme that provides a factual report on a particular subject.

Features	Language
◖ Interviews ◖ Expert opinion ◖ Voiceover ◖ Statistics ◖ Images ◖ Footage (audio or visual) ◖ Text on the screen ◖ Fly-on-the-wall footage	◖ Informative ◖ Language can be formal or informal and conversational, depending on the topic

The relics of St Valentine, some of his bones and a vial tinged with his blood, are kept in a small casket under a shrine in Whitefriar Street Church, a beautiful old church off a busy Dublin city street. On the shrine lies a simple, soft cover notebook, where locals and tourists write their prayers to St Valentine.

People write to St Valentine about what they long for, asking him to help, telling him their secret hopes or fears. It's an incredibly compelling document. Discovering it is almost like finding someone's diary – except it's public.

Listen to the following radio documentary about the relics of St Valentine, produced by comedian Maeve Higgins and aired on RTÉ Radio 1.

http://www.rte.ie/radio1/doconone/2013/1018/647545-documentary-podcast-valentines-bones-maeve-higgins-whitefriar-church/

 Understand

1. What evidence is there to suggest that Maeve Higgins is a comedian?
2. What does it say on the heavy cloth covering the statue?
3. What abbreviation does Jacinta use when talking about St Valentine?
4. What is inside the sturdy treasure chest?
5. How did Maeve contact visitors and people who had written in the book?
6. **(a)** When did Pope Gregory donate these relics?
   (b) How many years ago was this?
7. What is the role of Father Brian McKay?
8. Describe the types of messages that people write in the book.
9. What features of a documentary can you identify in this piece?
10. Aside from music, what other sound effects do you hear in this documentary?

Explore

1. What impression do you form of Maeve Higgins from the documentary?

2. Why do you think it helped Alan to write in the book?

3. Why do you think people write in the book?

4. Which word do you think best describes Father Brian McKay? Explain your answer.
   - Respectful
   - Considerate
   - Caring

5. Do you think those who write in the book would mind others reading their letters?

6. Would you ever consider writing in the book? Give a reason for your answer.

Investigate

1. Use your research skills to find out more information about St Valentine and share your findings with the class.

2. The speakers in this documentary share different experiences of love and Valentine's Day. Work in groups to find out what your classmates think about St Valentine's Day. You may gather information using surveys, interviews or questionnaires. Present your findings to the class in the form of a digital presentation.

Create

1. Maeve's final message in the documentary is about how brave it is to look for love, knowing that the loss one feels when it is gone is so painful. Write a short piece, in any form you choose (poem, song, diary, letter, article, etc.) about how loving is such an important part of living.

2. Using the information that you learned from your research about St Valentine, work in groups to create a short documentary. Record your documentary, using appropriate sound effects.

The following poem explores the many emotions that love can stir up, and how the people we love can have a lasting impact on our lives.

Valentine

By Carol Ann Duffy

Not a red rose or a satin heart.

I give you an onion.
It is a moon wrapped in brown paper.
It promises light
like the careful undressing of love.

Here.
It will blind you with tears
like a lover.
It will make your reflection
a wobbling photo of grief.

I am trying to be truthful.

Not a cute card or a kissogram.

I give you an onion.
Its fierce kiss will stay on your lips,
possessive and faithful
as we are,
for as long as we are.

Take it.
Its platinum loops shrink to a wedding ring,
if you like.
Lethal.
Its scent will cling to your fingers,
cling to your knife.

A **symbol** is something that represents another thing.

Discuss

1. What symbols do you associate with Valentine's Day?
2. Do you think Valentine's Day is an important occasion?

Understand

1. What gift does the speaker give to her Valentine?
2. What does the poet say this gift will do to the receiver?
3. What does the speaker say she is trying to be?
4. What does the poet say that she could have given to her lover instead?
5. What will the scent of this gift cling to?
6. This poem appeals to some of the senses. Identify one descriptive detail relating to each of the following senses:
   ◖ smell   ◖ sight   ◖ touch.

Explore

1. What kind of relationship do you think the speaker has with the person they are addressing? Give reasons for your answer.
2. The onion is described as having a 'fierce kiss'.
   (a) What poetic device is used here?
   (b) What do you think this means?
3. This poem can be described as an extended metaphor. What is the metaphor in this poem?
4. Compare this poem to 'Scaffolding' on page 257. Which metaphor do you think is stronger at conveying love?
5. How would you feel if someone sent you this poem on Valentine's Day?
6. Think of a relationship that is important in your life. Write down as many words as you can to describe the relationship (e.g. reliable, strong, complicated, caring). What object could you use to describe the way you feel about this person?
7. Write a personal response to this poem. Take into account the effect that the poetic devices have on the poem, the impact that the sentiment in the poem has on you and what you like or dislike about the poem.

Create

Over one billion cards are exchanged on St Valentine's Day, making it the most popular card-exchanging holiday after Christmas. Organise a class debate on the following motion: *This house believes that Valentine's Day has become too commercial.*

Enduring loss

Sadly, loss is a natural part of life and is something that we will all experience at some stage.

When a relationship breaks down it can be painful and have upsetting consequences for those involved. When we are hurt by someone we love, it can take time to feel ready to love and trust again.

The following song was written by Paul Simon and explores the ways people can cut themselves off after suffering a loss.

I Am a Rock

A winter's day
In a deep and dark December
I am alone
Gazing from my window
To the streets below
On a freshly fallen, silent shroud of snow

I am a rock
I am an island

I've built walls
A fortress, steep and mighty
That none may penetrate
I have no need of friendship
Friendship causes pain
It's laughter and it's loving I disdain

I am a rock
I am an island

Don't talk of love
Well, I've heard the word before
It's sleeping in my memory
And I won't disturb the slumber
Of feelings that have died
If I never loved, I never would have cried

I am a rock
I am an island

I have my books
And my poetry to protect me
I am shielded in my armor
Hiding in my room
Safe within my womb
I touch no one and no one touches me

I am a rock
I am an island

And a rock feels no pain
And an island never cries

Discuss

1. Can you think of the last time that you were alone?
2. How do you imagine life would be if you didn't have your friends?
3. Do you think that books could be a substitute for friendship?

Understand

1. What time of year is the song set in?
2. How does the speaker cut himself off from others?
3. What words does the speaker use to describe himself?
4. How does the speaker feel about love?

Explore

1. Why do you think the speaker does not want any form of friendship?
2. 'If I never loved, I never would have cried.' Do you agree with this sentiment?

Create

1. Write a blog entry about how we can help people who feel isolated and alone in the space provided on page 71 of your Portfolio.

2. Work in groups of four (two proposition and two opposition) to debate the following motion: *This house believes that alone time is essential for everyone.*
   Come up with three separate points to support your argument.

Letters are often mementos or keepsakes to remind us of loved ones who have passed away. We treasure these letters when our loved one is no longer with us.

Finding a Box of Family Letters

By Dana Gioia

The dead say little in their letters
they haven't said before.
We find no secrets, and yet
how different every sentence sounds
heard across the years.

My father breaks my heart
simply by being so young and handsome.
He's half my age, with jet-black hair.
Look at him in his navy uniform
grinning beside his dive-bomber.

Come back, Dad! I want to shout.
He says he misses all of us
(though I haven't yet been born).
He writes from places I never knew he saw,
and everyone he mentions now is dead.

There is a large, long photograph
curled like a diploma—a banquet sixty years ago.
My parents sit uncomfortably
among tables of dark-suited strangers.
The mildewed paper reeks of regret.

I wonder what song the band was playing,
just out of frame, as the photographer
arranged your smiles. A waltz? A foxtrot?
Get out there on the floor and dance!
You don't have forever.

What does it cost to send a postcard
to the underworld? I'll buy
a penny stamp from World War II
and mail it downtown at the old post office
just as the courthouse clock strikes twelve.

Surely the ghost of some postal worker
still makes his nightly rounds, his routine
too tedious for him to notice when it ended.
He works so slowly he moves back in time
carrying our dead letters to their lost addresses.

It's silly to get sentimental.
The dead have moved on. So should we.
But isn't it equally simpleminded to miss
the special expertise of the departed
in clarifying our long-term plans?

They never let us forget that the line
between them and us is only temporary.
Get out there and dance! the letters shout
adding, *Love always. Can't wait to get home!*
And soon we will be. *See you there.*

Discuss

Do you have any keepsakes from a loved one that you treasure?

Understand

1. What happened to the speaker's father?
2. What does the speaker want to shout to his father?
3. In the fourth stanza the speaker describes a photograph. Describe this photograph in your own words.
4. Why does the speaker think it is silly to be sentimental?
5. Who is the speaker talking to in the final line?

Explore

1. Choose your favourite image from the poem and explain why you like it.
2. 'They never let us forget that the line / between them and us is only temporary.' Explain what this line means to you.

Create

Write a letter to a loved one in which you share three things you appreciate about them. Give this letter to your loved one to have as a keepsake.

In the following speech from William Shakespeare's *Julius Caesar*, Brutus, alone in his garden, reveals that he must kill Caesar. He feels that Caesar is abusing his power and has ascended too quickly. This speech reveals his thoughts and emotions.

Julius Caesar

BRUTUS   It must be by his death: and for my part,
I know no personal cause to spurn at him,
But for the general. He would be crown'd:
How that might change his nature, there's the question.
It is the bright day that brings forth the adder;
And that craves wary walking. Crown him? – that; –
And then, I grant, we put a sting in him,
That at his will he may do danger with.
The abuse of greatness is, when it disjoins
Remorse from power: and, to speak truth of Caesar,
I have not known when his affections sway'd
More than his reason. But 'tis a common proof,
That lowliness is young ambition's ladder,
Whereto the climber-upward turns his face;
But when he once attains the upmost round.
He then unto the ladder turns his back,
Looks in the clouds, scorning the base degrees
By which he did ascend. So Caesar may.
Then, lest he may, prevent. And, since the quarrel
Will bear no colour for the thing he is,
Fashion it thus; that what he is, augmented,
Would run to these and these extremities:
And therefore think him as a serpent's egg –
Which, hatched, would, as his kind, grow mischievous,
And kill him in the shell.

adder:
snake

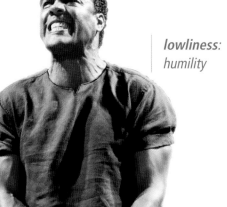

lowliness:
humility

Focus on ... **soliloquies**

A **soliloquy** is a speech in which a character speaks their thoughts aloud when alone or without addressing anyone.

The word 'soliloquy' comes from the Latin *solus* (alone) and *loqui* (speak). In drama, soliloquies give the audience insight into the thoughts and feelings of a character. The character may not be alone on stage, but the other characters will not be able to hear the soliloquy as it is used to represent the speaker's inner thoughts.

Discuss

1. What type of revelations do you imagine could come from a soliloquy?
2. Why do you think it is important that the other players on the stage are unable to hear a soliloquy?
3. If Shakespeare had not included soliloquies in his plays, do you think this would change our understanding of them?
4. Can you think of other examples of soliloquies in plays that you have read or watched? What did this soliloquy reveal to the audience?

Understand

1. What reason does Brutus give for why he must kill Caesar?
2. According to Brutus, why would you need to be careful walking in the daytime?
3. What does Brutus say could happen to Caesar if they crown him?
4. According to Brutus, what can happen to young men when they reach the top of the ladder?
5. At the end of the soliloquy, what does Brutus compare Caesar to and how does he say this should be dealt with?

Explore

1. What does this soliloquy reveal about the character of Brutus?
2. If you were playing Brutus, what tone would you use when speaking these words? Would your tone change at all throughout the soliloquy? Explain your answer.
3. Choose a play that you have studied in which a soliloquy exposed the private thoughts of a character.
   (a) Name the play, the playwright and the character.
   (b) What private thoughts does the character reveal in their soliloquy?
   (c) Explain how the revelations in this soliloquy added to your enjoyment of the play.

Investigate

1. Research a famous Shakespearean soliloquy.

   (a) Deliver three lines from the soliloquy to the rest of the class.

   (b) Add stage directions to this soliloquy in order to bring it to life.

   (c) Describe the costume you would wear if you were playing this character, and explain your choice.

Create

1. (a) In James Joyce's short story 'Eveline' (pages 249–251), Eveline struggles with a dilemma and Joyce succeeds in describing her state of mind. You have been asked to transform this story into a play. Write the soliloquy that you think would best capture Eveline's feelings as she struggles with the dilemma of whether to stay or go, in the space provided on page 72 of your Portfolio.

   (b) Practise performing your soliloquy. Consider:

   ◖ tone of voice

   ◖ movement

   ◖ facial expressions.

   (c) Perform your soliloquy to the class.

Losing a loved one is always a difficult experience, and people are often unsure as to how they can comfort those in mourning.

In the following extract from her memoir *Shop Girl*, famous retail consultant and broadcaster Mary Portas reflects on the experience of losing her mother.

Shop Girl

Condolences

'Ach, she was a saint your mother and no doubt about it,' the elderly Irish woman says, as we stand in the street. 'To think that she was right as rain one day and then gone. It's past thinking about. A woman like that. Five children too. She was a saint so she was.'

I stare at the woman, trying to get away, but she won't stop talking.

'I just couldn't believe it when I heard the news. "Not Theresa Newton," I said. It's a terrible thing. And her only a young woman. Tragic. Just tragic.'

Death, like birth, is a universal truth. But where one is celebrated, it felt to me that the other was often met with either too much talking or painful silence. I understood why my classmates didn't say much when I got back to school after the summer holidays. They simply gathered me up, carried me with them and I was thankful that they were there each day. School was something to cling to.

The only person in St Joan's who really talked to me about what had happened was Sister St James, who still came back occasionally and called me in to see her when the autumn term of my final A-level year started.

'I'm so terribly sorry about your mother, Mary,' she said gently. 'Where you're a nun, people often think that you have made the greatest sacrifice by giving your life to God. But the most important thing anyone can do is to bring children into the world and raise a family. Your mother brought up five so that means she did the biggest job anyone can.'

A tear had slipped down Sister St James's face as she looked at me and I'd stared wordlessly back at her.

There were other people who reached out too. Aunty Cathy, Ruth, Jean, Don, Sadie, Harry and Sheila dropped in whenever they could, arriving with meals and cakes as they bustled around making pots of tea and asking how we were or trying to get Dad to talk. But there were times when I almost wished they wouldn't come, moments when I saw grief etched so sharply on their faces that I wasn't sure I could face dealing with their loss as well as ours. I didn't want them to see us struggling, to know how hard we were finding it to cope.

Discuss

1. When you are going through a tough time, do you prefer to be left alone or to have people around you supporting you?

2. What do you think are the most appropriate things for people to do when trying to sympathise with someone suffering from grief?

 Understand

1. How many children did Theresa Newton have?

2. **(a)** Who was the only person at St Joan's to talk to Mary about what had happened?

   (b) What did this person say to Mary to comfort her?

3. What did others do to help comfort Mary and her family?

4. Why did Mary wish at times that other people would not call?

5. What features of a typical memoir to you recognise in this piece?

 Explore

1. What age do you imagine Mary to have been when her mother died? Use evidence from the extract to support your answer.

2. What do you think the author means when she says that death is 'often met with either too much talking or painful silence'?

3. Why do you think Mary's classmates didn't say much when she came to back to school?

 Create

Imagine you are Mary's friend. Write the text of what you would say to Mary to offer her the hope she needs during this time.

It is important to enjoy the small things and celebrate life as much as possible. This next poem centres on the theme of loss, but it is about celebrating life and not allowing death to be the end of love.

Death Is Nothing At All

By Henry Scott Holland

Death is nothing at all.
I have only slipped away to the next room.
I am I and you are you.
Whatever we were to each other,
That, we still are.

Call me by my old familiar name.
Speak to me in the easy way
which you always used.
Put no difference into your tone.
Wear no forced air of solemnity or sorrow.

Laugh as we always laughed
at the little jokes we enjoyed together.
Play, smile, think of me. Pray for me.
Let my name be ever the household word
that it always was.
Let it be spoken without effect.
Without the trace of a shadow on it.

Life means all that it ever meant.
It is the same that it ever was.
There is absolute unbroken continuity.
Why should I be out of mind
because I am out of sight?

I am but waiting for you.
For an interval.
Somewhere. Very near.
Just around the corner.

All is well.

Discuss

1. What symbols do you associate with death?
2. Do you agree that a funeral can be a celebration of life as opposed to a mourning of death?

Understand

1. Where does the speaker say they have gone?
2. What does the speaker urge their loved ones to do now that they are gone?
3. How does the speaker want their name to be treated?
4. What is the speaker waiting for?

Explore

1. In your opinion, what is tone of the speaker in this poem? Support your answer with reference to the poem.

2. This poem deals with the theme of death. Would you agree that the poem considers death in a positive light? Give reasons for your answer.

Create

You want to comfort a friend after the passing of a loved one. Write a list of three or four consoling ideas that you could relay to your friend to help them in their time of loss.

Losing a loved one is always hard. Coming to terms with the loss through grief is a part of life. At this difficult time, we might ask ourselves what the person we have lost would say. The following poem is written from the perspective of one who has passed away and it gives some comforting advice.

Do Not Stand at My Grave and Weep

By Mary Elizabeth Frye

Do not stand at my grave and weep,
I am not there. I do not sleep.
I am in a thousand winds that blow.
I am the softly falling snow.
I am the gentle showers of rain.
I am the fields of ripening grain.
I am in the morning hush,
I am in the graceful rush
Of beautiful birds in circling flight,
I am the starshine of the night
I am in the flowers that bloom,
I am in a quiet room.
I am in the birds that sing,
I am in each lovely thing.
Do not stand at my grave and cry,
I am not there. I do not die.

Discuss

1. What would you like to be able to say to comfort the people you leave behind after you pass away?
2. Do you think a funeral should be a celebration of life, an occasion to mourn or both?

 Understand

1. Why does the speaker tell us not to stand at their grave?
2. What does the speaker tell us that they are now?

 Explore

1. **(a)** How many times can you count the personal pronoun 'I' in this poem?

   (b) Do you think this repetition is effective? Give reasons for your answer.

2. **(a)** Identify the rhyming scheme in this poem.

   (b) What contribution do you think this rhyming scheme makes to the poem?

3. Would you agree that this is a comforting poem for someone who has lost a loved one?

4. What similarities do you notice between 'Do Not Stand at My Grave and Weep' and 'Death Is Nothing At All' (page 271)?

 Investigate

In small groups, research poems that deal with the theme of death. Find a poem that you consider to portray death in a comforting and consoling manner. Find a poem that you think portrays death as dark and final. Share your poems with the class.

The following letter is an extract from *Refugee Boy* by Benjamin Zephaniah. Alem is a refugee in Britain and receives news from his father in Ethiopia during the Eritrean-Ethiopian War.

Refugee Boy

My dearest son,

I do hope this letter finds you soon and that you are as well as can be. War is such a terrible thing, my son, I hope you never witness it again. Darkness is upon our land; it seems that every man that is alive is limping and that there are bloodstains on the dresses of all our women. Today I found the arm of a man lying at the side of a street. No body, just one arm. And I found myself asking trivial questions like, 'Is this an Ethiopian or an Eritrean arm?' Could you believe it? I was asking this question, I, the great Pan-Africanist. War is eating away at our souls, young man, it is terrible.

Sadly I must tell you that I have bad news. From the day I returned here I have been searching but I cannot find your mother. She left your auntie's house in Asmara to go visit your grandmother in Badme. Some people tell me she has been seen in Ethiopia, some say she is in Eritrea, but I have tried everywhere I can think of and I can't find her. When I came back I found that your auntie's house had been looted and burnt but your auntie got out in time. She is with your grandmother now. It has been very hard for me. I have hardly slept since I came back here. I did not want to give you such news but what can I do? You must know the truth, son. I can't find your mother. I ask myself, what kind of a place do I live in if I can't find your mother, my wife and our love? But I can casually find the arm of someone I don't know just lying in the streets.

The organisation of EAST has fallen apart and now there is not a single organisation working for peace in the region. It seems that our people are so busy dealing with war that there is no time to deal in peace. Our Eritrean office has been raided and our Ethiopian office has been raided too. It is so sad that our only surviving branch is in London.

I hope you understand why we had to leave you in England for a while. I have so much work to do, and I will not stop until I find your mother. Be strong, young man. Learn more English and remember to love your neighbour. I will write you another letter soon.

Your loving father

Pan Africanist: *part of a worldwide movement aiming to encourage and motivate the solidarity of all people of African descent.*

Understand

1. How does Alem's father describe the aftermath of the war in the opening paragraph of the letter?
2. What happened to Alem's auntie's house?
3. What advice does Alem's father offer him?
4. How does Alem's father sign off the letter?
5. What features of a letter are missing in the extract?

 Explore

 1. How would you describe the relationship between Alem and his father? Explain your answer.

 2. How likely does it seem that they will achieve peace in this region? Give reasons for your answer.

3. In your opinion, do you think Alem's father was right to deliver this news to his son through a letter?

 Investigate

 Research information about the war that took place between Ethiopia and Eritrea. Make a list of six pieces of information that you discovered about this war. Share your list with the class and add any new information that you learn from the lists other groups in your class have made.

 Create

Write the letter that Alem might have written in response to his father's letter.

Moving on

We all have times in our life when we struggle with challenges. During these tough times it is the love and support from those who love us that gives us the strength and encouragement we need to keep going.

The following song, written by Paul Simon, is about providing comfort to someone in a time of need.

Bridge Over Troubled Water

When you're weary, feeling small
When tears are in your eyes, I will dry them all
I'm on your side, oh, when times get rough, and friends just can't be found

Like a bridge over troubled water, I will lay me down
Like a bridge over troubled water, I will lay me down

When you're down and out, when you're on the street
When evening falls so hard, I will comfort you
I'll take your part, oh, when darkness comes, and pain is all around

Like a bridge over troubled water, I will lay me down
Like a bridge over troubled water, I will lay me down

Sail on silver girl, sail on by
Your time has come to shine, and all your dreams will run their way
See how they shine, oh, if you need a friend, I'm sailing right behind

Like a bridge over troubled water, I will lay me down
Like a bridge over troubled water, I will lay me down

Discuss

1. What kind of music would you expect to accompany these lyrics?
2. What is the purpose of a bridge?
3. Can you think of a time in your life when you needed comfort?
4. What advice would you offer to someone who needs emotional support?

 Understand

1. In your own words, describe three things that the speaker promises to do.
2. **(a)** Explain what the speaker means when he says 'Like a bridge over troubled water, I will lay me down'?
   (b) What poetic device is this?

 Explore

1. **(a)** Compare and contrast the message in this song and the message in 'I Am a Rock' (page 262). How do the speakers' experiences of love and relationships differ?

 (b) Choose a line from either song and explain why it stands out to you.

   (c) If you were creating a presentation to accompany one of these songs, what images would you include in order to capture the meaning of the song? Describe three images you would choose and explain your choice.

 Create

Some believe that 'it is better to have loved and lost than to never have loved at all'. Write a blog post describing your view of relationships.

The following poem traces different milestones within a relationship, from the first meeting through its development and breakdown and eventually to both parties moving on.

The Thickness of Ice

By Liz Loxley

At first we'll meet as friends
(Though secretly I'll be hoping
We'll become much more
And hoping that you're hoping that too).

At first we'll be like skaters
Testing the thickness of ice
(With each meeting
We'll skate nearer the centre of the lake).

Later we will become less anxious to impress
Less eager than the skater going for gold.
(The triple jumps and spins
Will become an old routine:
We will become content with simple movements).

Later we will not notice the steady thaw,
The creeping cracks will be ignored.
(And one day when the ice gives way
We will scramble to save ourselves
And not each other).

Last of all we'll meet as acquaintances
(Though secretly we'll be enemies,
Hurt by missing out on a medal,
Jealous of new partners).

Last of all we'll be like children
Having learnt the thinness of ice,
(Though secretly perhaps, we may be hoping,
To break the ice between us
And maybe meet again as friends).

Understand

1. What is the speaker hoping for in the first stanza?
2. What do the couple test in the second stanza?
3. What does the skater going for gold attempt to do?
4. What does the speaker say that they will become content with?
5. What will the couple begin to notice?
6. What does the speaker hope for at the end of the poem?

 Explore

 1. In your opinion, does the poem effectively capture a loving relationship? Explain your answer.
2. What do the 'creeping cracks' in the fourth stanza represent, in your opinion?
 3. Do you think the metaphor of ice-skating works well in this poem? Give two reasons for your answer.
4. Can you recognise any other poetic devices in this poem?
   (a) Give an example of one other device the poet uses.
   (b) How does this device contribute to the overall poem?
5. '"The Thickness of Ice" is a hopeful poem about a failed relationship.'

   Do you agree or disagree with this statement? Explain your answer.

 Create

1. The poem is divided into three separate sections: 'At first', 'Later' and 'Last of all'. Imagine you are the poet. Write three tweets summarising how the poet felt at each stage. Remember, a tweet can be no longer than 280 characters.
 2. In pairs, think of another metaphor that could be used to describe a broken relationship. Then work together to write one verse of a poem using the metaphor you have created.

Reviewing mapping milestones

Reflect and review

1. Look back at the images at the start of this unit on page 233. In your opinion, do any of the images fail to capture what this unit is about?
2. Think of some alternative images that could be used to represent milestones.
3. Why do you think writers choose to write about love and loss? Give 3–4 points.
4. Fill in the unit review on pages 73–74 of your Portfolio.

Language skills

Write out the following sentences in your copy, inserting 'its' or 'it's' as needed.

1. Hold the horse steady while I jump on _____ back.
2. I'm only going to go if _____ not raining.
3. How many times do I have to tell you, _____ her jacket.
4. The cat is in _____ bed.

Oral assessment

'Sometimes a poem about love can be more powerful than actions of love.' Find a love poem that you think captures the theme of love. Present this poem to your class and explain why you chose this poem. What poetic features are evident? Are there any strong images?

Written assessment

1. (a) Write an editorial for a school magazine in which you discuss ideas on how to overcome the challenges and pressures of teen life in the space provided on pages 75–76 of your Portfolio.

   (b) Redraft your editorial in the space provided on pages 120–121 of your Portfolio.

Exam skills

1. Think of a moment in a novel or a play you have studied that you regard as an important milestone for a character.

   (a) Name the novel or play, the author or playwright and the character.
   (b) Describe the moment that you regard as an important milestone for this character.
   (c) Explain why this milestone was important to the development of the plot.

   Write your answer in the space provided on pages 141–142 of your Portfolio.

Theme 7
Let Freedom Ring

What is freedom?

Freedom is living without being imprisoned or enslaved. When a person is free, they can act, think and speak as they choose.

Why study this theme?

Freedom is something that many of us take for granted, yet throughout history and in the world today some people do not know what it means to be truly free. Studying this theme will help you to value the freedoms you enjoy and recognise the importance of freedom for all.

Learning intentions

- Learn about different types of freedom.
- Assess situations where freedom is denied.

Writing With Purpose
- Learn about and write blurbs.

Poetry and Song
- Look at a selection of poems and songs that celebrate freedom.
- Learn about slavery both in the past and today.

Fiction
- Analyse extracts from three novels that relate to the theme of freedom.

Stage and Screen
- Look at the steps a character takes to feel free in a Shakespearean play.
- Read an inspiring speech against oppression in a film script.

Media and Advertising
- Examine images that portray the horrors of slavery.
- Read articles on the topic of freedom.

Language Skills
- Learn about prefixes and suffixes.

 Discuss

1. In pairs, discuss which of the images above show **(a)** someone enjoying their freedom and **(b)** someone whose freedom is denied.

2. What image would you add to the selection representing freedom above?

 Create

 Write your own definition of 'freedom' in the space provided on page 81 of your Portfolio, by completing the sentence 'Freedom is …'. You will return to this definition later on.

Valuing freedom

It is important to value the freedom you enjoy. Maybe you like to go out with your friends, make decisions for yourself and express your opinions. In order to do all of these things, you must be free. As you will see throughout this unit, there are many people in the world who have been denied such freedom.

Watch the music video for the song 'Freedom' by Pharell Williams and make a note of all of the images shown that are associated with freedom or a lack of freedom.

 https://youtu.be/LlY90lG_Fuw

Freedom!

Hold on to me

Don't let me go

Who cares what they see

Who cares what they know?

Your first name is Free

Last name is Dom

We choose to believe

In where we're from

Man's red flower

It's in every living thing

Mind, use your power

Spirit, use your wings

Freedom!

Freedom!

Freedom!

Freedom

Freedom

Freedom

Hold on to me

Don't let me go

Cheetahs need to eat

Run, antelope

Your first name is King

Last name is Dom

Cause you still believe

In everyone

When a baby first breathes

When night sees sunrise

When the whale hunts in the sea

When man recognizes

Freedom!

Freedom!

Freedom!

Freedom

Freedom

Breathe in

We are from heat

The electric one

Does it shock you to see

He left us the sun?

Atoms in the air

Organisms in the sea

The son and yes, man

Are made of the same things

Freedom!

Freedom!

Freedom!

Freedom

Freedom

Freedom

Freedom

Freedom

Discuss

In pairs, discuss the images in the music video for the song 'Freedom'.

1. What images stand out to you both?
2. What do you associate with the images you have chosen?
3. How are the images associated with freedom or a lack of freedom?
4. Choose the lyrics that stand out most. Compare your choices.

Understand

1. Describe the rhythm of the song.
2. Choose one example of the freedom of the natural world in the song's lyrics.
3. Explain your understanding of the following lines:
   ◖ 'Mind, use your power'
   ◖ 'Spirit, use your wings'

Explore

1. Reflect on the image that most stands out to you in the music video or song lyrics.

(a) Write a description of the image in the space provided on page 77 your Portfolio.

(b) Form groups of four to discuss your chosen images. Use the ranking ladder provided on page 77 of your Portfolio. Each person should write about their favourite image in the spaces provided in each corner of the ranking ladder. As a group, you should decide which three images are most relevant to the theme of freedom. List these in the ladder located in the centre of the page.

2. This song was included on the soundtrack to the film *Despicable Me 3*.
   (a) Name another film that this song could be used in.
   (b) Explain how the theme of this song is relevant to the plot of your chosen film.

Slavery and racial oppression

Slavery is the practice of people owning other people. Slaves have their freedom taken away and are forced to labour without payment. From the fifteenth century, most people who were enslaved were African or of African descent. Although slavery was abolished, many people continue to suffer from oppression due to their race, and an estimated 40.3 million people are still victims of modern slavery around the world.

Slavery was practised throughout the American colonies in the seventeenth, eighteenth and nineteenth centuries. Enslaved people were forced to toil without payment and in dreadful conditions. Their lives were stolen, their children were taken away and they lived in fear and without hope.

The images below depict scenes associated with slavery in America, before its abolition in 1865.

Discuss

Work in pairs to examine the images, using the discussion points below.

◖ Slaves lived in fear.

◖ White slave owners had all the power.

Understand

1. Describe what is happening in image A.
2. How do you think the man in the water feels in image B?
3. Choose one word to describe the atmosphere you imagine in image C. Explain your choice.

Investigate

Work in small groups to learn about slavery in America before 1865. You should visit your local or school library to source information. Use your skills to carry out secure internet searches. Share three interesting facts with the class when you have finished.

Create

1. Write a short story based on the events in one of the images on page 286.
2. **(a)** You are speaking at a rally to abolish slavery in 1864. Write the speech that you will deliver. Choose one of the images on page 286 to accompany your speech, and refer to this image in your speech.

   (b) Deliver your speech to your classmates.

In the following poem, the speaker describes the terrible suffering endured by slaves throughout history.

Form groups of four to read the poem aloud. Each member of the group should read two stanzas.

Bury Me in a Free Land
By Frances Ellen Watkins Harper

You may make my grave wherever you will,
In a lowly vale, or a lofty hill;
You may make it among earth's humblest graves,
But not in a land where men are slaves.

I could not sleep if around my grave
I heard the steps of a trembling slave;
His shadow above my silent tomb
Would make it a place of fearful gloom.

I could not rest if I heard the tread
Of a coffle gang to the shambles led,
And the mother's shriek of wild despair
Rise like a curse on the trembling air.

I could not rest if I heard the lash
Drinking her blood at each fearful gash,
And I saw her babes torn from her breast
Like trembling doves from their parent nest.

I'd shudder and start, if I heard the bay
Of the bloodhounds seizing their human prey;
If I heard the captive plead in vain
As they tightened afresh his galling chain.

If I saw young girls, from their mothers' arms
Bartered and sold for their youthful charms
My eye would flash with a mournful flame,
My death-paled cheek grow red with shame.

I would sleep, dear friends, where bloated might
Can rob no man of his dearest right;
My rest shall be calm in any grave.
Where none calls his brother a slave.

I ask no monument proud and high
To arrest the gaze of the passersby;
All that my spirit yearning craves,
Is – bury me not in the land of slaves.

coffle gang: a group of slaves chained together in a line

galling: make sore by rubbing

Understand

1. What would cause the speaker unrest after death?

2. What would bring about sleep for the speaker?

 Explore

 1. There are some harrowing images of slavery in this poem. Which image most poignantly (movingly) highlights the suffering experienced by slaves, in your view?

 2. Find two poetic techniques used by the poet. Are they effective? Explain your answer with reference to the poem.

 3. Do you agree that the tone of this poem is one of disapproval and condemnation? Use evidence from the poem to support your answer.

 4. One important theme in this poem is freedom. Identify and discuss one more theme that you feel is important in the poem.

5. Write about another poem you have studied that deals with a serious issue.

   (a) Name the poem and the poet.

   (b) Identify and discuss the issue.

   (c) How did the poet make the issue evident throughout the poem?

   (d) What did you learn about the issue addressed in the poem?

 Investigate

Use your research skills to learn about modern-day slavery. You should visit your local or school library to source information. Use your skills to carry out secure internet searches. You may find the following website helpful: ⟨⟩ www.antislavery.org

 Create

Write an article entitled 'Modern-Day Slavery' for a national newspaper. Use your findings from the Investigate task to help you.

Even in the decades that followed the abolition of slavery in the United States, black people were not free, safe or treated equally. Lynching is the unlawful public hanging of a person. In the United States, the majority of the victims of lynchings were black. Lynchings were carried out in front of a crowd, who often cheered in support of the act of racism and violence.

The following poem was written in 1937 by teacher Abel Meeropol. He said that he wrote it because he hates 'injustice and the people who perpetuate it'. The poem is a protest against racial violence, in particular, the violence and terror of the lynch mob.

 Listen to the poem being read aloud, then work in pairs to discuss the images that strike you most.

Strange Fruit

By Abel Meeropol

Southern trees bear strange fruit,
Blood on the leaves and blood at the root,
Black bodies swinging in the southern breeze,
Strange fruit hanging from the poplar trees.

Pastoral scene of the gallant south,
The bulging eyes and the twisted mouth,
Scent of magnolias, sweet and fresh,
Then the sudden smell of burning flesh.

Here is a fruit for the crows to pluck,
For the rain to gather, and for the wind to suck,
For the sun to rot, for the trees to drop,
Here is a strange and bitter crop.

Understand

1. What is the 'strange fruit' that the trees bear in the first stanza?
2. What two scents are compared in the second stanza?
3. What happens to the 'fruit' in the third stanza?
4. Select one image that stands out to you. Does the image appeal to any of the senses?
5. Find two poetic techniques that you found effective in the poem.

 ## Explore

 1. Discuss the use of metaphor in the poem 'Strange Fruit'.

 2. What do you think the poet wanted to achieve by writing this poem?

 3. Musician Nina Simone said that 'Strange Fruit' 'is violent and tears at the guts of what white people have done'. Do you agree that this is a violent poem? Explain your answer in detail.

 ## Investigate

'Strange Fruit' was made famous as a song by singer Billie Holiday, and there are many other versions of the song. Use your research skills to find a version of the song that you like. Share your favourite video by creating a Padlet page dedicated to the song.

 ## Create

Write a blog post about the issue of racism or inequality that you see in the world today. Share your blog post using WordPress.

The following poem addresses the lack of freedom experienced by those who suffer racial oppression.

Form small groups to read the poem aloud. Read the poem a minimum of two times, then discuss how the bird is represented throughout.

Caged Bird

By Maya Angelou

A free bird leaps
on the back of the wind
and floats downstream
till the current ends
and dips his wing
in the orange sun rays
and dares to claim the sky.

But a bird that stalks
down his narrow cage
can seldom see through
his bars of rage
his wings are clipped and
his feet are tied
so he opens his throat to sing.

The caged bird sings
with a fearful trill
of things unknown
but longed for still
and his tune is heard
on the distant hill
for the caged bird
sings of freedom.

The free bird thinks of another breeze
and the trade winds soft through the sighing trees
and the fat worms waiting on a dawn bright lawn
and he names the sky his own

But a caged bird stands on the grave of dreams
his shadow shouts on a nightmare scream
his wings are clipped and his feet are tied
so he opens his throat to sing.

The caged bird sings
with a fearful trill
of things unknown
but longed for still
and his tune is heard
on the distant hill
for the caged bird
sings of freedom.

Understand

1. How is the **free bird** described? Quote from the first and fourth stanzas in your answer.

2. How is the **caged bird** described? Quote from the second, third, fifth and sixth in your answer.

3. What does the speaker mean when she says that the bird who is trapped sings 'of things unknown / but longed for still'?

4. We learn that the caged bird's 'wings are clipped and his feet are tied'. What does this tell us about the bird's freedom?

Explore

  1. Discuss the metaphor presented in the poem 'Caged Bird'.

2. Do you sympathise with the caged bird? Give reasons for your answer.

  3. How is the theme of freedom explored in this poem?

4. Choose an image to accompany a reading of this poem. Describe the image you have chosen and explain why this image is a suitable accompaniment.

Investigate

Work in small groups to carry out research on the life of Maya Angelou. Find the following information:

◖ date of birth
◖ date of death
◖ where she grew up
◖ information about her achievements
◖ other poems she wrote
◖ pictures, articles or video links.

Create

You have been asked to give a radio talk, sharing your knowledge of Maya Angelou with listeners. In groups, write and deliver your radio talk. Use the checklist to help you.

Radio talks

✓ Address your audience
✓ Positive language
✓ Rhetorical questions
✓ Anecdotes
✓ Information
✓ Ask listeners to get involved by calling, tweeting or texting
✓ Go to commercial breaks, news or traffic
✓ Thank your listeners at the end
✓ Pass on to the next presenter

Focus on ... blurbs

A **blurb** is a short description of a book written for promotional purposes.

Blurbs appear on the back covers of books. They can be written by the author or the publisher and may contain quotations from others. Like reviews, blurbs briefly describe what the book is about without giving the plot away. Unlike reviews, blurbs are always positive and are designed to convince readers to buy and read the book.

Work in pairs to examine the blurb below. What stands out? What do you learn about the book?

"I KNOW WHY THE CAGED BIRD SINGS liberates the reader into life simply because Maya Angelous confronts her own life with such a moving wonder, such a luminous dignity."

—James Baldwin

Here is a book as joyous and painful, as mysterious and memorable, as childhood itself. I Know Why the Caged Bird Sings captures the longing of lonely children, the brute insult of bigotry, and the wonder of words that can make the world right. Maya Angelou's debut memoir is a modern American classic beloved worldwide.

Sent by their mother to live with their devout grandmother in a small Southern town, Maya and her brother endure the ache of abandonment and prejudice. At eight years old and back at her mother's side in St. Louis, Maya is attacked by a man many times her age—and has to live with the consequences for a lifetime. Years later, in San Francisco, Maya learns that love for herself, the kindness of others, her own strong spirit, and the ideas of great authors will allow her to be free instead of imprisoned. Poetic and powerful, I Know Why the Caged Bird Sings will touch hearts and change minds for as long as people read.

Poet and Civil Rights Activist Maya Angelou also published seven autobiographies. Here is the blurb from the back cover of one of them, titled *I Know Why the Caged Bird Sings*.

 Create

 Imagine you have written your autobiography. Write the accompanying blurb, in the space provided on page 78 of your Portfolio. In it you should appeal to the reader and encourage them to read your book.

Free to be me

Throughout history, many people have been unable to express themselves freely for various reasons. In the past, women were unable to live free and independent lives simply because of their gender. Even today, women are often still expected to conform to traditional gender roles. All people, irrespective of their gender, sexuality or cultural identity should be free to be true to themselves.

 In William Shakespeare's play *As You Like It*, Rosalind disguises herself as a man to enjoy a kind of freedom that she has never known as a woman.

In this scene, Rosalind (dressed as a man) encounters Orlando, who fell in love with her earlier in the play. Rosalind is empowered by her manly appearance and, in disguise, she tests Orlando's love.

 Work in pairs to read the scene aloud.

As You Like It

ORLANDO Where dwell you, pretty youth?

ROSALIND With this shepherdess, my sister; here in the skirts of the forest, like fringe upon a petticoat.

ORLANDO Are you native of this place?

ROSALIND As the coney that you see dwell where she is kindled.

ORLANDO Your accent is something finer than you could purchase in so removed a dwelling.

Orlando comments on Rosalind's refined accent

ROSALIND I have been told so of many; but indeed an old religious uncle of mine taught me to speak, who was in his youth an inland man; one that knew courtship too well, for there he fell in love. I have heard him read many lectures against it; and I thank God I am not a woman, to be touch'd with so many giddy offences as he hath generally tax'd their whole sex withal.

Rosalind makes a joke at Orlando's expense by saying that she is grateful not to be a 'giddy' woman

ORLANDO Can you remember any of the principal evils that he laid to the charge of women?

ROSALIND There were none principal; they were all like one another as halfpence are; every one fault seeming monstrous till his fellow-fault came to match it.

Rosalind says that women have many faults

ORLANDO   I prithee recount some of them.

ROSALIND   No; I will not cast away my physic but on those that are sick. There is a man haunts the forest that abuses our young plants with carving 'Rosalind' on their barks; hangs odes upon hawthorns and elegies on brambles; all, forsooth, deifying the name of Rosalind. If I could meet that fancy-monger, I would give him some good counsel, for he seems to have the quotidian of love upon him.

Orlando has been leaving notes expressing his love for Rosalind all over the forest. Here, Rosalind says that the man responsible for these notes is love-sick

ORLANDO   I am he that is so love-shak'd; I pray you tell me your remedy.

ROSALIND   There is none of my uncle's marks upon you; he taught me how to know a man in love; in which cage of rushes I am sure you are not prisoner.

Rosalind questions whether Orlando is really in love

ORLANDO   What were his marks?

ROSALIND   A lean cheek, which you have not; a blue eye and sunken, which you have not; an unquestionable spirit, which you have not; a beard neglected, which you have not; but I pardon you for that, for simply your having in beard is a younger brother's revenue. Then your hose should be ungarter'd, your bonnet unbanded, your sleeve unbutton'd, your shoe untied, and every thing about you demonstrating a careless desolation. But you are no such man; you are rather point-device in your accoutrements as loving yourself than seeming the lover of any other.

Rosalind says that the symptoms of being in love include a slim face, sunken eyes, an overgrown beard and being generally unkempt, and argues that Orlando has none of these symptoms

ORLANDO   Fair youth, I would I could make thee believe I love.

ROSALIND   Me believe it! you may as soon make her that you love believe it; which, I warrant, she is apter to do than to confess she does. That is one of the points in the which women still give the lie to their consciences. But, in good sooth, are you he that hangs the verses on the trees wherein Rosalind is so admired?

ORLANDO   I swear to thee, youth, by the white hand of Rosalind, I am that he, that unfortunate he.

ROSALIND   But are you so much in love as your rhymes speak?

ORLANDO   Neither rhyme nor reason can express how much.

ROSALIND   Love is merely a madness; and, I tell you, deserves
as well a dark house and a whip as madmen do; and
the reason why they are not so punish'd and cured
is that the lunacy is so ordinary that the whippers
are in love too. Yet I profess curing it by counsel.

Rosalind says that love is a kind of madness and promises to cure it

ORLANDO   Did you ever cure any so?

ROSALIND   Yes, one; and in this manner. He was to imagine me
his love, his mistress; and I set him every day to
woo me; at which time would I, being but a moonish
youth, grieve, be effeminate, changeable, longing
and liking, proud, fantastical, apish, shallow,
inconstant, full of tears, full of smiles; for every
passion something and for no passion truly anything,
as boys and women are for the most part
cattle of this colour; would now like him, now loathe
him; then entertain him, then forswear him; now weep
for him, then spit at him; that I drave my suitor
from his mad humour of love to a living humour of
madness; which was, to forswear the full stream of
the world and to live in a nook merely monastic.
And thus I cur'd him; and this way will I take upon
me to wash your liver as clean as a sound sheep's
heart, that there shall not be one spot of love in 't.

Rosalind says that she has previously cured a man who was in love by asking him to express his love to her

ORLANDO   I would not be cured, youth.

ROSALIND   I would cure you, if you would but call me Rosalind,
and come every day to my cote and woo me.

ORLANDO   Now, by the faith of my love, I will. Tell me
where it is.

ROSALIND   Go with me to it, and I'll show it you; and, by the way,
you shall tell me where in the forest you live.
Will you go?

Rosalind (still disguised as a man) says that she will cure Orlando if he comes to her cottage to woo her, pretending 'he' is Rosalind (Orlando still does not realise he is talking to Rosalind)

ORLANDO   With all my heart, good youth.

ROSALIND   Nay, you must call me Rosalind.
Come, sister, will you go?

Exeunt

Discuss

1. How does Rosalind treat Orlando?
2. What sort of freedom does Rosalind enjoy when disguised as a man?
3. Do you believe that Orlando truly loves Rosalind?

 Understand

Find quotes in the extract to match each of the following statements.

◖ I live on the outskirts of the forest with my sister.
◖ Women's faults are dreadful.
◖ There is a man in the forest carving 'Rosalind' on the barks of trees.
◖ You are well-presented and seem to love yourself more than any other.
◖ I am the one who is in love. Tell me the cure.

 Explore

 1. What evidence is there to suggest that Orlando really loves Rosalind?

 2. In your view, does Rosalind enjoy being in disguise?

3. Consider a female character in your studied play. Explain this character's experience of freedom – do they enjoy or lack freedom?
   (a) Name your play, the playwright and the character you will discuss.
   (b) Write about the freedom that this character lacks or enjoys. Quote from the play to support your answer.

  4. As a class, choose one female character from your studied play. One student should take on the role of this character. The student will take the hot seat, answering inventive questions from the rest of the class.

 Investigate

Find out more about the lives of women in Elizabethan England, when Shakespeare wrote many of his plays. Make a note of the main differences between the lives of women now and then. Share your findings with the class.

 Create

Imagine you could disguise yourself beyond recognition. Write a diary entry following your day in disguise.

◖ Describe your new appearance and persona.
◖ Give an account of what you did while in disguise.
◖ Say what you learned from being in disguise.

Women have historically been paid less than men for doing the same job. Although this is illegal in Ireland and in many countries throughout the world, the gender pay gap continues to exist.

The following scene is from the film *Made in Dagenham*, which is set in 1968 and follows the cause of female factory workers who were paid less than male employees. In this scene, Rita speaks to union members about the issue of equality for women who seek equal pay for equal work. She urges the male union members to support the women's cause.

Made in Dagenham

RITA

My best friend lost her husband recently. Durin' the war he was a gunner in Fifty Squadron in the RAF. He got shot down one time ... on a raid to Essen and even though he managed to bail out, he was badly injured. I asked him once, why he'd joined the RAF and he said ... they got the best women ...

(Laughter in the hall. She nods, upset)

Which they did ...

Eddie stares at Rita

RITA (CONT'D)

But then he said, you had to do somethin'. And he'd always wanted to go up in a plane ...

Her jaw tightens; she feels the cause start to flood through her veins.

RITA (CONT'D)

You had to do somethin' ... That was a given. 'Cause it was a matter of principle. You had to stand up; do what was right, 'cause otherwise you wouldn't be able to look yourself in the mirror.

(stares at hall)

When did that change? When did we, in this country, start bein' happy, to do nothin'? On what day did we decide we had no duty to fairness no more?

(the hall is silent. She nods slightly)

It has NOT changed. That is NOT us ... It is not you ... And we are only in this situation now, where women get paid less money than men for doing the same work ...

(lets it sink in. Nods)

– because we was tricked. Those in power kept tellin' us: it's fine. You don't need to do the right thing cause there's nothin' needs fixin'. And they said it for so long, we ended up believin' it was right ... Well it ain't right!

Calls of support. Heads nod in agreement.

RITA (CONT'D)

It was wrong at the start, it's wrong now, and it'll be wrong forever! –

(shouts of agreement)

– unless you back us, you stand up, you remember who *you* are and you accept, that *this* is a matter of principle. Women are entitled to the same rates of pay as men. And that is it. No matter the cost, no matter the difficulty, not matter them that are gonna lose out, no human being should be punished in the workplace cause've how they was born!

(Cheers. Rita calls above them –)

We are the working classes. The men *and* the women. We are the furnace which fires the world and without us no-body earns tuppence h'appeny!

(big cheer)

We are *not* separated by sex, only by the will of those who are not prepared to go into battle for what is right – and those who are!

The hall erupts. And leaps to its feet. Eddie sways.

Focus on ... audience

The **audience** are the people who hear, watch or read something.

In this scene, Rita addresses an audience. She encourages male union members to support equal pay for women. Find an example of where Rita directly addresses the audience in her speech.

In your own writing, you should always give consideration to your target audience. Ask yourself:

◖ Who will be reading or listening?
◖ How can I engage and connect with my audience?

Discuss

1. Discuss what you learned from **(a)** Rita's speech and **(b)** the directions in this script.
2. Identify the audience for each of the following:
    - an article in the school magazine
    - an acceptance speech at a televised awards ceremony
    - a bedtime story.

 Understand

1. Rita talks about her friend's husband. What do we learn about him?
2. What is Rita's message to the union members?
3. How do people react?

 Explore

1. The Feminist Movement calls for gender equality in all forms, advocating the rights of women. How do you know that Rita is a feminist?
2. Rita says that people 'had to stand up; do what was right, 'cause otherwise you wouldn't be able to look yourself in the mirror'. Do you agree?
3. Discuss two features of persuasive language used by Rita as she addresses the crowd.
4. Imagine you are playing the part of Rita. How would you deliver your speech? Comment on:
    - tone of voice
    - facial expressions
    - body language, movement and gestures
    - pacing.

 Investigate

The film *Made in Dagenham* is set in England in the 1960s, yet today there is still gender inequality. Use your research skills to find an example of gender inequality in the world today.

 Create

Compile your findings to write a news report for newspaper, radio or television. Identify your audience before writing.

Sometimes a person may struggle with their feelings when they realise that they are LGBT (lesbian, gay, bisexual or transgender). It can be a daunting time for some, who may feel that they will no longer be accepted by their family or friends. Living in an inclusive society like Ireland and having supportive friends and family means that people can be free to be themselves, regardless of their sexual orientation.

In the following extract from Jacqueline Wilson's novel *Kiss*, Carl has just told his best friend Sylvie that he is gay. It is in the presence of Sylvie that Carl feels free to be himself.

Kiss

'*I* was shocked. I mean, I kind of knew I liked boys, not girls – apart from you, I mean – but I didn't *want* to be different. But I couldn't help it. I just saw him that first day and it was like he was the only boy in the whole school. I couldn't stop watching him. It was OK because *everyone* watched him. He was the big-time football hero and everyone was desperate to be in his little gang. It was fine then, when we never even spoke to each other. But then we were paired up by this teacher in drama. I couldn't believe it. I was thrilled and yet so scared too. I was sure I'd make a complete berk of myself. Well, I did, I didn't have a clue what to say—'

'Oh, Carl, stop it, you're the most articulate person I've ever met.'

'I can say all sorts of stuff to *you*, Sylvie, but at first with Paul I could hardly say two words. Then we had to do this daft trust exercise when you take turns falling and the other guy has to catch you. You've no idea what it felt like, holding him in my arms. I can't explain, just touching him, it was electric. You wait till you feel that way about someone, then you'll understand.'

I was glad it was dark.

'Sylvie?' He didn't understand. 'You *are* shocked, aren't you?'

'No, no, it's just… a bit of a surprise.'

'It's a surprise for me too,' said Carl. I never ever thought I'd feel like this. I thought I'd just coast along somehow. I've always been careful not to act too girly or whatever. I hate being teased. I felt so safe, you and me and our own private world. I didn't have a clue what it's like to fall in love. It's frightening because it's so intense, it kind of takes you over. It's just like every stupid cliché, every silly song. You can't eat, you can't concentrate, you can't sleep. You just think about the other person all the time, even though you know it's crazy. You just can't help it. It's especially crazy to fall for Paul because he's the straightest boy ever. He's one of the worst for making stupid jokes. I knew I didn't stand a chance of him ever feeling the same way about me, and yet I still sort of hoped that somehow it would happen. How mad is that?

'It's mad,' I said.

'So I thought I'd just carry on, us being friends, Paul and me. I thought I could make it work. But it was so *difficult* never being able to say what I really felt. It made me feel so hopeless sometimes. I mean, even if Paul were gay too you could never ever come out at our school. You can call any of the guys any four-letter word you choose and they don't blink, but call one of them gay and he'll punch your head in, even if he *is*. I used to get called gay a lot because I'm arty and swotty and not too good at football, but they didn't really *mean* it. *Paul* called me hopelessly gay whenever I muffed a football move, but it was OK if I just laughed and clowned around with limp wrists, going *whoopsie* all the time to try to be part of the joke.'

'Carl, how can you love someone who treats you like that?'

'But I keep telling you, he didn't *mean* it. He didn't dream I was really gay. He always went on and on about girls and what he'd like to do to them so I did too.'

'About me?'

'No!' he said. 'I'd never talk about you like that, Sylvie, you know I wouldn't.' He said it fiercely, to be reassuring.

'So who did you talk about?'

'Oh. Just anyone. it was all so stupid and tacky. Whoever came into my head.'

'Miranda.'

'Well, she was an obvious candidate.'

'Did you tell Paul about kissing her at the party?'

'Yes, I did vaguely mention it.'

'So what did you tell him it was like?'

'Oh, Sylvie, I can't remember. It didn't mean anything to me. It felt a bit weird and threatening, if you really want to know. She opened her mouth so wide I thought she was going to swallow me whole. Plus she was wearing all this slippery lipstick. I was scared she was going to get it all over me. It tasted disgusting.'

I felt a pang for Miranda, but I couldn't help being pleased.

'So you tried to set Paul up with her instead?'

'I know it was mad and stupid but I hoped that the four of us could be friends and all go round together. It seemed a great idea at the time. I mean, I love Paul, I love you, you like Miranda, she likes *any* boy who pays her attention. I thought it might work.'

The Glass Hut whirled round me as I replayed what he'd said inside my head.

'You love me?' I whispered.

'Yes! Of *course* I love you, Sylvie. You know how much you mean to me. You're the one and only girl for me, ever. You know that.'

'But you're not *in* love with me?'

'Not the way I'm in love with Paul.'

'Still?'

'Yes. And you don't even know how he acted. You see, I tried to kiss him and—'

'You did *what*?'

'I know, I know. It was totally crazy. I didn't mean to. It was just a spur-of-the-moment thing. It was so lovely in Kew Gardens in the moonlight. I felt as if we'd stepped into another world and anything could happen.'

'I felt that too.'

It was like our own Midsummer Night's Dream. Then Miranda suggested playing Hide and Seek, and we all scattered and I didn't plan anything, I just set off and I spotted Paul almost straight away. It was as if he was waiting there in the bushes for me. He laughed when I walked up, and pulled me in to the bushes with him so we were all squashed up, hiding together. My head was right next to his and we were still laughing and fooling about, and without even thinking I kissed him. I couldn't believe it was happening. It felt so incredible – but then he pushed me away. He punched me. Then he said all these awful things.'

'Oh, poor poor Carl,' I said, but I couldn't help adding 'Still, what did you *expect*?'

'I know, I know. I was just totally mad. I kept telling him I was sorry and I'd never do it again but he kept on saying stuff, acting like I was this weird sick pervert.'

'You're not, you know you're not.'

'But *he* thinks I am. He acted like it's some contagious disease and I was trying to infect him too. He was so *angry* with me. I fell over and he actually started *kicking* me, even though we'd been best mates just two minutes ago. Then he stormed off, saying he never ever wanted to see me again.'

'Well, that's a bit silly, seeing as you're in the same form at school.'

'That's what I'm so worried about. It's not just the awfulness of making Paul hate me—'

'That's mad. I think you should hate him for being so horrible to you,' I interrupted.

'No, listen, what if he tells everyone at school that I kissed him?'

'He won't', I said firmly. 'Look, I know he didn't tell Miranda. He just said you'd had a fight. She thought it was over her.'

'That's so typical of Miranda. I don't know what you *see* in her, Sylvie.'

'Well. I don't get what you see in Paul. Especially now,' I said. 'You *still* want to be friends with him, don't you?'

'Yes, but he won't want anything to do with me. Yet the weirdest thing of all... for a second he kissed me back like he really cared about me too.'

A **character** is a person who appears in a story. We form opinions of characters based on their actions and behaviour.

Discuss

'People should always express themselves freely.'

◖ Your teacher will nominate one group to sit in the middle of the classroom to carry out their discussion aloud. Each student should take a turn contributing to the discussion.

◖ The remaining students should take their seats around the inner group. Listen carefully to the inner group as each student takes a turn expressing their view.

◖ Students in the outer group may contribute to the discussion at the end.

Understand

1. How does Carl feel about Paul?
2. What does Carl do to express his feelings for Paul?
3. How does Paul react?
4. According to Carl, what happens if you call boys 'gay'?

Explore

 1. How do you know that Carl feels free to express himself to Sylvie?

 2. Based on this extract, what do we know about the characters of Carl and Sylvie? Use evidence from the extract in your answer.

 3. Would you be interested in reading the rest of this novel, based on this extract? Explain your answer.

4. What do you enjoy most about reading a novel? Explain your answer.

5. One theme evident in this extract is freedom. Consider how a character's freedom may be limited in a novel that you have studied.

   (a) Name the novel, the author and the character you will discuss.

   (b) Describe the situation facing your chosen character.

   (c) How is the situation resolved?

Investigate

There are lots of supports available for LGBT (lesbian, gay, bisexual and transgender) teenagers. Use your research skills to find out the names of groups and organisations offering support to the LGBT community.

◖ Name the group or organisation.

◖ Find out more about the services offered.

◖ Note the contact information.

◖ Use ⊘ belongto.org as a starting point for your research.

 **Create**

You write an Agony Aunt column for your school magazine. Students are invited to email their problems or issues. Your column aims to resolve these problems by offering advice and support. Carl has written the following email seeking your advice:

To:	agonyaunt@schoolmag.ie
From:	carl01@mail.com
Subject:	Please help!

Dear Agony Aunt,

I do not want to give you my full name in case people figure out who I am.

I am having a hard time right now. It took me a while to figure out that I am a boy who likes boys – I'm gay. It is something I struggled with for a few years, but recently I came out to my best friend and she was supportive. I'm lucky to have her in my life because she is always there for me.

I am writing to ask for your advice with a situation I got myself into last week. I made a huge mistake when I kissed the guy I really like. He kissed me back for just a minute before pushing me away. Then he lost it. He started lashing out and calling me all sorts of names. Now I have ruined our friendship and really messed things up.

What should I do?

Please help me.

From,

Anonymous

Write a column for the school magazine in which you respond to Carl's email. You may like to inform him of the LGBT groups and organisations that you found in your previous investigation.

Prefixes and suffixes

A prefix is a group of letters added to the beginning of certain words.

Dis ...   *Mis ...*   *Em ...*   *Im ...*   *Un ...*

Prefixes are used to change the meaning of the root word. Notice how the spelling of the root word stays the same when a prefix is added.

Untrue   *Impatient*   *Misbehave*

 Do not change the spelling of the original word when adding a prefix.

A suffix is a group of letters added to the end of certain words.

... ery   *... ful*   *... ness*   *... ment*   *... ible*

Suffixes are used to create a variation of the root word. Notice how the spelling of the original word can sometimes change when a suffix is added.

Replacement   *Terrible*   *Friendliness*

 In most cases, change the spelling of the original word when adding a suffix.

Understand

1. What is a prefix? Write a definition in your own words.

2. Explain the spelling rule when adding a prefix.

3. **(a)** Match the prefixes 'dis', 'mis' and 'il' to the correct root words below to change their meaning.

    ◁ Legal   ◁ Agree   ◁ Understanding

   (b) Write a sentence using each of the new words you created by adding prefixes to the words above.

4. Identify the root word in each of these examples and use your dictionary to find a definition of each root word.

    ◁ Illogical   ◁ Unnecessary   ◁ Incomplete
    ◁ Malfunction   ◁ Television   ◁ Unfortunate

5. What is a suffix? Write a definition in your own words.

6. When adding a suffix, should you change the spelling of the original word **(a)** always or **(b)** sometimes?

7. **(a)** Write out these words, adding the suffix.

    ◁ Bake (ery)   ◁ Horror (ible)   ◁ Nutrition (ious)

   (b) Write a sentence using each of the new words you created.

8. Identify the root word in each of these examples and use your dictionary to find a definition of each root word.

    ◁ Reliable   ◁ Ambitious   ◁ Responsibly
    ◁ Malicious   ◁ Replacement   ◁ Audible

 9. Work with a partner to identify one example of a prefix and one example of a suffix in the extract from *Kiss* on pages 303–305.

   (a) Identify the root word.

   (b) Has the spelling changed?

   (c) Write a sentence containing both words.

Free from confinement

We often associate imprisonment with people who have been convicted of a crime and lose their freedom as a result. However, there are many other reasons people and animals can lose their freedom. Sometimes elderly people become more dependent on others, feeling confined by their circumstances. Inequality can mean that people are confined and suppressed in many ways throughout the world today. Often, animals are confined to cages and enclosures.

In the following opinion piece, comedian and actor Romesh Ranganathan argues that zoos serve to imprison animals that should be free in the wild. Read the article and consider your own viewpoint – do you agree with Romesh Ranganathan's perspective?

Zoos are prisons for animals – no one needs to see a depressed penguin in the flesh

In an age when David Attenborough can virtually take us inside an elephant's bottom, is there any or conservational value to keeping animals in captivity?

That a zoo in Cumbria is having its licence revoked as a result of nearly 500 animals dying there over a two-year period comes as no shock – but it still slightly surprises me that anybody thinks that we should have zoos at all. The animals always look miserable in captivity. If you don't believe me, visit a farm park. It's as likely as not that you will see a goat, pleading with its eyes to be euthanised, while a sign on the enclosure says: 'Gerry the goat is quite the character – he often plays a game in which he looks like he has been crying for many, many hours!'

A lot of zoos play the conservation angle, which is a rationale that has been reverse engineered. That's not really why zoos exist. Zoos exist so that we can wander round with our children and say: 'No, don't bang the glass, Timothy, he's getting agitated,' before going home to post on Facebook about the educational day that we have had.

The argument that zoos have educational merit might have once seemed convincing, but there is less reason to see animals in captivity than ever before. David Attenborough's Planet Earth shows you all the animals you could ask for in their natural habitat, with added drama and narrative arcs. We are surely only a few series away from filming inside the animals, with Attenborough using his dulcet tones to give the origin story of an elephant turd. Why, then, do we need to see them in prison?

The idea that kids only get excited about things they can see in the flesh is ridiculous. My kids are obsessed with dinosaurs that no longer exist, and Skylanders, which have never existed. One of our sons watches endless YouTube videos of Kinder Surprise eggs being opened, so the bar is set pretty low in terms of what will get him interested. I would, however, be delighted to hear that the YouTubers responsible for these videos had been put in a series of cages for our enjoyment.

I was struck by my own hypocrisy when I was looking to get a family pet. When I found myself Googling: 'How long will a puppy cry for its mother and siblings,' it occurred to me that I probably no longer wanted to do it. The idea that I don't want animals to be imprisoned, but that I quite fancy having a prisoner of my own doesn't sit comfortably. This might sound extreme and no doubt cat owners will tell me that their cats are free to go wherever they want but always return. I live in Crawley, however, and often when I'm out I immediately want to return straight home. I could never be sure if the cat coming back was a thumbs-up for the family, or a silent protest against the lack of amenities in town. I'm also starting to consider setting my children free.

Focus on ... vocabulary

Vocabulary refers to the words you know and use.

It is important to expand your vocabulary with new words. Try to include some new words in your own writing. Look out for ways of improving your expression when redrafting your work. Ask yourself the following questions:

◖ Can I find a better way of writing this sentence?

◖ Can I vary the words that I have used?

 In pairs, return to the article and find any words or phrases that are new to you. Can you guess what they mean, based on the context of the whole sentence?

Understand

1. **(a)** Use your dictionary to find definitions of each of the words below.

   ◖ Euthanasia   ◖ Endangered

   ◖ Conservation   ◖ Hypocrisy

   ◖ Agitate   ◖ Extreme

   ◖ Dulcet   ◖ Amenities

   (b) Add these words to your vocabulary builder on pages 1–2 of your Portfolio.

2. In the case of each of the following, write the numeral corresponding to the correct answer in your copy.

   (a) Why has a zoo in Cumbria had its licence revoked?

   i. Nearly 500 animals escaped.

   ii. Nearly 500 animals died.

   iii. Nearly 500 animals attacked visitors.

   (b) What does Romesh Ranganathan say about David Attenborough's television programme, *Planet Earth*?

   i. It shows animals in captivity, but has narrative qualities.

   ii. It shows animals and human beings interacting.

   iii. It shows animals in their natural habitat with added drama and narrative arcs.

   (c) Which of the following are Ranganathan's sons obsessed with?

   i. Dinosaurs, skyscrapers and Kinder Surprises.

   ii. Dinosaurs, skydivers and Kinder Surprises.

   iii. Dinosaurs, Skylanders and Kinder Surprises.

   (d) Why does Ranganathan feel like a hypocrite?

   i. He considered getting a family pet.

   ii. He doesn't really care about animals in captivity.

   iii. He regularly visits the zoo.

Explore

1. Does Ranganathan make a valid argument against zoos, in your view? Explain your answer.

2. Do you think that it is right or wrong to keep animals in zoos? Make three arguments to support your viewpoint.

Investigate

Organise a survey of students in your school or members of your family to learn more about how they feel about animals being kept in zoos.

◖ Make a list of questions.

◖ Ask people to complete your survey.

◖ Examine their answers.

◖ Share your findings.

Create

1. **(a)** Write a script about the Ranganathan family's trip to the zoo. You should structure your script like a play. Include:

   ◖ background information

   ◖ stage directions

   ◖ dialogue.

   (b) Redraft your script. Make sure that you vary your vocabulary.

In Jonas Jonasson's novel *The Hundred-Year-Old Man Who Climbed Out of the Window and Disappeared*, Allan Karlsson has had his freedom taken away from him when the authorities move him to a retirement home. In the opening of the novel below, Allan takes measures to regain his freedom.

The Hundred-Year-Old Man Who Climbed Out of the Window and Disappeared

Monday, 2nd May 2005

You might think he could have made up his mind earlier, and been man enough to tell the others of his decision. But Allan Karlsson had never been given to pondering things too long.

So the idea had barely taken hold in the old man's head before he opened the window of his room on the ground floor of the Old People's Home in the town of Malmköping, and stepped out – into the flowerbed.

This manoeuvre required a bit of effort, since Allan was one hundred years old. On this very day in fact. There was less than an hour to go before his birthday party would begin in the lounge of the Old People's Home. The mayor would be there. And the local paper. And all the other old people. And the entire staff, led by bad-tempered Director Alice.

It was only the Birthday Boy himself who didn't intend to turn up.

 The **opening** is the beginning of a piece of writing. A good opening hooks the reader and grabs their attention.

 Understand

1. Where is the opening of the story set?
2. When is Allan's birthday?
3. Who will be in attendance at Allan's party?
4. Choose one word to describe Allan, based on what you have read in this extract.

   ◁ Impulsive   ◁ Selfish   ◁ Independent

 Explore

1. Why do you think Allan left the nursing home?
2. This is the opening of a novel. In your opinion, is it a good opening?
3. What do you think happens next in Allan's story? Write a paragraph describing what may have happened once he left the nursing home.

 Investigate

Use your research skills to find a review of *The Hundred-Year-Old Man Who Climbed Out of the Window and Disappeared*. Does the reviewer:

◁ give an overview of the plot
◁ introduce some of the characters
◁ give their opinion
◁ recommend the film or book?

 Create

1. Write a review of a film or novel that you have studied as part of your Junior Cycle English course.

2. **(a)** Write the opening of a story that features an escape in the space provided on page 79 of your Portfolio. Include one unexpected element in the opening to your story.

   (b) Swap your opening with a partner. Choose one element of your partner's story that you liked. Suggest one way your partner could make their opening even better in their second draft. Fill in your suggestions in the space provided on page 80 of their Portfolio.

   (c) Redraft your opening based on the feedback you received, then write the rest of your story in the space provided on page 122 of your Portfolio.

In the following article, written by Nour Hassan, we learn about life in Saudi Arabia, where women do not enjoy the same freedoms as men.

As a woman who lived in Saudi Arabia, here's how I feel about them letting women drive for the first time

Friday Morning Prayer call echoed around the city – Jeddah was always the most peaceful at this time. This was the calm before the storm. I stuffed my swimsuit and a pair of jeans shorts into a small black duffel bag, zipped it up and sat on my bed. Helpless; the usual wait began.

I was rushing, late, stressed out and could not leave the house until my father got home from prayer. The driver was on vacation for the weekend, his wife was giving birth and so it would be impossible for him to be on call, as he usually was. Taking a local cab was unheard of for a woman, and there was absolutely no way would I risk riding in a car with one of my 'male' friends.

My best friend's sweet sixteen had already started, 20 minutes away at a Yacht Club at the coastal marina area of Obhur, near Jeddah City. The boat was leaving port at 2pm. It was now 12:45pm, and the mosque was five minutes from home. I was stranded. My mother came in to check up on me, reassuring me as always that I wouldn't be late, that I'd catch what promised to be the party of the year. At the time these things mattered, a lot, and it didn't feel good to be so dependent.

She couldn't help, she was a woman in Saudi Arabia, and she couldn't drive me anywhere …

I am an Egyptian female who grew up in Jeddah, Saudi Arabia. I spent 18 years of my life there – it is my second home and a place I have a lot of reverence for.

On Tuesday night King Salman ordered a reform allowing women to obtain a driver's licence if they so please, with no requirement of permission from a male guardian.

Saudi Arabia was the last country to allow women to drive. My inner feminist is confused and a little taken aback by this fact. Is this really still a topic of conversation in 2017? Growing up it seemed so normal to me; the constant frustration, the endless obstacles that came up when planning an outing due to having to organise rides there and back, the undeniable lack of equality and reliance on third parties. Subconsciously, I was forced to accept it.

Jeddah is a city that is buzzing with vitality. A beach side town, with a beautiful coast and access to some of the most coveted dining, shopping, and diving spots in the region.

As a woman in Jeddah you had to acknowledge a couple of things. Your freedom – a loose synonym for the ability to move around or do as you please – was always directly linked, connected or intertwined with that of a male counterpart, be it your father, husband, driver, or brother. Male friends were as taboo as they were useless in these situations. Being caught driving around with a male, who was not legally allowed to escort you from point A to point B, was just as bad an offence as stealing the car yourself.

Curiously enough, old habits really do die hard. I moved to Egypt in 2012 for college. Women are allowed to drive here; this should go without saying I suppose. However, I was so used to being driven around, to the comfort of the passenger seat or the passive daydreams of the backseat, that it took me three years to actually begin driving myself. I know this is not the case with most women, and many leave Saudi Arabia only to hop into a car the first chance they get and speed off into the distance.

I cannot imagine a Jeddah where you look to your left at a traffic light and see a woman at the driver's seat – the image is exhilarating and the impacts for such a monumentally overdue reform will most likely create a ripple effect unlike any other.

Mobility is powerful. Feeling as though you have the ability to escort yourself, plan your own day, give yourself permission to leave the house without making a single phone call or having to arrange for a car to come pick you up. These are all things that have small but very significant impacts of the psyche, on how a woman perceives herself and her freedom.

My experience was not a negative one, as the city became almost programmed to accommodate for this latent inconvenience for females. However, as a statement on equality, acceptance and progressive thinking this is undeniably 'one for the books'.

I visit Jeddah once every two months, and look forward to the day where I can drive myself to dinner. Abaya clad, music blasting, friends in tow and evidently fearless!

Abaya: loose robe worn by some Muslim women

Understand

1. Locate the underlined words in the article. Use your dictionary to find a definition of each word and add these terms to the vocabulary builder on pages 1–2 of your Portfolio.

2. In the case of each of the following, write the numeral corresponding to the correct answer in your copy.

   (a) Why does the writer have no one to drive her at the start of the article?
   i. Her father is at prayer and he is the only driver she knows.
   ii. Her driver is on holidays in Dubai.
   iii. Her father is at prayer and her driver's wife is giving birth.

   (b) Where was the birthday party being held?
   i. A hotel   ii. A restaurant   iii. A boat

   (c) What does the author tell us was unheard of for a woman to do?
   i. Take a bus   ii. Take a cab   iii. Walk

   (d) What does the writer describe as being 'normal' to her as she grew up?
   i. The lack of equality   ii. The lack of fun   iii. The lack of love

   (e) How does the writer describe Jeddah?
   i. Unsafe   ii. Buzzing with vitality   iii. Noisy

Explore

1. Compare the writer's life growing up in Saudi Arabia with your own. Consider similarities and differences.

 2. Based on the article you have read, is Jeddah a city you might like to visit?

3. The writer says that a woman's freedom 'was always directly linked, connected or intertwined with that of a male counterpart'. Do you think this is fair?

4. Do you think that this article belongs in a newspaper or magazine? Give reasons for your answer.

 Investigate

Use your research skills to find out more about day-to-day life in Saudi Arabia. Share your findings with the class.

◀ What similarities are there between life in Saudi Arabia and life in Ireland?

◀ What differences are there?

 Create

1. **(a)** Think about a reform that you would like to see in your school. Write a speech to be delivered to Third Year students and teachers. In your speech, you should clearly state the reform you wish to see and give valid reasons for implementing the change.

(b) Write a tweet about the reform that you wish to implement. Remember to limit the length of your tweet to 280 characters.

Free from threat

People's freedom is sometimes threatened by others who spread hatred and fear. This can result in the lives of innocent people being destroyed or inhibited, as many people live in fear of violence.

During the Miss Peru Pageant in 2017, competitors took the opportunity to highlight the issue of violence against women.

Miss Peru contestants accuse country of not measuring up on gender violence

Beauty pageant competitors refuse to list vital statistics during live TV broadcast, instead stating figures on violence against women in Peru

It was that moment in the beauty pageant where the contestants come forward, introduce themselves and then announce their bust, waist and hip measurements.

But in the opening segment of Sunday night's televised Miss Peru contest, a whole different set of figures were presented to the audience as each competitor listed a hard-hitting statistic about violence against women in the South American country.

'My name is Camila Canicoba and I represent the department of Lima. My measurements are: 2,202 cases of femicide reported in the last nine years in my country,' said the first.

'My name is Karen Cueto and I represent Lima and my measurements are: 82 femicides and 156 attempted femicides so far this year,' said the second.

Latin American beauty pageants are criticised as sexist and patriarchal in their portrayal of women. But the 23 Miss Peru contestants agreed with the pageant's organiser, former beauty queen Jessica Newton, to dedicate the event to empowering women in a country with an appalling record for gender violence.

'Greetings from Almendra Marroquín. I represent Cañete, and my measurements are: more than 25% of girls and teenagers are abused in their schools,' said another.

'My measurements are 3,114 female victims of trafficking since 2014': Romina Lozano, winner of Miss Peru 2017.

The eventual winner of the competition, Romina Lozano, said her 'measurements' were '3,114 female victims of trafficking have been registered since 2014'.

In one part of the televised competition, newspaper clippings about femicide killings or showing the faces of battered women were displayed behind the contestants as they spoke. Especially prominent was the bruised face of Lady Guillén, one of the widely publicised cases

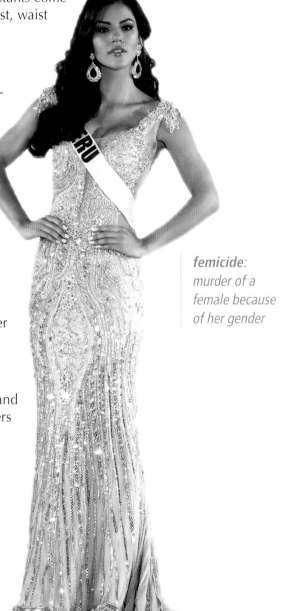

femicide: murder of a female because of her gender

that sparked a multitudinous Ni Una Menos (Not One Less) march against gender violence in Lima last year.

multitudinous: very numerous

Public indignation about violence against women peaked before the march in August 2016, when CCTV images of Cindy Arlette Contreras being dragged by the hair through a hotel reception by her naked ex-boyfriend Adriano Pozo were widely circulated on the internet. In March, Contreras was awarded the international women of courage award by Melania Trump, the US First Lady.

The Miss Peru competition concluded with each woman being asked what laws they would change to combat violence against women.

'Now, nobody can be indifferent to the level of violence,' said Susána Chavez, director of Promsex, a gender rights organisation in Peru.

'These competitions focus on many stereotypes about women and judge them by their physical characteristics, but they impact a broad group of women and men that we [feminist groups] do not reach.'

'We've never seen a time when there is more awareness about the problem [of gender violence].'

Understand

1. In what country was the beauty contest held?
2. What sort of statistics did the contestants share with the audience?
3. Locate one statistic that may have shocked the audience. Explain your choice.
4. What sort of violence was shown on CCTV?
5. How did the competition conclude?
6. Susána Chavez says that beauty pageants 'judge [women] by their physical characteristics'. Find evidence in the article to suggest that this is true.

Explore

1. In your view, is this an effective way of raising awareness of a serious issue? Give reasons for your answer.
2. We are told that people marched against gender violence in Lima. Suggest one other way for people to take a stand against gender violence or another serious issue.

Create

1. Write an article for a broadsheet or tabloid newspaper using one of the statistics shared above.
2. Write a short story that includes a character who takes a stand against something.
3. Write a poem from the perspective of someone who has experienced fear or intimidation.

Terrorism is the use of violence that targets civilians. Terrorists are often motivated by extreme political or religious views. Terror attacks threaten the freedom of ordinary, innocent people.

In 2017, twenty-three people were killed in a terror attack at an Ariana Grande concert in Manchester. The extract below is taken from the poem 'This is the Place', originally written in 2012. The poem celebrates the spirit of Manchester and the people of the city, and it came to represent the defiance of the people of Manchester in the face of such a horrific act.

Watch the following video of the poem being read by Tony Walsh at a vigil in the aftermath of the attack.

youtu.be/PszMmYpQjPo

Understand

1. Tony Walsh uses words like 'ace' to describe Manchester. Find three other words with positive connotations that are used to describe Manchester.

2. What evidence is there to suggest that the poet is proud of Manchester?

3. Give two examples of the 'hard times' that Manchester has faced, according to the poem.

4. Choose one line that shows Manchester's resilience.

Explore

 1. Write in detail about two aspects of 'This is the Place' that appeal to you.

 2. Do you think this poem was a good response to the terror attack in Manchester?

3. Imagine you are part of the crowd listening to Tony Walsh reading his poem. Describe how you are feeling as you listen to the poem.

4. Why do you think it is important to protect and defend the freedom of ordinary people?

Investigate

Find out more about the place where you live. Make a note of:

◖ important places in the area ◖ changes to the area

◖ important people ◖ facilities and amenities

◖ historical facts ◖ your favourite thing about the place.

Create

1. **(a)** Write a poem entitled 'This is the Place'. Your poem should be based on the place where you live. Include some of the information that you found in the previous Investigate task.

   (b) When you have finished, recite your poem for your classmates.

On 11 September 2001, two aeroplanes flew into the World Trade Center in New York in a terror attack. Both buildings collapsed, causing chaos and destruction and killing 2,606 people.

The protagonist in Jonathan Safran Foer's novel *Extremely Loud and Incredibly Close*, nine-year-old Oskar, lost his father in the attack on the World Trade Center. In the following extract, Oskar's grandmother recalls what happened on the day of the attacks.

Extremely Loud and Incredibly Close

You went to the bathroom. I told her to control herself. At least in front of you.

She called the newspapers. They didn't know anything. She called the fire department. No one knew anything.

All afternoon I knitted that scarf for you. It grew longer and longer. Your mother closed the windows, but we could still smell the smoke. She asked me if I thought we should make posters. I said it might be a good idea.

That made her cry, because she had been depending on me. The scarf grew longer and longer.

She used the picture from your vacation. From only two weeks before now. It was you and your father.

When I saw it, I told her she shouldn't use a picture that had your face in it. She said she wasn't going to use the whole picture. Only your father's face. I told her, Still, it isn't a good idea.

She said, There are more important things to worry about. Just use a different picture. Let it go, Mom. She had never called me Mom. There are so many pictures to choose from. Mind your own business. This is my business. We were not angry at each other.

I don't know how much you understood, but probably you understood everything.

She took the posters downtown that afternoon. She filled a rolling suitcase with them. I thought of your grandfather. I wondered where he was at that moment. I didn't know if I wanted him to be suffering.

She took a stapler. And a box of staples. And tape. I think of those things now. The paper, the stapler, the staples, the tape. It makes me sick. Physical things. Forty years of loving someone becomes staples and tape.

It was just the two of us. You and me.

We played games in the living room. You made jewelry. The scarf grew longer and longer. We went for a walk in the park. We didn't talk about what was on top of us. What was pinning us down like a ceiling. When you fell asleep with your head on my lap, I turned on the television.

I lowered the volume until it was silent.

The same pictures over and over.

Planes going into buildings.

Bodies falling.

People waving shirts out of high windows.

Planes going into buildings.

Bodies falling.

Understand

1. What did Oskar's grandmother spend the afternoon of 11 September 2011 doing?
2. Oskar's mother made posters. What was the purpose of this task?
3. What do we learn about the narrator's relationship with Oskar's grandfather?

Explore

1. Oskar's grandmother says that she felt sick to think that 'Forty years of loving someone becomes staples and tape.' What do you think she means by this?
2. Imagine you are Oskar's grandmother, sitting with your grandson asleep on your lap. Describe the thoughts that are running through your mind as you watch television.

Create

1. Imagine you are in New York when the attack took place. People are panicking and the city is in chaos. Write a paragraph in which you describe the scene using imagery and vivid descriptions.
2. Imagine you are the Mayor of New York. Write the speech you would deliver to the American people to help them through this sad time. Your speech should discuss the importance of protecting people's freedom.

Reviewing let freedom ring

Reviewing let freedom ring

Reflect and review

1. **(a)** Take a look at the images on page 283. Consider how each image is associated with the theme. Rank the images from most relevant (1) to least relevant (4).

   (b) Share the image that you feel ranks the highest. Explain your choice and listen as others share their choice with you.

   (c) What image would you choose to replace the image that you feel ranks the lowest? Describe the image you would replace it with and explain your choice.

2. Fill in the unit review on pages 81–82 of your Portfolio.

Language skills

1. What is the spelling rule when using **(a)** a prefix and **(b)** a suffix?

2. **(a)** Identify whether the underlined word in each of the sentences below has had a prefix or a suffix added to it.

   ◀ My project was <u>incomplete</u>.

   ◀ What a <u>horrible</u> sight!

   ◀ This is such a <u>spacious</u> room.

   ◀ We need to <u>declutter</u> our house.

   (b) Examine the underlined terms above carefully. Find the root words and explain the meaning of each.

3. **(a)** In this chapter, you focused on vocabulary. List five new words that you learned while studying the theme of freedom. You may like to look at your vocabulary builder on pages 1–2 of your Portfolio to remind you.

   (b) Work with a partner using your chosen words. You should take turns testing each other's understanding of the five words using the questions below.

   ◀ What does the word mean?

   ◀ Give one synonym of the word.

   ◀ Give one antonym of the word.

   ◀ Put the word into a sentence.

   Try to help each other if you get stuck!

Oral assessment

 Prepare a speech starting with the statement: 'In order to be free, people must be equal.'

(Consider the statement carefully.

(Plan what you would like to say.

(Write and practise the delivery of your speech.

When you are ready, speak in front of your classmates.

Written assessment

 1. **(a)** Write a radio talk about your understanding of freedom in the space provided on pages 83–84 of your Portfolio.

(Think carefully about your understanding of freedom.

(Plan what you would like to say.

(Show awareness of your audience by engaging your listeners.

(b) Redraft your radio talk in the space provided on pages 123-124 of your Portfolio.

Exam skills

 1. 'Freedom means different things to different people.'

Select a text that you have studied (novel, play or film) and explain how this statement applies to at least one of the characters.

(a) Name the text and the author/playwright/director.

(b) Explain what freedom means to at least one of the characters in your chosen text. Refer to the text throughout your answer.

(c) Explain how one key moment makes the reader or audience aware of the freedom or lack of freedom within the world of your chosen text.

Write your answer in the space provided on pages 143–144 of your Portfolio.

Theme 8
Facing Challenges

What are challenges?

Challenges are difficulties that we must deal with. We face challenges every day at school, at home and out in the world. Our daily lives are made up of difficulties of all types. They can range from getting out of bed on a cold morning, to being persecuted for your skin colour. It is how we deal with these challenges that makes us who we are.

Why study this theme?

It is important to understand the different challenges that people face and how they can inspire people to take action. Often, it is these challenges that make people react creatively and produce meaningful and thought-provoking literature. Understanding challenges also helps us to become better people, as we are more aware of the struggles and issues of those around us.

Learning intentions

- Learn about different obstacles that people face.
- See how writers use challenges as inspiration.

Writing With Purpose
- Read an extract from a memoir reflecting on a challenge.

Poetry and Song
- Understand how poetic techniques can help communicate emotions.

Fiction
- Look at how challenges motivate and develop characters.

Stage and Screen
- Explore how challenges can be addressed using humour.

Media and Advertising
- Read and write feature articles that address challenges people face.
- Learn about podcasts.

Language Skills
- Learn how and when to use conjunctions.
- Revise verbs and adverbs.

 Discuss

1. Choose one of the images above and explain why you think it best represents the theme of challenges.
2. Would you add any other image to this selection to represent challenges?
3. Can you think of a story you have read in which a character faces a challenge?
4. Think of a time when you faced a challenge.
   (a) What was the challenge?
   (b) How did it make you feel?
   (c) Did you share your feelings with anyone? Why or why not?
   (d) How did you deal with the challenge?
   (e) What kinds of challenges do people face every day?

 5. 'Ever tried. Ever failed. No matter. Try Again. Fail again. Fail better.' (Samuel Beckett)
   In groups or pairs, think about a time when someone might experience failure.
   (a) What do you think this quote means?
   (b) What kind of advice would you offer this person?
   (c) Do you think it is easy to take advice after failure?

 Create

 Write your own definition of challenges in the space provided on page 90 of your Portfolio, by completing the sentence 'Challenges are ...'. You will return to this definition later on.

Challenges young people face

There are many challenges that young people can face as they are growing up. The challenge of fitting in and being accepted by your classmates and friends is one that everyone has faced at one time or another.

It is important to remember that everyone faces different challenges, and that you should always feel comfortable reaching out if you need some help dealing with a problem.

The following poem reminds us not to define ourselves by material things, but instead to value ourselves for who we truly are on the inside.

Not

By Erin Hanson

You are not your age,
Nor the size of clothes you wear,
You are not a weight,
Or the colour of your hair.
You are not your name,
Or the dimples in your cheeks,
You are all the books you read,
And all the words you speak,
You are your croaky morning voice,
And the smiles you try to hide,
You're the sweetness in your laughter,
And every tear you've cried,
You're the songs you sing so loudly
When you know you're all alone,
You're the places that you've been to,
And the one that you call home,
You're the things that you believe in,
And the people that you love,
You're the photos in your bedroom,
And the future you dream of,
You're made of so much beauty,
But it seems that you forgot,
When you decided that you were defined
By all the things you're not.

Discuss

1. How do you define who you are?
2. What makes you different from others?
 3. Work with a partner to list each of your personality traits. Then, discuss some traits that you do not possess.

 Understand

1. What is the rhyming scheme in this poem?
2. 'You are not your name.' Explain the meaning of this line in your own words.
3. What do you think is the main message of this poem?

 Explore

 1. Choose one line of the poem that you can most relate to and explain why you have chosen this line.
2. Suggest an alternative title for the poem and explain your choice.

 Create

 1. In pairs, write an additional two lines that could be added anywhere in the poem. Try to maintain the existing rhyming scheme.
 2. **(a)** Choose a line from the poem that would work as a slogan for an advertising campaign to promote positive mental health in your school. In groups, create an advertisement for this campaign that includes your chosen slogan. Your advertisement can be in any of the following formats:

      ◖ poster
      ◖ video or short film
      ◖ radio advertisement.

   (b) Create a hashtag for a social media campaign to accompany your advertisement.

 3. **(a)** Write your own poem about a personal challenge in the space provided on page 85 of your Portfolio.
 (b) Perform your poem for the class and choose one image to accompany your reading of it. After you have performed your poem, explain why you chose this image.

Conjunctions

Conjunctions are words that link phrases or other words together.

Some sentences are made up of more than one clause. These clauses are often joined together using conjunctions to make more interesting sentences.

*I like when my room is neat **and** tidy, **but** I really hate doing the vacuuming.*

*Our teacher wasn't well, **yet** she came to school.*

The word 'and' in the first example links the list of words in the first clause, while the word 'but' links the second clause with the first. In the second example, 'yet' links the two phrases, as the second is in spite of the first – even though the teacher was sick, she still came to school.

*I didn't do my homework **because** I was busy.*

In this sentence, the word 'because' introduces the reason behind the first clause.

The following are examples of commonly used conjunctions.

although	by	just	supposing	whereas
as	even if	nor	unless	wherever
as long as	despite	providing	until	whether
before	for	so	when	while

 Understand

1. Using the list of common conjunctions above, link each phrase in column one with a phrase in column two. Then write out the full sentences in your copy.

He passed his exams	the weather is fine.
Michelle arrived to her interview on time	you practise more.
You can go to the cinema this evening	he didn't do much revision.
They will go to the beach	the heavy traffic.
You won't pass your driving test	you have finished your homework.

2. Find the conjunctions in the poem 'Not' on page 326.

3. Complete the following sentences using a conjunction to add further information.

   (a) I missed the bus …

   (b) He dropped his phone in a puddle …

   (c) We bought him a new bicycle …

   (d) She was in hospital …

   (e) I don't know …

 **Discuss**

 With a partner, rank the following challenges in order, 1 being the toughest and 5 being the easiest. Discuss your reasons and share your thoughts with the class.

- Starting at a new school
- Failing an exam
- Losing your phone
- Fighting with a friend
- Breaking your leg

In the following short play, Emer faces the difficult challenge of starting at a new school.

Pastoral Care

Fade up lights.

A career guidance teacher's office in a second-level school. A small, cramped space overwhelmed by books, pamphlets, filing systems, posters.

Sitting behind a desk is **Ms Flynn** *(50s). She wears spectacles on a cord around her neck.* **Mr Gormley** *(40s) is standing to the side of* **Emer** *(12). He has a copybook in his hand.* **Ms Flynn** *and* **Mr Gormley** *are dressed in aged, faded clothing.* **Emer** *wears a tidy school uniform.*

Ms Flynn *is smiling at* **Emer**. **Emer** *is not sure why she has been brought here. She never gets into trouble.*

Emer:	(*to* **Ms Flynn**, *in response to a question, uncertain*) … Is it when someone steals something? … Like the thoughts or writing of someone else and they pretend that it's their own?
Flynn:	… That's exactly what it is!
Gormley:	(*still not entirely convinced*) … Can you spell it?
Emer:	… Em … p – l – a – g – i – a – r – i – s – m.
Flynn:	Wonderful!
Gormley:	… You're new to the area – aren't you?
Emer:	(*uncertain*) … Yeah.
Flynn:	And how are you finding it?
Emer:	(*uncertain*) … All right.
Gormley:	(*presenting the copybook and quoting from it*) This is a terrific essay.
	'Freedom of opinion and expression, tolerance, understanding, the right to an education' – you're just at a whole other level.
Emer:	(*Is that good or bad?*) … Oh. Thanks?
Gormley:	(*while walking over to the door*) … But it's just …

(**Mr Gormley** *opens the door. SFX:The roar of noisy corridors*)

Gormley:	(*with door open*) … They'll eat you alive.

(**Mr Gormley** *closes the door. SFX:The roar ceasing*)

SFX: sound effects

Flynn:	(*to* **Emer**) … We thought you might benefit from some words of advice, Emer.
Gormley:	(*returning to the desk*) … What's your name?
Emer:	(*again uncertain, seeing as they already know her name*) … em … Emer Mc Evoy?
Flynn:	If a teacher asks your name – just say 'What?'
Emer:	(*doesn't respond*)
Flynn:	'What?'
Emer:	… What?
Flynn:	… A little more impertinence.
Emer:	(*tries being impertinent*) … What?
Gormley:	… Not bad.
Flynn:	If a teacher asks you to perform a task in class – don't do it straight away –
Gormley:	or just pretend you can't do it –
Flynn:	– or complain and say something like, 'It's stupid!'

impertinence: rudeness

(**Emer** *doesn't respond.*)

Gormley:	… Go on.
Emer:	… It's stupid.
Gormley:	(*with an accent*) 'Stupid!'
Emer:	(*tries the accent*) … Stupid.
Gormley:	Yeah better – good!
Flynn:	… Make sure you get caught using your phone in class –
Gormley:	And if the teacher says 'Are you texting?'
Flynn:	Just say, 'No I'm on Facebook.'
Emer:	(*not sure if she has to repeat this*) … No …

(**Mr Gormley** *is encouraging* **Emer** *to continue.*)

Emer:	… I'm on Facebook.
Gormley:	That's it.
Flynn:	Otherwise only speak when you're spoken to.
Gormley:	And for God's sake don't use big words.
Flynn:	… And don't forget to work on your accent.

(*Both teachers smile at* **Emer**. *She smiles back uncertainly.*)

Discuss

1. What are the hardest things about starting at a new school?
2. What advice would you give to someone starting at a new school?

Understand

1. Where does this scene take place?

2. According to Emer, what is plagiarism? Add this word to your vocabulary builder on pages 1–2 of your Portfolio.
3. What do the words in brackets represent?

Explore

1. Choose one of the words below to describe Mr Gormley and give two reasons to explain your choice.
   - Friendly
   - Caring
   - Funny
   - Encouraging

2. What evidence from the scene suggests that this is a difficult school to attend?

3. Sound effects are used in this scene, both inside and outside the office. What do we learn about the setting from the sounds?

4. This scene depicts a conversation between three people. The exchange of ideas and thoughts between two or more characters in drama is called dialogue. Based on the dialogue, choose one of the characters in this scene and explain what you learned about him or her.

Create

1. In groups of three, act out this scene. Play close attention to the stage directions and the movements of each character.

2. (a) Imagine Emer leaves the office and goes back to the classroom, where she meets two of her classmates. Write a short dialogue that takes place between them in the space provided on page 86 of your Portfolio. Use the format of the script of *Pastoral Care* as a guideline.

   (b) Redraft your dialogue, improving on your first and adding in any sound or light effects, in the space provided on page 125 of your Portfolio.

331

The following short story is from a collection called *Owning It* by Donald R. Gallo, which contains stories about young people facing different challenges.

 **Discuss**

1. From the title 'Fatboy and Skinnybones', what do you think this story might be about?

2. Can you think of a time when somebody's words had a lasting effect on you?

3. People say hurtful things to each other all the time. What kinds of things do young people often tease each other about? Why do you think this is?

4. Can you think of a time when words failed you?

Fatboy and Skinnybones

So, yesterday I was walking to the supermarket down the street a couple of blocks. This is part of my regimen. I do this at least three afternoons a week, seeing how I work there part-time. I'll tell you what, though: I'm so big I've had to borrow one of the store's shopping carts to lean myself onto and make my way there easier. Otherwise my back would just crumble to bits. But it's a workout.

regimen: diet and exercise plan

I can feel the strain on my heart and lungs, and the south Texas heat doesn't help any. Amá, as a matter of fact, read that stress like this may even be worse for me because of the exertion. But what else am I going to do? I need some kind of workout, and this is it, really. The bike at home's a joke. I'm too big for it. Besides, I like the time I get to myself walking to work.

Amá: (Spanish) mum

I was maybe a half block away when a car pulled up beside me.

'That's quite a load you're carrying there, Gordilongo.'

Gordilongo: a variation of 'gordo', Spanish for 'fat boy'

I looked over. It was none other than Pimple-Faced Skinnybones. 'Nice ride,' I told him, but meant it sarcastically. He didn't get it. He was driving one of those small foreign jobs made up with a ground-effects kit, a spoiler on the trunk, and the funniest paint job I'd ever seen. Almost like he'd done it himself: purple flames along the green side panel that then petered out in sparks or stars or spiky dots. But the paint was textured. I could see the thickness of the brushstrokes.

'You like it?' he said, hanging his left arm out the door and caressing the bad paint.

'Sure,' I said. 'It's really you.' Meaning more loud and showy than cool.

'Thanks. I like it OK. Where you going?' He lowered the volume on some rap music.

'What do you care?' I said. I kept pushing the cart, looking forward mostly.

'Whoa, man. I'm just asking. I'm headed to H.E.B. to start work today. I'm training on the registers. How hard can that be? Take product, scan it, take people's money. A monkey can do that. I heard you work there, too?'

'Yeah, what of it?' Him working the registers meant I'd probably be training him. What kind of cosmic joke was God playing on me?

'That's some chip you got on your shoulder, man. You got to get over whatever it is bothering you.'

'You think so?'

'Sure. Like a duck – water off your back. In your case, lots of back, lots of water. He he he he.' He adjusted the left sideview mirror.

'Drive on, jerk. You don't want to be late on your first day.'

'I'd offer you a ride, but, well, I'm already low enough to the ground. And it looks like you're riding low and slow, too.' He revved his engine and screeched the back tires, leaving me behind.

What a jerk!

When I got to work, I left my buggy outside and went into the workroom to drop off my lunch. I saw Skinnybones sitting quiet in the corner. He looked up briefly and I noticed his eyes were red, like he'd been crying. He had a produce apron draped over his lap, which was funny because I'd looked at the schedule posted on the door and he was supposed to be training on the register (lucky for me, Mary had been assigned to work with him). I opened my locker and took out my back brace and my specially made stool.

He looked up, then down again.

'What? No joke about the size of the brace, how it can lift a horse, or a house? Nothing about why it is I get to sit down on the job? Fat *and* lazy?' I said.

He shook his head and sniffed.

'What's your problem? Work a bit too much for you already?'

'Shut up, why don't you?' he said

'Sure I will. Later.' *The dude can dish it out, but he can't take it*, I thought.

I left the workroom. I saw Jimmy, the day manager, just outside. He was talking to a couple of guys from produce and one from the bakery. They were all laughing but stopped when they saw me coming. When I got closer, Jimmy said, 'Gordo, how's it going?'

I shrugged. 'Not much to tell. What's up with the new kid in there?'

'That's what these guys were just telling me about,' Jimmy said. 'Get this – the kid comes in like he owns the place, telling everybody everything about everything and how he knows it all. Like working a register's beneath him. Luis here told him, "You've got no clue, kid." Can you believe it? The kid got in Luis's face and said, "You got no clue," and didn't get out of Luis's face.'

'Yeah,' said Luis. 'Real dumb. I mean, look at me.'

He was right – all muscle. 'I stared at him real mean and said, "Talk like that? You wanna go outside and back it up?" And I gave him a shove. Just a little one, you know. You should've seen the look in the kid's eyes. It was hilarious. I told him I was only joking, but to watch out who he talked like that to. The next guy might not be so nice.'

'So why's he crying?' I asked.

'I scared him so much, I guess, I spooked the pee out of him, literally. He looked down at his legs, then I did, too. He started crying right then. It'd be funnier if it wasn't so sad.'

I asked Jimmy if I could see what I could see about the kid. He gave me the go-ahead. So I stepped back into the workroom, set up my stool, and sat opposite the lockers. To my surprise, Skinnybones had pulled off his pants and was over by the sink, running them under the water.

'You know,' I said, 'girls come in here, too.'

'So?' he said. 'They don't need to look if they don't want. If they do, then they'll get an eyeful of all of me.'

The kid had the skinniest, longest legs I'd seen ever. He had knobs for knees, no sign of muscle anywhere.

'What you looking at?' he said.

'Just looking.'

'It's like you've never seen a slender build like mine.'

'Slender? That's what you call it?'

'Call it whatever you want to.' He was running the wet pants under the heat of the hand dryer now. After a few moments, he started putting them on. 'It's all words, man.' He wrapped the apron around his waist. 'I mean, look at this,' he said, pointing at the apron. 'It's supposed to be one-size-fits-all. Does this look like it fits? And would it fit you? I don't think so.'

The kid was right. The store had to special order mine off the Internet. 'So, you going out like that?' I asked.

'Like what?'

'They told me outside you'd peed yourself,' I said.

'They got it wrong. They must've meant I was all wet. Or wet behind the ears. It's all words, I tell you.' He finished tying the apron on. He looked up at me. 'You and me, we're not so different. You know how it goes for people like us. We've got to make do with what we've got.' He started out the workroom, then turned back. 'What's your name, anyway?' he asked.

'My name?'

'Yeah, what your mom called you when you were born?'

'It's Miguel. You?'

'Me? I'm Tony, but my friends call me *El Hueso*, the bone. I kind of like it.' He ran a hand through his hair and left me sitting on the stool.

I couldn't believe he liked being called El Hueso. Something else I couldn't wrap my brain around was that he'd wet himself and it didn't faze him one way or the other.

The door opened slightly. El Hueso stuck his head in.

'About at school the other day: sorry I made fun of you, Miguel.'

'Don't do it again, and we're OK.'

He smiled and the door closed.

He was right. If he could go out to the store wet like he was, I could be fat and pushing myself home on a buggy or sitting at my own special table at school instead of at a desk for regular-sized kids, or ordering super-size clothes from specialty stores online. I could be fatter than fat. Besides, it wasn't like I wasn't doing anything about it. I was trying my best to eat right, to get what exercise I could without hurting myself. I'd keep doing it.

I pushed myself off the stool, took a good breath, and headed out to the store myself.

But life isn't so easy as that; sometimes they're not *just* words, and words *are* like rocks. Sometimes, people can take it too far saying what they're saying, and really it's not what people say that hurts the most, but that they say it without thinking it might hurt. Like we aren't even there.

Understand

1. **(a)** Who is the narrator?

   (b) What kind of narrative voice is this, first-person or third-person?

2. What challenge does the narrator face?

3. Why does Miguel find it so difficult to exercise?

4. What is Jimmy's role in the supermarket?

Explore

1. Do you think that Miguel is motivated to lose weight? How do you know?

2. What impression do you get of Tony? Explain your answer.

3. What advice would you offer to Miguel at the end of the extract?

4. 'Words are just words, but I got something better.' This is something that Miguel says later on in the story. What valuable lesson do you think Miguel may have learned?

Create

1. Write a continuation to the story, outlining what might happen between Tony and Miguel.

2. Choose a genre of writing (opinion piece, short story, poem, play, etc.) and write 300 words in the space provided on pages 87–88 of your Portfolio on one of the following topics:

   ◖ The Power of Words

   ◖ Time Heals All Wounds

   ◖ What Motivates Bullies?

3. What if the story about Tony got around school the next day? Imagine the confrontation he might have with another school bully. Write an article for a school newspaper reporting the details of the confrontation.

4. Work in groups to create a digital presentation on how to deal with the issue of bullying. You may want to use PowerPoint, Prezi or Keynote to create your presentation.

In the following feature article, novelist Dave Rudden discusses his experiences of being bullied as a teenager, and explains why it is important to speak out instead of struggling alone.

Why teenage boys are told not to feel, and why that's so wrong

Author Dave Rudden was bullied when he was at school for being sensitive and bookish. He stayed silent about it for 10 years and now wishes he had spoken out instead of struggling on and suppressing the pain until the wound festered

I'm lucky enough to be able to say that words are my job. I've loved them since I was a kid – the sheer power of the right phrase in the right place. There's a magic to them – these simple sounds that can cause fights, mend friendships, inspire armies and create monsters. A well-chosen word is a weapon, and the wrong word can work its way like a splinter into your head so you never forget it, no matter how hard you try.

Weak. Cry-baby. Soft. Gay. Girl. Loser. Freak. Not a real man.

I was bullied as a teenager. I don't say this with any shame, because it's been 10 years and I've made my peace with it, and also because 43% of the UK's young people are going through it right now. It's your story as well, or a story you see out of the corner of your eye every lunch break. And for most of us, for a long time, it will be a story of silence.

BE A MAN.

We learn that on the playground and we have to learn it quick, because if we don't the next lesson has knuckles attached. I've never been good at not having feelings, to be honest. Things affect me. I worry. I care. I get invested in causes and people and books. I have so many emotions I had to invent fictional people to put them in, and because I think about words so much …

I wonder when *BEING A MAN* meant shutting up and toeing the line. I wonder when the Council of the Rules of Men (not a real thing) got together and decided that *open* meant *weak* and that bottling things up was better. That's not how science works (and that is, at base, what feelings are – chemicals reacting in your brain, as natural and human as the beating of a heart) They don't go anywhere just because you pretend they have.

Is lying to yourself strength?

I kept quiet for years, because I thought that was the way to make the bullying stop. I was quiet for years after the bullying *did* stop, because in order to survive I convinced myself not talking about it meant it wasn't real, because if it was real I'd talk about it.

And I've watched too many time travel shows to obsess a lot about changing my past. I am who I am because of my experiences, good and bad. The parts of me they targeted – being sensitive, being bookish, being the kid who handed in essays five pages too long because I loved words – are the parts of me I am proudest of now, the parts that allow me to do what I do.

But I wish I had told someone. I wish I hadn't decided I was alone in a room, a class, a school of guys deciding they were alone as well because no-one was willing to say the first word.

There's this movie scene. You know the one – the hero gets injured but manfully struggles on, refusing the help his companions know he needs. They continue, he struggles, lashes out in anger and –

dramatic music

– he collapses. The wound is infected. People recoil. Cue boiling water and sutures.

We're taught to ignore injury, to keep going, to not make a fuss. And we suppress the pain until the wound festers, and you get angry at yourself for getting hurt in the first place. As if being human was your fault. As if the smart thing to do isn't to treat the pain instead.

The boys who teach us to stay quiet do so because they're in pain, and like the lantern-jawed hero we're all supposed to be, they're afraid to look beneath the bandage. The pain of treatment would be too great, they think, and they attack others because if they're in pain others must be too.

Anger and fear are all we boys are allowed. Seems a bit of a raw deal.

I wouldn't go back and talk to Younger Me, if I could. He'd have far too many questions about how I got there, for one thing, and I don't want to be different than I am now. But I've watched bullies live like rats in a wheel, playing out the same patterns over and over again because they can't admit that they're in pain, and I've seen young men resolutely fight to hold onto the things that make them human, instead of hiding them just to fit in with everybody else. *That's* strength – the strength to speak up, for yourself and for others, the strength to be yourself, instead of what other people decide you should be. There's no power in spending your life in retreat from yourself, and I'd rather not wait until I drop from a wound I'm pretending not to have.

I care too much for that.

Focus on ... clichés

A **cliché** is an overused phrase or idea.

There are many sayings that people use regularly. For example, 'It's OK to be different', 'Sticks and stones may break my bones, but words will never hurt me' and 'Act your age'. The more we hear these phrases, the more they lose their meaning.

In literature, there are many clichés. For example, 'It was all a dream', 'They lived happily ever after'.

 Work in pairs to find some common sayings or phrases in Dave Rudden's article.

Discuss

1. Share some clichés that you know.
2. What do these clichés mean?
3. Is there any truth in them?
4. Discuss some well-known sayings that bother you and explain why they bother you.
5. Name some bullies from well-known television programmes, books and films.
6. Does seeing characters dealing with bullying in films and television shows help us to deal with the bullies in real life?

Understand

1. What is Dave Rudden's occupation?
2. What percentage of young people in the UK are being bullied, according to the article?
3. Name one of Dave Rudden's interests or hobbies.
4. Why did Dave Rudden stay silent for years after the bullying had stopped?

 ## Explore

 1. What kind of person do you think Dave Rudden is? Give reasons for your answer.

 2. What do you think Dave Rudden's issue is with the phrase 'Be a man'? Explain your answer.

3. Is there any difference between the bullies from Dave Rudden's youth and bullies today? Explain your answer.

4. Explain the difference between a news article and a feature article in your own words.

5. Compare and contrast Dave's experience of bullying with Jim's experience in the extract from *The Bully* on page 143.

 ## Create

 1. (a) In groups, discuss how you think bullying should be tackled in your school.

 (b) Work with your group to create a video for your anti-bullying campaign, inspired by the following quote from Dave Rudden's article:

> 'There's this movie scene. You know the one – the hero gets injured but manfully struggles on, refusing the help his companions know he needs. They continue, he struggles, lashes out in anger and –
>
> *dramatic music*'

OR

Work with your group to create a poster for your anti-bullying campaign.

 (c) As a group, show your video or poster to the class and give a presentation explaining how you think bullying could be tackled in your school.

Challenges of a changing world

The world is constantly changing. Technology is continually being developed to address challenges that we face in areas such as health, education and communication. However, these changes can also create new challenges.

A major challenge facing the newspaper industry is online news. Many people now choose to access the news through websites, social media and streaming services. This has had a negative effect on the print industry, as fewer physical papers are sold.

In the following article from thejournal.ie, journalist Paul Hosford reports on the decision of the British newspaper *The Independent* to become an online-only news source.

The final edition of The Independent newspaper is on newsstands today

The paper has been going for 30 years.

After 30 years, British newspaper The Independent will disappear from newsstands.

The paper last month announced its intention to become an online-only outlet, after circulation dropped from an all-time high of 420,000 to just 10% of that.

A wrap-around front page carries the words 'Stop Press'.

The newspaper will now be available online only, with its final editorial claiming history would be the judge of its 'bold transition … as an example for other newspapers around the world to follow'.

In its final front-page exclusive, the 'Indie' reported that British-based dissident Mohammed al-Massari was being pursued through the courts over a plot ordered by former Libyan leader Moamer Kadhafi to assassinate Saudi king Abdullah.

The paper carries an interview with Alistair Campbell, Tony Blair's former spin doctor, who had a running battle with the paper over their opposition to the 2003 invasion of Iraq.

spin doctor: a person employed (e.g. by a political party) to make information or events seem favourable to the press

The Independent was set up by three former journalists in 1986 and became known for its eye-catching, campaigning front pages and emphasis on photos.

In an editorial, The Guardian paid tribute to a 'really rather wonderful newspaper' that had suffered from dramatic changes to the advertising market, notably the shift in revenues to sites such as Facebook.

'Great newspapers which have survived for centuries find their business models challenged as never before. So no one will celebrate the end of the Independent in print,' it said.

The paper is the first British daily to close since 1995, when Today folded.

The Independent's Russian-born British owner, Evgeny Lebedev, who announced the closure of the print edition last month, wrote that journalism had 'changed beyond recognition' and the newspaper 'must change too'.

Discuss

1. List some advantages of print media over digital media.
2. List some advantages of digital media over print media.
3. What is the most effective way to get information to young people today?

Understand

1. What has happened to *The Independent* newspaper?
2. Has *The Independent* stopped all publication?
3. We are told that circulation dropped from 'an all-time high of 420,000 to just 10% of that.' What is 10% of 420,000?
4. When was *The Independent* set up?

Explore

1. Why do you think *The Independent* had to become an online-only outlet?
2. Give two reasons why the news about *The Independent* has not been welcomed by most people.
3. In what way has journalism 'changed beyond recognition', in your opinion?
4. Think of all the ways that you and your classmates use apps every day. How could you use these apps in order to combat a serious issue among young people?

Investigate

As a class, conduct a survey to find out how many people read online news. Try to survey people from different age groups (classmates, siblings, teachers, parents, grandparents, etc.). Collate and discuss your findings.

Create

1. Identify a challenge facing young people today. Create a mini-documentary about your classmates' thoughts on this challenge.

2. Carry out a class debate on the following motion: *This house believes that printed newspapers are a thing of the past.*

Mary Robinson served as the first female President of Ireland from 1990 to 1997. She went on to become the United Nations High Commissioner for Human Rights until 2002.

The following extract from her book *Everybody Matters: A Memoir* details her opinion of Ireland joining the European Economic Community (EEC) (the body that the European Union developed out of) in 1973. She reflects on the challenges facing Ireland at this time, and explains why she felt Ireland should become a member of the EEC.

Everybody Matters

I felt strongly that it was in Ireland's interests to become part of a wider European grouping of states. This would help us to stop seeing ourselves always reflected in the mirror of Britain, next door. Even then Ireland still had some of the feeling of inferiority of a post-colonial country. There had long been the sense that the English looked down on or tried to ignore Northern Ireland and didn't really think very highly of Ireland or Irish society, whereas the French were interested in our culture, the Germans were interested in our writers, the Italians were interested in the beauty of our landscape. I thought that joining the EEC and becoming part of a community of nine would help Ireland come out of the shadow of its more dominant neighbour and negotiate with the other member states in the context of EEC regulations and directives. I believed we could find common ground with France, for example, in agriculture, and with Britain on other aspects of legislation where we would have a common tradition, so that instead of a post-colonial semi-dependency, we would be more mature. I felt that it would actually reinforce our sense of identity, because we would take our place proudly as one of the members of the EEC.

post-colonial
after colonial rule (e.g. British rule in Ireland)

Discuss

1. Mary Robinson is speaking about challenges that faced Ireland as a nation in the 1970s. What challenges do you feel that Ireland faces today?
2. What do you know about the European Union?

Understand

1. What major challenge existed for Ireland at this time, according to Mary Robinson?
2. Identify one argument that Mary Robinson gave in support of joining the EEC.
3. According to Mary Robinson, what aspect of Ireland and Irish life and culture were **(a)** the French, **(b)** the Germans and **(c)** the Italians interested in?

Explore

 Do you think Mary Robinson is proud of her country? Give reasons for your answer.

Investigate

 Carry out some research on the European Union and its origins. Try to find the following information:

◖ when it was established
◖ who it was established by
◖ what its objectives are
◖ who are the current members
◖ at least one other interesting fact or statistic.

Write up a short fact file on the European Union and present your findings to the class.

Create

 Carry out a class debate on the following motion: *This house believes that Britain's exit from the European Union is good news for Ireland.*

Nowadays, environmental changes due to human activity are one of the biggest challenges the world is facing.

Discuss

What kind of environmental challenges does our world face today?

Focus on ... podcasts

A **podcast** is a digital audio file available online.

Popular podcasts are often series that subscribers can follow and get the automatic download of recent episodes. Some popular podcasts are:

- Radiolab
- The Second Captains Podcast
- HowStuffWorks
- TED Talks Daily
- The Daily

Are there any podcasts that you like to listen to? Discuss them with your classmates.

In the following podcast, Avi Steinberg looks at the effects of global warming on the polar ice caps. NASA has been charting their retreat for 10 years. Listen to the first 13 minutes of this podcast and answer the questions. You can listen to the whole podcast when you have finished.

https://www.theguardian.com/environment/audio/2017/aug/11/where-global-warming-gets-real-inside-nasas-mission-to-the-north-pole-podcast

Understand

1. According to the podcast, how does Greenland compare in size to the United States?
2. How was the ice sheet formed?
3. What is Operation IceBridge?
4. How can a person access information from the NASA dataset?
5. What is John Sonntag's major concern?

 Explore

1. How would you describe Sonntag in your own words?
2. Podcasts are audio only. How does the presenter succeed in bringing the subject matter of this podcast to life?

 Investigate

 In groups, discuss how images could be used to inform people of the effects of global warming and climate change. For example:

◖ graphs
◖ bar charts
◖ pie charts
◖ symbols
◖ colours.

Brainstorm your ideas on a large sheet of paper to create a poster. Present your ideas to the class, using the poster as a stimulus.

 Create

1. Using the description of the ice sheets in the Arctic, create an infographic to present the data in an engaging and interesting way.

 2. Work in groups to choose a topic that you are interested in and write a short script for a podcast. You may have more than one speaker. When you have practised the script, record yourselves to create your podcast.

Inequality and discrimination

Unfortunately, inequality and discrimination are on-going problems in the world. Many people face challenges due to their environment, poverty, being denied their human rights or being discriminated against due to their race, sex or gender.

The following infographics deal with various inequalities people in different parts of the world face.

VERY POOR PEOPLE SPEND

50-75%

OF THEIR INCOME ON FOOD.

Source: Ivanic & Martin, 2008

Climate change will affect food security and human health in many ways, including via food safety.

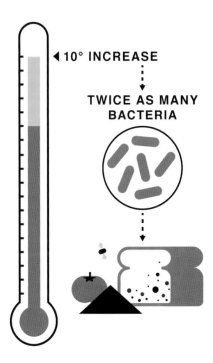

◄ 10° INCREASE

TWICE AS MANY BACTERIA

Bacterial growth rates approx. double with every 10 °C rise in temperature above 10 °C.

Source: James and James 2010

In drought-prone countries, children under five are up to

50% MORE

likely to be malnourished if born during a drought.

Source: UNDP 2007

If women had access to resources,
on-farm yields could **INCREASE BY 20-30%.**

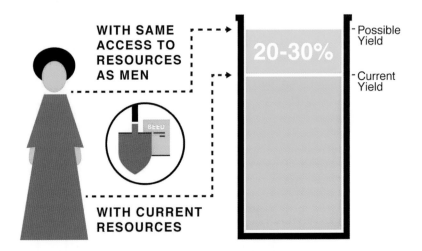

WITH SAME ACCESS TO RESOURCES AS MEN

WITH CURRENT RESOURCES

20-30%

- Possible Yield
- Current Yield

This extra output could reduce the number
of hungry people in the world by

12-17%.

Source: FAO, 2011

265 MILLION PEOPLE

will face a **5% DECREASE** in growing
season in the next 40 years.

Source: Ericksen et al., 2011

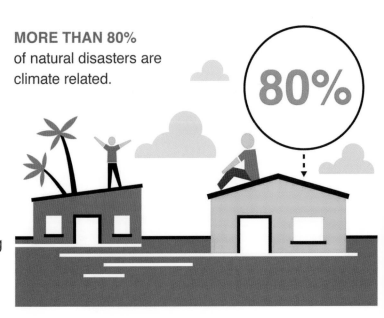

MORE THAN 80%
of natural disasters are
climate related.

80%

Source: GAR 2013

Understand

1. What is most likely to happen to half of the children under five in drought-prone countries?
2. If women had access to resources, the extra output would be between 12 and 17%. True or false?
3. How much of a decrease in the growing season will 265 million people see over the next 40 years?

Explore

1. Why do you think climate change might have an impact on the increase of bacteria in food?
2. According to the infographic, children born during a drought are at a disadvantage when it comes to nutrition. Can you explain why this might be?

3. Which infographic do you find most effective? Explain your choice.
4. **(a)** Choose one of the infographics and express the information in words. For example:

   According to a study from 2008, extremely poor people worldwide spend between a half and three-quarters of their income on food.

   (b) Write a personal response to the information you have just described.

Investigate

Think of a challenge that people face today. Research this issue and find one or two statistics that explain the issue further. Carefully check your sources and make sure your statistics are correct.

Create

Create an infographic to represent your findings in the Investigate task above, in the space provided on page 89 of your Portfolio. List the sources for your information underneath your infographic.

Throughout history, people have been discriminated against due to their race. This persecution has inspired some very thought-provoking work. The poetry and writing of Langston Hughes, an African-American poet, social activist, novelist and playwright, is an example.

The following poem is written exactly as it would be spoken.

Mother to Son
By Langston Hughes

Well, son, I'll tell you:
Life for me ain't been no crystal stair.
It's had tacks in it,
And splinters,
And boards torn up,
And places with no carpet on the floor—
Bare.
But all the time
I'se been a-climbin' on,
And reachin' landin's,
And turnin' corners,
And sometimes goin' in the dark
Where there ain't been no light.
So boy, don't you turn back.
Don't you set down on the steps
'Cause you finds it's kinder hard.
Don't you fall now—
For I'se still goin', honey,
I'se still climbin',
And life for me ain't been no crystal stair.

 **Focus on ...** **writing phonetically**

Phonetic writing is writing that is written as it sounds, instead of using the correct spelling.

Phonetic writing can be used to illustrate the accent of a speaker.

Discuss

1. Do you remember any other poems by Langston Hughes from First Year?
2. Share what you know about Langston Hughes.

Understand

1. What kind of life has the mother in the poem led?
2. The mother says that her life 'ain't been no crystal stair'. What device is the poet using here?

Explore

1. What do you think the 'tacks' and 'splinters' are that the mother is referring to?
 2. What kind of person is the mother in this poem, in your opinion? Explain your answer.
 3. What is the main message behind the poem, in your opinion? Back up your answer using quotations from the poem.
4. Suggest an alternative title for this poem and explain your choice.
5. **(a)** Choose a line from the poem and rewrite it as if it is being said in one of the accents below (use YouTube to listen to your chosen accent):
   ◖ Scottish
   ◖ Australian
   ◖ Welsh
 (b) Swap your line with a partner and each guess which accent your partner has rewritten the line in.
   (c) Why do you think phonetic language might appeal to the reader?

Create

1. Draw a picture of life as described in this poem.
 2. **(a)** In pairs, discuss other metaphors for life that you have heard of. For example:
   ◖ Life is a climb, but the view is great.
   ◖ All the world's a stage ...
 (b) Now, come up with your own metaphors for life and share your ideas with the class.

The characters in the following extract from Mildred D. Taylor's novel *Roll of Thunder, Hear My Cry* face similar challenges to those faced by the mother and son in the Langston Hughes poem on page 348.

The story follows the Logan family, a poor African-American family living in rural Mississippi in the 1930s. This was a time in the United States known as the Great Depression. Poverty was widespread, and black people were segregated in all aspects of life.

In this extract, Cassie Logan describes her experience with her younger brother, Little Man, on his first day at an elementary school for black children only.

 **Discuss**

What challenges do you think Cassie and her family might face in their day-to-day lives?

Roll of Thunder, Hear My Cry

'Cassie Logan!'

'Yes, ma'am?' I jumped up quickly to face Miss Crocker.

'Aren't you willing to work and share?'

'Yes'm.'

'Then say so!'

'Yes'm,' I murmured, sliding back into my seat as Mary Lou, Gracey, and Alma giggled. Here it was only five minutes into the new school year and already I was in trouble.

By ten o'clock, Miss Crocker had rearranged our seating and written our names on her seating chart. I was still sitting beside Gracey and Alma but we had been moved from the third to the first row in front of a small potbellied stove. Although being eyeball to eyeball with Miss Crocker was nothing to look forward to, the prospect of being warm once the cold weather set in was nothing to be sneezed at either, so I resolved to make the best of my rather dubious position.

Now Miss Crocker made a startling announcement: This year we would all have books.

Everyone gasped, for most of the students had never handled a book at all besides the family Bible. I admit that even I was somewhat excited. Although Mama had several books, I had never had one of my very own.

'Now we're very fortunate to get these readers,' Miss Crocker explained while we eagerly awaited the unveiling. 'The county superintendent of schools himself brought these books down here for our use and we must take extra-good care of them.' She moved toward her desk. 'So let's all promise that we'll take the best care possible of these new

books.' She stared down, expecting our response. 'All right, all together, let's repeat, "We promise to take good care of our new books."' She looked <u>sharply</u> at me as she spoke.

'WE PROMISE TO TAKE GOOD CARE OF OUR NEW BOOKS!'

'Fine,' Miss Crocker beamed, then proudly threw back the tarpaulin.

Sitting so close to the desk, I could see that the covers of the books, a motley red, were badly worn and that the gray edges of the pages had been marred by pencils, crayons, and ink. My anticipation at having my own book ebbed to a sinking disappointment. But Miss Crocker continued to beam as she called each fourth grader to her desk and, recording a number in her roll book, handed him or her a book.

As I returned from my trip to her desk, I noticed the first graders <u>anxiously</u> watching the disappearing pile. Miss Crocker must have noticed them too, for as I sat down she said, 'Don't worry, little ones, there are plenty of readers for you too. See there on Miss Davis's desk.' Wide eyes turned to the covered teacher's platform directly in front of them and an audible sigh of relief swelled in the room.

I glanced across at Little Man, his face lit in eager excitement. I knew that he could not see the soiled covers or the marred pages from where he sat, and even though his penchant for cleanliness was often annoying, I did not like to think of his disappointment when he saw the books as they really were. But there was nothing that I could do about it, so I opened my book to its center and began browsing through the spotted pages. Girls with blond braids and boys with blue eyes stared up at me. I found a story about a boy and his dog lost in a cave and began reading while Miss Crocker's voice droned on <u>monotonously</u>.

Suddenly I grew conscious of a break in that monotonous tone and I looked up. Miss Crocker was sitting at Miss Davis's desk with the first-grade books stacked before her, staring fiercely down at Little Man, who was pushing a book back upon the desk.

'What's that you said, Clayton Chester Logan !' she asked.

The room became gravely silent. Everyone knew that Little Man was in big trouble for no one, but no one, ever called Little Man 'Clayton Chester' unless she or he meant serious business.

Little Man knew this too. His lips parted slightly as he took his hands from the book. He quivered, but he did not take his eyes from Miss Crocker. 'I – I said may I have another book please, ma'am,' he squeaked. 'That one's dirty.'

'Dirty!' Miss Crocker echoed, appalled by such temerity. She stood up, gazing down upon Little Man like a bony giant, but Little Man raised his head and continued to look into her eyes. 'Dirty! And just who do you think you are, Clayton Chester? Here the county is giving us these wonderful books during these hard times and you're going to stand there and tell me that the book's too dirty? Now you take that book or get nothing at all!'

Little Man lowered his eyes and said nothing as he stared at the book, For several moments he stood there, his face barely visible above the desk, then he turned and looked at the few remaining books and, seeming to realize that they were as badly soiled as the one Miss Crocker had given him, he looked across the room at me. I nodded and Little Man, glancing up again at Miss Crocker, slid the book from the edge of the desk, and with his back straight and his head up returned to his seat.

Miss Crocker sat down again. 'Some people around here seem to be giving themselves airs. I'll tolerate no more of that.' she scowled. 'Sharon Lake, come get your book.'

I watched Little Man as he scooted into his seat beside two other little boys. He sat for a while with a stony face looking out the window; then, evidently accepting the fact that the book in front of him was the best that he could expect, he turned and opened it. But as he stared at the book's inside cover, his face clouded, changing from sulky acceptance to puzzlement. His brows furrowed. Then his eyes grew wide, and suddenly he sucked in his breath and sprang from his chair like a wounded animal, flinging the book onto the floor and stomping madly upon it.

Miss Crocker rushed to Little Man and grabbed him up in powerful hands. She shook him vigorously, then set him on the floor again. 'Now, just what's gotten into you, Clayton Chester?'

But Little Man said nothing. He just stood staring down at the open book, shivering with indignant anger.

'Pick it up,' she ordered.

'No!' defied Little Man.

'No? I'll give you ten seconds to pick up that book, boy, or I'm going to get my switch.'

switch: wooden stick

Little Man bit his lower lip, and I knew that he was not going to pick up the book. Rapidly, I turned to the inside cover of my own book and saw immediately what had made Little Man so furious. Stamped on the inside cover was a chart which read:

PROPERTY OF THE BOARD OF EDUCATION Spokane County, Mississippi			
CHRONOLOGICAL ISSUANCE	DATE OF ISSUANCE	CONDITION OF BOOK	RACE OF STUDENT
1	September 1922	New	White
2	September 1923	Excellent	White
3	September 1924	Excellent	White
4	September 1925	Very Good	White
5	September 1926	Good	White
6	September 1927	Good	White
7	September 1928	Average	White
8	September 1929	Average	White
9	September 1930	Average	White
10	September 1931	Poor	White
11	September 1932	Poor	White
12	September 1933	Very Poor	nigra
13			
14			
15			

Understand

1. **(a)** Match the following words with the correct definition.

Dubious	Boring, unwavering tone
Ebbed	A strong liking for something
Penchant	Boldness or confidence
Monotonously	Declined or decreased
Temerity	Of questionable quality

    (b) Find these words in the extract. Read the sentences again, keeping in mind the correct definitions. Now, write your own sentences for each of these words.

    (c) Add these words to your vocabulary builder on pages 1–2 of your Portfolio.

2. Why does Cassie get in trouble at the start of the lesson?

3. What is Ms Crocker's startling announcement?

4. What is Clayton Chester's nickname?

5. According to the chart, how old was the book by the time Little Man receives it?

Explore

1. 'Although Mama had several books, I had never had one of my very own.' What does this tell you about Cassie's family background?

2. What kind of relationship do you think Cassie and Little Man have?

3. In your opinion, what was it about the books that made Little Man so angry?

4. Miss Crocker says that some people are 'giving themselves airs'. What do you think she means by this?

5. How might the story be different if it were written from Miss Crocker's point of view?

6. Contrast Cassie's school to your own. List at least three differences.

7. The poem 'Mother to Son' (page 348) and the novel *Roll of Thunder, Hear My Cry* were both written by African-American writers. What themes do they both deal with? Are these themes still relevant today?

Create

1. Is there anything that you feel you and your classmates are lacking regarding learning material and resources? Write a letter to the principal requesting this material.

2. Write a diary entry from the perspective of Little Man after the school day is over.

Verbs and adverbs

Verbs are action words.

In the present tense, there are two main tenses: the present simple and the present continuous.

The present simple is used to talk about things in general.

*Elizabeth **reads** the newspaper every day.*

*Bill does not drink coffee, he **drinks** only tea.*

The present continuous is used to describe something that you are currently doing, and ends in –ing.

*I am **looking** for a job.*

*Maria is **learning** French.*

Now, let's improve our sentences even more by adding some adverbs.

Adverbs change verbs, adjectives or other adverbs.

Adverbs often end in -ly, but not always! There are many types of adverbs.

- Adverbs of manner tell us how an action occurs: *He walked **slowly**.*
- Adverbs of place tell us where an action occurs: *She ran **down** the street.*
- Adverbs of time tell us when an action occurs: *I went to the shop **yesterday**.*
- Adverbs of frequency tell us how often an action occurs: *I **usually** walk to school.*
- Adverbs of degree tell us about the intensity or degree of something: *The water is **extremely** cold.*
- Interrogative adverbs appear at the beginning of a question: ***What** is happening?*

Adverbs can be used to change adjectives: *The house is **very** small.* 'Very' (adverb) modifies 'small' (adjective).

 Understand

1. Improve the three present continuous examples above by adding adverbs.
2. Look back at the extract from *Roll of Thunder, Hear My Cry* (pages 350–352). Three adverbs have been underlined in this extract: sharply, monotonously and anxiously.
   (a) Find five more adverbs in the extract.
   (b) Decide what category each adverb you find falls into.
3. Write out the following sentences, adding adverbs where possible.
   (a) She walked to the door.
   (b) Every morning we get on the bus and read the newspaper.
   (c) Tim spoke, stood up and ran to the door.

 4. Look at your last piece of written homework or classwork and try to improve it by adding some adverbs.

Facing challenges

There are endless different challenges that people can face, and we all deal with challenges in different ways.

In the following interview, adventurer, athlete and motivational speaker Mark Pollock explains how he has faced up to many challenges in his life.

'The way I faced up to my blindness and paralysis was just replicating what I'd learned through sport'

We caught up with two-time Commonwealth medallist, adventurer and cure for paralysis activist Mark Pollock.

'I'M STANDING THERE, my hips are forward and the physios were blocking my knees. He pushes the knees back and I drive my hips forward.

With the electrical simulator turned on and me trying to straighten my legs, my hips went forward and my knees came back and I'm in the standing position.

Because I can't see it or feel it, I needed the guy in front of me to say "I'm not holding, I'm not holding." As unusual as it was for me, the guy holding my knees was really nervous that I was just going to collapse.'

10 November 2015. Mark Pollock remembers, as clear as day, the first time he stood unassisted since the accident which left him paralysed from the waist down in 2010.

Many people may be aware of his story, but if you aren't here's a quick run-through.

Pollock has said before that the present is almost like his third life. The first was his life before he lost his sight, the second was after blindness and before paralysis, and the third is now – dealing with both blindness and paralysis.

Born in Belfast, he was a talented rower and sailor growing up, but always had problems with his sight.

'I wasn't allowed to pick up a contact sport so sailing and rowing were originally what I did whenever I could see and walk,' he tells *The42*.

Aged 22 and coming towards the end of his time in Trinity College Dublin, over a period of two weeks, Pollock lost his sight. His vision started to go blurry, and his left retina became detached. He went through various operations and procedures, but nothing could be done.

In a matter of days, his world was turned upside down.

'When you acquire a disability, everything changes. Everything.

When I went blind, I didn't have a watch. When I opened my eyes, I didn't know if it was night or day, I couldn't tell what time it was. You can't leave the house on your own.

Everything is new, from telling the time to the way you find your clothes to put on in the morning, to how you move about the house and then outside.

Everything was different, and I spent those years after blindness trying to just rebuild my identity – which was to go and get a job, to study, and more particularly, to go back rowing.

Getting back into rowing – it took three years to – that was the big change where I really felt like I was confident again, that I was competing again. It's probably the other way around. Through the competition was where I gathered my confidence again.'

He picked himself up, dusted himself off and got on with life.

Pollock won silver and bronze rowing medals at the 2002 Commonwealth Games. He recalls how he kayaked across the Irish Sea, did the Round Ireland Yacht Race and took part in the North Pole Marathon.

In 2009, to mark the 10th anniversary of his blindness, he completed one of the biggest adventures possible and became the first blind man to reach the South Pole.

'All of those were races, and had a competitive element to it which is where I felt at home,' he smiles.

Then came July 2010. And his life took another incredulous turn.

Just weeks before his wedding, Pollock fell through a second-storey window onto a patio, and critically damaged his spinal cord. He was left paralysed from the waist down, and subsequently, a wheelchair user.

'I'm certainly getting a chance to learn how to deal with challenges,' he laughs, his remarkable positivity shining through. 'I'm getting good at it now it would seem.

I go back to the days when I was 12, 13 and 14, rowing on the Lagan River in Belfast or sailing around, club racing on the Belfast Lough in my boat, and you learn through sport how to win.

You learn how to succeed. And you also learn what it feels like to fail, and be beaten. You learn that neither success nor failure defines you for the rest of your life. You just go back to training, learn from it and move on, whether it's a win or a loss.

I think, in fact, the way I faced up to my blindness, and ultimately faced up to my paralysis, was just replicating what I'd learned on the water as a rower and a sailor.

Acknowledge that it's there, acknowledge that that's the challenge and then decide what you're going to do about it.'

And that, in a nutshell, is what he has done.

Understand

1. What was the first major challenge that Mark Pollock faced?
2. According to Mark, what change does a person go through after acquiring a disability?
3. What happened to Mark that resulted in his paralysis?

 Explore

 1. Based on this interview, how would you describe Mark? Give reasons for your answer.

 2. Do you think that Mark is a good example of someone who has faced a challenge? Use evidence from the article in your answer.

3. What message do you take from this piece? Explain your answer.

 Investigate

 1. Work in groups to research some new technologies being developed that could help people with visual impairments. Share your findings with the class.

 2. Work in groups to assess how accessible your school is for people who use wheelchairs. Write a report on your findings.

 Create

1. 'You learn that neither success nor failure defines you for the rest of your life.' Write a letter to Mark, inviting him to come in and speak to your classmates about challenges in life.

 2. **(a)** In pairs, write a short scene in which you explore a challenge facing two or more characters.

 (b) When you have finished writing your scene, practise acting it out together, then perform it for the rest of the class.

Many people face the challenge of poverty and hunger. In the past, people who were not able to support themselves were offered accommodation and employment in workhouses. Unfortunately, conditions in workhouses were harsh and the food was monotonous and portions were rationed.

In the following extract from *Oliver Twist* by Charles Dickens, the boys in the workhouse try to find a way to obtain more food for themselves.

Oliver Twist

The room in which the boys were fed, was a large stone hall, with a copper at one end: out of which the master, dressed in an apron for the purpose, and assisted by one or two women, ladled the gruel at mealtimes. Of this festive composition each boy had one porringer, and no more— except on occasions of great public rejoicing, when he had two ounces and a quarter of bread besides.

porringer: small bowl

The bowls never wanted washing. The boys polished them with their spoons till they shone again; and when they had performed this operation (which never took very long, the spoons being nearly as large as the bowls), they would sit staring at the copper, with such eager eyes, as if they could have devoured the very bricks of which it was composed; employing themselves, meanwhile, in sucking their fingers most assiduously, with the view of cathcing up any stray splashes of gruel that might have been cast thereon. Boys have generally excellent appetites. Oliver Twist and his companions suffered the tortures of slow starvation for three months: at last they got so voracious and wild with hunger, that one boy, who was tall for his age, and hadn't been used to that sort of thing (for his father had kept a small cook-shop), hinted darkly to his companions, that unless he had another basin of gruel per diem, he was aftaid he might some night happen to eat the boy who slept next to him, who happened to be a weakly youth of tender age. He had a wild, hungry eye; and they implicitly believed him. A council was held; lots were cast who should walk up to the master after supper that evening, and ask for more; and it fell to Oliver Twist.

assiduously: carefully

voracious: greedy

per diem: per day

implicitly: wholeheartedly

The evening arrived; the boys took their places. The master, in his cook's uniform, stationed himself at the copper; his pauper assistants ranged themselves behind him; the gruel was served out; and a long grace was said over the short commons. The gruel disappeared; the boys whispered to each other, and winked at Oliver; while his next neighbours nudged him. Child as he was, he was desperate with hunger, and reckless with misery. He rose from the table; and advancing to the master, basin and spoon in hand, said: somewhat alarmed at his own temerity:

'Please, sir, I want some more.'

The master was a fat, healthy man; but he turned very pale. He gazed in stupefied astonishment on the small rebel for some seconds, and then clung for support to the copper. The assistants were paralysed with wonder; the boys with fear.

stupefied: dazed

'What!' said the master at length, in a faint voice.

'Please, sir,' replied Oliver, 'I want some more.'

Understand

1. Why did the bowls never need washing?
2. How do you know the boys were hungry?
3. Why did the boys decide finally to ask the master for more food?
4. How did they decide which boy would ask the master for more?
5. **(a)** Put the following words into sentences.
   - Assiduously
   - Voracious
   - Implicitly
   - Stupified

   (b) Add these words to the vocabulary builder on pages 1–2 of your Portfolio.

Explore

1. Do you think the master also experienced extreme hunger? Give reasons for your answer
2. **(a)** Why do you think the master was so surpised at Oliver Twist's request?
   (b) What does this tell you about the relationship that existed between the master and the boys?
3. You are a director and you have decided to transform this extract into a dramatic scene. Describe how you would direct this scene, using the headings below.
   - Props
   - Stage direction and movement
   - Costume

Create

Imagine the conversation that took place between the boys on the evening they decided to approach the master requesting more food. Write the dialogue that might have taken place between Oliver Twist and the other boys.

In Unit 2: The World Around Me, we discovered how humour can be an important tool when viewing the world. The following comedy sketch from *Monty Python's Flying Circus*, series 1, episode 8 (1969) uses humour to explore a rather unusual social challenge. You can watch the sketch on Monty Python's YouTube channel: https://youtu.be/UY-I3QTT8mY

Hell's Grannies

Opens with a pan across Bolton. Voice of reporter.

Voice Over   This is a frightened city. Over these houses, over these streets hangs a pall of fear. Fear of a new kind of violence which is terrorizing the city. Yes, gangs of old ladies attacking defenseless fit young men.

Film of old ladies beating up two young men; then several grannies walking aggressively along street, pushing passers-by aside.

First Young Man   Well they come up to you, like, and push you – shove you off the pavement, like. There's usually four or five of them.

Second Young Man   Yeah, this used to be a nice neighborhood before the old ladies started moving in. Nowadays some of us daren't even go down to the shops.

Third Young Man   Well Mr. Johnson's son Kevin, he don't go out anymore. He comes back from wrestling and locks himself in his room.

Film of grannies harassing an attractive girl.

Voice Over   What are they in it for, these old hoodlums, these layabouts in lace?

First Granny *(voice over)* Well it's something to do isn't it?

Second Granny *(voice over)* It's good fun.

Third Granny *(voice over)* It's like you know, well, innit, eh?

Voice Over   Favorite targets for the old ladies are telephone kiosks.

Film of grannies carrying off a telephone kiosk; then painting slogans on a wall.

Policeman *(coming up to them)* Well come on, come on, off with you. Clear out, come on get out of it. *(they clear off; he turns to camera)* We have a lot of trouble with these oldies. Pension day's the worst – they go mad. As soon as they get their hands on their money they blow it all on milk, bread, tea, tin of meat for the cat.

Cut to cinema.

Cinema Manager Yes, well of course they come here for the two o'clock matinee, all the old bags out in there, especially if it's something like 'The Sound of Music'. We get seats ripped up, hearing aids broken, all that sort of thing.

A policeman hustles two grannies out of the cinema.

Cut to reporter walking along street.

Reporter The whole problem of these senile delinquents lies in their complete rejection of the values of contemporary society. They've seen their children grow up and become accountants, stockbrokers and even sociologists, and they begin to wonder if it is all really ... *(disappears downwards rapidly)* arggh!

Shot of two grannies replacing manhole cover.

Cut to young couple.

Young Man Oh well we sometimes feel we're to blame in some way for what our gran's become. I mean she used to be happy here until she started on the crochet.

Reporter *(off-screen)* Crochet?

Young Man Yeah. Now she can't do without it. Twenty balls of wool a day, sometimes. If she can't get the wool she gets violent. What can we do about it?

Film of grannies on motorbikes roaring down streets and through a shop. One has 'Hell's Grannies' on her jacket.

Understand

In the case of each of the following, write the letter corresponding to the correct answer in your copy.

1. Who is terrorising the city of Bolton?
   (a) Gangs of young people
   (b) Gangs of motorcyclists
   (c) Gangs of old ladies

2. What does the voice over describe as a 'favorite target' for the grannies?
   (a) Tea, bread and milk
   (b) Shop windows
   (c) Telephone kiosks

3. According to the reporter, what three professions does he associate with contemporary society?
   (a) Accountants, psychologists and sociologists
   (b) Accountants, stockbrokers and sociologists
   (c) Accountants, stockbrokers and social workers

4. Crochet is:
   (a) the creation of fabric using a needle and wool.
   (b) a game played with dice.
   (c) a type of food.

Explore

1. What kind of behaviour would you typically expect from a group of elderly ladies?

 2. Explain how parody is used in this piece. Support your answer with reference to the script.

 3. Why do you think Mr Johnson's son Kevin does not go out much anymore? Is this surprising?

4. How is this comedy sketch similar to the play *Pastoral Care* on pages 329–330? Write a short paragraph comparing the two.

Create

 In this parody, the general perception of grannies is turned upside down. In groups, discuss a social challenge that you may have experienced. Using 'Hell's Grannies' as an example, create a news broadcast or short film to present this topic in an extreme and humourous way. Possible social challenges that could be explored are:

◖ teenagers and technology
◖ gender roles
◖ the arts.

Sometimes we struggle to come up with new and interesting ideas. In the arts, people are always trying to create something new and beautiful, whether it's with words, music, colour or movement. Unfortunately, inspiration does not always come.

In the following poem, the poet gives some advice to those facing the challenge of trying to write.

'Do You Have Any Advice For Those of Us Just Starting Out?'

By Ron Koertge

Give up sitting dutifully at your desk. Leave
your house or apartment. Go out into the world.

It's all right to carry a notebook but a cheap
one is best, with pages the color of weak tea
and on the front a kitten or a space ship.

Avoid any enclosed space where more than
three people are wearing turtlenecks. Beware
any snow-covered chalet with deer tracks
across the muffled tennis courts.

Not surprisingly, libraries are a good place to write.
And the perfect place in a library is near an aisle
where a child a year or two old is playing as his
mother browses the ranks of the dead.

Often he will pull books from the bottom shelf.
The title, the author's name, the brooding photo
on the flap mean nothing. Red book on black, gray
book on brown, he builds a tower. And the higher
it gets, the wider he grins.

You who asked for advice, listen: When the tower
falls, be like that child. Laugh so loud everybody
in the world frowns and says, 'Shhhh.'

Then start again.

Understand

1. On what subject is the speaker offering advice?
2. What common challenge are writers faced with?
3. Identify three main pieces of advice offered by the speaker.
4. The poem describes a small child building a tower out of books in the library.
   (a) What does the tower of books represent in the poem?
   (b) What poetic device is this?

 Explore

1. Why do you think the notebook's pages are described as being the 'color of weak tea'?
2. Do you think the speaker is an experienced writer?
3. Writing poses many challenges. How do the challenges differ, would you say, when writing fiction instead of poetry?

 Create

Imagine a place where you feel most creative or where you might be inspired. Write a descriptive paragraph explaining the details of this place and why you feel so at ease there. Use a variety of adjectives and descriptive language to bring your place to life for the reader. Use the following checklist to help you:

Descriptive writing
- ✓ What do you see?
- ✓ What do you hear?
- ✓ What do you smell?
- ✓ What can you feel or touch?
- ✓ What can you taste?

The following song, written by Bob Dylan, encourages people not to worry about questions they cannot answer.

Blowin' in the Wind

How many roads must a man walk down
Before you call him a man?
Yes, 'n' how many seas must a white dove sail
Before she sleeps in the sand?
Yes, 'n' how many times must the cannonballs fly
Before they're forever banned?
The answer, my friend, is blowin' in the wind
The answer is blowin' in the wind

How many years can a mountain exist
Before it's washed to the sea?
Yes, 'n' how many years can some people exist
Before they're allowed to be free?
Yes, 'n' how many times can a man turn his head
Pretending he just doesn't see?
The answer, my friend, is blowin' in the wind
The answer is blowin' in the wind.

How many times must a man look up
Before he really sees the sky?
Yes, 'n' how many ears must one man have
Before he can hear people cry?
Yes, 'n' how many deaths will it take till he knows
That too many people have died?
The answer, my friend, is blowin' in the wind
The answer is blowin' in the wind

Focus on ... rhetorical questions

A **rhetorical question** is a question that is asked to make a point and not to get an answer. For example, 'Who cares?'

Rhetorical questions are used in literature to make a statement or to draw the reader's attention to something.

Work in pairs to identify all of the rhetorical questions in 'Blowin' in the Wind'. What point is Bob Dylan trying to make by asking these questions?

Understand

1. Identify one literary device used in this song.

2. Find an example of phonetic language in this song.

3. Where does the songwriter suggest that we will find the answers to these questions?

Explore

1. Choose one of the questions asked in this song and explain what it is asking in your own words.

2. Do you think the songwriter has his own answers to some of these rhetorical questions?

 3. Do you like this song? Explain your answer.

 4. **(a)** Choose a line from the song to represent each one of the following themes and explain your choice:

   ◖ conflict
   ◖ nature
   ◖ inequality.

   (b) Identify another theme in this song and discuss what the songwriter has to say about this theme.

Create

Think about questions that you have no answers to. Write your own poem or song addressing these questions.

   ◖ Include a rhetorical question.
   ◖ Write phonetically in a specific dialect.

Reviewing facing challenges

Reflect and review

1. Look back at the images at the start of this unit (page 325).
   (a) Do you think they represent the theme well?
   (b) Are there any images that you would add to represent this theme?
2. Fill in the unit review on pages 90–91 of your Portfolio.

Language skills

1. In the final song of the unit, the speaker says that 'the answer is blowin' in the wind'. What is the word 'blowing' an example of?
2. Write out the following sentences in your copies, filling in the gaps with an appropriate conjunction.
   (a) This is the hotel _____ we stayed the last time we were here.
   (b) Deirdre is such a strong leader _____ everyone looks up to her.
   (c) She has not finished her homework _____ she should have.
   (d) I would have been here sooner _____ I could not get a parking space.

Oral assessment

1. Organise a class debate on the following motion: *This house believes that using social media is the best way to deal with the challenges facing young people today.*

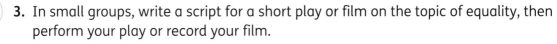

2. Make a presentation to your class on a personal challenge that you faced in your life. You may wish to discuss:
   - what the challenge was
   - how you dealt with it
   - what you learned from it.

3. In small groups, write a script for a short play or film on the topic of equality, then perform your play or record your film.

Written assessment

1. **(a)** Write a feature article for a popular magazine on the challenges facing young people today in the space provided on pages 92–93 of your Portfolio.
   (b) Redraft your feature article in the space provided on pages 126–127 of your Portfolio.

Exam skills

1. Choose a character from a novel or short story that you have studied who faces some sort of challenge.
   (a) Name the novel or short story, the author and the character.
   (b) Describe the challenge that the character faces.
   (c) Explain how the character succeeded or failed in overcoming this challenge.
   Write your answer in the space provided on pages 145–146 of your Portfolio.

Theme 9

Looking Back

What is looking back?

This unit is all about looking back to past events that have shaped our lives. These may be personal triumphs or tragedies, or they may be historical celebrations or crises. Either way, they are etched in our memories.

Why study this theme?

In society, it is vital that we remember the past accurately. We tend to try to forget the negative and traumatic events, but they are equally important in the development of our world. For example, we remember the events of the Holocaust, so that such horror can be avoided by future generations. Literature both celebrates and criticises the past, creating art in the process.

Learning intentions

- Discover how the past can shape people and events.
- Learn how to compare texts across different genres.

Writing With Purpose
- Listen critically and analyse a podcast.
- Read a reflective personal essay.

Poetry and Song
- Experience spoken-word poetry.
- Compare audio and visual experiences.

Fiction
- Learn about stereotypes.
- Revise the importance of the narrator.

Stage and Screen
- Consider the importance of props and set.
- Learn about the past by watching a documentary.

Media and Advertising
- Engage in critical analysis of advertisements.
- Learn about eye-witness accounts.

Language Skills
- Learn how to use semicolons and colons.
- Recognise and form compound nouns.

Discuss

1. Which of the images above best represents 'looking back', in your opinion?
2. Do you keep things at home that remind you of the past?
3. Do you have any photographs, postcards, letters, souvenirs or other mementos?
4. Why would someone choose to keep these things?
5. Does your social media profile allow you to look back at activity from this date in previous years?
6. How do you feel when looking at old pictures, posts or messages?

Create

Write your own definition of 'looking back' in the space provided on page 100 of your Portfolio, by completing the sentence 'Looking back is …'. You will return to this definition later on.

Heirlooms and mementos

We often keep objects that link to a certain memory. An heirloom is an object that is passed from one generation to the next, such as jewellery or certain pieces of furniture. Mementos are objects that we keep to remind us of a significant person or event. For example, you might keep ticket stubs from a concert you attended or a souvenir from a holiday. Objects can link us to our past, and looking at mementos and heirlooms can help us to reflect on our personal history.

The following scene is from the play *The Wardrobe* by Sam Holcroft. The play is centred around an object, a large wardrobe, and the action takes place across several centuries.

The Wardrobe

An auction house, an industrial city in Great Britain, 19 June 1916.

We hear a recording of 'It's a Long Way to Tipperary' by John McCormack or similar.

The First World War has raged throughout Europe since 1914. In January 1916 a military service bill is introduced providing for the conscription of single men aged eighteen to forty-one. In May conscription was extended to married men.

Nell, *eighteen years old, opens the door of the wardrobe. She carries a Sotheby's catalogue under her arm. Her fiancé,* **Anthony**, *also eighteen years old, stands close behind. Beyond them can be heard the sounds of a busy English furniture sale.* **Nell** *inspects the wardrobe as* **Anthony** *reads from his own catalogue. The wardrobe is empty.*

Anthony (*reading*)   'A classic wardrobe of Tudor design with detailed carving including the classic Tudor arch and beautifully panelled doors. Handmade, solid mahogany. Believed to have originated in the late 1480s.' (*Looking up from the catalogue.*) That makes it … 1480 to 1917 … ? Four hundred and thirty years old. I'm surprised it's still standing.

This rouses no response from **Nell**. *She checks the wardrobe meticulously for flaws.*

Anthony   'It is believed that it first belonged to Elizabeth of York, daughter of King Edward the Fourth, and mother of King Henry the Eighth, to whom the wardrobe passed on her death.' Isn't that astonishing? We are touching what royalty once touched.

Nell   Why would Elizabeth of York ever have touched her wardrobe? With all the servants she had, I bet she never even saw the inside of a wardrobe.

Beat.

Anthony (*reading*)   'It was lately the property of Downside Abbey in Somerset. The monks used it to house the robes of choirboys. It was purchased from them privately before being professionally restored for resale. It is estimated to fetch a price at auction of –'

He breaks off.

Nell   How much?

Anthony   Didn't you want a painting?

Nell   How much do they say?

Anthony   Or what about that Victorian vanity table?

Nell *tries to snatch the catalogue from him, but he whisks it away. She opens her own catalogue and begins to search for the wardrobe,* **Anthony** *stops her.*

Anthony   Nell, if you want it, it's yours.

Nell   They've done an adequate job of restoring it, I suppose, but there are still signs of wear.

Anthony   It's four hundred years old.

Nell   Look at that stain.

Anthony   It could be a *royal* stain.

Nell *is not amused.*

Anthony   Then what about a mirror?

He is about to turn away when **Nell** *climbs into the wardrobe.*

Anthony   Nell … ! Nell, I don't think you're allowed inside it.

Nell (*pulling him inside and shutting the doors*)   Shhh.

Anthony   If we're found in here –

Nell   Anthony, just be quiet.

Anthony *falls silent.* **Nell** *looks around the wardrobe.*

Nell   I always wanted a walk-in wardrobe.

Anthony   I don't think you're supposed to walk into this one.

Nell   I used to say, 'Ma, one day I'm going to have so many clothes they'll need to custom build a wardrobe big enough.' 'Fat chance,' she said. 'People like us have two outfits to their name: a set of flannel pajamas and a serving-apron. That's all you'll ever need.'

Anthony   Then why on earth are we hunting for antiques? I'll build you a wardrobe.

Nell   I don't want you to build me a wardrobe.

Anthony   Then … I don't understand. I'm bending over backwards to buy you the perfect wedding present. And if I didn't know you better I'd call you ungrateful.

Nell   I don't want a wedding present for a wedding I might never have.

Beat.

I know we said we wouldn't talk about it. I thought shopping would help. But it's not working. I think we should go home.

She stands to leave. **Anthony** *stops her.*

Nell   Anthony …

Anthony *rifles through the catalogue. Finding what he's looking for, he tears a corner from a page.*

Nell   I'm just not in the mood to buy anything.

Anthony (*reading*)   'Eighteen-carat rose-gold Georgian artisan-made wedding band.'

He folds the picture of the ring in half and tears a chunk out of the corner so that when he opens it again the ring has a hole in the middle.

Anthony   'Amazing condition for its age. You can still see the hallmarks. No visible wear.'

He presents her with the paper ring.

Nell   Anthony …

Anthony (*taking her hand*)   I, Anthony Edward Leveson-Gower, take you, Ellen Anne Rigby, to be my wedded wife, to have and to hold, for richer for poorer, in sickness and in health from this day forward until death us do part.

He slips the paper ring on to her ring finger.

Anthony   Do you, Ellen Anne Rigby, take me, Anthony Edward Leveson-Gower, to be your wedded husband?

Nell *nods.*

Anthony   You have to say it.

Nell   I, Ellen Anne Rigby, take you, Anthony Edward Leveson-Gower – why do you have to have such a long name? – to be my wedded husband.

Anthony   To have and to hold.

Nell   To have and to hold.

Anthony   For richer for poorer.

Nell   For richer for poorer.

Anthony   In sickness and in health from this day forward –

Nell   In sickness and in health from this day forward –

Anthony   Until death us do part.

Beat.

I'm coming back, Nell.

Nell   If you were just a year younger –

Anthony (*he's heard many times before*)   Nell …

Nell   If your birthday had been in January –

Anthony   Not December, I know.

Nell   Then you wouldn't qualify for conscription.

Anthony   Maybe the moment I arrive they'll call a victory. Maybe I'll never see the trenches. And if I do … well, I won't take any risks or show off or anything like that. I'll be sensible.

Nell   No you won't.

Anthony   Yes I will.

Nell   No, you won't be sensible because you're too bloody … *good*. There's nothing you wouldn't do for someone you cared for. Like going back for a man fallen. Sometimes I wish you were a bit more of a bastard and put yourself first.

They smile at one another.

       Until death us do part, then.

Anthony (*smiling with joy*)   A marriage isn't legal until you've signed the register!

He grabs the catalogue and scribbles on the page. He offers it to her.

       Sign your name, here.

Nell *signs her name.*

Anthony   Well. I now pronounce us husband and wife.

He tears the signed sheet out of the catalogue and feeds it through a gap in the wooden boards at the base of the wardrobe into the secret space underneath.

Anthony   I swear upon my honour that I will come back for you, and I will dig it out we'll take it to the town hall and have it signed officially by the mayor.

Nell   But how will you know where to find this wardrobe?

Anthony   Because we're going to buy it.

Nell   But it's so expensive.

Anthony   So what? I might die next week.

Nell (*slapping him on the shoulder*)   You can't make jokes like that.

Anthony   Sorry, from now on consider me silent as the dead.

Nell   Anthony!

Anthony   Come on. This wardrobe isn't going to buy itself!

He exits the wardrobe. **Nell** *follows close behind.*

 **Props** are moveable objects used in plays and films in order to help tell the story.

 Discuss

1. Share what you know about conscription.
2. Do you think conscription is fair or unfair?

 Understand

1. Where does this scene take place?
2. What are Anthony and Nell doing there?
3. What is Nell's real name?
4. For what purpose did the monks use the wardrobe?
5. Conscription is when all men aged 18 to 41 must:
   (a) get married.
   (b) vote.
   (c) enlist in the military.

 Explore

 1. Do you think this is an expensive wardrobe? Give reasons for your answer.

 2. In your opinion, why does Nell think the wedding may not happen?

3. Name one prop you would give the actors to bring this scene to life, and explain your choice.

4. How would you direct the actors playing Nell and Anthony in this scene? Use the headings below to guide your answer.
   ◖ Movements and gestures
   ◖ Facial expression
   ◖ Tone of voice
   ◖ Costumes
   ◖ Hair and makeup

In the next two scenes, the same wardrobe is used at more recent points in history.

The Wardrobe

Anywhere in the United Kingdom, anytime post the publication of The Lion, The Witch and The Wardrobe *by C. S. Lewis in 1950, but before the present day.*

We hear music or sounds relevant to the time and place.

A *leads* **B** *into the wardrobe.* **B** *shows some signs of being ill, perhaps s(he) wears a nightgown while* **A** *wears day-clothes, or perhaps s(he) has bandages on her arms, or perhaps s(he) wears a hospital gown.* **A** *carries a copy of* The Lion, The Witch and The Wardrobe *by C. S. Lewis.*

The object of this scene is for **A** *to read to* **B** *from the first chapter of the book while at the same time trying to re-create for* **B** *the experience as described by C. S. Lewis of Lucy's first adventure into the wardrobe.*

I suggest you begin at the moment in Chapter One, when Lucy first steps into the wardrobe. **A** *reads the relevant lines from the text while ushering* **B** *into the wardrobe.* **B** *is initially reluctant and resentful. S(he) interrupts occasionally with protests similar to 'This is so childish' or 'I can't believe you're making me do this'. However,* **A** *insists and they carry on.* **A** *encourages* **B** *to read aloud Lucy's lines of dialogue whenever they occur in order to give her the full 'Lucy experience'. As they continue, it becomes clear that* **A** *has planted props within the wardrobe.*

A *prises open a board at the base of the wardrobe and rummages around underneath for props – for example, a fur hat to represent the fur coats; scrunched newspaper or polystyrene peanuts underfoot to create the sound of crunching snow; a fir branch to brush against* **B**'s *hand; a sieve of icing sugar shaken overhead to re-create falling snow, etc.*

At one point **A** *retrieves the signed catalogue page hidden down there by Anthony in the previous scene.*

A *(reading from the catalogue page)* Anthony Edward Leveson-Gower … Ellen Anne Rigby … Who are they?

B Ellen Rigby is my – *(Insert appropriate relation depending how long it's been since the previous scene.)*

A Who's Anthony Edward Leveson-Gower?

B No idea …

A *tosses the catalogue sheet aside and continues.*

I suggest that **A** *read through the text to the point at which Lucy steps out of the wardrobe into Narnia and feels the snow falling from the sky. At this point* **A** *opens her/his satchel and* *attempts to set the scene of Narnia using household props. Please improvise the lines as necessary, but in a similar vein to the following:*

A   See … imagine this is the lamp post where she meets … and this is the White Witch and this is … (*Revealing a stuffed toy.*) Well, I expect you can imagine who this is. And me.

           I'm … (*throwing a scarf around his neck, collecting an umbrella.*) I'm Mr Tumnus.

B *is lost for words*

A   It's okay … Don't cry.

A *reads the relevant lines from the book about Lucy feeling frightened yet inquisitive.* **B** *nods in response to this.* **A** *has won her/him over. They smile at each other and continue to read.*

· ·

A museum, somewhere in Britain, 2014.

We hear music or sounds relevant to the time and/or place.

The doors to the wardrobe open and **Friend One**, *any age between fifteen and seventeen, enters. (S)he sits on the floor, takes out her/his phone and begins playing a game. The light of the phone illuminates the wardrobe. The door opens and* **Friend Two**, *also between the ages of fifteen and seventeen, pokes his/her head inside.*

Friend Two   I knew it was you – what are you doing? You can't be in there, get out.

Friend One *ignores him/her.* **Friend Two** *climbs into the wardrobe and closes the door behind her.*

Friend Two   You know this is probably alarmed.

Friend One *ignores* **Friend Two**

Friend Two   Are we going to talk about this?

Friend One *ignores* **Friend Two**

Friend Two   Hello?

Friend One   Talk about what?

Friend Two   Eh, we're in a wardrobe. In a museum.

Friend One *concentrates on her/his phone.*

 **Staging** is the way a play is presented on stage.

 Explore

1. Ellen Anne Rigby seems to be a relative of B. Why is it that B has no idea who Anthony Edward Leveson-Gower is? What does this suggest?

2. Most of the action in this play takes place in the wardrobe. Describe how you would depict this on stage.

3. Think of a play you have studied. Choose a scene where the main action centres around a prop or object.

   (a) Name the play and the playwright.

   (b) Explain why this object was significant.

   (c) Discuss how the object added to your enjoyment of the play.

 Investigate

A and B are re-enacting a scene from the well-known novel, *The Lion, the Witch and the Wardrobe*. Find a copy of this book in your school or local library then read the opening scene that is used in this piece.

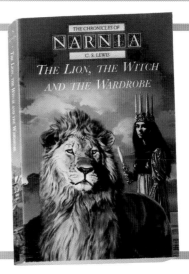

 Create

1. Read back over the dialogue between A and B. Choose a time and place, give each character a name and imagine what they might discuss inside the wardrobe. Then, in pairs, act out the scene.

2. Write a scene for a play that takes place in a cramped place, with limited performing space and where characters might come and go regularly. Here are a few ideas to help you:

   ◖ a lift

   ◖ a taxi

   ◖ a park bench

   ◖ a sauna.

   Remember to include stage direction in your script.

The following extract comes from a novel called *Click*, a work of collaborative fiction, which means it was written by several different authors. The novel is about a well-known photo journalist and his two grandchildren, Jason and Margaret, and how they affected the lives of different people. This extract is from 'Chapter 3: Jason', written by Eoin Colfer.

Click

Kronski Antiques was an old junk shop on the third floor, up above the Gaps and Burger Kings – up with all the other small-time operators that couldn't afford prime spots. But the proprietor, Dr Kronski, wasn't like all the other shopkeepers on that level. When you came in the door, he looked at you like you were interrupting something important and he certainly did not need your business.

Jason had been here once before. Grandpa Gee had an old Civil War spyglass that he kept in a travel chest in their basement. Dr Kronski had given him twenty bucks for it. Grandpa hadn't even noticed it was missing. Jason had felt guilty about stealing it for a couple of days, but soon the feeling had faded from neon to dull. He didn't even think about the theft most of the time. Then Grandpa Gee died, and the guilt had flared up again like an infected wound, even though now his crime would never be discovered. He thought about what he had done every day, and the act made him sick to the pit of his stomach. Yet here he was back at Kronski's shopfront again. But this time it was different, wasn't it? This time he was only selling what he owned.

A brass bell tinkled as he pushed through the door. Jason could barely see the counter for all the junk, sorry, '*antiques*', stacked on almost every inch of floor space. Whatever rent old Kronski was paying per square foot, he was definitely getting his money's worth.

There were harpsichords, and candelabras, and stuffed animals, and reconstructed battle scenes, and shrunken heads, and candles made from fat and blood. Of course Jason's brain didn't catalogue any of this. All he saw was junk that people would pay money for.

Kronski was behind the counter. A tall, slight man wearing a fitted black suit. His complexion was sallow, and his bald head shone orange from the overhead lights. He was busy painting a lead Napoleonic soldier, held in place with carpenter's clamps.

He glanced up from his work, brow creased with irritation.

'I really don't think I can help you, boy. Perhaps you are lost. There is an arcade one floor down.' Kronski's accent was clipped. European. Jason didn't know enough geography to pin it down, but definitely something on the other side of the Atlantic.

Jason raised his face. 'Hey, Doc. It's me, Jason.'

Kronski removed a jeweller's glass from his eye. 'Ah, yes. The light-fingered boy. The one with the eyeglass.'

Jason scowled. 'About that spyglass. I looked that up on the Internet. It was worth eight hundred dollars; you gave me twenty.'

Kronski smiled. His teeth were small and square, like an infant's.

'Eight hundred, with papers of provenance. Do you have such papers?'

Jason's silence was ample reply.

provenance: details of past ownership that prove an object is genuine

'I thought not. That twenty dollars was a finder's fee. Now, are you here to waste my time or to make some money?'

Jason turned his back for a moment, sliding one photograph from the package. It was a blurred black-and-white of two boxers in action. Their sinews were stretched, sweat streamed from their limbs, and their lips were drawn back over white gum shields.

The photograph made you feel like you were ringside. There was a message scrawled across the top in black felt-tip. *To Jason*, it read. *You are the greatest*. And below that, a flamboyant signature: *Muhammad Ali*.

Jason stared at the photo for a minute. Grandpa Gee must have taken this photo in the seventies, and then somehow got Muhammad Ali to sign it after Jason was adopted. Amazing. Unique.

'What are you hiding there, boy? The crown jewels? Let me see, or get out.'

Jason was suddenly reluctant to part with the picture, but he conjured an image of Tobago in his mind, and it bolstered his resolve.

He slapped the picture down on the counter.

'What will you give me for this, Doc?'

Kronski took tweezers from a rack and picked up the picture by the corner.

'This is genuine, I suppose.'

'Absolutely.'

Kronski smiled thinly. 'Let's say I get a friend of mine to check it out. After all, you are not known for your honesty.' The doctor heaved open a leather-bound book bigger than a couple of bibles, flicking through the pages.

'If it is genuine, then the almanac says I can let you have five dollars.'

'Five dollars,' gasped Jason. 'But Muhammad Ali is a legend.'

Kronski sighed. 'These days, legends spend most of their time signing things. The average celebrity signs more than ten thousand pieces of assorted paper in a lifetime. I'll give you five dollars, or a hundred and fifty for that entire envelope.'

A hundred and fifty dollars. Could he sell his inheritance for that little?

Kronski leaned across the counter. 'Now, if you want to make some serious money …'

Jason felt his stomach churn. There was no way he was going to like whatever came next.

Dr Kronski drew the Civil War spyglass from a desk drawer.

'When you brought this to me, you mentioned an old box camera. I would really like that. I'm something of an enthusiast.'

Jason's stomach lurchings increased in speed and intensity. All the old feelings of guilt resurfaced. He could pretend that selling the pictures meant nothing, but theft was theft, no matter how you looked at it.

'How much?'

Kronski shrugged. 'A decent price this time. Five hundred if it's in good repair.'

Jason calculated. With five hundred, plus the seven fifty he had saved, he could be ready to go on his birthday.

Kronski returned to his lead soldier.

'Think before you decide, young man. Decisions like this one tend to affect your entire future. It's not too late to go home to your family and be boring and happy.'

Tobago, thought Jason. *Tobago. That's what I have always wanted.*

'I'm sure,' he said. 'I'll be back later. Count on it.'

Kronski nodded thoughtfully. 'I think you might.'

Jason took the long way home. The house was in darkness except for an outside light that his mother always left on to guide him back. For some reason, the light made him feel even guiltier than the theft he was planning to commit.

He let himself in, creeping downstairs to the basement where Grandpa Gee kept his old junk. He stepped around the stacks of *National Geographic* and over boxes of toy cars from the last century. Grandpa Gee had almost as much junk as old Doc Kronski.

Finally Jason reached the old chest at the rear of the room and whipped back the tablecloth laid over it. The cloth snapped through the air and Jason froze, waiting for a reaction from above. None came. The house was as silent as space.

Jason opened the chest, searching the interior with a penlight. The camera was there, lying on the velvet lining of a wooden presentation box. And in the space left by the stolen spyglass was an envelope. The envelope was addressed to him.

Jason balanced the chest's lid on his forehead, reaching inside for the envelope. There was a letter inside. The handwriting was Grandpa Gee's. Jason recognized it from the dozens of letters he had received from faraway places.

Dear Jason, it read. I am sorry for all the things that have built a wall between us. I am sorry that I am not your real grandfather, but I should not have tried to be. This lesson has cost me your affection and respect.

I am sorry that there is no place for me in your world, because if there was, my life would be just about perfect.

I am sorry that your mother loves you so much, because she will be heartbroken when you leave for Tobago, as we all know you will. Frank and Maggie will be devastated too. Like it or not, you are Maggie's hero. When you go, she will wonder what she did to drive you away.

Finally, I am sorry that you feel you have to steal from me. Do you need money for your Tobago fund? Is that it, Jason, my dearest boy? All you have to do is ask.

If stolen money takes you to a place, you will never be truly happy there. In time, you will be driven from the island by guilt. I know this is true, because I made a similar mistake once, and because you are a good person on the verge of a bad decision.

Think about what you are doing, Jason. We give you love, food, and shelter, and you throw them all back at us. And for what? For a father who deserted you. Can't you find your father without discarding your family?

This is my last letter to you. I have a week left and a lot of people to write to. So my final gift to you is this:

Take what you need, Jason. I would not expose you even if I was around to do so. But think about the people who love and need you, and think about the road you are on and where it leads. Believe me, this advice is worth more than a few dusty antiques.

> *All my love,*
>
> *Your friend,*
>
> *G*

The letter rustled slightly in Jason's trembling hands. Grandpa Gee had known all the time. He had spent the last few weeks praying for his grandfather's ignorance, and he himself had been the ignorant one. Grandpa had known of the theft, and the thief.

Jason dropped the chest lid. It crashed in the darkness, but he didn't care. He jumped to his feet, knocking over a stack of *Rolling Stone* magazines.

He had been so close. So close. Jason could almost smell the Caribbean. He'd stuck it out through funerals and Brendan blasted Murphy and lactose-intolerant kids. And now his resolve was being unravelled by a letter.

Take the camera, screamed his dark half. *Take it and go.*

But he could not. He was too much his mother's son and his little sister's hero. What kind of hero steals from his own family?

Jason mounted the stairs, putting some distance between himself and temptation. He sat glumly on the top step, head in hands. Now he had a new problem. If he was staying for a while longer, he had to get the spyglass back. How could he ever remember Grandpa Gee if he didn't retrieve the telescope?

The answer was obvious, of course, though it took Jason several minutes to admit to thinking of it. He had seven hundred and fifty dollars stashed in a *Lord of the Rings* boxed-set binder. His Tobago fund. The spyglass had been valued at eight hundred dollars.

Jason trudged down the corridor to his bedroom. He would go down to the mall and haggle with the Doctor. He would go down tomorrow right after he had finished grovelling to Brendan. Maybe Kronski would do a deal.

Understand

1. Why had Jason been in the antique shop before?
2. Name one other item for sale in the shop.
3. Grandpa Gee was a:

    (a) photo journalist.　　　**(b)** travel writer.　　　**(c)** boxer.

Explore

1. What kind of person do you think Grandpa Gee was? Give reasons for your answer.

2. Choose one of the following words to describe Jason and explain your choice.
    - Angry
    - Guilty
    - Sad
    - Conflicted
    - Greedy

3. What valuable lesson do you think Jason learned from his grandfather?

Investigate

Work in pairs to find answers to the following questions.
- Who was Muhammad Ali?
- Where was he from?
- What was he famous for?
- Why would these pictures have been valuable?

Create

1. Write a descriptive paragraph painting a vivid picture of the basement and all the things that Grandpa Gee had kept there.

2. A time capsule is a container in which one puts pictures, souvenirs and mementos representing a specific time in history. It is to be opened at a date in the future. As a class, create a time capsule. Explain each of your choices in a presentation to the class. You may like to include:
    - pictures
    - letters to your future selves
    - popular music, films or books
    - news and magazine articles about current events or trends.

Discuss

1. What is an heirloom?
2. Does an heirloom always have to be something with monetary value?
3. Do you have any family heirlooms? If so, what are they?

In the following poem, the speaker is inspired by a family heirloom to reflect on the experiences of his ancestor.

Heirloom

By Gerard Smyth

Among family heirlooms
I find a postcard written on a voyage
to America: the barely legible last goodbye of a steamship emigrant.

I imagine him, my ancestor
on the journey west: homesick, heartstruck.
Like a fledgling thrown from the nest
to take a chance
under Liberty's outstretched hand.

I imagine him, sad to leave his bogbanks,
grassland, the sound of the latch,
but ready to seek with rolled-up sleeves
the better life in Queens, the Bronx,
streets with their entourage,
streets that spawned hard tasks.

Flashback   **Mood** is the feeling or atmosphere in a poem or a piece of fiction.

Understand

1. What is the heirloom that the speaker describes?

2. What relationship exists between 'him' (mentioned in the second stanza) and the speaker?

3. Where is he going?

4. Explain the meaning of the line 'but ready to seek with rolled-up sleeves' in your own words.

 Explore

1. How do you think the speaker's ancestor feels about the journey?

2. Do you think the speaker's ancestor is from the countryside or the city? Explain your answer.

 3. What is the mood in this poem? Explain your answer with reference to the poem.

 4. In groups, choose one image from the poem and create a freeze frame. A freeze frame is like a snapshot of a scene. There is no sound or movement.

5. Choose one of the following images to accompany a reading of this poem and explain your choice.

Investigate

Find out about an heirloom belonging to your family, friends or neighbours. Even the simplest thing can be an heirloom – once it is passed on from one generation to the next, it becomes valuable. You may find letters, photographs, postcards, jewellery, etc. If possible, take a picture of your heirloom (or maybe you can get permission to bring it to school) and prepare a three-minute presentation for your class. You may want to consider the questions below to get you started.

- What is the heirloom?
- Where did it come from?
- How old is it?
- What does it mean to the people who own it?
- Why did you choose to talk about this particular heirloom?

Create

Write your own version of the poem 'Heirloom'. For example:

Heirloom

Among family heirlooms

I find an old tarnished engagement ring, given to a relative

in the sixties: the last remaining evidence of a loving relationship ...

Compound nouns

Compound nouns are nouns that are made up of two words joined together.

We use compound nouns every day and do not always realise that we are combining words to make new meanings.

Different combinations of words can be used to create compound nouns. Some common examples are:

- noun + noun   *football, shoelace*
- adjective + noun   *blackboard, homesick*
- verb + preposition   *outbreak, breakthrough*
- verb + noun   *washing machine, driving licence, swimming pool*

Many more combinations of words can be joined together to make compound nouns.

There are three main types of compound nouns.

- Open   *bus stop, swimming pool, tennis racket*
- Hyphenated   *part-time, long-term*
- Closed   *tablecloth, sunset*

 If you can separate a word into two words and they each mean something independently, it is probably a compound noun.

 ## Understand

1. See how many compound nouns you can make by combining some of the following words:

   - Black
   - Smart
   - Road
   - Book
   - Bird
   - Down
   - Light
   - Sports
   - School
   - Fire
   - Life
   - Cross

 2. In the poem 'Heirloom' on page 383 the word 'steamship' is a compound noun. Work with a partner to find the other compound nouns in this poem. For each compound noun you find, state:

   - what type of compound nouns it is
   - what types of words (nouns, verbs, adjectives) are added together to create the compound noun.

Looking back in history

It is important to study past events in order to understand how the world today was shaped and to learn from previous mistakes. In literature, the past is often used as a backdrop to create interesting worlds for the characters.

Memories can be powerful, and not all are described in a fond way. Sometimes, if something traumatic happens, visual reminders are not necessary. The memories alone are vivid and upsetting. Can you think of any incidents for which this might be the case?

J. Bruce Ismay was the chairman of the White Star Line, the company famous for its 'unsinkable' ship, the *Titanic*. *Titanic* sank on its maiden voyage in April 1912 and more than 1,500 people lost their lives. The following poem, by Derek Mahon, is written from Ismay's point of view, describing his life since he survived the tragedy.

After the Titanic

By Derek Mahon

They said I got away in a boat
And humbled me at the inquiry. I tell you
I sank as far that night as any
Hero. As I sat shivering on the dark water
I turned to ice to hear my costly
Life go thundering down in a pandemonium of
Prams, pianos, sideboards, winches,
Boilers bursting and shredded ragtime. Now I hide
In a lonely house behind the sea
Where the tide leaves broken toys and hatboxes
Silently at my door. The showers of
April, flowers of May mean nothing to me, nor the
Late light of June, when my gardener
Describes to strangers how the old man stays in bed
On seaward mornings after nights of
Wind, takes his morphine and will see no one. Then it is
I drown again with all those dim
Lost faces I never understood, my poor soul
Screams out in the starlight, heart
Breaks loose and rolls down like a stone.
Include me in your lamentations.

pandemonium:
noisy chaos

ragtime:
a type of music usually played on the piano in the late nineteenth/ early twentieth centuries

morphine:
pain medication

lamentations:
expressions of grief

Understand

1. Find a quote from the poem that illustrates each of the following statements:
   (a) I suffered so much that night, I might as well have died.
   (b) My life was in a state of chaos.
   (c) I am constantly reminded of the horrors of that night.
2. Who is the speaker in the poem?
3. Ismay survived the sinking of the *Titanic*. True or false?
 4. Put the following words into a sentence, then add them to your vocabulary builder on pages 1–2 of your Portfolio:
   ◖ pandemonium   ◖ lamentations.

 Explore

 1. Do you feel sorry for the speaker in the poem? Give reasons for your answer.
2. Do you think that much time has passed for the speaker since the tragedy occurred?
3. **(a)** Find examples of each of the following in the poem:
   ◖ simile   ◖ alliteration   ◖ metaphor.
   (b) Did you find any of these particularly effective? Explain your answer.

 Investigate

 Work in groups to find out what you can about the *Titanic*.
   ◖ Where and when was it built?
   ◖ What was the planned route for the maiden voyage?
   ◖ What happened in the early hours of the 15 April 1912?
   ◖ What happened in the aftermath?
Share your findings with the class.

 Create

1. Think about another tragedy you have learned about in History or Geography. Assume the role of someone who experienced that tragedy and write a personal essay describing your thoughts and feelings.
 2. Write a monologue describing your thoughts and feelings based on a tragic event from the past in the space provided on page 94 of your Portfolio.
 3. When filling the lifeboats on the night the *Titanic* sank, the crew prioritised the safety of women and children before that of the men. Start a class debate on the motion: *This house believes that the lives of women and children should be prioritised in life-threatening situations.*

Discuss

Discuss what you know about the *Titanic* with a partner.

1. Have you seen any films or documentaries based on the tragedy?
2. Were these factual or fictional?
3. Have you ever visited the Titanic Belfast museum?

The following documentary, *Titanic: The New Evidence*, looks at new evidence that reveals a fire was raging in *Titanic*'s boiler rooms before she left port, that it was kept secret and, it's now believed, that it led to the tragedy.

Watch the first ten minutes of the documentary and answer the questions.

 www.channel4.com/programmes/titanic-the-new-evidence

 Understand

1. How tall was the *Titanic*?
2. Where was it built?
3. Who is Senan Molony and why was he involved in this documentary?
4. Identify some features of a typical documentary in this piece.
5. Where does the new evidence come from?

 Explore

1. There were no cameras recording the events of the night in April 1912, so what technique is used by the creator of the documentary to show what happened?
2. What other voice do you hear in the opening few minutes of the documentary? Is this a common feature of documentaries?
3. What other visuals appear in the first few minutes? Do you find these effective?
4. Why do you think this 'new evidence' was not discovered for over 100 years?

 Investigate

Have you heard any other theories about the sinking of *Titanic*? Find out more about the tragedy and share your findings with the class.

  Create

Fill in the documentary analysis worksheet on pages 95–96 of your Portfolio.

The following article outlines accounts that were given by people who experienced the sinking of the *Titanic*.

Titanic's 100th Anniversary: 6 Survivor Stories

One hundred years after the RMS Titanic met its fatal end, the story of the tragic wreck continues to fascinate people worldwide. Out of over 2,200 people on board, approximately 700 lived to tell about it. Though many survivors and their family members disappeared into obscurity or were hesitant to talk about what they went through, others were willing to share their experiences during the wreck and in its aftermath. These are some of their stories.

Elizabeth Shutes

Elizabeth Shutes served as a family governess on board Titanic and was 40 years old at the time; she was among the passengers quickly ordered to the Sun Deck after the ship hit an iceberg. She later described the chaotic scene on the lifeboat, shortly before they were rescued by Carpathia: 'Our men knew nothing about the position of the stars, hardly how to pull together. Two oars were soon overboard. The men's hands were too cold to hold on … Then across the water swept that awful wail, the cry of those drowning people. In my ears I heard: "She's gone, lads; row like hell or we'll get the devil of a swell."' Shutes was among those who reflected on 'needless luxuries' aboard Titanic, which had been prioritized over lifeboats and other safety features.

Survivors in lifeboats

Laura Mabel Francatelli

Laura Mabel Francatelli, a 30-year old secretary from London, reflected later on the dramatic arrival of Carpathia: 'Oh at daybreak, when we saw the lights of that ship, about 4 miles away, we rowed like mad, and passed icebergs like mountains, at last about 6:30 the dear Carpathia picked us up, our little boat was like a speck against that giant. Then came my weakest moment, they lowered a rope swing, which was awkward to sit on, with my life preserver 'round me. Then they hauled me up, by the side of the boat. Can you imagine, swinging in the air over the sea, I just shut my eyes and clung tight saying "Am I safe,?" at last I felt a strong arm pulling me onto the boat ...'

Survivors aboard the *Carpathia*

Charlotte Collyer

Passengers lucky enough to have been picked up by Carpathia arrived in New York City days later and started a frantic search for their loved ones, desperately hoping they too had been saved. Collyer, a second-class passenger who was 31 years old, later described her panicked search for her husband: 'There was scarcely anyone who had not been separated from husband, child or friend. Was the last one among the handful saved? … I had a husband to search for, a husband whom in the greatness of my faith, I had believed would be found in one of the boats. He was not there.'

Collyer and her daughter

Lawrence Beesley

Lawrence and a fellow passenger in *Titanic*'s gymnastic room

Lawrence Beesley, a young widower and science professor in London, left his young son at home to board Titanic, hoping to visit his brother in Toronto. At left is a photo of Beesley and a fellow passenger in Titanic's gymnastic room. Just nine weeks after the tragedy, Beesley published the famous memoir *The Loss of the S. S. Titanic*. The book contained stern recommendations for avoiding further tragedies. He also had a powerful reason to be skeptical about certain superstitions: 'I shall never say again that 13 is an unlucky number. Boat 13 is the best friend we ever had.'

Florence Ismay, wife of J. Bruce Ismay, Chairman of the White Star Line

Bruce Ismay being questioned by the Senate Investigating Committee

White Star Chairman Bruce Ismay boarded a lifeboat to safety and was criticized by many for his decisions regarding Titanic. A letter from his wife, Florence, reveals the relief she felt upon realizing he had made it through the disaster alive:

'... Only a week ago today ... I watched that magnificent vessel sail away so proudly. I never dreamt of danger as I wished her Godspeed ... I know so well what bitterness of spirit you must be feeling for the loss of so many precious lives and the ship itself that you loved like a living thing. We have both been spared to each other, let us try to make our lives of use in the world.'

Eva Hart

Crowd awaiting *Titanic*'s survivors in New York

At left is a picture of the crowd awaiting the ship's survivors in New York City. Eva Hart was seven years old at the time of the Titanic disaster. A second-class passenger with her parents, Eva lost her father in the tragedy. She went on to live a vibrant life, and spoke frequently about the sinking of Titanic and her approach to life. 'People I meet always seem surprised that I do not hesitate to travel by train, car, airplane or ship when necessary. It is almost as if they expect me to be permanently quivering in my shoes at the thought of a journey. If I acted like that I would have died of fright many years ago—life has to be lived irrespective of the possible dangers and tragedies lurking round the corner.'

Focus on ... eyewitness accounts

An **eyewitness account** is when someone experiences an event and gives a first-hand account of it.

These accounts can be used when trying to piece together facts about the event and they give important insight into how it felt for the people involved.

With the growth in popularity of smartphones, people are often able to record footage (audio or visual) of an event as it happens. Broadcasters are using this material more and more to provide their viewers with a clearer and more detailed picture of what happened. This is called citizen journalism.

Discuss

1. Do you think a tragic event can change your view on life?
2. Have you ever experienced something that changed your outlook?

Understand

1. Match the people with their profiles.

Florence Ismay	31-year-old second-class passenger
Charlotte Collyer	Secretary from London
Eva Hart	Science professor
Laura Mabel Francatelli	Seven-year-old second-class passenger
Elizabeth Shutes	Wife of the chairman of White Star Lines
Lawrence Beesley	Governess

2. How many people survived the tragedy?
3. What was the name of the ship that picked up survivors a few hours later?

Explore

1. Do you think Florence Ismay had a point when she said 'We have both been spared to each other, let us try to make our lives of use in the world'? Explain your answer.
 2. What kind of person is Eva Hart, in your opinion? Give reasons for your answer.

Investigate

Ask a classmate, teacher, parent or guardian to tell you about an event they experienced first-hand. Record what they say to create an eyewitness account of the event.

Create

1. Write an article about the event you were told about in the Investigate task above. Make sure to include some direct quotations from the first-hand account you were given.
2. Imagine you are one of the six people whose eyewitness accounts are given in this article. Write a diary entry from their perspective, written after the events that they have detailed in their eyewitness account took place.
3. Write the script of a radio interview with a *Titanic* survivor for a programme entitled *The History Hour*. You can use one of the people mentioned above or you can come up with your own.

We all take in and process information in different ways. Some people prefer to see things presented in numbers and figures, some prefer wordy explanations and some prefer visual aids and symbols. This infographic provides us with some very interesting facts about the famous *Titanic*. Examine it carefully and answer the questions that follow.

TITANIC BY NUMBERS

Construction

3 YEARS TO BUILD

3,000 WORKERS

$7.5 MILLION (EQUAL TO **$167 MILLION TODAY**)

Technical specifications

Height: **53 m**

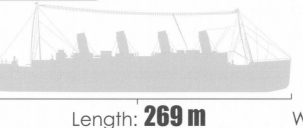

Length: **269 m**

Width: **28 m**

Weight: **46,000 tonnes**

On board

Approximately **2,200** people: **1,300** passengers and **900** crew

Titanic set sail less than **75% full** – it had room for **1,100** more people

20 lifeboats – enough for half of its passengers (this was more than they were required to carry by law)

April 14–15, 1912

3,330 km Distance *Titanic* sailed between April 11 and the evening of April 14, 1912

644 km Distance from land when it sank

93 km Distance of the nearest rescue vehicle, *Carpathia*, which didn't arrive until 4 a.m.

SITE OF SINKING

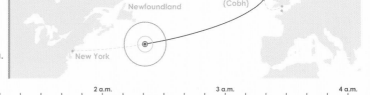

Queenstown (Cobh)

Newfoundland

New York

| 11:30 p.m. | 12 a.m. | 1 a.m. | 2 a.m. | 3 a.m. | 4 a.m. |

30 seconds elapsed between the first sighting of the iceberg and impact **at 11:40 p.m.**

60 minutes elapsed between collision and **launch of first lifeboat**

160 minutes When he saw the damage, *Titanic's* builder said it would sink within 90 minutes. It didn't – it stayed afloat for 160 minutes.

Odds of survival

	1ST CLASS		2ND CLASS		3RD CLASS (steerage)		CREW	
Women & children:	93%	7%	81%	19%	47%	53%	87%	13%
Men:	31%	69%	9%	91%	14%	86%	22%	78%

KEY
- Survived
- Perished

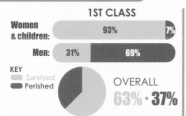 OVERALL **63% · 37%**

 OVERALL **42% · 58%**

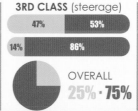 OVERALL **25% · 75%**

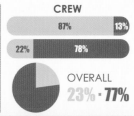 OVERALL **23% · 77%**

ONLY 700 PEOPLE made it into a lifeboat – almost all of them left **with empty seats.**

Understand

1. **(a)** Pick three pieces of information you find interesting and rephrase the information into a question. For example:

   ◖ The *Titanic* took two years to build: true or false?

   ◖ How many boilers did the *Titanic* have?

   Try to come up with three different types of questions. For example, questions that require answers in the form of:

   ◖ true/false

   ◖ a number

   ◖ a sentence.

 (b) Divide into groups. Each member of the group should take a turn posing their three questions to the rest of the group.

 Explore

1. What is the most shocking piece of information that you discovered from the infographic? Explain why you found this information shocking.

2. Find a piece of information or statistic that supports any of the eyewitness accounts on pages 390–391 and explain how the information backs up their account.

 Create

1. Using the information in the infographic, write a report about the *Titanic*, from its creation to its destruction.

2. Write a news article for the local paper issued the day after the tragedy.

Compare the following two images, which advertise the *Titanic* ship on its maiden voyage.

 Understand

1. According to poster A, how much does the ship weigh?
2. What was the name of the company who owned the *Titanic*?
3. According to poster B, where will the ship start its voyage?

 Explore

 1. Do think the *Titanic* was an impressive ship? Explain your answer.

 2. Which advertisement do you think is more effective? Explain your choice. You may wish to consider:
   ◄ colour
   ◄ images
   ◄ text/font
   ◄ details and information
   ◄ language.

 Create

Based on the information you have learned about the *Titanic*, create your own poster advertising the ship. Include details that you think would be most persuasive.

Childhood

Childhood is an important time in our lives. Our experiences in childhood help to form who we become as adults. For some, childhood is a time of freedom and innocence, but others have more challenging experiences. Many writers look back at childhood and celebrate it, while others use literature to explore difficult experiences.

 Discuss

1. What is your earliest memory?
2. Did you ever ask your parents what your first words were?

 In the following poem, Welsh poet Gillian Clarke describes the experience of a baby learning their first words.

First Words

By Gillian Clarke

The alphabet of a house – air,
breath, the break of the stair.
Downstairs the grown-ups' hullabaloo,
or their hush as you fall asleep.

You're learning the language: the steel slab
of a syllable dropped at the docks; the two-beat word
of the Breaksea lightship; the golden sentence
of a train crossing the viaduct.

Later, at Fforest, all the words are new.
You are your grandmother's Cariad, not Darling.
Tide and current are *llanw, lli*.
The waves repeat their *ll-ll-ll* on sand.

Over the sea the starlings come in paragraphs.
She tells you a tale of a girl and a bird,
reading it off the tide in lines of longhand
that scatter to bits on the shore.

The sea turns its pages, speaking in tongues.
The stories are yours, and you are the story.
And before you know it you'll know what comes
from air and breath and off the page is all

you'll want, like the sea's jewels in your hand,
and the soft mutations of sea washing on sand.

Fforest:
a holiday location in Wales

Cariad:
(Welsh) sweetheart or darling

llanw:
(Welsh) tide

lli:
(Welsh) current

ll-ll-ll:
a soft hissing sound used in the Welsh language, made by touching your tongue off the roof of your mouth and blowing air through your cheeks

Welsh is a Celtic language, like Irish. The longest place name in Europe can be found in Wales, and it is quite a mouthful! Have a go at pronouncing it, then look it up online to see if you got it right.

Llanfairpwllgwyngyllgogerychwyrndrobwllllantysiliogogogoch

The English translation of this place name is: St Mary's Church in the hollow of the white hazel near to the rapid whirlpool and the Church of St Tysilio of the red cave.

 Understand

1. What three sounds can you hear in the first stanza? Describe them in your own words.
2. Write six sentences describing the setting of this poem.
3. Find examples of the following poetic devices in this poem. Write the line from the poem which corresponds with each.

   ◖ Enjambment   ◖ Onomatopoeia   ◖ Simile

 Explore

1. Do you think the child and the grandmother have a good relationship? Explain your answer.
2. What do you think the relationship is between the speaker and the person they are talking to? Give reasons for your answer.
3. What do you think is the theme of this poem? Explain your answer with reference to the poem.
4. If you had to rename this poem, what title would you give it and why? Choose one of the following alternative titles or come up with your own title and explain your choice.

   ◖ 'Memories by the Sea'   ◖ 'Living Language'   ◖ 'Growing Up'

5. Suggest a song or piece of music to accompany a reading of this poem and give reasons for your choice.
6. Choose a poem you have studied that has a strong sense of place.

   (a) Name the poem and the poet.
   (b) How does the poet succeed in creating this sense of place? Write three paragraphs to illustrate your point.

 Investigate

Use your research skills to find out three interesting facts about the Welsh language and share your findings with the class.

 Create

Imagine you are at the place described in 'First Words'. Write a postcard to a friend describing your surroundings.

Colons and semicolons

A colon is used to introduce relevant information.

For this class you will need three things: a pen, some paper and scissors.

Colons often introduce a list that is linked to the initial phrase.

'For this class, you will need three things' is the introductory statement. The colon then introduces the list of the things needed: ': a pen, some paper and scissors.'

A colon may also be used to offer a definition or explanation of something. The phrase 'For example' is often followed by a colon. This indicates that further explanation is to follow.

A semicolon is used to break up two separate but related clauses.

I have an exam tomorrow; I need to study tonight.

A semicolon is stronger than a comma, but not as final as a full stop.

A clause is a phrase that can exist on its own, but can be joined with others to form more complex sentences.

Clause 1   **Clause 2**

She was texting while walking;   *now her phone needs to be fixed.*

These phrases could be made into two separate sentences, but the semicolon joins them together and provides a clearer context.

Sometimes the semicolon is used to join two separate clauses. In order to link them, conjunctions such as 'otherwise', 'however' or 'therefore' may be used.

You shouldn't eat too many sweets; otherwise your teeth will rot.

I have to walk home in the rain; however, I have my umbrella.

Understand

Write out the following sentences, adding colons or semicolons as needed.

1. For this cake you will need sugar, flour, eggs and chocolate.
2. I recognised the feeling straight away butterflies.
3. The conservatives were voting in favour Labour were voting against.
4. I nominate the following people for class representatives James, Michael, Luke and Molly.
5. As a great woman once said 'I've learned that people will forget what you said, people will forget what you did, but people will never forget how you made them feel.'

The friends we make when we are young often help to mould us into the adults we become. The change from Primary to Secondary School can be difficult, and it can sometimes take a while to make new friends and feel like we belong. It is only in later years that we are able to look back and see how far we have come.

In the following personal essay, Rebekah Hare reflects on her first few years in Secondary School.

Scrabble

At the beginning of First Year I was excited, yet the question of 'who do I want to be?' riddled me with confusion and uncertainty. First Year was like the beginning of a six-year-long game of Scrabble, where the entire board was empty and we had only begun to choose our letters to hopefully develop a word we would be proud of.

All the American High School movies had convinced me that I was prepared for any challenge that school could throw at me. Yet, no movie can help you to figure out who you want to be, or which letter you want to become in the ongoing game of Scrabble.

My journey began in assessing the competition, which was fierce. There were the vowels at the lunch table, towards the back of the hall. A, E, I, O and, of course, U. These girls could fit into any word. U soon moved to the next table with Q and the two became inseparable. These best friends were deemed the power couple of the canteen. Q was the shy one, yet was popular enough to be given a high value of 10 points. However, she was nothing without her trusty U. I loved the idea of joining forces with Q and U, yet as my mother always told me, 'Three's a crowd', and I wasn't ready to endure the next six years as a third wheel. If I wanted to score high points in the game I had to be careful where I laid my allegiances.

W, X and Z always seemed iconic to me. They were highly valued and able to create memorable and interesting words. Their letters were well-known to school management, causing trouble as frequent flyers in detention. The problem was, they knew where they stood in the game. Despite being worth high points, they were often forgotten. Being so near to the end of the alphabet, they needed to cause trouble to be noticed. This crowd wasn't for me, as I love to learn and wasn't thrilled with the idea of spending all that time in the principal's office. I needed to choose my letters very carefully.

The feeling of uncertainty followed me around for the first few years of secondary school. I couldn't help but feel lost, unable to fit into a group. I found myself among the letters left behind in the flimsy green sack. I was wasting so much time deciding where I wanted to be, but I really wanted to feel comfortable with my letters.

After some searching, I found M. M had been cast aside by O and replaced with N. 'A better fit', O had described it, as in their union made up the word 'NO'.

One day M and I were sitting in the lunch room, when we were joined by E and F. F had recently been swapped out of her word for a more valuable letter. E no longer could stand the fierce competition among the vowels, and wanted an escape. She yearned for stability and friendship, and found us.

In the following weeks our word began to take shape, as we were joined by S and Y. I had always noticed S – she was friendly and chatty and had the locker next to mine. Initially I wasn't sure about her, but later was charmed by her sassy nature. Once she came into the group, she and I became very close. It's funny how quickly you can develop tight bonds with people, especially in school, where we most need the comforts of friendship.

Finally, our word was complete. I knew at that point who I wanted to be. I never wanted to be false or competitive. I never wanted to be something I wasn't. On my quest to fit in I had figured out that what I really wanted was to be happy. I needed to find other letters to help me to be comfortable in my own skin, while feeling safe and valued.

Now, as I look back, I find myself thinking about who I could have been if I hadn't chosen these letters. When I look at other words, I realise the strength and loyalty in my word. My friends, M, Y, S, E and F occupy a really valuable space on the board, and we earn double points due to our combination! As the letter L, I truly found myself through my friends and their support. I was originally the lone wolf, but together we score a respectable 10 points in the prolonged game of Scrabble.

Understand

1. What convinced Rebekah that she was prepared for Secondary School?
2. What was the main challenge Rebekah faced in Secondary School?
3. In terms of forming words, why are Q and U inseparable?
4. Which letters in the Scrabble game are described as trouble makers?
5. What word do Rebekah and her friends create together?
6. What features of a typical personal essay can you identify in this piece?

Explore

1. Do you like the way the author described the different people in her year group as letters on a Scrabble board? Explain your answer.
2. Suggest an alternative title for this essay and explain your choice.
3. If you were a letter in Scrabble, which one would you be? Give reasons for your answer.

Investigate

Find five words that would score high points in a game of Scrabble. Write their definitions in the vocabulary builder on pages 1–2 of your Portfolio, then put each word into a sentence in your copy.

Create

Write a personal essay describing your experience of making friends in First Year.

In the following extract from *Reading in the Dark* by Seamus Deane, the narrator looks back at the first novel he read while growing up in the 1940s in Ireland.

Reading in the Dark

The first novel I read had a green hardboard cover and was two hundred and sixteen pages long. It was called *The Shan van Vocht*, a phonetic rendering of an Irish phrase meaning The Poor Old Woman, a traditional name for Ireland. It was about the great rebellion of 1798, the source of almost half the songs we sang around the August bonfires on the Feast of the Assumption. In the opening pages, people were talking in whispers about the dangers of the rebellion as they sat around a great open-hearth fire on a wild night of winter rain and squall. I read and re-read the opening many times. Outside was the bad weather; inside was the fire, implied danger, a love relationship. There was something exquisite in this blend, as I lay in bed reading while my brothers slept and shifted under the light that shone on their eyelids and made their dreams different. The heroine was called Ann, and the hero was Robert. She was too good for him. When they whispered, she did all the interesting talking. He just kept on about dying and remembering her always, even when she was there in front of him with her dark hair and her deep golden-brown eyes and her olive skin. So I talked to her instead and told her how beautiful she was and how I wouldn't go out on the rebellion at all but just sit there and whisper in her ear and let her know that now was forever and not some time in the future when the shooting and the hacking would be over, when what was left of life would be spent listening to the night wind wailing on graveyards and empty hillsides.

'For Christ's sake, put off that light. You're not even reading, you blank gom.'

And Liam would turn over, driving his knees up into my back and muttering curses under his breath. I'd switch off the light, get back in bed, and lie there, the book still open, re-imagining all I had read, the various ways the plot might unravel, the novel opening into endless possibilities in the dark.

The English teacher read out a model essay which had been, to our surprise, written by a country boy. It was an account of his mother setting the table for the evening meal and then waiting with him until his father came in from the fields. She put out a blue-and-white jug full of milk and a covered dish of potatoes in their jackets and a red-rimmed butter dish with a slab of butter, the shape of a swan dipping its head imprinted on its surface. That was the meal. Everything was so simple, especially the way they waited. She sat with her hands in her lap and talked to him about someone up the road who had had an airmail letter from America. She told him that his father would be tired, but, tired as he was, he wouldn't be without a smile before he washed himself and he wouldn't be without his manners to forget to say grace before they ate and

squall
sudden,
powerful
wind

gom
(slang)
fool

that he, the boy, should watch the way the father would smile when the books were produced for homework, for learning was a wonder to him, especially the Latin. Then there would be no talking, just the ticking of the clock and the kettle humming and the china dogs on the mantelpiece looking, as ever, across at one another.

'Now that,' said the master, 'that's writing. That's just telling the truth.'

I felt embarrassed because my own essay had been full of long or strange words I had found in the dictionary – 'cerulean', 'azure', 'phantasm' and 'implacable' – all of them describing skies and seas I had seen only with the Ann of the novel. I'd never thought such stuff was worth writing about. And yet I kept remembering that mother and son waiting in the Dutch interior of that essay, with the jug of milk and the butter on the table, while behind and above them were those wispy, shawly figures from the rebellion, sibilant above the great fire and below the aching, high wind.

 Understand

1. What was the first novel the narrator ever read?

2. How do you know that the narrator shares a room?

3. What kind of narrator is used in this story: first-person or third-person?

4. **(a)** Look up the meaning of each of the following words in a dictionary:

   ◖ cerulean   ◖ azure   ◖ phantasm   ◖ implacable.

    (b) Add these words to your vocabulary builder on pages 1–2 of your Portfolio.

   (c) Put each of these word into a sentence.

 Explore

 1. Do you think the boy enjoys reading? Explain your answer.

 2. In your opinion, why was the narrator surprised that the essay was written by a country boy?

 3. What important lesson do you think the boy learns about writing?

4. '... that's writing. That's just telling the truth.'

   Do you think this is good advice from the teacher? Give reasons for your answer.

 Create

1. You have decided to organise a writing competition. Design or describe the poster that you would use to promote the competition around the school.

2. Write an article for the school magazine on the importance of reading in the lives of young people.

Discuss

1. Can you name any of Roald Dahl's books?
2. Which is your favourite?
3. Have you seen any film adaptions of his books?

In the following podcast, Sarah McInerney talks to one of Roald Dahl's daughters, Lucy Dahl, about the centenary celebrations for her father.

http://www.newstalk.com/podcasts/The_
Hard_Shoulder/Highlights_from_The_Hard_
Shoulder/157452/Roald_Dahl_Centenary

 Understand

1. At the time of this recording, how long has it been since Roald Dahl's birth?
2. Name one of Dahl's books.
3. What reasons do the children give for reading his books? Give at least one.
4. One of the children does a performance of one of Roald Dahl's most famous characters. Which character is this?
5. According to his daughter, was Roald Dahl always famous?
6. How does she describe her father?
7. Name one thing that Lucy remembers doing with her father when she was younger.
8. What famous character, created by Roald Dahl, used to visit Lucy during the night?
9. According to the interviewer, what made Roald Dahl a good writer for children?

 Explore

 1. Do you think Roald Dahl was a good father? Explain your answer.

2. Do you think Sarah McInerney does a good job as the interviewer? Give reasons for your answer.

 3. Come up with three more questions that you would ask if you were conducting this interview.

Investigate

Conduct a survey to establish which of Roald Dahl's books is most popular in your class.

 Create

 Choose a character from any Roald Dahl book or a chararcter from your studied text and write the script of the interview you would record if you met them.

◖ Start by finding out a bit about the person or character.

◖ Devise a list of questions that you would ask, bearing in mind that you want detailed answers.

◖ Write the script and ask a classmate to read the part of the interviewee.

◖ Record your interview.

Special occasions

Special occasions, such as birthdays and family celebrations, are usually more memorable than everyday events. These occasions can often cause us to reflect and take stock of where we are in our lives.

Birthdays are a time for celebration, but they can sometimes be difficult as people can feel unsatisfied with their accomplishments. In the following extract from *The Art of Being Normal* by Lisa Williamson, David is celebrating his 14th birthday.

The Art of Being Normal

My party guests are singing 'Happy Birthday'. It does not sound good.

My little sister Livvy is barely even singing. At eleven, she's already decided family birthday parties are tragically embarrassing, leaving Mum and Dad to honk out the rest of the tune, Mum's reedy soprano clashing with Dad's flat bass. It is so bad Phil, the family dog, gets up from his basket and slinks off mid-song in vague disgust. I don't blame him; the whole party is fairly depressing. Even the blue balloons Dad spent the entire morning blowing up look pale and sad, especially the ones with 'Fourteen Today!' scrawled on them in black marker pen. I'm not even sure the underwhelming events unfolding before me qualify as a party in the first place.

'Make a wish!' Mum says. She has the cake tipped at an angle so I won't notice it's wonky. It says 'Happy Birthday David!' in blood-red icing across the top, the 'day' in 'birthday' all scrunched up where she must have run out of room. Fourteen blue candles form a circle around the edge of the cake, dripping wax into the butter cream.

'Hurry up!' Livvy says.

But I won't be rushed. I want to do this bit properly. I lean forward, tuck my hair behind my ears and shut my eyes. I block out Livvy's whining and Mum's cajoling and Dad fiddling with the settings on the camera, and suddenly everything sounds sort of muffled and far away, a bit like when you dunk your head under water in the bath.

I wait a few seconds before opening my eyes and blowing out all the candles in one go. Everyone applauds. Dad lets off a party popper but it doesn't 'pop' properly and by the time he's got another one out of the packet Mum has opened the curtains and started taking the candles off the cake, and the moment has passed.

'What did you wish for? Something stupid, I bet,' Livvy says accusingly, twirling a piece of golden brown hair around her middle finger.

'He can't tell you, silly, otherwise it won't come true,' Mum says, taking the cake into the kitchen to be sliced.

'Yeah,' I say, sticking my tongue out at Livvy. She sticks hers out right back.

'Where are your two friends again? she asks, putting extra emphasis on the 'two'.

'I've told you, Felix is in Florida and Essie is in Leamington Spa.'

'That's too bad,' Livvy says with zero sympathy. 'Dad, how many people did I have at my eleventh?'

'Forty-five. All on roller skates. Utter carnage,' Dad mutters grimly, ejecting the memory card from the camera and slotting it into the side of his laptop.

The first photo that pops up on the screen is of me sitting at the head of the table wearing an oversized 'Birthday Boy' badge and pointy cardboard party hat. My eyes are closed mid-blink and my forehead is shiny.

'Dad,' I moan. 'Do you have to do that now?'

'Just doing some red-eye removal before I email them over to your grandmother,' he says, clicking away at the mouse. 'She was gutted she couldn't come.'

This is not true. Granny has bridge on Wednesday evenings and doesn't miss it for anyone, least of all her least favourite grandchild. Livvy is Granny's favourite. But then Livvy is everyone's favourite. Mum had also asked Auntie Jane and Uncle Trevor, and my cousins Keira and Alfie. But Alfie woke up this morning with weird spots all over his chest that may or may not be chicken pox, so they had to give their apologies, leaving the four of us to 'celebrate' alone.

Mum returns to the living room with the sliced cake, setting it back down on the table.

'Look at all these leftovers,' she says, frowning as she surveys the mountains of picked-at food. 'We're going to have enough sausage rolls and fondant fancies to last us until Christmas. I just hope I've got enough cling film to wrap it all up.'

Great. A fridge full of food to remind me just how wildly unpopular I am.

After cake and intensive cling-film action, there are presents. From Mum and Dad I get a new backpack for school, the *Gossip Girl* DVD box set and a cheque for one hundred pounds. Livvy presents me with a box of Cadbury Heroes and a shiny red case for my iPhone.

Then we all sit on the sofa and watch a film called *Freaky Friday*. It's about a mother and daughter who eat an enchanted fortune cookie that makes them magically swap bodies for the day. Of course everyone learns a valuable lesson before the inevitable happy ending, and for about the hundredth time this summer I mourn my life's failure to follow the plot of a perky teenage movie. Dad drops off halfway through and starts snoring loudly.

That night I can't sleep. I'm awake for so long, my eyes get used to the dark and I can make out the outlines of my posters on the walls and the tiny shadow of a mosquito darting back and forth across the ceiling.

I am fourteen and time is running out.

Focus on ... stereotypes

A **stereotype** is a set idea that people have about what someone or something is like.

These ideas are often widely held, but are not based on any evidence and are largely untrue.

People are often stereotyped based on the way they are dressed. For example, people can be quick to assume that teenagers in hoodies are hooligans or people who like makeup and fake tan are not intelligent.

Can you identify any stereotypes associated with the following groups?

◀ Men   ◀ Smart people   ◀ Teenagers
◀ Women   ◀ Sporty people   ◀ People without a home

Are these stereotypes fair?

In literature people are often stereotyped. Sometimes the author is trying to prove a point. Can you think of any novels, plays or films you have studied where there was a stereotyped character? What effect did this have on you as a reader?

 ## Discuss

1. What was your most memorable birthday? Why was it so memorable?
2. David is trying to be a 'normal' teenager. What does this mean?
3. Do you think it is difficult to be 'normal'?
4. Have you ever been the victim of stereotyping? How did it make you feel?

 ## Understand

1. Find a synonym for each of the following words in the extract from *The Art of Being Normal*:
   ◀ crooked
   ◀ hurried
   ◀ coaxing
   ◀ twisting
   ◀ destruction.
2. How old is David?
3. Name one present that David receives for his birthday.

Explore

1. In your view, how does David feel about his birthday?

2. Do you think David's parents are loving people? Explain your answer.

3. Do you think this is a typical 14-year-old's birthday celebration? Give reasons for your answer.

4. '... for about the hundredth time this summer I mourn my life's failure to follow the plot of a perky teenage movie.'

   (a) Do you think young people are heavily influenced by what they see on television and in films?

   (b) List some teenage films that are not considered 'perky'.

Investigate

Conduct a survey to find out how people in your community feel about birthdays. You may wish to ask your classmates, other members of your school community, family and friends. One way to conduct an informal survey is to ask people at random and record their responses. This is called a **vox pop**. The term 'vox pop' comes from the Latin phrase *vox populi*, meaning 'voice of the people'. Reporters frequently use vox pops to obtain a snapshot of public opinion.

Create

1. Design the front cover for the book *The Art of Being Normal*.
2. Write the next paragraph, continuing the story.
3. Write a speech to be delivered to your classmates entitled 'The Art of Being Normal'.
4. Write a feature article for your school magazine on the subject of birthdays.

Our fondest memories are often associated with happy occasions and celebrations. Christmastime can offer a mix of happy and sad memories for a lot of people. It is a time for togetherness and family, but can also be a time when people are at their most vulnerable and lonely.

The following spoken word poem is a fun and lively way of reflecting on the lighter side of Christmas. This poem is meant to be spoken out loud, rather than read, and it is written phonetically, in the language and accent of the performer.

Talking Turkeys!!

By Benjamin Zephaniah

Be nice to yu turkeys dis christmas
Cos turkeys just wanna hav fun
Turkeys are cool, turkeys are wicked
An every turkey has a Mum.
Be nice to yu turkeys dis christmas,
Don't eat it, keep it alive,
It could be yu mate an not on yu plate
Say, Yo! Turkey I'm on your side.

I got lots of friends who are turkeys
An all of dem fear christmas time,
Dey wanna enjoy it, dey say humans destroyed it
An humans are out of dere mind,
Yeah, I got lots of friends who are turkeys
Dey all hav a right to a life,
Not to be caged up an genetically made up
By any farmer an his wife.

Turkeys just wanna play reggae
Turkeys just wanna hip-hop
Can yu imagine a nice young turkey saying,
'I cannot wait for de chop'?
Turkeys like getting presents, dey wanna watch christmas TV,
Turkeys hav brains an turkeys feel pain
In many ways like yu an me.

I once knew a turkey called Turkey
He said 'Benji explain to me please,
Who put de turkey in christmas
An what happens to christmas trees?'

I said, 'I am not too sure turkey

But it's nothing to do wid Christ Mass

Humans get greedy an waste more dan need be

An business men mek loadsa cash'.

Be nice to yu turkey dis christmas

Invite dem indoors fe sum greens

Let dem eat cake an let dem partake

In a plate of organic grown beans,

Be nice to yu turkey dis christmas

An spare dem de cut of de knife,

Join Turkeys United an dey'll be delighted

An yu will mek new friends 'FOR LIFE'.

Understand

1. According to the speaker, in what way are turkeys like people?
2. Name one thing that turkeys want to do.
3. Find an example of a poetic device in the poem.

Explore

1. What do you think the title 'Talking Turkeys!!' means?
2. Write out the first stanza with the correct punctuation and with full words instead of abbreviations. Now read it aloud. What do you think is lost by taking away the poem's original style?

 3. Do you like this poem? Explain your answer.

Create

1. Write another stanza to complete the poem. Begin with 'Be nice to yu turkeys dis christmas ...'.

 2. Create an advertising campaign to stop people eating turkeys at Christmas. You can use whatever media format you wish (poster, social media page, video, etc.). You may wish to consider some of the following:

   ◖ slogans
   ◖ hashtags
   ◖ images
   ◖ endorsement
   ◖ information.

People often get nostalgic around Christmastime. Nostalgia is when people think back on the past in a fond and sentimental way.

Here are two advertisements, both shown at Christmastime.

 https://youtu.be/BbPGxO2ZWrw

 https://youtu.be/u8hRUQTt8MQ

 Discuss

Can you think of any other advertisements that make you feel nostalgic?

Understand

1. In the first advertisement, why do the children decide to leave out Corn Flakes?
2. What time does Santa arrive?
3. Why does the child suggest that Santa liked the Corn Flakes?
4. In the second advertisement, how do you know in the first few seconds that it is a Christmas advertisement?
5. List three things the family do to improve the conditions in the house.

Explore

 1. How do you know what product is being advertised in the first advertisement?

 2. Christmas is a time for nostalgia. What items do the family find in the second advertisement that might add to this sense of reflecting fondly on the past?

 3. In the second advertisment, whose house do you think this was before? Explain your answer.

 4. Choose one family relationship in either of the advertisements and explain why you think it is a strong bond.

 5. Compare and contrast these advertisements using the advertising comparison worksheet on pages 97–98 of your Portfolio.

 Create

 The theme of these advertisements, as well as Christmas, is family. Imagine you work for an advertising company. Work in groups to come up with some other themes that you would use to create a Christmas advertisement.

   ◖ Choose a product.   ◖ Choose a theme.

Create a presentation explaining how you would advertise this product.

Discuss

What is your favourite month and why?

The following poem journeys through the different months of the year, and discusses the typical features of each.

The Months

By Sara Coleridge

January brings the snow,
Makes our feet and fingers glow.

February brings the rain,
Thaws the frozen lake again.

March brings breezes loud and shrill,
Stirs the dancing daffodil.

April brings the primrose sweet,
Scatters daisies at our feet.

May brings flocks of pretty lambs,
Skipping by their fleecy dams.

June brings tulips, lilies, roses,
Fills the children's hands with posies.

Hot July brings cooling showers,
Apricots and gillyflowers.

August brings the sheaves of corn,
Then the harvest home is borne.

Warm September brings the fruit,
Sportsmen then begin to shoot.

Fresh October brings the pheasant,
Then to gather nuts is pleasant.

Dull November brings the blast,
Then the leaves are whirling fast.

Chill December brings the sleet,
Blazing fire, and Christmas treat.

JANUARY

FEBRUARY

MARCH

APRIL

MAY

JUNE

JULY

AUGUST

SEPTEMBER

OCTOBER

NOVEMBER

DECEMBER

Understand

1. What does April bring, according to the poem?
2. List three types of flowers and three animals mentioned in the poem.
3. How many months bring weather, according to the poem?

Explore

1. Look at the adjectives used to describe July, October and November in the poem. Would you agree that these are appropriate descriptions?
2. Suggest an alternative title to this poem and give reasons for your choice.
3. Looking back over your own childhood, what other things would you associate with each of the months of the year?
4. Choose a poem you have studied that deals with change.
   (a) Name the poem and the poet.
   (b) What change(s) does the poem describe?
   (c) Give your favourite quote from the poem and explain why you like this quote.

Investigate

Work in small groups to choose one year from the past and document a list of important events that took place throughout the year. You can present your findings in whatever format you wish (poem, video, visual presentation, dramatic re-enactment, news article, etc.). Try to include something news-worthy from every month of your chosen year. Use the headings below to guide you.

◖ News and current affairs
◖ Politics
◖ Sports
◖ Music
◖ Entertainment

Create

Using the same rhyming scheme and couplets as 'The Months', write your own version of this poem in the space provided on page 99 of your Portfolio. Include all the things that are important in your calendar.

Reviewing looking back

Reflect and review

1. **(a)** Take a look back at the images on page 369. Consider the association each image has with the theme. Rank the images from most relevant (1) to least relevant (5).

   (b) Share the image that you feel ranks the highest. Explain your choice and listen as others share their choice with you.

   (c) What image would you choose to replace the one that you feel ranks the lowest? Describe the image you would replace it with and explain your choice.

2. 'Life can only be understood backwards; but it must be lived forwards.'

   Do you agree with this statement? Discuss the texts that you have studied in this chapter in your answer.

3. Fill in the unit review on pages 100–101 of your Portfolio.

Language skills

Write out the following sentences, inserting colons and semicolons where needed.

1. I like tomatoes Mary likes cucumbers.
2. I have visited three Italian cities Milan, Venice and Rome.
3. She listens to three types of music rock, jazz and hip-hop.
4. She cannot eat burgers red meat of any kind does not agree with her.
5. There are a lot of things to enjoy at the circus bright lights, flying acrobats and candy floss.

Oral assessment

Using a visual text as a stimulus, prepare a two-minute oral presentation for the class. You may use an image from the chapter, an old photograph or a newspaper or magazine cut-out.

◖ Consider carefully what the image means to you.

◖ Plan what you would like to say.

◖ Write your presentation.

◖ Practise the delivery of your presentation. Make sure it is two minutes long.

When you are ready, deliver your presentation to your classmates.

Written assessment

1. (a) Write a short story entitled 'Looking Back' in the space provided on pages 102–103 of your Portfolio. Remember to include:
- vivid descriptions
- well-developed characters
- an interesting setting.

(b) Redraft your short story in the space provided on pages 128–129 of your Portfolio.

Exam skills

1. Choose a film or play you have studied in which the characters have been affected by past events.

(a) Name the film or play and the director or playwright.

(b) Explain the past event(s).

(c) How does this affect the characters and the way they relate to each other?

(d) What advice would you offer to one of the main characters in order to help them move on from the past?

Write your answer in the space provided on pages 147–148 of your Portfolio.

Acknowledgements:

'A Whole New World' by Alan Menken and Tim Rice, by kind permission of Hal Leonard LLC; 'A World Without Limits' by kind permission of Euronews; 'After the Titanic' from *New Collected Poems* (2011) by Derek Mahon. Reproduced by kind permission of the author and The Gallery Press, Loughcrew, Oldcastle, County Meath, Ireland; *All the Light We Cannot See* by Anthony Doerr. Reproduced by kind permission of ICM; 'Another Planet' by Dunya Mikhail. Reproduced by kind permission of New Directions Publishing; 'As a woman who lived in Saudi Arabia, here's how I feel about them letting women drive for the first time' by Nour Hassan. Reproduced by kind permission of *The Independent*; 'Berlin Wall – readers' memories: "It's hard to remember how scary the Wall was"' by *Guardian* readers and Caroline Bannock. Reprinted by kind permission of Guardian News & Media; 'Blowin' in the Wind' by Bob Dylan, by kind permission of Special Rider Music; 'Caged Bird' by Maya Angelou. Reproduced by kind permission of Little, Brown Book Group; 'California' words and music by Joni Mitchell © 1971 (Renewed) Crazy Cow Music. All Rights Administered by Sony/ATV Music Publishing, 8 Music Square West, Nashville, TN 37203, All Rights Reserved. Used by Permission of Alfred Music (100% administered by Alfred); 'Christmas 1914' by Mike Harding. Reproduced by kind permission of the author; *Click* by Eoin Colfer. Reproduced by kind permission of the author c/o The Sophie Hicks Agency; 'Clonmel driver finally makes switch to electric cars – at age 100' by Tim O'Brien. Reproduced by kind permission of *The Irish Times*; *Dreamland* by Sarah Dessen. Reproduced by kind permission of Hodder & Stoughton; 'Do You Have Any Advice For Those of Us Just Starting Out?' from *Fever* (2006) by Ron Koertge. Reproduced by kind permission of Little Red Hen Press; *Educating Rita* by Willy Russell. Reproduced by kind permission of Negus-Fancey Agents Ltd.; 'Fabulous Places' words and music by Leslie Bricusse EMI United Partnership Ltd., by kind permission of Music Sales Group; 'Fatboy and Skinnybones' by René Saldaña Jr. Reproduced by kind permission of the author; 'Finding a Box of Family Letters' from *99 Poems: New and Selected* by Dana Gioia. Copyright © 2012 by Dana Gioia. Reprinted with the permission of The Permissions Company, Inc., on behalf of Graywolf Press, Minneapolis, Minnesota, www.graywolfpress.org; *First Crossing* by Pam Muñoz Ryan. Reproduced by kind permission of BookStop Literary Agency; 'First Words' by Gillian Clarke. Reproduced by kind permission of Carcanet Press; 'Freedom' words and music by Pharrell Williams, Anthony Criss, Keir Gist and Vincent Brown © 2015, by permission of More Water from Nazareth/EMI Pop Music Publishing Ltd, London W1F 9LD; 'Heirloom' by Gerard Smyth. Reproduced by kind permission of Dedalus Press; *Hell's Grannies* from Monty Python's Flying Circus Series 1, Episode 8 (1969) courtesy of Python (Monty) Pictures Limited; *Holes* © Louis Sachar 2000, Bloomsbury Publishing; 'Home is so Sad' from COLLECTED POEMS by Philip Larkin. © the estate of Philip Larkin. Reproduced by permission of Faber & Faber Ltd.; 'I Am A Rock' and 'Bridge Over Troubled Water' words and music by Paul Simon © Universal Music Publishing Group by kind permission of The Music Sales Group; 'It Wasn't the Father's Fault' by Rita Ann Higgins from *Throw in the Vowels: New & Selected Poems* (Bloodaxe Books, 2005). Reproduced by kind permission of Bloodaxe Books; 'It's Time for Teens to Vote' from *The New York Times*, 2018 © 2016 The New York Times. All rights reserved. Used by permission and protected by the Copyright Laws of the United States. The printing, copying, redistribution, or retransmission of this Content without express written permission is prohibited; *Kiss* by Jacqueline Wilson. Reproduced by kind permission of David Higham Associates; 'Miss Peru contestants accuse country of not measuring up on gender violence' by Dan Collyns. Reproduced by kind permission of Guardian News & Media; *Made in Dagenham* by William Ivory. Reproduced by kind permission of Number 9 Films; *Matilda* by Roald Dahl. Reproduced by kind permission of David Higham Associates; 'Mother to Son' by Langston Hughes. Reproduced by kind permission of Alfred A. Knopf Inc. c/o David Higham Associates; 'My Digital Utopia' by Oscar Mann. Reproduced by kind permission of the poet; *Pastoral Care* by Gerald Murphy. Reproduced by kind permission of the author c/o The Agency; 'Raising Kids During War: A Syrian Mom's Story'. Reproduced by kind permission of SOS Children's Villages USA. SOS Children's Villages is an international nonprofit organization that builds loving, stable families for orphaned, abandoned and other vulnerable children. In doing so, we make sure that every child has the support and care he or she needs to grow, thrive, and lead a fulfilling life. Learn more at http://sos-usa.org; *Reading in the Dark* by Seamus Deane. Reproduced by kind permission of Shiel Land Associates Ltd.; *Refugee Boy* © Benjamin Zephaniah, 2001, Bloomsbury Publishing; 'Refugees' by Brian Bilston. Reproduced by kind permission of Unbound; 'Review of Hitler's Canary by Sandi Toksvig' by The Lightening Readers. Reproduced by kind permission of Guardian News & Media; *Roll of Thunder, Hear My Cry* by Mildred D. Taylor. Reproduced by kind permission of Penguin Random House; 'Scaffolding' by Seamus Heaney. First appeared in DEATH OF A NATURALIST. © The estate of Seamus Heaney. Reproduced by permission of Faber & Faber Ltd.; "Someday the Wall will fall" – Letter from an East German Penpal (Hausarchiv)'. Copyright © 2009–2013 William C. Dawson III; 'Song in Space' by Adrian Mitchell. Reproduced by kind permission of the Estate of Adrian Mitchell, c/o United Agents; 'Strange Fruit' words and music by Abel Meeropol. Reproduced by kind permission of Carlin America Inc.; 'Thank you, Ma'am' by Langston Hughes. Reproduced by kind permission of Alfred A. Knopf Inc. c/o David Higham Associates; *The Art of Being Normal* by Lisa Williamson. Reproduced by kind permission of David Fickling Books; 'The Boy' by P. J. Harvey. Reproduced by kind permission of Bloomsbury; 'The Émigreé' by Carol Rumens. Reproduced by kind permission of the author; 'The final edition of The Independent newspaper is on newsstands today' by Paul Hosford. Reproduced by kind permission of TheJournal.ie; *The Island at the End of Everything* © Kiran Millwood Hargrave, 2017. Reproduced with permission of Chicken House Ltd. All rights reserved; 'The Landlady' by Roald Dahl. Reproduced by kind permission of David Higham Associates; 'The Limits of the Earth' by Ramez Naam. Reproduced by kind permission of the author; 'The Listeners' by Walter de la Mare. Reproduced by kind permission of The Society of Authors; *The Maddie Diaries* by Maddie Ziegler. Reproduced by kind permission of Simon & Schuster; 'The Process of Being Yourself: For Simon, It Began with Blue Hair Dye' by Simón Maracara Diaz. Reproduced by kind permission of the author; 'The Road Not Taken' by Robert Frost from *The Poetry of Robert Frost* edited by Edward Connery Lathem. Copyright © 1916, 1939, 1969 by Henry Holt and Company. Copyright © 1944, 1958 by Robert Frost. Copyright © 1967 by Lesley Frost Ballantine. Used by permission of Henry Holt and Company. All rights reserved. *Collected Poems* by Robert Frost. Published by Vintage. Reprinted by permission of The Random House Group Limited. © 1930; *The Road Home* by Rose Tremain, published by Chatto & Windus. Reproduced by kind permission of The Random House Group Ltd. © 2007; 'The Thickness of Ice' by Liz Loxley. Reproduced by kind permission of the poet; *The Silver Donkey* by Sonya Hartnett. Text Copyright © 2006 Sonya Hartnett. Originally published by Pearson Australia Pty Ltd. Reproduced by kind permission of Walker Books Ltd., London SE11 5HJ www.walker.co.uk; 'The Umbrella Man' by Roald Dahl. Reproduced by kind permission of Penguin Random House c/o David Higham Associates; *The Wardrobe* by Sam Holcroft. Reproduced by kind permission of Bloomsbury; 'The way I faced up to my blindness and paralysis was just replicating what I'd learned through sport' by Emma Duffy. Reproduced by kind permission of TheJournal.ie; *The Wardrobe* by Sam Holcroft. Reproduced by kind permission of Bloomsbury; *The Wizard of Oz* by Noel Langley, Florence Ryerson and Edgar Allen Woolf. Reproduced by kind permission of Warner Bros.; 'There Came a Day' by Ted Hughes. © The estate of Ted Hughes, first appeared in SEASON SONGS. Reproduced by permission of Faber & Faber Ltd.; 'To a Daughter Leaving Home' ©1988 by Linda Pastan. Used by permission of Linda Pastan in care of the Jean V. Naggar Literary Agency Inc. (permissions@jvnla.com); 'Top Maldives Points of Interest You Must Visit' by Janet Newenham. Reproduced by kind permission of the author; 'Valentine' from *Mean Time* by Carol Ann Duffy. Published by Anvil Press, 1993. Copyright © Carol Ann Duffy. Reproduced by permission of the author c/o Rogers, Coleridge & White Ltd., 20 Powis Mews, London W11 1JN; 'War' Words and Music by Norman Whitfield and Barrett Strong © 1970, Reproduced by permission of Stone Agate Music/EMI Music Publishing Ltd, London W1F 9LD; 'When All the Others Were Away at

Mass' by Seamus Heaney. © The estate of Seamus Heaney, first appeared in CLEARANCES III - In Memoriam M.K.H., 1911-1984. Reproduced by permission of Faber & Faber Ltd.; 'When Immigration Agents Came Knocking' by Krystal A. Sital from *The New York Times*, 2018 © 2016 The New York Times. All rights reserved. Used by permission and protected by the Copyright Laws of the United States. The printing, copying, redistribution, or retransmission of this Content without express written permission is prohibited; 'Why teenage boys are told not to feel and why that's so wrong' by Dave Rudden by kind permission of Guardian News & Media; 'Zoos are prisons for animals – no one needs to see a depressed penguin in the flesh' by Romesh Ranganathan. Reproduced by kind permission of Guardian News & Media

Photo acknowledgements:

AF archive / Alamy Stock Photo; AF Fotografie / Alamy Stock Photo; Alison Wright / Alamy Stock Photo; Allstar Picture Library / Alamy Stock Photo; Archive PL / Alamy Stock Photo; Ben Molyneux / Alamy Stock Photo; Dough Productions; NITV; Catharine Collingridge (The Bright Agency); CGIAR Research Program on Climate Change, Agriculture and Food Security CCAFS; cineclassico / Alamy Stock Photo; Classic Image / Alamy Stock Photo; Collection Christophel / Alamy Stock Photo; Design Pics Inc / Alamy Stock Photo; Don Powers; Everett Collection Inc / Alamy Stock Photo; Geraint Lewis / Alamy Stock Photo; GL Archive / Alamy Stock Photo; Glasshouse Images / Alamy Stock Photo; Granger Historical Picture Archive / Alamy Stock Photo; Heritage Image Partnership Ltd / Alamy Stock Photo; INTERFOTO / Alamy Stock Photo; intrepidcamera / Alamy Stock Photo; JERSEY FILMS / TRISTAR PICTURES / Ronald Grant Archive / Alamy Stock Photo; Jocelyn Kao (The Bright Agency); Laperruque / Alamy Stock Photo; LiamMcArdle.com / Alamy Stock Photo; Little, Brown Book Group; Loop Images Ltd / Alamy Stock Photo; Lordprice Collection / Alamy Stock Photo; Moviestore collection Ltd / Alamy Stock Photo; NASA Archive / Alamy Stock Photo; Neil McKay / Alamy Stock Photo; Niday Picture Library / Alamy Stock Photo; PackStock / Alamy Stock Photo; Photo 12 / Alamy Stock Photo; Pictorial Press Ltd / Alamy Stock Photo; PjrTravel / Alamy Stock Photo; reallifephotos / Alamy Stock Photo; Roberto Herrett / Alamy Stock Photo; RooM the Agency / Alamy Stock Photo; Science History Images / Alamy Stock Photo; Sebastian Kroll / Stockimo / Alamy Stock Photo; Shawshots / Alamy Stock Photo; Shutterstock; SPUTNIK / Alamy Stock Photo; Steven May / Alamy Stock Photo; TC / Alamy Stock Photo; The Advertising Archives / Alamy Stock Photo; The Granger Collection / Alamy Stock Photo; Trinity Mirror / Mirrorpix / Alamy Stock Photo; United Archives GmbH / Alamy Stock Photo; Vibrant Pictures / Alamy Stock Photo; WALT DISNEY ENT / Ronald Grant Archive / Alamy Stock Photo; WENN Ltd / Alamy Stock Photo; Wikimedia Commons; World History Archive / Alamy Stock Photo; ZUMA Press Inc / Alamy Stock Photo.

Special thanks to EmojiOne.com for emoji icons © 2018, EmojiOne, Inc.

The author and publisher have made every effort to trace all copyright owners, but if any material has inadvertently been reproduced without permission, they would be happy to make the necessary arrangement at the earliest opportunity and encourage owners of copyright material not acknowledged to make contact.